Mike Tiple

3 6 4 2 6 95

<u>Dorean Krimsky</u>
593 West Wilson Hall
Phone 35-30544

Modern Elementary Mathematics

Modern Elementary
Mathematics

by

MORGAN WARD

Department of Mathematics
California Institute of Technology

and

CLARENCE ETHEL HARDGROVE

Department of Mathematics
Northern Illinois University

ADDISON-WESLEY PUBLISHING COMPANY, INC.

READING, MASSACHUSETTS · PALO ALTO · LONDON

PREFACE

This book is devoted to the development of the basic ideas of mathematics. The authors hope that the content and the method of presentation will appeal to all those interested in gaining a general grasp of the ideas underlying mathematics. The book is written especially for teachers and administrators of elementary schools; the content of the book will help them to gain an understanding of the content of a modern elementary school mathematics program.

Special emphasis is placed on understanding the structure and relationship of mathematical ideas, showing how these ideas are related to the mathematics which lies beyond. The treatment is largely inductive, rather than deductive, because elementary mathematics is more easily taught and learned inductively. However, the reader is given ample opportunity to understand and use simple deductive reasoning, especially in Chapter 3 and in the Exercise Sets, which are an essential part of the text.

Because geometry is an integral part of mathematics and because it is assuming a greater role in elementary school programs, this book devotes two chapters to a consideration of the topic. In Chapter 8, which discusses the elements of geometry, a systematic use is made of a convex figure. In Chapter 13 the connection between number and geometry by use of coordinate systems is described; the necessity for extending the rational number system is shown; and the real numbers are introduced by means of their decimal representation.

The book permits the reader to gain a general grasp of the ideas underlying mathematics, but its primary use is as a textbook for pre-service elementary teachers. The book is planned for a year's work, but it can easily be adapted to a one-term course. As a possible sequence for such a course the authors suggest Chapters 1, 2, 4, 6, 7, 9, 10, and 15.

It is assumed that the reader has enough familiarity with elementary arithmetic and geometry to understand the examples and illustrations given in the first few chapters. More precise meanings for technical terms such as number, fraction, and triangle are developed as the text proceeds.

We hope that in the process of learning more about mathematics the reader may also experience the pleasure and excitement of personal discovery. The Exercise Sets are designed to provide these opportunities.

The authors wish to acknowledge the help given by Sigrid Ward, Audrey Ward Gray, Anne Bacon, Margaret Wood, John Todd, and many other friends and students, with special thanks to Edward G. Begle, Director of School Mathematics Study Group, for his leadership in mathematics education.

M. W.
C. E. H.

October 1963

Publisher's Note:

It is especially tragic that Professor Ward, who, because of his concern for improved mathematics education, had devoted so much time and energy to the writing and proofreading of this volume, did not live to see the text in book form.

CONTENTS

Chapter 4. The Whole Numbers

Chapter 5. Induction

CHAPTER ONE

MATHEMATICS, WHAT IT IS AND WHY IT IS IMPORTANT

1. INTRODUCTION

Mathematics results from the discovery, the formulation, the systematic development, and the application of patterns of inductive and deductive thinking. Mathematics consists of patterns of related ideas and patterns of thought. Many of these are familiar to you. You use them to add 276 and 167, to distinguish a square from a rectangle, to compare a set of twelve objects with a set of three dozen objects, to find the circumference of a circle of diameter five inches, and even to count the chairs in a room.

If the two numbers 276 and 167 are to be added, a mathematical pattern guides the procedure unerringly to a sum of 443. The pattern is the result of a long period of development. Other forms were developed and discarded before the simple convenient one now used was formulated. It is learned by every child in elementary school.

The development of simple convenient mathematical patterns is an important part of the evolution of our culture. This is illustrated by the fact that we do not think of 276 + 167 as "many," that we do not count to find the sum of these numbers but rather that we use an efficient procedure to find a unique sum.

Many mathematical patterns are presented in this book for your discovery and for your study. These will suggest still others. Some of them will be familiar to you; others will be new. All have a place in mathematics and, as discovered, will lead to a greater understanding of mathematics and its applications.

2. REASONS FOR STUDYING MATHEMATICS

The principal reason that mathematics is widely studied is its usefulness. It was easy in the past to identify a minimum amount of useful mathematics. The present, however, is a time of change. New developments in industry and science and new applications call for a greater knowledge of mathematics than was required from the early settlers of the United States or even from the people of the 1950's. Mathematics is needed not only as a part of the language for effective everyday living but as a language of industry and science.

Very little modern science can be learned without an understanding of mathematics. Physical sciences state their basic laws in mathematical language and use mathematics continuously to formulate results and to make predictions. Social and behavioral sciences are using mathematics to an ever-increasing extent.

If the mathematics necessary to industry and science consisted merely of routine skills, the curriculum of mathematics would be simple and unchanging. Such is not the case. The needs are expanding too rapidly for a simple unchanging curriculum to suffice. New patterns which result in new routines are continuously being discovered; mathematics is not static. The nature of the subject must be learned so that the most useful and productive patterns may be selected and intelligently used. The mathematics needed in industry and science consists of a knowledge of mathematical patterns, as well as of how they were originally discovered from experience, how they were formulated into patterns, how they were developed into the overall growing pattern called mathematics, and how the patterns are applied. Without this knowledge routine skills are almost valueless.

3. PATTERNS IN MATHEMATICS

The giant sunflower of Fig. 1–1* reveals a geometric pattern occurring in nature. The small blossoms of the flower naturally arrange themselves in interlacing spiral curves. It is easier to perceive the small blossoms as part of an orderly arrangement than to view them as having been randomly placed in the flower head. Recognizing patterns in nature gives pleasure. They have been copied by man in objects of art and architecture giving the creations a mathematical form and structure.

The mathematical patterns occurring in nature and art are usually geometric. There are, however, many patterns which are arithmetical. For example, the successive sums,

$$1 + 3 = 4, \quad 1 + 3 + 5 = 9, \quad 1 + 3 + 5 + 7 = 16, \ldots,$$

form a pattern. From the study of these you may predict the sum of $1 + 3 + 5 + 7 + 9$, and if the pattern is understood, you can predict the sum of

$$1 + 3 + 5 + 7 + 9 + 11 + 13 + 15 + 17 + 19 + 21 + 23$$

without adding. The pattern that you perceive is a number relationship.

FIGURE 1-1

There are more complicated and more abstract patterns in geometry and in arithmetic than the examples just examined. As the material of this book develops you will be perceiving both geometric and arithmetic patterns, ideas which are the basis of the subject called mathematics, as well as patterns of thought themselves. The last chapter will be devoted to a reexamination of the mathematics you have studied from the standpoint of its basic patterns.

4. GAMES AND MATHEMATICAL PATTERNS

Games are dependent on mathematical patterns. Hopscotch, tennis, croquet, and shuffleboard, for example, have a geometric plan in their mode of play and an arithmetical plan in their mode of scoring. Any game has an abstract mathematical pattern embodied in its rules which govern the manner in which the game is played. The rules are formulated clearly and carefully so that there may be no doubt how the game continues. The rules correspond to the assumptions which underlie a subject such as geometry and set the pattern for the entire game.

More complicated games such as bridge and chess have been studied mathematically. Some of the studies have given rise to important branches of mathematics. Statistics and probability theory originated in the seventeenth century from the study of gambling games played with cards and dice. An important and actively growing branch of twentieth-century mathematics is called game theory. It studies games in general and how they should be played even when chance plays an essential role in the outcome. It has important practical applications in economic planning.

5. OTHER ASPECTS OF MATHEMATICS

The historical aspect. A knowledge of how mathematics has developed, of the relationship of mathematics to other cultural factors, and of how mathematics has met cultural demands in the past helps you realize the importance and meaning of mathematics. Since history shows that mathematics has continuously developed and changed with changing needs, it is known and expected that in the future it will continue to develop and change. The mathematics of the school curricula must also change since mathematics itself is growing.

The theoretical and practical aspects. The part of mathematics related to theoretical concepts is called pure mathematics and that related to practical affairs is called applied mathematics. Pure mathematics studies patterns of thought without regard to their application. Applied mathematics uses the patterns developed in pure mathematics to understand and control the world around us.

Until very recently, all pure mathematics rose from applied mathematics; that is, from the need to develop new methods to solve problems of everyday life. The developments in pure mathematics often were carried far beyond their original applications and led to further developments quite remote from practical experience. Later, what initially developed as pure mathematics often proved to be extremely useful in applied mathematics. For example, an electrical engineer designing a new electronic device uses mathematical methods created over one hundred and fifty years ago by pure mathematicians investigating properties of the complex numbers. Mathematicians developed these methods with no prevision of their use in modern electrical engineering. Indeed, at the time of their work, the knowledge of electricity was in a rudimentary stage.

Mathematics differs in no way from science in this respect. Discoveries in pure science are continuously being put to use in applied science, and problems in applied science in turn inspire investigations in pure science. In view of the close relationship between pure and applied mathematics it is unwise to consider one aspect without the other. Both aspects are therefore blended in this book.

The generality of mathematics. Another important aspect of mathematics is its generality. For example, the pattern of addition may be applied to any two numbers, and the methods of mathematics which the electrical engineer uses in designing a circuit may be applied to any circuit he considers. This generality is one of the reasons that mathematical patterns are useful, but it creates a difficulty for one who is studying mathematics. He may confuse his ability to state a general principle with his ability to use it effectively. Until considerable experience has been attained in thinking mathematically, it is best to understand the general by examining its meaning in particular cases. Indeed it is precisely by such examination that general mathematical principles were originally discovered.

Mathematics as a language, the last aspect of mathematics to be considered, is so important that a separate section will be devoted to it.

6. MATHEMATICS AS A LANGUAGE

Ideas and symbols. Some mathematical language is known by everyone. For example, you have ways of telling others both in spoken and written language the number of chairs in a room or the shape of this book. The language you use conveys mathematical ideas.

Mathematical language consists of spoken or written symbols which represent the ideas of mathematics. You must always distinguish between the idea and its symbol. The distinction is usually clear from the context. For example, the following sentences make it clear whether the idea or the symbol is being considered:

A square is a mathematical object.

'Square' is printed on this page.

The name or mark which represents an idea is chosen arbitrarily. It matters not what symbol is used; what is important is that a mathematical idea is understood or communicated. For example, number names are not universal; there are many names for each number idea. The English number names "one," "two," and "three" are "moja," "mbili," and "tatu" in Swahili. A German names them "eins," "zwei," and "drei." The ideas represented are the same in each case; only the written and spoken languages differ.

It is the mathematical ideas which are characteristic of mathematics, not the symbols which express them. The symbols are used so that the ideas may be grasped, retained, and used more easily, and so that the ideas may be thought about and discussed with others. In general, the ideas are more important than the symbols which represent them. For example, a number is more important than its symbol. Mathematical objects are different. A number is an idea and is abstract in nature; a number symbol, or numeral, is a thing which exists and is concrete in nature.

Some difficulties arise if the distinction between an idea and its symbol is not clear. This can be avoided, however, if the idea is clearly understood before the symbol or symbols for it are adopted. Once the idea is understood and a language to express it is available, the idea and its symbol merge into the working body of mathematics.

Translations of symbols. A sentence may be translated from a foreign language into English in many ways. The translation may be literal, that is, word for word, or it may endeavor to convey the thought in a natural style.

Sentences in mathematics may also have many translations. For example, the sentence,

$$7 + 4 = 11,$$

is translated literally into the English sentence,

Seven plus four equals eleven.

It may also be translated as

Seven plus four is eleven,

Seven and four are eleven,

The sum of seven and four is eleven,

and

Four added to seven equals eleven.

For the student learning to use the language of mathematics the literal translation is preferable; however, a different type of translation will sometimes lead to better understanding. For example, a six-year old finds more meaning in "Seven and four are eleven" than in "Seven plus four equals eleven."

Every mathematical symbol and every mathematical sentence have a literal English translation. This does not mean, however, that the literal translation can be understood. For example, since you know names for the symbols "Γ," "z," "1," "sin," and "π," and since you understand the convention of expressing division by writing one number over another, you can translate the following mathematical sentence into literal English:

$$\Gamma(z)\Gamma(1 - z) = \frac{\pi}{\sin \pi z}.$$

The translation is

> Gamma z times gamma one minus z equals pi divided by sine of pi times z.

This translation conveys no meaning to you if you are unfamiliar with the ideas of advanced mathematical analysis which are being expressed. The translation of symbols can only be accomplished when the ideas which symbols represent have meaning.

Conciseness of mathematical language. Mathematical language is a concise language. When it is applicable, all irrelevances are stripped away. The language is translated and used literally, and it is not necessary to recast the thought in a more elaborate way. The result is compactness which allows concentration on the essential idea and also contributes to its comprehension. This can best be understood by an example.

An important principle, the distributive property of multiplication, is frequently useful in the multiplication of numbers. The principle, discussed in Chapter 6 and elsewhere in this book, may be illustrated by the following examples:

$$(a) \quad (10 + 3) \times 5 = (10 \times 5) + (3 \times 5);$$
$$(b) \quad (5 + 8) \times 7 = (5 \times 7) + (8 \times 7).$$

These statements may be tested by first performing the operations shown in parentheses and then comparing the indicated results. For example, in statement (a)

$$(10 + 3) \times 5 = 13 \times 5, \quad (10 \times 5) = 50, \quad \text{and} \quad (3 \times 5) = 15.$$

Since $13 \times 5 = 65$ and $50 + 15 = 65$, statement (a) is verified. You may verify the second statement in the same manner. Other illustrations of the principle are:

$$(4 + 6) \times 13 = (4 \times 13) + (6 \times 13);$$
$$(100 + 5) \times 7 = (100 \times 7) + (5 \times 7).$$

If the principle just illustrated is stated in words, it might read:

> "If three numbers are chosen, and the first two numbers are added, and their sum is multiplied by the third number, then the result is the same as if the first number and third number are multiplied, the second and third number multiplied, and the resulting two products added."

The statement of the principle in mathematical language is as follows: "if a, b, and c denote any three numbers, then

$$(a + b) \times c = (a \times c) + (b \times c)."$$

The brevity and compactness of the statement in mathematical symbols make the principle easier to understand than when it is stated in words.

7. MATHEMATICS AS AN ECONOMY OF THOUGHT

An important practical benefit of mathematics is the economy of thought and mental effort which results when it is properly applied. Once a mathematical method has been discovered, it can be used by anyone willing to take the time to learn it. The common pattern for addition is an illustration of this economy of thought. Consider, for example, the following problem:

> A dress shop had a two-day sale of dresses. The first day of the sale, 276 dresses were sold, and the second day of the sale, 167 dresses were sold. How many dresses were sold during the entire sale?

You have already found the mathematical solution for this problem when you performed the addition $276 + 167$ in Section 1 of this chapter. It was pointed out then that the method used, that is, the pattern for the addition process, is the final result of a long historical development. Four thousand years ago in Egypt only a highly skilled mathematician would have been able to add 276 and 167.

It is not known how the Egyptians would have performed this feat. It is known that whatever the method, it was clumsy and inefficient compared to ours. A less familiar example of the economy of thought which mathematics can effect is the simplification of the following rules adopted by a large department store.

> *Rule 1:* All floor managers shall be chosen from among the sales clerks.
>
> *Rule 2:* No one shall be both a buyer and a sales clerk.
>
> *Rule 3:* No buyer shall be a floor manager.

These rules may be simplified by a routine method requiring little more thought than that needed for adding 276 and 167. The method, though difficult to discover, can be learned and used by anyone.

The solution is as follows: Retain rule 1 and eliminate rule 3. Replace rule 2 with the following.

> *Rule 2:* No sales clerk shall be a buyer.

These examples help to demonstrate that the effect of increasing mathematical knowledge is to widen the scope of application of thought and simultaneously reduce the amount of thought required to attain a desired result. Once a new method has been discovered, experience has shown that it will have many useful applications, and furthermore, the method can eventually be simplified so that anyone may learn and use it with confidence.

8.   CONVEYING INFORMATION IN MATHEMATICAL LANGUAGE

A student of mathematics sometimes feels that the difficulty of the subject is due to the use of unfamiliar symbols and to the arbitrary manner in which symbols are selected to represent ideas. This is partly true, but the difficulty is not peculiar to mathematics. The relation between the meaning of an idea and a symbol is arbitrary in any language. We may illustrate this fact by conveying information in a nonsense language.

Suppose that "ootza" means one, "throotza" means three, while "flumf" means foot and "yorbak" means yard. Then the following sentence conveys information:

(1)   There are throotza flumfs in ootza yorbak.

This is a true statement if the meaning of the nonsense words which appear in it are understood.

Compare statement (1) with the mathematical sentence,

(2) $\triangle ACF \cong \triangle BDE.$

The meaning of statement (2) is familiar from the study of high-school geometry. The information which it conveys might refer to Fig. 1–2, as well as to others.

FIGURE 1–2

There is a similarity between statements (1) and (2). The symbols $\triangle$, ACF, BDE and $\cong$ are used in the same way in (2) as the nonsense words ootza, throotza, flumf, and yorbak are used in (1); that is, they are used to express ideas. And in both (1) and (2), the symbols for the ideas have been assigned arbitrarily.

The meaning of the nonsense statement (1) is clear from its literal translation,

There are three feet in one yard.

The meaning of the mathematical statement (2) is not immediately clear from its literal translation,

Triangle ACF is congruent to triangle BDE.

You must also remember facts about triangles and the meaning of congruent triangles. The information which (2) conveys is more complicated than the information which (1) conveys, and it requires more knowledge to understand it.

It may be concluded from this discussion that the principal obstacle to understanding mathematics is an inadequate understanding of ideas. Paradoxically, only information which is already known can be conveyed in mathematical language. Once the ideas are understood, mathematical language is the best language for retaining and recalling the information and for applying it effectively to new situations.

Sets. During the twentieth century mathematicians all over the world have been using the idea of a set in the formulation and development of mathematical patterns, both new and old. The set idea has proved to be of advantage in elementary mathematics as well as in advanced mathematics; it is employed continually in this book. The next chapter is devoted to an explanation of the idea of a set, some of its useful consequences, and how mathematics may be communicated in set language.

Like many ideas of merit, the idea of a set is basically simple. You will realize as you study Chapter 2 that you have been using the idea of a set ever since you began to think. What is new is its applications, and the mathematical language employed to describe it. The wide-spread systematic use of set ideas is a distinguishing characteristic of modern mathematics and is one of the principal reasons for its greater scope and power as compared with mathematics of the past.

9. THEME AND PURPOSE OF BOOK

The theme and purpose of this book are the seeking and unfolding of the patterns of mathematics which underlie arithmetic and elementary geometry. Emphasis is placed on the inductive techniques of discovery of such patterns rather than on their formal development by the techniques of deductive logic. You will be guided to look for patterns and to regard the numerous problems as an opportunity to apply mathematical patterns to new situations. The language and ideas of set theory are used throughout the book in order to carry out these purposes in the simplest and most effective manner.

Note: It is assumed that you have some skill with the basic operations of arithmetic. You may evaluate your ability by performing one or more of the practice tests of Appendix II. You may continue with other tests of Appendix I if more practice is needed for development of greater skill.

EXERCISE SET 1–1

1. (a) Describe briefly two patterns you know for subtracting 89 from 191.
   (b) Place an asterisk next to the pattern which is most convenient for use with any two numbers.
2. You have learned a pattern for counting. Describe briefly the pattern used when counting the following objects:

3. Identify three other mathematical patterns you have learned.
4. Explain why mathematics is useful to you, giving three reasons other than reasons related to the intelligent handling of your money.
5. Why is the study of mathematics becoming more important for every elementary and high-school student?
6. Find an illustration from a book or magazine which illustrates geometric patterns and describe briefly the patterns illustrated.
7. (a) Sketch a pattern for linoleum, using dots.
   (b) Sketch a pattern for linoleum, using triangles.
   (c) Sketch another linoleum pattern.
8. Study the patterns in the two squares below and answer the following questions.

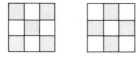

   (a) Name three ways in which the patterns in the two squares are similar.
   (b) Name one way in which they differ.
   (c) The second pattern may be obtained from the first in a simple way. How?
9. Observe the pattern in each of the following divisions and make a general statement which predicts the results of continuing the pattern.

   (a) $\dfrac{1\frac{1}{2}}{8)\overline{12}}$; $\dfrac{3}{4)\overline{12}}$; $\dfrac{6}{2)\overline{12}}$; $\dfrac{12}{1)\overline{12}}$; $\dfrac{24}{\frac{1}{2})\overline{12}}$; ...

   (b) $\dfrac{6}{2)\overline{12}}$; $\dfrac{5}{2)\overline{10}}$; $\dfrac{4}{2)\overline{8}}$; $\dfrac{3}{2)\overline{6}}$; $\dfrac{2}{2)\overline{4}}$; $\dfrac{1}{2)\overline{2}}$; $\dfrac{\frac{1}{2}}{2)\overline{1}}$; ...

10. Observe the pattern in each of the following sequences and list the next five numbers in each.

   (a) 0, 2, 4, 6, 8, . . .

   (b) 1, 4, 9, 16, 25, . . .

   (c) $\frac{1}{2}$, $\frac{1}{4}$, $\frac{1}{8}$, $\frac{1}{16}$, $\frac{1}{32}$, . . .

   (d) 2, 5, 11, 23, 47, . . .

   (e) 1, 2, 1, 4, 1, 6, . . .

11. Study the patterns of the numbers 1 through 16 in the squares below.

1	2	3	4
6	5	8	7
9	10	11	12
14	13	16	15

(i)

7	4	2	1
11	8	5	3
14	12	9	6
16	15	13	10

(ii)

   (a) Describe the arrangement of the numbers in (i).

   (b) Describe the arrangement of the numbers in (ii).

   (c) Arrange the numbers in another way and describe the pattern you followed.

12. (a) Name three games not mentioned in the text which have an arithmetic plan of play.

   (b) Name three games not mentioned in the text which have a geometric plan of play.

   (c) Name three games not mentioned in the text which have both a geometric and an arithmetic plan of play.

13. Answer the following questions about the game of tic-tac-toe which is played on the grid in the accompanying diagram.

   (a) Does the game have a geometric or an arithmetic plan?

   (b) Write simple rules for the game.

14. Simplify the following rules for Wythoff's game.*

   (a) Arrange a number of objects in two heaps each containing a different number of objects.

   (b) One of two players, in his turn, may take one, two, three, . . . or any number of objects from one heap; or he may take one, two, three, . . . or any number of objects from both heaps, provided he takes the same number from both heaps.

   (c) The game is completed when all objects have been removed.

   (d) The winner is the person removing the last object.

---

* Ball, W. W. Rouse, *Mathematical Recreations and Essays.* (Revised by H. S. M. Coxeter.) London: Macmillan and Co., Ltd., 1942, p. 38.

15. Play the following game with a friend and answer the question below.

> *Adding game.* First player selects a number less than 7. Each player in turn adds a number less than 7 to the sum. The person who obtains a sum of 24 is the winner.

What pattern of play should you follow to ensure that you always win if you are the first to mention a number?

16. Identify which of the following statements belong to pure mathematics and which belong to applied mathematics.
    (a) The sum of a number and zero is the number itself.
    (b) The circumference of a circle is π times the diameter.
    (c) The unit of length, one foot, is twelve times the unit, one inch.
    (d) A circle is a set of points.
    (e) An automobile traveling 50 miles per hour can travel 150 miles in three hours.

17. Using a and b as any two numbers, generalize the pattern you observe in each of the following.
    (a) $3 \times 4 = 4 \times 3$; $10 \times 8 = 8 \times 10$; $12 \times 728 = 728 \times 12$;...
    (b) $3 + 4 = 4 + 3$; $10 + 8 = 8 + 10$; $12 + 728 = 728 + 12$;...

18. Using a, b, and c as any three numbers, generalize the pattern in the following.

$$(12 + 9) \div 3 = 12 \div 3 + 9 \div 3; \quad (25 + 15) \div 5 = 25 \div 5 + 15 \div 5;...$$

19. List ten widely used symbols which convey meaning, without using number symbols, words, or abbreviations.

20. List seven symbols for conveying the idea of four.

21. How do the statements in each of the following differ in meaning? Distinguish in each between idea and symbol.
    (a) Anne is pretty; Anne has four letters.
    (b) Penelope is shorter than Anne; Penelope is longer than Africa.
    (c) The subject of the paragraph is "3"; the subject of the paragraph is three.
    (d) Mile and inch are rather short; mile and kilometer are rather long.
    (e) Foot is longer than rod; a rod is longer than a foot.

22. Tell whether each "three" which is italicized in the following refers to the number three or to the number symbol "3."

> *Three* is a difficult idea for a one-year old child to understand.
> A *3* is difficult for a *three*-year old to write.
> The *three* in the number symbol 235 represents a number which is *three* times ten.

23. Make three translations of each of the following mathematical sentences. Mark the literal translation of each with an asterisk.
    (a) $5 \times 2 = 10$ (b) $12 \div 2 = 6$ (c) $\angle 1 + \angle 2 = 90°$

24. (a) What is a pictograph and how does it convey information?

(b) What is a rebus and how does it convey information?

25. Simplify the following statements by eliminating any statements that are superfluous in each case.

(a) I like green dresses. I like your green dress. You dress is green.

(b) Mary is my friend. My friends are pretty. Mary is pretty.

(c) A square has four sides. A square is a rectangle. A rectangle has four sides.

26. Simplify this series of statements by eliminating any that are unnecessary to the situation.

(a) Today is the first Sunday after the first full moon on or after the vernal equinox.

(b) The first Sunday after the first full moon on or after the vernal equinox is Easter.

(c) Today is Easter.

27. Given: "tootza" means two, "throotza" means three; "knuk" means equal, and "chook" means plus.

(a) What is the meaning of the following:

$$2 + 2 + 2 = 3 + 3$$

Tootza chook tootza chook tootza knuk throotza chook throotza?

(b) Translate the sentence into language which is more widely understood.

28. Study the pattern in the first diagram below and finish the others in a similar way.

5	2	7
9	4	13
14	6	20

12	8
7	9

75	39
39	24

a	b
c	d

(a)   (b)   (c)

29. (a) What two ways may be used to obtain the number in the lower right corner of the patterns of Exercise 28?

(b) Why is the result the same for each method?

30. Study the pattern in the first diagram below and finish the others in a similar way.

2	4	8
3	5	15
6	20	120

5	6
8	10

10	50
8	25

a	b
c	d

(a)   (b)   (c)

31. (a) What are the two ways you may use to obtain the number in the lower right corner of the patterns of Exercise 30?

(b) Why is the result the same for each method?

32. Arrange the following in a pattern so that each square selected is enclosed by the last one selected. In what order will they be selected?

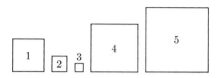

33. Given the following girls names: Rose, Violet, Sue, Janet, Geraldine.
    (a) Arrange them alphabetically.
    (b) Arrange them by the number of letters in each name.
    (c) Arrange them in any other order you may wish to choose. Define the order in words.

34. Arrange the three letters p, t, i in three different sequences. Describe each sequence chosen in words.

35. Examine the number sequence:

$$0, 1, 1, 2, 3, 5, 8, 13, 21, 34, 55, 89, 144, 233, 377, 619, 981$$

Each number after the first two is obtained by adding the two preceding numbers. For example,

$$0 + 1 = 1, \qquad 1 + 1 = 2, \qquad 1 + 2 = 3, \qquad 3 + 2 = 5, \quad \text{etc.}$$

As many numbers can be written in the sequence as desired. For example, the next two numbers are $21 + 34 = 55$ and $34 + 55 = 89$.
    (a) Write the next five numbers in the sequence after 89.
    (b) Place a circle around each even number in the sequence.
    (c) Identify and describe the pattern formed by the even numbers of the sequence.
    (d) The tenth number in the sequence is the even number 34. Can you predict whether the sixteenth number of the sequence will be odd or even? Explain.

36. Pascal used the arithmetic triangle below. The numbers in it form many patterns.

```
            1
          1   1
        1   2   1
      1   3   3   1
    1   4   6   4   1
  1   5  10  10   5   1
```

    (a) Discover and describe three patterns formed by the numbers of the arithmetic triangle.
    (b) Study the patterns of each horizontal row of numbers and describe the pattern in each.

37. The numbers in the two squares below have been chosen to form a simple addition pattern.

1	6	8
5	7	3
9	2	4

9	4	2
5	3	7
1	8	6

(a) What is the pattern formed?
(b) The pattern of the second may be obtained from the pattern of the first square in a simple way. What is it?
38. (a) Find three examples of magic squares in a reference book and explain their pattern.
    (b) Develop three magic squares of your own and explain their pattern.

REFERENCES

BALL, W. W. ROUSE, *Mathematical Recreations and Essays.* (Revised by H. S. M. Coxeter.) London: Macmillan and Co., Ltd., 1942, 418 pp.

BANKS, J. HOUSTON, *Elements of Mathematics.* Boston: Allyn and Bacon, Inc., 1961, pp. 1–6.

BRUMFIEL, CHARLES F., ROBERT E. EICHOLZ, and MERRILL E. SHANKS, *Fundamental Concepts of Elementary Mathematics.* Reading, Mass.: Addison-Wesley Publishing Company, Inc., 1962, pp. 1–11.

BRUNE, IRVIN H., "Language in Mathematics," in *The Learning of Mathematics*, Twenty-first Yearbook of the National Council of Teachers of Mathematics. Washington, D. C.: The Council, 1953, pp. 156–191.

CAJORI, FLORIAN, *A History of Mathematics.* New York: The Macmillan Company, 1919, 515 pp.

FOUCH, ROBERT S., and EUGENE D. NICHOLS, "Language and Symbolism in Mathematics," in *The Growth of Mathematical Ideas*, Twenty-fourth Yearbook of the National Council of Teachers of Mathematics. Washington, D. C.: The Council, 1959, pp. 327–369.

OSBORN, ROGER, M. VERE DeVAULT, and W. ROBERT HOUSTON, *Extending Mathematical Understanding.* Columbus, Ohio: Charles E. Merrill Books, Inc., 1961, pp. 1–11.

SANFORD, VERA, *A Short History of Mathematics.* Boston: Houghton Mifflin Co., 1930, 402 pp.

School Mathematics Study Group, "Number Systems," in *Studies in Mathematics*, Volume VI. New Haven, Conn.: Yale University, 1961, pp. 1–13.

SMITH, DAVID EUGENE, *History of Mathematics*, Volume II. Boston: Ginn and Company, 1925, 725 pp.

CHAPTER TWO

SETS

The distinct objects in a well-defined collection of things are said to form a *set*. It is common to speak of a set of dishes or a set of dominoes when referring to a specific collection of dishes or dominoes. You also use the set idea when speaking of a "school" of fish, a "herd" of cattle, a stamp "collection" or the "membership" of a club.

1. SETS AND THEIR IMPORTANCE

The set idea is used tacitly every time objects are classified by their properties, and is of the greatest importance in science. The classification of plants and animals in biology is essentially an arrangement in hierarchies of well-defined sets. Most scientific laws are statements about well-defined sets of objects, such as electrons, chemical elements, stars, and nebulae. Finally, the idea of a set is of major importance for mathematics. In fact, logicians have shown that the whole of pure mathematics may be reduced to statements about sets.

The paragraphs which follow contain nothing which is new in principle. What is new is that significant and useful statements will be made about sets and their relations to one another which in no way depend upon the nature of the objects of which the sets are composed. Although such statements are of primary interest to logicians and mathematicians, they are useful to anyone interested in thinking effectively in any situation, because they furnish patterns for thinking which have wide applicability.

Defining sets. There are two general methods of defining a set. The first method is simply to name each of the objects in the set. For example, if the objects are the letters in the word "constitution," the set formed of these objects consists of the seven letters, i, o, u, c, n, s, t. The second method is to state a property possessed by each object in the set, and by no object not in the set. For example, the set mentioned above could be defined as the different letters of the English alphabet which appear in the word "constitution." The second method allows many possible definitions for the same set. For example, the set could also be defined as the different letters of the alphabet appearing in the phrase, "no coins to count."

17

The first method is a method of defining by *enumeration* or listing, and the second method is defining by *stating a property.* Any set considered must be well defined; that is, the definition must ensure that it is possible to decide whether any given object does or does not belong to the set.

Examples of sets. You should examine each of the following examples and decide whether the set is best defined by enumerating each object or by stating a property possessed by each object of the set. If possible, think of other defining properties of each set.

(1) The former presidents of the United States alive today.

(2) The vowels of the English alphabet.

(3) The seven deadly Sins.

(4) The cities of the United States with a population of over three million.

(5) The cities and towns of the United States with a population of over three thousand.

(6) All the different species of insects.

(7) The first hundred billion whole numbers.

You should identify other sets and define them; if a defining property is used, be sure that all objects of the set are included and all objects not in the set are excluded.

In the seven examples of sets above, there is an obvious similarity among the objects making up each set. Thus in the third example, the objects are all vices: Pride, Gluttony, Sloth, Greed, Anger, Envy, and Lust. There is, however, no requirement that the objects making up a given set have anything in common beyond the mere fact that they belong to that set. The only requirement is that it be clear what objects are in the set. For example, the collection made up of the Empire State Building, a particular sneezing cat, and a particular grain of sand from the Sahara Desert is a trivial thing to think about, but is nevertheless a well-defined set.

Notation for sets. In the discussion of general properties of sets, it is convenient to use capital letters, $A, B, C, \ldots$, to denote specific sets, and lower-case letters, $a, b, c, \ldots$, to denote the objects in the sets. Since these objects may be of diverse kinds, they are called elements or members of the sets to which they belong. Thus, if d is an element of set A, you indicate this fact by saying "d is an element of A" or "d belongs to A."

Mathematicians use a convenient notation for defining sets by enumeration. This notation is best explained by an example. The set consisting of the first three odd numbers is denoted by

$$\{1, 3, 5\}$$

and read:

the set consisting of (the numbers) 1, 3 and 5

or

the set whose members are 1, 3 and 5.

Although symbols are used to denote the objects which are the members of a set, the set itself consists of the objects and not the symbols unless it is so stated. The order in which the members appear between the braces is unimportant. Thus

$$\{1, 3, 5\}, \qquad \{3, 5, 1\}, \qquad \{5, 1, 3\} \qquad \text{and} \qquad \{1, 5, 3\}$$

all denote the same set.

A set may consist of a single member. Thus, if the set A has only one member "a," we write

$$A = \{a\}.$$

Note that the set $\{a\}$ is different from the object "a." For example, a set consisting of a pillow is not itself a pillow.

EXERCISE SET 2–1

1. Write an English sentence for the following mathematical sentences.
    (a) $A = \{\text{Mary, Jane, Joseph}\}$
    (b) $B = \{2, 4, 6, 8\}$
2. In each of the following indicate whether the set is described or listed.
    (a) The set of all houses in Little Rock
    (b) $\{\text{English, French, Spanish, Russian}\}$
    (c) $\{\text{Matthew, Mark, Luke}\}$
    (d) The set of all states in the United States which border Mexico
    (e) The set of all your aunts and uncles
3. Define each of the sets below by enumerating its members.
    (a) The set of persons who live in your home
    (b) The set of whole numbers less than 19 which are multiples of 4
    (c) The set of all the states of the United States whose names begin with I
    (d) The set of all letters in your name and not in your mother's name
    (e) The set of all fractions equal to $\frac{2}{5}$ with a denominator of 25
4. Define each of the sets below by stating a property possessed by every member of the set. (Several correct descriptions may be possible.)
    (a) Set $A = \{0, 1, 2, 3, 4, 5, 6, 7, 8, 9\}$
    (b) Set $B = \{\text{Erie, Huron, Michigan, Ontario, Superior}\}$
    (c) Set $C = \{\text{Washington, Adams, Jefferson, Madison}\}$
    (d) Set $D = \{\text{cent, nickel, dime, quarter-dollar, half-dollar, dollar}\}$
    (e) Set $E = \{\frac{8}{4}, \frac{12}{4}, \frac{16}{4}, \frac{20}{4}\}$

5. List the following sets.
  (a) The letters of the alphabet used to spell "NED"
  (b) The letters of the alphabet used to spell "DEN"
  (c) The letters of the alphabet used to spell "END"
6. What do you note about the three sets listed in Exercise 5?
7. Think of five sets of which you are a member.
  (a) Define each set either by listing or stating a property of the set.
  (b) Name the sets which have in common members other than yourself.
  (c) Which of the sets have exactly the same members?
  (d) Define a set which contains all the members of all the sets you have listed.
8. Define three sets to which any horse belongs.
9. Describe the difference between

$$A = \{1, 2, 3\} \quad \text{and} \quad B = \{\{1\}, \{1, 2\}, \{1, 2, 3\}\}.$$

10. Define these sets by stating at least two properties for each.
  (a) $A = \{$New York, Chicago$\}$ (b) $B = \{3, 6, 9\}$
11. In the paragraph below, identify as many of the sets referred to as you can.

James Brown was twenty-five years old, unmarried, and good looking. His young married friends liked him as a guest at their parties, but he hated parties unless they promised him an evening of dancing. So it was with reluctance that he accepted Grace Jackson's invitation to dinner and bridge.

2.   RELATIONS BETWEEN SETS

Set equality. Two sets are said to be equal if they consist of the same elements. If A and B are equal sets, $A = B$ may be written and read, "A equals B." If the statement $A = B$ refers to sets in general, it adds nothing to knowledge, since it merely means that either the symbol A or the symbol B may be used to denote the same set.

The situation is very different if two specific sets A and B defined by distinct properties are being considered. In this case, the statement "$A = B$" may be true, or it may be false, but determining its truth or falsity increases the information we have about A and B. For example, if the statement can be shown to be true, it is known that the same objects possess two different properties. This situation occurs constantly in every-day life, and it is also of fundamental importance in the sciences, particularly in mathematics. For example, A whose members are multiples of two, and B whose members are numbers which are exactly divisible by two have the same members and are equal sets. You should supply other examples.

The relation of equality between sets is a good example of a property which is independent of the nature of the elements making up the sets.

The relation is meaningful; that is, given any two sets A and B, the statement $A = B$ is either true or false. Other properties of equality to which attention is called below establish a pattern to be encountered many times in the study of mathematics. These properties will be stated in mathematical language, that is, in symbols. State their meaning in ordinary language and convince yourself that each of the three properties which follow is true irrespective of the nature of the objects making up the sets A, B, and C.

If A, B, and C are any three sets, then:

    (a) $A = A$.

    (b) If $A = B$, then $B = A$.

    (c) If $A = B$ and $B = C$, then $A = C$.

Finally, if the two sets A and B do not have the same members, we say they are unequal and write $A \neq B$, read, "A is not equal to B." You should determine whether properties of inequalities follow the pattern just given for equalities.

Set inclusion. Set A is said to include set B if every element of B is also an element of A. This fact is denoted by $A \supseteq B$, read "A includes B." The relation $\supseteq$ is called set inclusion. Note that since every element of A is also an element of A, A includes itself or, in symbols, $A \supseteq A$.

The inclusion language $A \supseteq B$ is used when the sets A and B are given equal consideration. But it often happens in mathematics that there is one set which is predominant because it includes all the other sets considered at the time. The set of whole numbers is an example of such a set from elementary arithmetic, and the set of all points in a plane is an example from geometry. If A is such a set, and $A \supseteq B$, the subordinate character of B as compared with A is best expressed by calling B a *subset* of A.

If A includes B but does not equal B, we say that A properly includes B. If the set B also has at least one member, we call B a *proper subset** of A. For example, the natural numbers are a proper subset of the whole numbers. On the other hand, the set $\{1\}$ has no proper subsets. The symbol $A \supset B$* denotes that "A properly includes B."

The relation of set inclusion has four important properties which are stated below in mathematical symbols. State what the properties mean in ordinary language and convince yourself that the properties given are true

---

* Some authors prefer to use the symbol $\supset$ for any set inclusion and to allow the empty set to be a proper subset. Here, as in all mathematics, a symbol or definition once accepted should be followed. When other books are consulted, you should be sure you understand how symbols are used and terms are defined.

irrespective of the elements in the sets. Note first that if A and B are two well-defined sets, the statement $A \supseteq B$ is meaningful; that is, it is either true or false.

Let A, B, and C be any three sets. Then:

(a) $A \supseteq A$.

(b) If $A \supseteq B$ and $B \supseteq A$, then $A = B$.

(c) If $A = B$, then $A \supseteq B$ and $B \supseteq A$.

(d) If $A \supseteq B$ and $B \supseteq C$, then $A \supseteq C$.

Many applications of these properties of inclusion will be given later. Like the properties of equality of sets, they will also serve as a pattern which appears many times in mathematics.

3. FINITE AND INFINITE SETS

The sentence $A = \{a, b, c\}$ defines the set A by enumerating or listing its members. Any set which consists of a small number of objects often can best be defined by enumeration. Nevertheless, modern logicians and mathematicians usually prefer to define sets by properties. To understand why this is so, consider the following three sets: A is the set of even whole numbers less than 13; B is the set of even whole numbers less than 133; C is the set of all even whole numbers. A simple definition by enumeration of set A is possible:

$$A = \{0, 2, 4, 6, 8, 10, 12\}.$$

In theory, set B is capable of the same kind of definition by enumeration; every element of B can be named explicitly:

$$B = \{0, 2, 4, 6, 8, 10, 12, \ldots, 130, 132\}.$$

Note that with both these definitions, you do not need to know what an even number is in order to know what the sets A and B are; for, since all their elements are known, the sets are known. But the situation with set C is quite different. Not every even number can be listed; there are too many of them. Consequently, a definition of C by enumeration is impossible. This fact may be described by saying that "the set C is infinite." A set such as A or B which can be defined by enumeration is called a finite set. A set such as C which cannot be defined by enumeration is called an infinite set.

The root meaning of the word infinite is "not finite." The word "infinite" does not imply that the set C is more difficult to think about, or any less real than the finite sets A and B. However, to understand what the set C is, the defining phrase, "even whole number," must be understood. For the collection of objects making up C to be well defined, a definition must be devised which will tell what objects belong to C, and what objects do not belong to C. Since it is assumed that you know what the whole numbers are, the definition must provide a rule which will make it possible to decide whether a given whole number does or does not belong to C.

Such a rule is easily stated. Divide the number in question by two. If the division is exact, the number is an element of C. If the division leaves a remainder of one, the number is not in C. For example,

$$7 = 3 \times 2 + 1$$

is not in C, but

$$18 = 9 \times 2 + 0$$

is in C.

Thus, if it is understood that "an even whole number" simply means a whole number exactly divisible by two, the set C is defined. It is often convenient to denote C as follows:

$$C = \{0, 2, 4, 6, \ldots\}.$$

The three dots within the braces serve two purposes. First, they indicate that set C is infinite and cannot be defined by enumeration. Second, they suggest that you may write as many elements of C as you please, following the pattern set by the first few elements. The sentence, "C consists of the numbers 0, 2, 4, 6, etc.," expresses the meaning of the symbol. Other more precise ways of describing infinite sets by mathematical symbols will be used later.

From this discussion it should be clear that if a set is infinite, it is important that it be well defined. Until you are familiar with precise definitions, it is wise to make certain that any definition given for an infinite set does in fact enable you to decide whether a given object is or is not a member of the set.

4. THE EMPTY SET

A set is often best defined by stating a property which every element in the collection must have. However, a property might be defined which none of the objects considered could have. For example, consider the collection of all human beings in Chicago over nineteen feet tall. This definition states a property which makes it possible to decide what inhabitants of Chicago belong to the collection, and what inhabitants do not. It may be said in this particular situation that the set considered does not exist. It turns out to be much more useful to say that the set does exist, but it is an *empty* set; that is, it has no members. The notation { } is used to denote an empty set. For example, the set A of human beings over nineteen feet tall may be denoted by $A = \{ \}$, read, "A is the empty set."

The situation is similar to that of regarding zero as a number. The natural numbers one, two, three, . . . are used for counting; hence they are called the counting numbers. Zero is not a counting number; nevertheless, it is advantageous to have some way of describing the situation when there is nothing to count; the number zero serves this particular purpose and many others. It is also advantageous to consider a collection containing no elements as a set.

There is only one empty set. Since two sets were defined to be equal if they consisted of the same elements, any two empty sets are equal. They both have no elements. Therefore, *there is only one empty set*. The empty set is a subset of every set. { } is a subset of the set of natural numbers, of the set of members of your family, and of the set of kings of England.

$$\text{If} \quad A = \{a, b, c\} \quad \text{and} \quad B = \{ \},$$
$$\text{then}$$
$$A \supseteq B.$$

5. VARIABLES AND CONSTANTS

There is another useful way of defining the elements of a given set. A symbol which is used to denote any element of a specified set is called a variable over the set. The set is referred to as the domain of the variable. The letters $m, n, . . . , x, y, z$ from the second half of the alphabet will often be used to represent variables. The domain will always be defined unless it is understood from the context. For example, an important domain is the set of whole numbers. This set will be referred to as set W.

If a variable is definable over a set, the set must be nonempty. In the special case when the set consists of exactly one element, the variable is called a constant. The letters $a, b, . . . , k$ from the first half of the alphabet will be used to represent constants. A constant may be equally well defined as a symbol denoting a specific element of a set.

Variables allow the extension of the brace notation $\{. . .\}$ used for the definition of finite sets by enumeration to the definition of a set by its property. For example, let n be a variable over the set W. The whole numbers of the set $A = \{0, 1, 2\}$ all have the property of being less than three. Therefore, A may be defined in the following way:

$$A = \{n \mid n < 3\}.$$

To the left of the vertical bar, |, is the variable, and on its right is the defining property which a number n must have to belong to set A. The expression is read, "A is the set of all whole numbers n such that n is less than 3."

Other examples of this notation will make the use clearer. The set B of all numbers with the property "multiple of 3" is denoted by

$$B = \{n \mid n \text{ is a multiple of } 3\}, \quad \textit{domain}$$

as well as by

$$B = \{0, 3, 6, 9, \ldots\}.$$

Similarly,

$$C = \{n \mid n \text{ is a power of } 3\}$$

defines the set

$$C = \{1, 3, 9, 27, \ldots\}.$$

The expression

$$B = \{n \mid n \text{ is a multiple of } 3\}$$

is read,

Set B is the set of all n such that n is a multiple of 3.

In each of the examples just given, the sets may be defined by using the letter a to represent a constant, that is, a specific whole number. For example,

$$A = \{n \mid n < a\},$$
$$B = \{n \mid n \text{ is a multiple of } a\},$$

and

$$C = \{n \mid n \text{ is a power of } a\}.$$

If $a = 3$, the sets A, B, and C are the sets described previously. However, if $a = 12$, the sets are not the same.

It is very important to know the domain of a given variable; that is, to know the set over which the variable is defined. For example, the sentence below does not define A; further information is needed.

$$A = \{x \mid 0 < x < 1\}.$$

If the domain of x is the set of the whole numbers, A is the empty set. If the domain of x is the set of common fractions, A is the infinite set of all proper fractions. If the domain of x is the set of all common fractions whose denominators are less than four, A is the finite set $\{\frac{1}{2}, \frac{1}{3}, \frac{2}{3}\}$.

The methods for operating with variables whose domain is some specified kind of number are a part of algebra and will not be discussed here. The purpose of using variables in this book is to help you think more effectively about arithmetic and geometry. The usefulness of variables as an aid in understanding complicated ideas will be clearer as further reading is done. The concept of a variable is almost indispensable to an understanding of modern mathematics and its applications. It is therefore important that you learn to state simple mathematical ideas by means of variables, in order to be able to use them intelligently in more complicated situations.

EXERCISE SET 2–2

1. Each of the following defines a set. Are the sets finite or infinite?
   (a) The set of all the countries in North America
   (b) $\{0, 1, 2, \ldots, 9\}$
   (c) The set of all whole numbers greater than 100
   (d) The set of all fractions greater than $\frac{1}{2}$
   (e) The set of elephants in the Chicago zoos today
   (f) $\{0, 2, 4, 6, \ldots\}$
   (g) The set of leaves on a three-leaf clover
2. Define each of the following sets by enumeration.
   (a) The set of odd numbers less than 15 and greater than 3
   (b) The set of all women who have been president of the United States
   (c) The set of all women who have been members of the cabinets of the presidents of the United States
   (d) The set of digits used in the decimal system of notation
3. State a general method for testing whether any finite set is well defined.
4. Which of the following are empty sets?
   (a) The women who are heads of the governments of the world
   (b) The readers of this book who are 45 feet tall
   (c) The grains of sand on the beaches of the world
   (d) The citizens of the United States who have visited the sun
   (e) The numbers used in counting
5. Which of the following pairs of sets are equal?
   (a) $\{m, n, p, q\}$ and $\{n, p, m, q\}$
   (b) $\{\frac{1}{2}, \frac{1}{4}\}$ and $\{.25, .5\}$
   (c) $\{\Box, \triangle, \nabla, \bigcirc\}$ and $\{\Box, \triangle, \bigcirc, \diagup\!\!\!\!\Box\}$
   (d) $\{0\}$ and $\{ \}$
   (e) $\{2, 1, 3\}$ and $\{1, 2, 3, \ldots\}$
6. Given: Set A, the set of whole numbers greater than five and less than nine; and set B, the set of whole numbers denoted by the individual digits of the number eight thousand eight hundred sixty-seven. Show that set $A =$ set B.

7. For each set in the left column, choose an equal set in the right column.

(a) $\{x, y, z\}$

(b) Set of numbers with one-digit number symbols

(c) The set of numbers used to name the number 792

(d) The set of letters in the word "pool"

(e) $\{\frac{1}{2}, \frac{1}{3}\}$

(f) The set of numbers whose symbols are used on a clock face

(g) $\{1, 2, 6, 7\}$

(h) The set of even numbers that are odd numbers

(1) $\{2, 90, 700\}$

(2) Set of digits

(3) $\{.5, .3\}$

(4) $\{\ \}$

(5) The sum of 996 and 730

(6) $\{y, x, z\}$

(7) $\{7, 6, 2, 1\}$

(8) The set of letters in the word "polo"

(9) $\{\frac{3}{9}, \frac{25}{50}\}$

(10) $\{12, 11, 10, 9, 8, 7, 6, 5, 4, 3, 2, 1\}$

8. Define five subsets of the set of all living men.

9. For each set in the left column, choose the sets from the right column which are subsets of it.

(a) $\{x, y, z\}$

(b) Set of even numbers

(c) The set of numbers used to name the number 792

(d) The set of letters in the word "pool"

(e) $\{\frac{1}{2}, \frac{1}{3}\}$

(f) The numbers whose symbols are used on a clock face

(g) $\{1, 2, 6, 7\}$

(h) The set of even numbers which are odd numbers

(1) $\{\ \}$

(2) $\{2, 7\}$

(3) $\{1, o, p\}$

(4) $\{1, 2, 6, 7\}$

(5) $\{33\frac{1}{3}\%\}$

(6) $\{x\}$

(7) $\{0\}$

(8) $\{2\}$

10. From the sets listed in Exercise 9, identify the proper subsets.

11. List all the subsets of set M, given that M has as members the last three letters of the English alphabet.

12. List the proper subsets of M from the previous exercise.

13. (a) Describe the sets which have no proper subsets.

(b) Describe the sets which always have proper subsets.

14. Indicate whether each of the following statements is true or false.

(a) $\{Mark\} \supseteq \{Matthew, Mark, Luke, John\}$

(b) $\{a, b, c\} \supseteq \{c, a, b\}$

(c) $\{5, 6, 7, 8\} \supseteq \{6, 7, 8\}$

(d) $\{.2, .4\} \supseteq \{.2, .4, .6, .8\}$

(e) $\{0, 1, 2, 3, \ldots\} \supseteq \{3, 4, 5, \ldots\}$

15. If $\{\ \} \supseteq A$, what do you know about A?

16. (a) $A \supseteq B$ means "A includes B." Mathematicians and logicians also use a relation, $\subseteq$, defined as follows:

$$A \subseteq B$$

if and only if

$$B \supseteq A.$$

What is the relation $\subseteq$?

(b) How would you write the sentence below in symbols?

B is a subset of A.

(c) State four properties of the relation $\subseteq$ analogous to the four properties of the relation $\supseteq$ given in the text.

17. (a) Identify a property P so that $D = \{x \mid x \text{ with property } P\}$ is the set of odd numbers.

(b) What set is defined by $\{2x + 1 \mid x \text{ a variable over } W\}$?

(c) Does the notation $D = \{1, 3, 5, \ldots\}$ define set D?

(d) Consider the property,

D consists of all whole numbers which are not multiples of two.

Does this property differ from the property stated in (a)?

(e) Define D by stating yet another property.

18. (a) Set G is defined as the collection of all multiples of 853. Is 566,127 a member of G?

(b) How did you decide whether 566,127 is a member of G?

(c) How can you decide whether any given member is or is not in G? in any set?

19. Write an English sentence for each of the following mathematical sentences.

(a) $A = \{x \mid x \text{ is a living ex-president of the United States}\}$

(b) $B = \{x \mid x \text{ is a whole number} > 9\}$

(c) $C = \{x \mid x \text{ is an even number}\}$

(d) $D = \{x \mid x \text{ is a whole number} > 2 \text{ and } < 9\}$

20. Define the finite sets of Exercise 19 by enumeration and indicate the infinite sets by listing some typical members.

21. Define each of the following, using the notation

$$A = \{x \mid x \text{ with property } P\}.$$

(a) Set B of all federal judges

(b) Set C of all numbers greater than $\frac{1}{2}$

(c) Set D of all numbers less than 20 and greater than 8

(d) Set E of all multiples of three which are also less than 15

6. FORMING SETS FROM GIVEN SETS

Union of sets. Given any two sets, there are two simple ways of forming a new set, ways that do not depend on the nature of the elements in the sets. The first one is as follows: if A and B are any two sets, the set consisting of all elements which belong to A, or to B, or to both A and B is called the set union of A and B. The set union of A and B is denoted by $A \cup B$, read "A union B."

For example, if A has as members the number zero and B has as members the natural numbers, $A \cup B$ is the set of whole numbers; when $A = \{$ham, coffee$\}$ and $B = \{$juice, toast, egg$\}$, then $A \cup B = \{$juice, ham, egg, toast, coffee$\}$; or, when $A = \{1, 2, 3, 4\}$ and $B = \{3, 4, 6\}$, then $A \cup B = \{1, 2, 3, 4, 6\}$.

It is always true that $(A \cup B) \supseteq A$ and $(A \cup B) \supseteq B$. If

$$C \supseteq A \qquad \text{and} \qquad C \supseteq B,$$

then

$$C \supseteq (A \cup B).$$

The reason for this is that every element belonging to A or B or to both A and B also belongs to C.

Intersection of sets. If A and B are any two sets, the set consisting of all elements which belong to both A and B is called the set intersection of A and B. The set intersection of A and B is denoted by $A \cap B$, read "A intersection B."

The sets A and B may have no elements in common. In this case, $A \cap B = \{ \ \}$, and A and B are said to be *disjoint sets*. The set of your fingers and the set of your eyes are disjoint sets. So are the set of odd numbers and the set of even numbers.

If A and B are not disjoint sets, they are called *intersecting sets*. Intersecting sets always have at least one member in common. The set of states north of the Ohio River and the set of states east of the Mississippi River are intersecting sets. The set of multiples of 4 and the set of multiples of 9 are also intersecting sets. But the set of factors of 4 and the set of multiples of 9 are not intersecting sets; they are disjoint sets. If

$$A = \{1, 2, 3, 4\}, \qquad B = \{3, 4, 6\}, \qquad \text{and} \qquad C = \{5, 6\},$$

then

$$A \cap B = \{3, 4\}, \qquad B \cap C = \{6\},$$

but

$$A \cap C = \{ \ \}.$$

Hence A and B are intersecting sets, and so are B and C, but A and C are disjoint sets.

It is always true that $A \supseteq (A \cap B)$ and $B \supseteq (A \cap B)$. If $A \supseteq D$ and $B \supseteq D$, then

$$(A \cap B) \supseteq D,$$

for every element of D belongs to both A and B and hence belongs to $A \cap B$.

7.   UNIVERSAL SETS AND SET COMPLEMENTS

It often happens in mathematics that all the sets being considered are subsets of one specified set. Such a set is called a universal set. Indeed, in investigating any one kind of object, such as stars, plants, poems, or schools, the set consisting of all the objects under consideration will form a universal set for that investigation.

Let U be a universal set, and let A be any subset of U. The collection of all elements of U which do not belong to A is the complement of A in U, or simply the complement of A if it is clear what universal set is considered. The complement of A will be denoted by comp A, read "complement of A." The two sets A and comp A give a simple classification of the elements of the universal set U. For every element of U belongs to A or to comp A, but not to both.

For example, if the universal set is the people in a school, the complement of the set of students in a particular classroom is the set of all people in the school who are not students in that classroom. But if the universal set is the people in a classroom, the complement of the set of students in a classroom is the set of teachers in that classroom. If the universal set is the collection of whole numbers less than eight, the complement of

$$\{4, 7, 2\} \quad \text{is} \quad \{0, 1, 3, 6, 5\}.$$

Two further properties of complements are of importance. The complement of comp A is A, for the elements of U which do not belong to comp A are precisely the elements of A. Every subset of U has a complement. This fact is clear from the definition of a complement except perhaps for the set U and the empty set $\{\ \}$. But since there are no elements of U which do not belong to U,

$$\text{comp } U = \{\ \}.$$

And since every element of U belongs to U but not to $\{\ \}$,

$$\text{comp } \{\ \} = U.$$

8. FAMILIES OF SETS, SUBSETS, AND DISTINGUISHED SUBSETS OF A SET

It is often necessary to consider sets all of whose elements are sets. Such a set is called a family of sets. For example in a school, the set of children age six, the set of children age seven, the set of children age eight, etc., form a family of sets.

If E is the set of even numbers and O is the set of odd numbers, the family $\{E, O\}$ may be formed.

Families of all subsets of a set. There is a particularly important family associated with every set, namely, the family of all of its subsets. It is not difficult to define this family by enumeration if there are just a few elements in the set. For example, the family of subsets of $\{1, 2\}$ consists of the sets

$$\{\ \}, \quad \{1\}, \quad \{2\}, \quad \text{and} \quad \{1, 2\}.$$

The enumeration rapidly becomes more difficult as the number of elements in the set increases.

Families of distinguished subsets of a set. If the number of elements of a set is infinite, it is impossible to define the family of all of its subsets by enumeration, for the number of the subsets is also infinite. The family of subsets of the whole numbers is too vast and inclusive to be of use in studying the properties of whole numbers themselves. It is, however, important to study the properties of certain subfamilies of whole numbers. Examples of these are the set of multiples of n, and the set of powers of n. Because of their importance, the elements of these families are called distinguished subsets of the whole numbers. There are many distinguished subsets of the set of whole numbers, such as the set of primes, the set of squares, and numbers that can be expressed as the sum of two squares or the sum of three squares.

The concept of a family of distinguished subsets of a set is also used in geometry. The universal set for plane geometry is the set P of all points of a plane. The family of all the subsets of P has been studied intensively by mathematicians. Nevertheless, it has proved impossible to obtain a comprehensive understanding of it. The progress which has been made has resulted from identifying and studying important families of distinguished subsets of P. The properties of some of the simplest of these, such as triangles and circles, are traditionally the subject matter of elementary geometry. These subsets and many other, more recently identified, distinguished subsets of P are the topics for study in Chapters 8 and 13.

9. FORMING SETS BY CLASSIFICATION

The elements of a set are frequently classified into smaller, more convenient subsets. Botanists classify the huge set of all the different kinds of plants on earth into smaller, more easily studied subsets which they call plant families. Geographers classify the cities and towns of the United States by population, grouping together cities with a population of over one million, cities with population between nine hundred thousand and one million, and so on, down to hamlets of less than one thousand inhabitants. The set of children in a given school are classified in various ways: by grade, by age, by I.Q., alphabetically by the initial letters of their last names.

Classification procedures are also common in mathematics. For example, whole numbers are classified as even and odd, and geometric figures are classified as lines, circles, triangles, quadrilaterals, etc.

The most useful and important classifications are those which are mutually exhaustive and exclusive; that is, each element of the set must be classified, and classified in one way only. In the examples above the classification of whole numbers as odd and even is exhaustive and exclusive, but the classification of geometric figures is not. If every element of a set is classified, the classification is said to be exhaustive. If every element is classified once, and only once, the classification is said to be exclusive. If the classification is both *exhaustive* and *exclusive* and every subset contains at least one element, the classification is *mutually exhaustive and exclusive.*

For example, if the first twenty-one whole numbers are classified according to the remainder obtained on division of each number by three, the subsets have as elements the numbers leaving no remainder, remainder 1 and remainder 2. Thus

$$M = \{0, 1, 2, 3, \ldots, 17, 18, 19, 20\},$$

and the family of subsets of M determined by this classification consists of three sets:

$$R_0 = \{0, 3, 6, 9, 12, 15, 18\},$$
$$R_1 = \{1, 4, 7, 10, 13, 16, 19\},$$
$$R_2 = \{2, 5, 8, 11, 14, 17, 20\}.$$

10. VISUALIZING RELATIONS BETWEEN SETS

Sets and the relations between sets may be visualized by representing the sets as regions in a plane.

Figure 2–1 illustrates the relations between two sets A and B when (a) A and B are disjoint, (b) A and B intersect, (c) A properly contains B. In

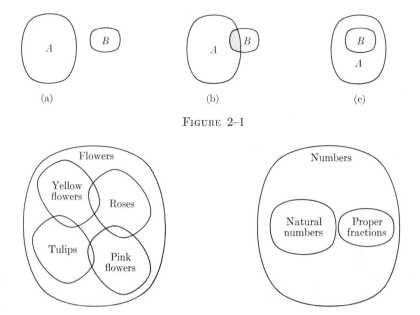

FIGURE 2–1

FIGURE 2–2

(b), the shaded area refers to $A \cap B$. Such figures are called *Euler diagrams* after the mathematician Euler (1707–1783), who first employed them. (Euler is pronounced "Oiler.")

Euler diagrams may be used to visualize much more complicated relations among sets. Figure 2–2 illustrates a classification of the set of all flowers and of the set of all numbers. The classifications are neither exhaustive nor exclusive. The diagrams show some subsets of flowers and of numbers but not all. In neither case are all the members of the universe classified. The diagrams allow you to identify some subsets, disjoint sets, and intersecting sets.

EXERCISE SET 2–3

1. Find the indicated sets:
   (a) $\{\bigcirc, \triangle\} \cup \{\square, \square\}$
   (b) $\{a, b, c\} \cup \{x, y\}$
   (c) $\{0, 1, 2, \ldots, 9\} \cup \{\ \}$
   (d) $\{1, 9, 25\} \cup \{4, 16\}$
   (e) $\{\bigcirc, \triangle\} \cap \{\square, \square\}$
   (f) $\{a, b, c\} \cap \{b, c, d, e\}$
   (g) $\{0, 1, 2, \ldots, 9\} \cap \{\ \}$
   (h) $\{0, 1, 2, 3, \ldots, 9\} \cap \{1, 3, 5, 7, 9\}$

2. Find the indicated sets, given that the domain of x is the set of whole numbers.
   (a) $\{x \mid x < 1\} \cup \{x \mid x > 3\}$
   (b) $\{x \mid x > 4\} \cup \{x \mid x < 6\}$
   (c) $\{x \mid x < 1\} \cap \{x \mid x > 3\}$
   (d) $\{x \mid x > 4\} \cap \{x \mid x < 6\}$

(e) $\{x \mid x$ is a multiple of $2\} \cup \{x \mid x$ is a multiple of $5\}$

(f) $\{x \mid x$ is a multiple of $2\} \cap \{x \mid x$ is a multiple of $5\}$

3. If A and B are any two sets, show that $A \supseteq B$ if and only if the criterion $A \cup B = A$ is true.

4. If A and B are any two sets, discover a criterion for $A \supseteq B$, using set intersection analogous to the criterion in the previous exercise for set union.

5. In each of the following classify A and B as: equal or unequal sets; disjoint or intersecting sets; and A, a subset of B or B, a subset of A.

(a) $A = \{5, 10, 15, \ldots\}$
   $B = \{ \ \}$

(b) $A = \{0, 5, 7, 9\}$
   $B = \{95, 70\}$

(c) $A = \{\square, \triangle, \bigcirc\}$
   $B = \{\square, \square, \triangle\}$

(d) $A = \{2, 4, 6, 8\}$
   $B = \{\frac{24}{2}, 2, \frac{8}{2}, 2^3\}$ $\{12, 2, 4, 8\}$

6. What is a suitable universal set for each of the following pairs of sets?

(a) $A = \{$rose, tulip, dandelion$\}$
   $B = \{$cherry, apple, pear, plum$\}$

(b) $E = \{0, 2, 4, 6, \ldots\}$
   $F = \{1, 3, 5, 7, \ldots\}$

(c) $C = \{\frac{1}{2}, \frac{1}{4}, \frac{1}{6}, \frac{1}{8}\}$
   $D = \{\frac{10}{20}, \frac{10}{40}, \frac{10}{80}\}$

(d) $G = \{x \mid x < 9\}$
   $H = \{x \mid x > 10\}$

7. Given: U, the universal set, has as members the students of a college. Define five subsets of U.

8. Use the sets defined in Exercise 7 to illustrate the following: (a) intersecting sets, (b) disjoint sets, (c) empty set. (If you did not define subsets which may be used as illustrations, define others.)

9. Define the complement of each of the following:

(a) $A = \{1, 3, 5, 7, 9\}$ when U is the set of all whole numbers less than 10.

(b) $B = \{0, 1, 2, 3\}$ when U is the set of all whole numbers.

10. Given that U is the set W of all whole numbers, define explicitly the complement of each of the following:

(a) A is the set of all numbers whose number symbols have two digits.

(b) B is the set of all even numbers.

(c) C is the set of all the multiples of 4.

11. Given that $U = \{0, 1, 2, \ldots, 9\}$, $A = \{0, 1, 2, 3\}$, and $B = \{2, 3, 4, 5\}$, enumerate the following:

(a) comp A

(b) comp B

(c) $A \cup B$

(d) $A \cap B$

(e) comp $(A \cup B)$

(f) comp $(A \cap B)$

12. Can a subset of U have more than one complement in U? Explain your answer.

13. If $A \cap$ comp $B = \{ \ \}$, what relationship must exist between A and B?

14. Let U be the universal set, and C and D any two subsets of U with properties $C \cup D = U$ and $C \cap D = \{ \ \}$.

(a) Show that $C =$ comp D.

(b) Show that $D =$ comp C.

15. Given any two subsets A and B of U.

(a) If $A \supseteq B$, prove that comp $B \supseteq$ comp A.

(b) If comp $B \supseteq$ comp A, does $A \supseteq B$? Prove your answer.

16. Let $U = \{1, 2, 3, \ldots, 10\}$, $A = \{1, 3, 4, 7\}$, and $B = \{1, 2, 3, 8\}$.

(a) Verify: comp $(A \cup B) =$ comp $A \cap$ comp B.

(b) Verify: comp $(A \cap B) =$ comp $A \cup$ comp B.

(c) Do the formulas in parts (a) and (b) suggest a pattern to you? Give other evidence for the pattern.

17. Translate the following mathematical sentences into English sentences.
    (a) $A \cup B = C$ (b) $\{x \mid x$ is a multiple of $a\} = H$
    (c) $\{5, 2, 0\} \supseteq \{2, 0\}$ (d) comp $A \neq$ comp B
    (e) $\{1, 3, 5, \ldots\} \cap \{0, 2, 4, \ldots\} = \{\ \}$ (f) $E \subseteq F$
18. Translate the following sentences into mathematical sentences.
    (a) A is the set of all whole numbers x such that x is less than twelve.
    (b) B is the set of all whole numbers x such that x is both a power of three and less than thirty.
    (c) Set D contains set A.
    (d) The union of $\{1, 2, 3\}$ and $\{0, 4\}$ is the set M.
    (e) The intersection of $\{1, 2, 3\}$ and $\{0, 4\}$ is the set N.
    (f) The complement of the set of multiples of two is the set of odd numbers.
19. Given: D_x denotes the set of whole numbers which divide x exactly, and M_x denotes the set of multiples of x.
    (a) What set is defined by D_0? by D_{15}?
    (b) What set is defined by M_4? by M_{20}?
20. Given $U = \{$sticks, stones, bones$\}$ classified into the following family of subsets: $\{$sticks, stones$\}$; $\{$stones, bones$\}$.
    (a) Is the classification exhaustive? Why?
    (b) Is the classification exclusive? Why?
21. Classify the elements of the following sets in as many ways as possible.
    (a) $D = \{$pencil, paper, eraser, paper clip$\}$
    (b) $E = \{a, b, c\}$
22. If the universal set is the people who live in your block, show with Euler diagrams at least two different classifications of this universe. Is each classification exhaustive and exclusive?
23. Why is the classification of a universal set U into B and comp B both exhaustive and exclusive?
24. Prepare a Euler diagram to show relations between the following subsets of a student body.

A: members of the student council,

B: male students,

C: female students,

D: senior class,

E: junior class.

25. Which of the following are true statements for the sets of Exercise 24? (U is the student body.)
    (a) $A \cup B = U$ (b) $B \cap C = \{\ \}$
    (c) $A \cup D \cup E = U$ (d) comp $B = C$
    (e) $B \supseteq A$ (f) $B \cup C = U$
    (g) B and C are disjoint sets (h) B and D are disjoint sets
26. Show by Euler diagrams the relationship of the sets referred to in each of the sentences below.
    (a) Most of my friends are students and/or bridge players.
    (b) All my brothers live in Columbus, Ohio, United States of America.

(c) The set {5, 15, 20} is contained in the set of all counting numbers which are multiples of five.

27. Given that U is the set of natural numbers, A is the set of multiples of three, and B is the set of multiples of four. Diagram the relationship of the three sets.

28. Show with Euler diagrams all the possible relationships of A and B if $A \neq B$.

29. Show with Euler diagrams six possible relationships of A, B, and C if $A \neq B \neq C$. Are these all the possible relationships of the three sets?

*30. Suppose $A = \{1, 2, 3, 4\}$, $B = \{1, 2, 4, 6, 7\}$, and $C = \{2, 3, 4, 7\}$.

    (a) What is the smallest set containing A, B, and C? Call this set D.

    (b) What is the largest set contained in A, B, and C? Call this set E.

    (c) Working by analogy with the text, develop a satisfactory symbolism and mathematical names for the sets D and E.

    (d) Suppose A, B, and C are any three sets. Extend your thinking about the special case of (a), (b) and (c) to make a general statement for finding D and E.

    (e) Formulate a generalization for finding the smallest set D containing any four sets and the largest set E contained in any four sets. Use illustrations to test your generalizations.

11. ORDERED SETS

Frequently the objects of a set present themselves naturally in a definite order. For example the set N of the natural numbers is most simply thought of as arranged in order of magnitude: 1, 2, 3, 4, . . . Similarly the set of points on a horizontal line are arranged in order, either from left to right or from right to left.

If the distinct objects of a collection are arranged in a definite order, the collection is called an ordered set. A very simple method of ordering any finite collection of distinct objects is to count them off one by one as the first, second, third, etc., and then take them in the order in which they were counted. For example, if the set of distinct letters in the word "constitution" are counted off as they appear in the word the result is: c, o, n, s, t, i, u. If the vowels are counted first and then the consonants, the result is: o, i, u, c, n, s, t. As this example shows, there are usually many ways of ordering a given set.

A set as such is not ordered. For example, the set

$$\{2, 4, 6, \ldots, 1, 3, 5, \ldots\},$$

with all the even natural numbers considered first and all the odd natural

---

    * Starred problems are more challenging than others.

numbers considered next, is simply another way of thinking of the set N of natural numbers. In effect, it corresponds to visualizing U as the set union of the even natural numbers and the odd natural numbers.

An ordered set consisting of the elements b, g, a in that order is written (b, g, a) with parentheses to distinguish it from the unordered set $\{b, g, a\}$; (b, g, a) is read "the ordered set whose members are b, g, and a." Note that

$$\{b, g, a\} = \{a, g, b\},$$

but

$$(b, g, a) \neq (a, g, b)$$

unless $a = b$.

The ordered set of natural numbers is called the counting numbers. The subsets

$$(1), (1, 2), (1, 2, 3), (1, 2, 3, 4), \ldots,$$

so useful in counting, are called the *counting sets*.

12. THE CARTESIAN PRODUCT OF TWO SETS

If any two objects are thought of simultaneously in a definite order, they are called an ordered pair. If a and b are the objects, the *ordered pair* of first a and then b is denoted by (a, b). Thus if $a \neq b$, (a, b) and (b, a) are different ordered pairs. Note that the concept of an ordered pair is different from the concept of a set of two objects. For example,

$$\{a, b\} = \{b, a\},$$

but

$$(a, b) \neq (b, a)$$

unless $a = b$.

Let A and B be any two sets. Then if a is any member of A and b is any member of B, the set made up of all ordered pairs (a, b) is called the Cartesian product of A and B. This set is denoted by $A \otimes B$ and is read "the Cartesian product of A and B."

For example, suppose that $A = \{1, 2, 3\}$ and $B = \{I, II\}$. Then

$$A \otimes B = \{(1, I), (2, I), (3, I), (1, II), (2, II), (3, II)\}.$$

Another way of describing the Cartesian product $A \otimes B$ is to say that it consists of all possible matchings of each element of A with each element of B. Thus in the example above, the element 1 of A is matched both with the element I of B, and with the element II of B, and the two ordered pairs $(1, I)$ and $(1, II)$ which describe these possibilities are both elements of $A \otimes B$.

This fact suggests that a useful method of grouping the elements in the Cartesian product so as to show the matchings at a glance is to arrange the elements in a rectangular pattern as below:

		Set B	
		I	II
Set A	1	(1, I)	(1, II)
	2	(2, I)	(2, II)
	3	(3, I)	(3, II)

Extensive use will be made of the Cartesian product in the discussion of multiplication and division of whole numbers. The concept is also extensively used in modern geometry and other branches of mathematics.

13. ONE-TO-ONE CORRESPONDENCE

It is not necessary to count all the elements of two sets in order to find whether the sets have or do not have the same number of elements. For example, if milk is brought for a group of children in individual cartons and an attempt is made to match each child with a carton, it is immediately evident whether enough cartons were purchased. If no cartons or children are left unmatched, there is the same number of cartons of milk as there are children. The members of the set of milk cartons and the members of the set of children are matched one to one. The sets are in a one-to-one correspondence.

Consider the two sets $A = \{a, b, c\}$ and $B = \{\bigcirc, \triangle, \square\}$. There are several alternatives of pairing the elements of these sets with each other. For example,

Pairing of this nature is called a one-to-one correspondence between the sets A and B. Because there is such a one-to-one correspondence the sets are said to be *equivalent*. On the other hand, if we consider the two sets $A = \{a, b, c\}$ and $C = \{\star, \odot, \triangle, \square\}$, no one-to-one correspondence between the sets A and C is possible.

The symbolism $M \approx N$, read, "M and N are in one-to-one correspondence" or "set M is equivalent to set N," is used when it is possible to find a one-to-one correspondence between the sets M and N; when it is impossible to find such a correspondence, then the appropriate symbolism is $M \not\approx N$. Thus, $A \approx B$, but $A \not\approx C$.

If A, B and C are any sets, they have the following properties:

(a) $A \approx A$.

(b) If $A \approx B$ then $B \approx A$.

(c) If $A \approx B$ and $B \approx C$, then $A \approx C$.

When the meaning of the symbol $\approx$ is considered, the properties stated above become almost self-evident. The first property states that a set may be placed in a one-to-one correspondence with itself. Property (b) states that if A can be put in a one-to-one correspondence with B, then B can be put in a one-to-one correspondence with A. Property (c) states that if A can be put in a one-to-one correspondence with B, and B can be put in a one-to-one correspondence with C, then A can be put in a one-to-one correspondence with C.

Many other relations which are important in logic and mathematics have the same three properties that the relation $\approx$ has. For example, the relation of equality between sets and the relation of similarity between triangles also have these properties. (See Section 2.) The properties have accordingly been given special names. They are called, respectively, the *reflexive property*, the *symmetric property*, and the *transitive property*. In general, any meaningful relation between the elements of a set or the elements of a family of sets which is reflexive, symmetric and transitive is called an *equivalence relation*. Many equivalence relations will be discussed in the chapters on arithmetic and geometry.

14. THE NUMBER OF A SET

The relation $\approx$ makes it possible to state what is meant by number. Consider the following sets:

$$\{\Box, \bigcirc, \star\}, \qquad \{\text{red, grey, blue}\}, \qquad \{5, 8^2, \tfrac{2}{3}\}, \qquad \{\text{Bob, Pat, Roy}\}.$$

All these sets may be put into one-to-one correspondence with each other. The common property which any member of this family of sets has is called *number*; in this case, the number is three. The counting set $(1, 2, 3)$ also has the number three.

The property, *number of a set*, is denoted by $n(A)$, read, "number of set A." If $A \approx B$, then $n(A) = n(B)$ for A belongs to the family of all sets which may be put into one-to-one correspondence with B. For example, if

and

$$A = \{\bigcirc, \Box, \triangle, \star\}$$

cardinal number

$$B = \{\because, \vdots, \therefore, \vdots\}$$

then

$$A \approx B, \qquad \text{and} \qquad n(A) = n(B).$$

The latter statement is read, "the number of A equals the number of B."
Each of these sets may be put into a one-to-one correspondence with the
counting set N_4. The set $N_4 = (1, 2, 3, 4)$. The number of set A, set B,
and set N_4 is four.

The purpose of counting is to find the number of a set. As a set is
counted, a one-to-one correspondence is set up by eye or by pointing.
The diagram below illustrates the establishment of a one-to-one correspondence between the set A to be counted and the counting set N_4. N_4 is
ordered, and its last member, four, is the number of set N_4, and therefore
is also the number of set A.

$$A = \{\square, \; \bigcirc, \; \triangle, \; \square\}$$
$$N_4 = (\text{one, two, three, four})$$

The number of a set as defined by the idea of one-to-one correspondence
does not depend in any way on the nature of the elements belonging to the
set. Note that the number of the empty set is zero.

The number of a finite set. If L and K are finite sets and $L \approx K$, then
$n(L) = n(K)$, that is, L and K have the same number of elements. It is
also true that if L and K are finite sets with the same number of elements,
then $L \approx K$. For example, suppose that L is the set of letters of the alphabet which precede j, while K is the set of letters of the alphabet which
follow q. That is,

$$L = \{a, b, c, d, e, f, g, h, i\}$$

and

$$K = \{r, s, t, u, v, w, x, y, z\}.$$

Let $N = (1, 2, 3, 4, 5, 6, 7, 8, 9)$. By counting both L and K, they are
each put in one-to-one correspondence with the counting set N; therefore,
both L and K have nine members. Since $L \approx N$ and $N \approx K$, it follows
by the transitive property of equivalence of sets that $L \approx K$. You should
find other examples, if necessary, to convince yourself that for finite sets
the assertions,

Two sets have the same number of elements,

and

Two sets may be put into one-to-one correspondence with each other,

have the same meaning.

It is also possible to use the idea of one-to-one correspondence to explain what is meant by the statement that one set has more elements than another set. If M and T are two finite sets, M has more elements than T if there exists a proper subset H of M such that $H \approx T$. For example, suppose that

$$M = \{\star, \bigcirc, \bigtriangledown, \square\} \quad \text{and} \quad T = \{a, b, c\}.$$

Then if $H = \{\star, \bigcirc, \bigtriangledown\}$, it is a proper subset of M and $H \approx T$. Clearly M has more elements than T.

In view of this discussion, it seems appropriate to think of $H \approx T$ as meaning, "H and T have the same number of elements," and to conclude that if H is a proper subset of M, then $M \not\approx H$ and M has more elements than H. But unexpected things happen when the sets involved are infinite.

Let N be the set of natural numbers and E the subset of even natural numbers:

$$N = \{1, 2, 3, 4, \ldots\},$$
$$E = \{2, 4, 6, 8, \ldots\}.$$

The matching

$$\{1, 2, 3, 4, \ldots\}$$
$$\{2, 4, 6, 8, \ldots\}$$

defines a one-to-one correspondence between N and E. Hence $N \approx E$, but E is a proper subset of N; that is, N is in one-to-one correspondence with a proper subset of itself. This situation cannot occur if N is finite. That is, if N is a finite set and E is a proper subset of N, $N \not\approx E$. On the other hand, any infinite set may be put into one-to-one correspondence with one of its proper subsets, so that the example above is typical for infinite sets. Mathematicians have shown, however, that not all infinite sets have the same number.

EXERCISE SET 2–4

1. Which of the following statements are true? Which are false?
   (a) $(a, b) = (a, b)$
   (b) $(m, n, p) \neq (n, m, p)$
   (c) $\{a, b, c\} = \{b, c, a\}$
   (d) $(1.5, a) \neq (1\frac{1}{2}, 0)$
   (e) $\{6, 5\} = (5, 6)$
   (f) $(a, b, c) = (b, a, c)$

2. G is a set of ordered pairs of numbers such that the first member is three times the second member. Supply the missing member in each pair where necessary. The letters a and b denote numbers and are constants.

$$G = \{(3, 1), (12, 4), (3a, a), (15, \ ), (\ , \tfrac{1}{3}), (\ , \tfrac{3}{5}),$$
$$(1, \ ), (b, \ ), (\ , 2b), (3a, \ ), (2a, \ ), (15b, \ )\}$$

3. Given $A = \{m, n, p\}$ and $B = \{x, y\}$.
   (a) List all the ordered pairs of $A \otimes B$ in a rectangular pattern.
   (b) List all the ordered pairs of $B \otimes A$ in a rectangular pattern.
   (c) Are the members of the set $A \otimes B$ the same as those of the set $B \otimes A$? Why?

4. (a) Define the Cartesian product $C \otimes D$ by enumeration when

$$C = \{1, 2, 3, 4\} \quad \text{and} \quad D = \{1, 2\}.$$

   (b) Are all the elements of this Cartesian product defined?

5. Write the following sentences in mathematical symbols.
   (a) The Cartesian product of A and B is not the same as the Cartesian product of B and C.
   (b) A and B may be put in a one-to-one correspondence.
   (c) C and D are equivalent.
   (d) Sets A and B have the same number.
   (e) The number of C is less than the number of $\{5, 7, 9, 8\}$.

6. Express the following mathematical sentences in English sentences.
   (a) $M \approx P$ (b) $A \otimes B = B \otimes A$
   (c) $n(A) = n(B \cup C)$ (d) $A \cap B \neq C$
   (e) $n(1, 2, 3) > n(B)$ (f) $n(E) = 5$

7. Given: $A = \{\text{Jane, Mary, Susan, James, Robert, Tom}\}$.
   (a) List the counting set used to find the number of A.
   (b) What is the number of set N? How do you know?
   (c) What is the number of set A? Why?

8. Give a definition of "two" similar to the definition of "three" given in the text.

9. Is the relationship among people that is usually described by the term "love" reflexive, symmetric, and transitive? Give examples to illustrate your answers.

10. Examine the relations "ancestor of" and "sister of" as they apply to human beings and determine whether each is reflexive, symmetric, and transitive.

11. Is the equality relation of sets reflexive? symmetric? transitive? If your answer is "yes," state the properties for any sets A, B, and C.

12. Is the relation of set inclusion, $\supseteq$, reflexive? symmetric? transitive? If your answer is "yes," state the properties for any sets A, B, and C.

13. Is the relation of inequality, $\neq$, between sets always, never, or sometimes reflexive? symmetric? transitive? Give examples to illustrate each of your answers.

14. Rewrite the statements of Exercise 13, for the relationship greater than, $>$, making all other necessary changes in the statement.

15. (a) Is the relation "equality of numbers" an equivalence relation?
    (b) Is the relation "nonequality of numbers" an equivalence relation?

16. Show that set T whose members are powers of two may be put in one-to-one correspondence with the set N of natural numbers. State what you have shown in a mathematical sentence.

17. Define another subset, Q, of the set of natural numbers which may be put in one-to-one correspondence with the set of natural numbers.
18. Show that the set of whole numbers and the set of natural numbers may be put in one-to-one correspondence.
19. State the difference between finite and infinite sets, using only the ideas of one-to-one correspondence and proper subsets.
*20. Show that if D is a set which may be placed in a one-to-one correspondence with the set of natural numbers, there exists a proper subset E of D such that $D \approx E$.
21. State whether the following are true or false statements.
    (a) $\{a, b, c\} = \{a, c, b\}$ (b) $(a, b, c) = (a, c, b)$
    (c) $n\{a, b, c\} = n\{a, c, b\}$ (d) $\{a, b, c\} \approx \{a, c, b\}$
    (e) $\{x \mid 2 < x < 7\} = \{3, 4, 5, 6\}$ when the domain of x is the set of whole numbers.
    (f) $A \supseteq \{ \}$
    (g) If $A \supseteq B$, then $B \subseteq A$.
    (h) $\{1, 2\} \otimes \{3\} = \{(1, 3), (2, 3)\}$
22. If A, B, and C are given sets, state a relationship between A and C for each situation below.
    (a) $A = B$ and $B = C$ (b) $A \supseteq B$ and $B \supseteq C$
    (c) $A \subseteq B$ and $B \subseteq C$ (d) $A \neq B$ and $B \neq C$
23. Do you observe a common pattern among any of the situations of Exercise 22?

REFERENCES

BRUMFIEL, CHARLES F., ROBERT E. EICHOLZ, and MERRILL E. SHANKS, *Fundamental Concepts of Elementary Mathematics.* Reading, Mass.: Addison-Wesley Publishing Company, Inc., 1962, pp. 63–64, 169–186.

JOHNSON, DONOVAN A., and WILLIAM H. GLENN, *Exploring Mathematics on Your Own.* Garden City, N. Y.: Doubleday and Company, Inc., 1961, pp. 139–196.

OSBORN, ROGER, M. VERE DeVAULT, and W. ROBERT HOUSTON, *Extending Mathematical Understanding.* Columbus, Ohio: Charles E. Merrill Books, Inc., 1961, pp. 97–114.

McSHANE, E. B., "Operating with Sets," *Insights into Modern Mathematics,* Twenty-third Yearbook of the National Council of Teachers of Mathematics. Washington, D. C.: The Council, 1957, pp. 36–45.

PETERSON, JOHN, and JOSEPH HASHISAKI, *Theory of Arithmetic.* New York: John Wiley and Sons, Inc., 1963, pp. 20–36.

SCHAAF, WILLIAM L., *Basic Concepts of Elementary Mathematics.* New York: John Wiley and Sons, Inc., 1960, pp. 10–23.

SWAIN, ROBERT L., *Understanding Arithmetic.* New York: Rhinehart and Company, Inc., 1957, pp. 27–45.

WILLIAMS, SAMMIE M., H. GARLAND READ, JR., and FRANK L. WILLIAMS, *Modern Mathematics in the Elementary and Junior High Schools.* Syracuse, N. Y.: The L. W. Singer Company, Inc., 1961, pp. 74–93.

CHAPTER THREE

DEDUCTIVE LOGIC

1. IMPORTANCE AND HISTORY

The importance of logic, that is, the systematic study of the procedures of correct reasoning, is obvious to everyone. Yet no formal courses in this subject are usually taught in high school. Traditionally considered a part of philosophy, the study of logic is today offered by the philosophy departments of universities.

It was the ancient Greeks who developed both philosophy and logic as areas of study. Indeed, the great Greek philosopher Aristotle (384–322 B.C.), who is traditionally recognized as the founder of logic, did his work so well that until quite recently the logic taught in universities was essentially as he conceived it.

The tremendous growth of mathematics in the nineteenth century caused mathematicians to examine critically the reasoning procedures which had been used in developing mathematics. It was discovered that many arguments which had convinced earlier mathematicians were either incomplete or incorrect. Efforts to correct these mistakes and to avoid similar ones renewed interest in logic and resulted in a great extension and development of the subject. This new development which began about the middle of the nineteenth century is called "mathematical logic," or "symbolic logic," to distinguish it from the older, traditional logic of Aristotle.

Symbolic logic makes extensive use of variables instead of expressing all reasoning processes in words as the Greeks did. People engaged in developing this powerful and flexible instrument of thought are called logicians. They may also be philosophers or mathematicians, but need not be either; for symbolic logic has developed into an important subject in its own right with many applications in science and technology and with far-reaching influence on its parents, philosophy and mathematics. This chapter will be concerned with some of the ideas of symbolic logic that are particularly useful to any student of elementary mathematics.

2. DEDUCTIVE AND INDUCTIVE LOGIC

Traditionally, logic is divided into two parts, *deductive logic* and *inductive logic*. Both Aristotelian logic and symbolic logic are parts of deductive logic. Roughly speaking, the difference between deductive and inductive logic is the following: deductive logic analyzes the reasoning process that leads from accepted general principles, or hypotheses, to valid conclusions; inductive logic examines the reasoning process that leads from particular cases to acceptable general conclusions. Deductive logic is used constantly in mathematics and in science. Inductive logic is used principally by scientists but also by others when they endeavor to pass from specific facts and observations to general laws, or hypotheses, which can explain them.

A few examples may make the distinction between deductive and inductive logic clearer. Statements such as

All whales are mammals,

There are 110 fathoms in a furlong,

The number of prime numbers is infinite

may be established by deductive reasoning. Scientific hypotheses such as the Darwinian theory of natural selection in biology or the existence of the Ice Age in geology may be established only by inductive reasoning. Today the word "logic" usually refers to deductive logic, and the word "induction" refers to reasoning done inductively.

In this chapter only deductive logic will be discussed and shall often be referred to simply as logic. Induction will be discussed in Chapter 5.

One of the principal concerns of logic is the analysis of the process of establishing the truth of general statements. In mathematics, this process of establishing the truth of general statements is called "proof." In solving some of the exercises of Chapter 2 you used deductive logic in this manner when you proved general statements about sets. This was done so naturally that there may have been no awareness of the process. The discussion which follows presents a specific problem, analyzes its proof in detail and uses it to point up the general characteristics of any mathematical proof.

3. AN ILLUSTRATION OF DEDUCTIVE PROOF

The problem (from Chapter 2, Exercise Set 2–3) is to prove that statement (S) is true:

(S): If set A contains set B, then the set union of A and B is A.

The *hypotheses* on which the proof will be based are listed below. These are general principles which you must understand and accept before you begin reading the proof.

Hypothesis 1.   If X and Y are any sets, then $X \cup Y \supseteq Y$ and $X \cup Y \supseteq X$.

Hypothesis 2.   If X is any set, then $X \supseteq X$.

Hypothesis 3.   If X, Y, and Z are any sets and $Z \supseteq X$, $Z \supseteq Y$, then $Z \supseteq X \cup Y$.

Hypothesis 4.   If X and Y are any sets and $X \supseteq Y$, $Y \supseteq X$, then $X = Y$.

Before proceeding further, be sure that you understand and accept all four of the hypotheses listed. Otherwise, reread Sections 2 and 6 of Chapter 2.

The proof of (S) is as follows.

PROOF

Steps of proof	Reasons for steps
(1) $A \supseteq B$	Hypothesis of the statement (S) to be proved
(2) $A \supseteq A$	Hypothesis 2 with $X = A$
(3) From steps (2) and (1): $A \supseteq A \cup B$	Hypothesis 3 with $X = A$, $Y = B$, and $Z = A$
(4) $A \cup B \supseteq A$	Hypothesis 1 with $X = A$ and $Y = B$
(5) From (3) and (4): $A \cup B = A$	Hypothesis 4 with $X = A$ and $Y = A \cup B$

It may be concluded that *if $A \supseteq B$, then $A \cup B = A$* which is the statement (S) in mathematical symbols.

The argument given here is not the only way of proving statement (S), nor is it the shortest way. It is probably longer and more complicated than the argument that you used in solving the problem. Many of the hypotheses that were stated explicitly were probably immediately recognized to be true, so that you used them implicitly without stating them or writing them down. The primary object of the proof developed here is not to convince you of something that you already know, but to illustrate clearly the nature of a deductive argument.

4.   CHARACTERISTICS OF DEDUCTIVE PROOF

The illustration in Section 3 is a typical example of a formal, deductive proof. Every proof of this type begins with *hypotheses*, that is, statements for which no proof is offered. These hypotheses, along with whatever definitions are necessary, are called the premises of the proof. For example, the premises of the illustrated proof are the four hypotheses listed.

Ideally a proof should use no premise not explicitly stated and should proceed by a series of short, *closely linked steps*, each of which should be obviously true. The final step should be the *conclusion* which the proof was designed to establish. In the illustrative example, there are five such steps numbered (1), (2), (3), (4), and (5). The conclusion which the proof establishes is that $A \cup B = A$, as is stated in the last step of the proof.

The linking of steps in a proof is illustrated in step (3) of the illustration, where the statement $A \supseteq A \cup B$ is established. Here two previously established statements, namely, (1) $A \supseteq B$ and (2) $A \supseteq A$, are linked together with the third step by hypothesis 3.

In a briefer, more informal proof for those of you who thoroughly understand Sections 2 and 6 of Chapter 2, the first three steps of the proof might be condensed into one step:

Assume that $A \supseteq B$; then $A \supseteq A \cup B$.

Here the word "then" indicates that there is a linkage between the two statements $A \supseteq B$ and $A \supseteq A \cup B$. But in this informal proof the nature of the linkage and the reasons which justify the statement $A \supseteq A \cup B$ are left for you to supply.

On the other hand, a logician might feel that the proof given here was incomplete from his standpoint and would amplify its premises, increase the number of its steps, and give more reasons. If you are interested in such refinements, consult texts on symbolic logic.

The most important characteristic of a correct deductive proof is its *certainty*. Once the premises are accepted, the conclusion follows inevitably. It is in this respect that a deductive proof of some statement or assertion differs most markedly from the kind of proof accepted for most of the statements read or heard. A deductive argument does not merely make an assertion seem plausible or develop reasons why the assertion might, or should, be true; it compels the acceptance of the conclusion if the hypotheses are accepted.

It was doubtless the desire for an objective process of establishing truth, a process acceptable to all human beings, which led the Greek philosophers to discover and develop deductive logic. They were also convinced that there existed premises whose truth was self-evident. As a result they attached great importance to deductive reasoning, and firmly believed in the possibility of arriving at the truth by reasoning. This belief still is one of the driving forces in the development of our culture. Today, however, fewer people believe in the existence of completely certain, self-evident truths as the starting point for our reasoning. In mathematics, in particular, the question of whether premises are accepted because they are self-evident truths or merely because they are a convenient starting point is left undecided. For example, such fundamental hypotheses as the existence of the set of whole numbers or the existence of points are left undecided in a deductive development of the subject. All that is asserted is that *if* whole numbers (or points) exist with certain properties, they must have certain other stated properties. The utility and value of the conclusions arrived at and their applicability to the world around us are the reasons for the acceptance of the initial hypotheses—not the certainty of the hypotheses themselves.

In summary, the important characteristics of a formal deductive proof are:

(1) Every deductive proof begins with a set of hypotheses, its premises, which must be understood and accepted.

(2) A proof proceeds by a series of short, closely linked steps.

(3) Once the premises are accepted, the conclusion follows inevitably.

5. PROPOSITIONS

An analysis of the nature of the steps in deductive proof from another standpoint will provide a useful general pattern of reasoning.

The raw materials of both traditional logic and mathematical logic are propositions. *A proposition is a declarative statement which is either definitely true or definitely false.* The following are declarative statements. Some are propositions, some are not.

(1) Too many cooks spoil the broth.

(2) Many hands make light work.

(3) Progress is a comfortable disease.

(4) Time is the school in which we learn.

(5) Socrates is a man.

(6) All reptiles are cold blooded.

(7) Pigs can fly.

(8) Some mammals are whales.

(9) If X, Y, and Z are sets and $X \supseteq Y$, $Y \supseteq Z$, then $X \supseteq Z$.

(10) Seven is an even number.

(11) If x is any whole number, then $x + 1$ is greater than x.

(12) If x and y are odd numbers, then x times y is an odd number.

The first four examples will not be considered here, since it is difficult to secure agreement as to their truth or falsity. The next four examples belong to traditional logic; they are statements which are either true or false. They may be thought of as stating relations between sets and elements of sets. The last four examples also state relations between sets and since these four utilize either constants or variables, they belong to mathematical logic.

6. STATEMENTS INVOLVING VARIABLES

Statements like the examples given above are common in mathematics. Bear in mind in the discussion which follows that a proposition is a statement that is always either definitely true or definitely false. Not every statement involving variables is a proposition. For example, if x and y are variables whose domain is the finite set $\{1, 2, 3, 4\}$, then the statement "$x < y$" is not a proposition, for it is true for some values of x and y ($x = 1$; $y = 3$), but false for other values of x and y ($x = 3$; $y = 2$). Consequently, the statement "$x < y$" is sometimes true and sometimes false, and is not a proposition.

On the other hand, with the same domain for the variables x and y,

$$x < 5 \qquad \text{and} \qquad x \text{ times } y \text{ is less than twenty}$$

are both propositions, since they are true for all possible values of the variables x and y. Similarly,

$$x < 1 \qquad \text{and} \qquad x \text{ times } 2 \text{ equals zero}$$

are also propositions, since these statements are false for all the possible values 1, 2, 3, 4 of the variable x. A statement which is always false is a proposition just as is a statement which is always true. But a statement is *not* a proposition if, like "$x < 2$," it is sometimes true and sometimes false depending on the value of the variable x.

7. PROPOSITIONAL FORMS

A propositional form is a statement involving variables over a prescribed domain. The statement is a proposition for all values of the variables. Some propositional forms are true propositions for all values of the variables, some are false propositions for all values of the variables, and others are sometimes true and sometimes false propositions.

The statements $x^2 = x$ and $x > 1$ are both examples of propositional forms. If x is a variable whose domain is the set of whole numbers, then the first statement is true if $x = 0$ or $x = 1$, but false for all other values of x; the second statement is false for $x = 0$ or $x = 1$, but true for all other values of x.

The set of values of x for which a propositional form becomes a true proposition is called the *truth set* of the propositional form. If a truth set is either the entire domain of x or the empty set, the statement is not a propositional form, but a proposition. For example, with the domain of x as the set of whole numbers, $x^2 \geq x^*$ and $x > x + 1$ are both propositions because one is true and one is false.

From this discussion and from the solutions of the exercises you should recognize the importance of knowing the domain of the variable in statements involving variables. For example, if the domain of the variable x is the set $\{2, 4, 6\}$, the statement,

> (i) x is a multiple of two,

is a proposition. But if the domain of the variable x is the set $\{3, 4, 6\}$, then (i) is a propositional form. If the domain of the variable x is the set of whole numbers, the statement,

> (ii)   2 times $x = 5$

is a proposition. But if the domain of x is the set of fractions, then (ii) is a propositional form whose truth set is $\{\frac{5}{2}\}$. When working with variables always be sure that the domains of the variables are known.

8. ALGEBRAIC FORMULAS

Mathematical formulas such as $A = lw$ for computing the area of a rectangle or $d = rt$ for solving a distance (a rate and time problem) are already familiar to you. However, there exists another kind of mathematical formula.

If the domain of the variable is a set which can be regarded as a universal set, certain propositions stated as equalities are true for all values of the variables. These propositions are called algebraic formulas. For example, if the domain of X is the family U of all subsets of a set, the proposition $X \cup X = X$ is an algebraic formula. It is true for every element of U. If the domain U of the variables r and s is the set W of whole numbers, the propositions,

$$r \times s = s \times r \quad \text{and} \quad (r + s) \times (r + s) = r^2 + 2rs + s^2,$$

are algebraic formulas, since they are true for all whole numbers r and s. In general, then, *an algebraic formula is a proposition stating an equality which is true for all values of the variables.*

---

* The symbol $\geq$ symbolizes "greater than or equal to." $x^2 \geq x$ is read "x squared is greater than or equal to x"; $x^2 \leq x$ is read "x squared is less than or equal to x."

9. PROPOSITIONAL FORMS AND THE OPERATIONS OF ARITHMETIC

From the standpoint of mathematical logic, the process of subtracting the number 13 from 187 may be thought of as determining the truth set of the propositional form

$$x + 13 = 187$$

(see Exercise Set 3–1, Exercise 11). This truth set has only one element. If a and b are any whole numbers, the process of subtracting a from b may be thought of as determining the truth set of the propositional form

$$x + a = b.$$

This discussion and the solutions of the exercises will make it clear that propositional forms whose truth sets consist of one element are of importance in arithmetic. Try to identify other examples of this type of propositional form.

EXERCISE SET 3–1

1. Let P denote the set of all pigs, F the set of beings that fly, and B the set of all birds.
   (a) Is the statement

   $$(B \cup P) \cap F \neq \{ \, \}$$

   true or false?
   (b) What does the statement $P \cap F \neq \{ \, \}$ mean?
   (c) Illustrate the answers to (a) and (b) with Euler diagrams.
2. Using the sets of Exercise 1, answer the following.
   (a) Which of these statements are true?

   $$B \supseteq F, \qquad B = F, \qquad F \supset B$$

   (b) Is $F \supseteq B$ a true proposition?
3. Translate each of the propositions below into the language of sets.
   (a) Some mammals are whales.
   (b) All reptiles are cold blooded.
   (c) Pigs can fly.
4. Translate each of the propositions below into the language of sets. (Let E denote the set of even numbers, O the set of odd numbers, and W the set of whole numbers.)
   (a) If x and y are odd numbers, $x \times y$ is an odd number. (*Answer:* If x and y are elements of O, $x \times y$ is an element of O.)
   (b) If x is any whole number, $x + 1$ is greater than x.
   (c) Seven is an even number.

5. (a) There is a similarity in pattern between the statements, "Socrates is a man" and "Six is an even number." What is it?

(b) Is the pattern identified in (a) applicable to the statement "My cat is gray"?

(c) Is the pattern identified in (a) applicable to the following statements?

All men are mortal.

All numbers whose symbols have the digit 6 in the units place are even.

All cats are mammals.

(d) If any of the statements in (c) are different from those in (a), show the difference with Euler diagrams.

6. List three other examples for each of the two patterns identified in Exercise 5.

7. (a) Do the statements below differ in kind from the statements of Exercises 4 and 5?

Too many cooks spoil the broth.

Many hands make light work.

Progress is a comfortable disease.

Time is the school in which we learn.

(b) If so, how?

8. If x and y are variables whose domain is the set $\{1, 2, 3, 4\}$, which of the following statements are propositions and which are propositional forms?

(a) $x > 0$

(b) $(x + y) < (x \times y)$

(c) $(x + y) \leq 2 \times (x + y)$

(d) $(4x - y) \geq 0$

(e) $(5x - y) > 18$

(f) $x + 3$ is an even number

(g) $2y$ is an odd number

(h) $x < y$

9. (a) Are the following statements propositions or propositional forms?

Sometimes men are happy   and   Perhaps men are happy.

(b) Give two examples of statements that are propositions and two of statements that are propositional forms.

10. Assume that set C consisting of the children of one man and his wife has six elements, and that x and y are variables whose domain is C. Under what circumstances are the following statements propositions?

(a) x and y have the same parents.   (b) If $x \neq y$, x and y are brothers.

(c) x has no brothers.

(d) If $x \neq y$, x and y are different ages.

11. Which of the following statements are propositional forms and which are propositions? The domain of the variables x and y is the set of whole numbers.

(a) $x + 13 = 187$

(b) $x \div 182 = 14$

(c) $x + y = y + x$

(d) Either $x^2 = x$ or $x > 1$

(e) $x^2 = x$ and $x > 1$

(f) $x > (2 \times x) + 1$

(g) $x > (2 \times x) - 1$

(h) $y = 2 \times x$ and $y < 5$

(i) $3 \times y > x \times y$ and $0 < x < 5$

(j) $5 < x + y < 10$

12. Determine the truth set for each propositional form identified in Exercise 11. Note that in (h), (i), and (j) the truth sets consist of collections of ordered pairs of values of x and y; for example, since $4 = 2 \times 2$ and $4 < 5$, the pair $(2, 4)$ belongs to the truth set of (h).

13. If x and y are variables whose domain is the set $\{0, 1, 2, 3\}$, determine for each value of y whether the statement $x \geq y$ is a proposition or a propositional form.

14. If x and y are variables whose domain is the set of whole numbers, which of the following statements are propositions?
(a) $(4 \times y) \div 2 = 2 \times x$ (b) $x + y + 2 > 1$ (c) $x + y < 2(x \times y)$

15. Choose a domain and make two statements involving variables that are propositions and two that are propositional forms. Do not choose the set of whole numbers.

16. (a) State two algebraic formulas different from those used as examples. (An algebra textbook may be needed.)
(b) State as a formula: For any pair of whole numbers, the order in which the members of the pair are added does not alter the sum.
(c) Does the formula stated in (b) apply to pairs of fractions?

10. NOTATION FOR PROPOSITIONS, RELATIONS BETWEEN PROPOSITIONS, IMPLICATIONS

To facilitate the discussion which follows, the symbols **a**, **b**, . . . , **p**, **q**, . . . will be used to denote propositions. In the discussion of sets, only relations and operations on sets which were independent of the nature of the members of the sets were important. Similarly, the relations and operations on propositions are independent of the nature of the propositions and depend only on whether the propositions are true or false.

The negation of a proposition. If **a** is any proposition, the statement,

a is false,

is another proposition called the negation of **a**. This new proposition is denoted by $-$**a**, read, "not **a**" or "**a** is false." For example, if **a** is the proposition,

2 is greater than 3,

then $-$**a** is the proposition,

It is false that 2 is greater than 3, or 2 is not greater than 3.

If **a** is the proposition, "There are seven days in a week," then $-$**a** is the proposition, "There are not seven days in a week." The operation of forming the negation of a proposition is somewhat analogous to the operation of forming the complement of a set.

Incompatible propositions.   Two propositions are said to be incompatible if they cannot both be simultaneously true.   For example, **a** and −**a** are always incompatible.   If S is a set of points, the propositions, "S is a circle" and "S is a square," are incompatible, but not negations of one another.

Implications.   A fundamental relation between propositions can now be defined.   Proposition **a** is said to imply proposition **b** if **a** and −**b** are incompatible.   This is denoted by

$$\mathbf{a} \Rightarrow \mathbf{b},$$

read, "a implies **b**."   Note that for any propositions **a** and **b**, the statement, "a implies **b**," is another proposition.   Propositions of this form are called implications.

For example, if **a** is the proposition, "New Year falls on Sunday," and **b** is the proposition, "January 2 is a holiday in the United States," then **a** implies **b**.   Think of some other examples of this type of implication.

11.   IMPLICATION AND THE LAW OF DEDUCTION

Implications occur continually in deductive logic because of the following very important general pattern of reasoning.

> THE LAW OF DEDUCTION.   *If proposition **a** is true and if proposition **a** implies proposition **b**, then proposition **b** must be true.*

For since **a** implies **b**, the two propositions **a** and −**b** cannot both be true.   But by hypothesis, the proposition **a** is true.   Therefore, the proposition −**b** must be false; that is, the proposition **b** is true.   You have been applying this law subconsciously since you began to think.   For example, let **a** be the proposition, "Jack is snoring," and let **b** be the proposition, "Jack is sleeping."   Then **a** implies **b**, for if Jack is snoring now, he must be sleeping.

In the illustrative proof of Section 3, all four of the hypotheses used are essentially implications.   For example, the first hypothesis may be restated as follows: "If it is true that X and Y are sets, then $X \cup Y \supseteq X$ and $X \cup Y \supseteq Y$."   Let **a** denote the proposition, "X and Y are sets," and let **b** denote the proposition, "$X \cup Y \supseteq X$ and $X \cup Y \supseteq Y$."   Then hypothesis 1 may be restated as "a implies **b**."   In the actual proof, the law of deduction is used repeatedly.   For example, steps (1) and (2) together state that the proposition, "$A \supseteq A$ and $A \supseteq B$," is true.   Hypothesis 3 states in effect that if $A \supseteq A$ and $A \supseteq B$, then $A \supseteq A \cup B$; that is, it asserts that **a** implies **b**, where **a** is the proposition, "$A \supseteq A$ and $A \supseteq B$," and **b** is the proposition, "$A \supseteq A \cup B$."   Thus in step (3), the assertion that $A \supseteq A \cup B$ is true is a consequence of the law of deduction.

In a deductive proof the different steps commonly consist of establishing implications and then applying the law of deduction. The certainty of a deductive proof thus ultimately rests on the law of deduction. There are other ways in which the steps of a deductive proof may be linked, but the most important linkage is by implications and the law of deduction.

12. FURTHER PROPERTIES OF IMPLICATION, LOGICAL EQUIVALENCE

It is an interesting fact that the relation of implication, $\Rightarrow$, between propositions has properties which are similar to the relation of inclusion, $\supseteq$, between sets. If **a** and **b** are two propositions such that both of the statements "**a** $\Rightarrow$ **b**" and "**b** $\Rightarrow$ **a**" are true, then the propositions **a** and **b** are said to be logically equivalent. This is symbolized by **a** $\Leftrightarrow$ **b**, read, "**a** is equivalent to **b**."

The relation of equality between sets is an equivalence relation; that is, set equality is a reflexive, symmetric, and transitive relation (Chapter 2, Sections 2 and 13). The relation of logical equivalence, $\Leftrightarrow$, between propositions is also an equivalence relation; that is, for any propositions **a**, **b**, and **c**:

(a) **a** $\Leftrightarrow$ **a**.

(b) If **a** $\Leftrightarrow$ **b**, then **b** $\Leftrightarrow$ **a**.

(c) If **a** $\Leftrightarrow$ **b** and **b** $\Leftrightarrow$ **c**, then **a** $\Leftrightarrow$ **c**.

The relation of inclusion between sets, $\supseteq$, is reflexive and transitive. If A and B are sets and $A \supseteq B$ and $B \supseteq A$, then $A = B$; and if $A = B$, then $A \supseteq B$ and $B \supseteq A$ (Chapter 2, Section 2). The analogous properties of the relation of implication, $\Rightarrow$, between propositions are as follows:

(d) **a** $\Rightarrow$ **a**.

(e) If **a** $\Rightarrow$ **b** and **b** $\Rightarrow$ **c**, then **a** $\Rightarrow$ **c**.

(f) If **a** $\Rightarrow$ **b** and **b** $\Rightarrow$ **a**, then **a** $\Leftrightarrow$ **b**.

(g) If **a** $\Leftrightarrow$ **b**, then **a** $\Rightarrow$ **b** and **b** $\Rightarrow$ **a**.

You may verify and prove properties (b), (f), and (g). Property (d) is true because both **a**, $-$**a** and $-$**a**, **a** are incompatible pairs of propositions. Therefore property (a) is true by the definition of $\Leftrightarrow$.

Property (e) is proved as follows. Assume that **a** $\Rightarrow$ **b** and **b** $\Rightarrow$ **c**. Then **a** and $-$**b** are incompatible. Suppose that **a** is false. Then **a** and $-$**c** are not both true. Consequently **a** and $-$**c** are incompatible and

$$\mathbf{a} \Rightarrow \mathbf{c}.$$

Suppose that **a** is true. Then **b** must be true by the law of deduction. Hence **c** must be true, and **a** and $-$**c** are incompatible.

Finally, property (c) is proved as follows. Assume that $\mathbf{a} \Leftrightarrow \mathbf{b}$ and $\mathbf{b} \Leftrightarrow \mathbf{c}$. Then by property (g)

$$\mathbf{a} \Rightarrow \mathbf{b} \qquad \text{and} \qquad \mathbf{b} \Rightarrow \mathbf{c}.$$

Therefore by property (e), $\mathbf{a} \Rightarrow \mathbf{c}$. Similarly, $\mathbf{c} \Rightarrow \mathbf{a}$. Consequently, $\mathbf{a} \Leftrightarrow \mathbf{c}$ by property (f).

Property (e), the transitivity of implication, is not particularly useful in deductive reasoning when $\mathbf{a}$ is false, since it then gives no information about the truth or falsity of $\mathbf{c}$. But it is very useful when $\mathbf{a}$ is known to be true. Assume that $\mathbf{a}$ is true and $\mathbf{a} \Rightarrow \mathbf{b}$ and $\mathbf{b} \Rightarrow \mathbf{c}$. Then by (e), $\mathbf{a} \Rightarrow \mathbf{c}$. Consequently, $\mathbf{c}$ is true by the law of deduction.

13. THE LANGUAGE OF IMPLICATION

An implication $\mathbf{a} \Rightarrow \mathbf{b}$ is seldom stated as "Proposition $\mathbf{a}$ implies proposition $\mathbf{b}$." A common form of the statement is: "If $\mathbf{a}$, then $\mathbf{b}$." For example, the proposition, "If x is exactly divisible by 6, then x is exactly divisible by 3," means that the proposition, "x is divisible by 6," implies the proposition. "x is divisible by 3."

Another frequently used method of stating implications in mathematics is as follows. If $\mathbf{a} \Rightarrow \mathbf{b}$, we say that "$\mathbf{a}$ is a sufficient condition for $\mathbf{b}$ to be true." For the law of deduction does indeed allow the inference that if $\mathbf{a} \Rightarrow \mathbf{b}$ and if $\mathbf{a}$ is true, then $\mathbf{b}$ is true. Mathematicians also frequently say that "$\mathbf{b}$ is a necessary condition for $\mathbf{a}$ to be true." The logical meaning of this statement is the same as the preceding statement; namely $\mathbf{a} \Rightarrow \mathbf{b}$. But the psychological meaning is different. Suppose that $\mathbf{a}$ is a proposition and it is not known whether it is true or false, but you wish to prove it true. By the law of deduction, if $\mathbf{a}$ is true, and $\mathbf{a}$ implies $\mathbf{b}$, $\mathbf{b}$ must be true. Thus the truth of $\mathbf{b}$ is a necessary condition for the truth of $\mathbf{a}$.

If, on the other hand, $\mathbf{a} \Rightarrow \mathbf{b}$, but $\mathbf{b}$ is false, then $\mathbf{a}$ must also be false because $\mathbf{a}$ and $-\mathbf{b}$ are incompatible. For example, the implication, "If all even numbers are divisible by 4, 6 must be divisible by 4," is true. But 6 is not divisible by 4; therefore, not all even numbers are divisible by 4. This example illustrates a very useful logical principle: *in order to disprove a general statement, one example to the contrary is sufficient.*

The same kind of language is used for the logical equivalence $\mathbf{a} \Leftrightarrow \mathbf{b}$. This relationship is indicated by the statement, "$\mathbf{a}$ is true if and only if $\mathbf{b}$ is true," or by "$\mathbf{b}$ is both a *necessary* and *sufficient* condition for $\mathbf{a}$."

However, if $\mathbf{a}$ is the proposition, "It is raining," and if $\mathbf{b}$ is the proposition, "It is cloudy," then "It is raining" is a sufficient condition for "It is cloudy." "It is cloudy" is a necessary condition for "It is raining." "It is cloudy" is not, however, a sufficient condition for "It is raining." These two propositions are a simple example of two nonequivalent propositions.

14. DIFFICULTIES OF DEDUCTIVE PROOF

It was pointed out in Section 4 that an important advantage of deductive proof is its certainty. But since to be convinced by a proof you must accept its premises, a difficulty arises: how are acceptable hypotheses found to serve as premises from which a deductive argument can begin?

It is this difficulty which makes the use of deductive logic comparatively rare in matters of any complexity. The involved situations with which human beings must deal, not to mention their hopes and fears and other emotions, prevent the identification, the formulation, and the acceptance of the hypotheses necessary for deductive proof. It is a commonplace to emphasize the distinction between the real reasons and the alleged reasons for various conclusions human beings accept as true. A college text on logic invariably devotes much space to the discussion of mistakes and abuses in reasoning.

Outright mistakes in reasoning are minimized in symbolic logic by using variables systematically and by formulating precisely how they may be used. But the danger of proofs becoming unintelligible without extensive preliminary study of logic increases as more symbolism is introduced.

The difficulty of selecting adequate premises appears also in mathematics. It was only at the beginning of this century, after elementary geometry had been studied for over two thousand years, that a completely adequate set of premises for plane geometry was formulated by the great German mathematician Hilbert (1862–1943). Before that time, all the alleged proofs of theorems of geometry were logically incomplete. Moreover, by using only the premises stated by the Greek founders of plane geometry, absurd theorems can be proved, such as "Every two intersecting lines intersect at right angles" or "All angles are either straight angles or right angles." The various theorems of plane geometry, e.g., "The sum of the interior angles of a triangle equal two right angles," are not false. The deductive proofs of these theorems traditionally given are, nevertheless, defective.

Luckily, none of these difficulties need be faced in the mathematics of this book. The proofs given will be, so far as they go, logically correct. The aim of the proofs is to help you comprehend and apply useful mathematical ideas rather than to give a rigorous, deductive development of elementary mathematics. Such developments do indeed exist. The references at the end of the chapter will give you more information.

15. MATHEMATICAL MODELS

In the application of mathematics to science and industry it is frequently possible to combine the advantage of the certainty of deductive proof with the advantage of not having to pre-establish the truth of the premises necessary for the proof. This is brought about by the construction of what is known as a mathematical model.

The most famous example of a mathematical model is probably that devised by Isaac Newton (1642–1727) to explain the motion of the earth in its orbit around the sun by means of the law of gravitation. The actual orbit of the earth is extremely complicated, because the motion of the earth is influenced by the nearby planets, as well as by the sun. The model which Newton chose was, however, very simple. He assumed:

(1) The attraction of the other planets could be neglected.
(2) The sun could be represented by a fixed point S at which the entire mass of the sun was concentrated.
(3) The earth could be represented by a moving point E at which the entire mass of the earth was concentrated.
(4) The mass points S and E were acted on by the law of gravitation.

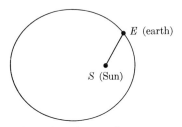

Orbit of earth around sun

FIGURE 3–1

Newton then proved deductively from the laws of mechanics that for this simple model, the orbit of E around S would be a plane curve, called an ellipse, having S at one of its foci.

The close agreement that was found to exist between the motion predicted for E in this model and astronomical observations of the positions of the earth and the sun was a striking confirmation of Newton's law of gravitation. And it was precisely this agreement between predictions deduced mathematically from the model and the actual observations that justified the premises on which Newton based his model.

Since the time of Newton, the method of constructing a simple mathematical model by choosing premises suggested by the physical situation, elaborating and developing their consequences as properties of the mathematical model, and then comparing these properties with the observed facts has been applied over and over again in the exact sciences with great success. In the last twenty-five years, the same method of constructing mathematical models has been employed successfully in biology and in the social and behavioral sciences. Consult references for examples of other models. Mathematical models useful in arithmetic and geometry will be developed in later chapters of this book.

A successful mathematical model bears the same kind of relation to the physical situation or process to which it applies that a well-drawn map bears to the actual surface of the earth. By necessity, much must be left out in any map; and the conventions employed by the maker of the map do not necessarily correspond to the actual reality the map describes. For example, in mapping a small portion of the earth's surface, the map-maker may assume the earth to be flat. Even if this assumption is not made, the map itself is usually flat, while the earth's surface is curved.

Again, any geometrical figure or diagram is a kind of mathematical model; for example, the Euler diagrams for sets are models of abstract relations such as inclusion and disjointness which hold between sets. Such models are especially useful in geometry. Nevertheless, a triangle drawn on a blackboard is quite different from the triangle as a set of points which is the object of geometrical reasoning.

EXERCISE SET 3-2

1. State in words the negations of each of the following propositions about whole numbers.
   (a) If x is any whole number greater than zero, then $2x$ never equals x.
   (b) Seven is an odd number.
2. Write in words the negation of each of the following, restricting yourself to the fewest number of elements that it is possible to consider.
   (a) $A \supseteq B$ (b) $A \cap B = \{ \}$
3. What is the negation of the proposition, "There exists at least one whole number whose square is equal to itself"?
4. Write the negation of the following statements regarding whole numbers.
   (a) $a \leq b$ (b) $a > b$ (c) $a < b$
5. Verify each of the following if a is any proposition.
   (a) One and only one of these propositions must be true: a, $-a$.
   (b) a is the negation of $-a$.
   (c) The propositions a and $-(-a)$ are either both true or both false.
6. State hypotheses 2 and 3 of the illustrative deductive proof in Section 3 as implications.
7. Analyze the remainder of the illustrative deductive proof in Section 3 and indicate precisely where the law of deduction was used.
8. Write two pairs of propositions such that the second proposition of a pair is implied from the first. One pair should be of a nonmathematical nature and the other of a mathematical nature.
9. Which of the following pairs of propositions are compatible?
   (a) I am older than 21. I am younger than 100.
   (b) My dog is 3 years old. My cat is 3 months old.
   (c) $\pi > 5$. $\pi < 14$
10. State the relation of implication which holds between each pair of the following statements, assuming that both a and b are true.
    (a) a is "John is the cousin of Mary"; b is "Mary is the cousin of John."
    (b) a is "m and n are odd numbers"; b is "$m + n$ is an even number."
11. Which of the statements in Exercise 10 are also equivalence relations?

12. Prove that if $a \Leftrightarrow b$, the propositions a and b must both be true or both false.

13. Give one simple illustration of your own of each of the five properties of $\Rightarrow$ and $\Leftrightarrow$ listed in Section 12.

14. The statement, "If x is exactly divisible by 6, then x is exactly divisible by 3," is logically defective since a premise has been omitted. State the missing premise.

15. Under what conditions can you prove, by citing examples, that a general statement is true?

16. Prove deductively that if a is true and $a \Rightarrow b$ is false, then b must be false.

17. If c is a whole number, which of the following propositions is necessary and which is sufficient for the others? (Pair the propositions in all possible ways.)
    (a) c is exactly divisible by 4.
    (b) c is exactly divisible by 6.
    (c) c is exactly divisible by 8.

18. If c is a whole number, prove that the following two statements are not equivalent.

    c is exactly divisible by 4,   and c is exactly divisible by 6.

19. Make up a pair of propositions from everyday life to illustrate each of the following concepts:
    (a) Necessary conditions
    (b) Sufficient conditions
    (c) Necessary and sufficient conditions
    (d) Neither necessary nor sufficient conditions

REFERENCES

ALLENDOERFER, CARL B., "Deductive Methods in Mathematics," in *Insights into Modern Mathematics*, Twenty-third Yearbook of the National Council of Teachers of Mathematics. Washington, D. C.: The Council, 1957, pp. 65–86.

ALLENDOERFER, CARL B., and C. O. OAKLEY, *Principles of Mathematics*. New York: McGraw-Hill Book Company, Inc., 1955, pp. 1–33.

BANKS, J. HOUSTON, *Elements of Mathematics*. Boston: Allyn and Bacon, Inc., 1961, pp. 9–46.

FAWCETT, HAROLD P., *The Nature of Proof*, Thirteenth Yearbook of the National Council of Teachers of Mathematics. Washington, D. C.: The Council, 1938, 146 pp.

SACHS, JEROME M., RUTH B. RASMUSEN, and WILLIAM J. PURCELL, *Basic College Mathematics*. Boston: Allyn and Bacon, Inc., 1960, pp. 1–27.

SCHAAF, WILLIAM L., *Basic Concepts of Elementary Mathematics*. New York: John Wiley and Sons, Inc., 1960, pp. 30–58.

SMITH, EUGENE P., and KENNETH B. HENDERSON, "Proof," in *The Growth of Mathematical Ideas*, Twenty-fourth Yearbook of the National Council of Teachers of Mathematics. Washington, D. C.: The Council, 1959, pp. 111–181.

CHAPTER FOUR

THE WHOLE NUMBERS

The set of pages of a book has many properties, such as size, color, shape, and number. The set of fingers in a glove may be black, short, and five in number. The "sevenness" of the set of days of a week, and the "fourness" of the set of legs of a dog are a property of sets called number. *Number* is a property of any set; but here only the numbers of finite sets shall be considered.

The early history of man's development of number ideas and the stages of your awareness of the number property of sets and of other elementary number ideas are similar. You learned, as early man learned, to identify sets which have the same or different numbers. Before you had an awareness of "twoness" or "threeness," you recognized that a set of two red blocks has the same number as a set of two blue blocks, and that three cookies is more than two cookies. One of the first concepts a child develops is the distinction between a set of one member and a set of more than one member. At one stage you may have known only two number names, "one" which identified a unit set and "two" which identified any set of more than one member.

As you became more familiar with sets of things, the number property of sets became more important. You recognized sets of one, two, three, and possibly four or five members and became aware of the empty set which you identified as "not any." For you, as for early man, the awareness of the importance of the number property of a set led to the learning of the number names of model sets for the purpose of distinguishing and describing any set. Today you use the number names of your culture; early man invented the names he used.

As the sets of a few members are assigned number names, they are also arranged both physically and mentally into a sequence from least to greatest, that is, into an ordered set (Chapter 2, Section 11). If the sets whose number properties are known are those shown in Fig. 4–1, they will soon be reorganized as shown in Fig. 4–2. (The number names used in Figs. 4–1 and 4–2 are those of the English culture. Other number names have been and are being used.)

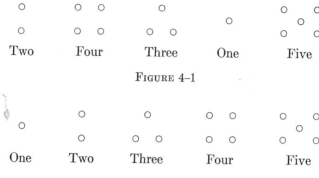

FIGURE 4–1

FIGURE 4–2

The result of this activity is an ordered set of number names, each name describing a set which has one more element than the preceding named set. The set is expanded as the need arises. This ordered set of number names is the set of names used in the process of counting. The names are those of the *natural numbers*. When the natural numbers are ordered, they are called the *counting numbers* (Chapter 2, Section 11).

1. HISTORIC NOTE

Early man probably first became aware of number as a way of expressing the difference or sameness of the quality of two sets. Sets were matched, each member of one set to a member of a second set, to determine whether the sets had the same number. If the members of the two sets could be placed in a one-to-one correspondence, the sets had the same number. Thus, for example, an ancient herdsman may have set up an equivalence between the sheep of his herd and a pile of stones when the herd left for grazing and again on its return, to check for missing animals. Today the principle of one-to-one correspondence is used often in such activities as matching a set of chairs whose number is known to the set of people occupying the chairs, keeping score by making a tally mark for each event as it happens, and counting a set of objects.

2. COUNTING

Counting is a process of applying the principle of one-to-one correspondence to two sets one of which is the set to be counted and the other is a counting set (Chapter 2, Section 11). As the letters in the word "hand" are counted, a number name from a counting set is matched to each letter of the word, one by one, as shown in Fig. 4–3. The counting set selected is that set which is needed to complete the matching, $N_4 =$ (one, two, three, four).

Given set: { h,   a,   n,   d}

Counting set: (One, Two, Three, Four) $= N_4$

FIGURE 4–3

The number of the counting set selected is four, the last number named in the set. Since the set of letters in the word "hand" and the set (one, two, three, four) were placed in a one-to-one correspondence, they are equivalent sets. Therefore, the number of letters in the word "hand" is the last number named in the selected counting set, N_4.

$$n\{h, a, n, d\} = n(\text{one, two, three, four}) = 4.$$

All counting is done in this manner. A counting set is selected which can be placed in a one-to-one correspondence with the set of objects being counted. The last number of the counting set is the number of objects in the set being counted.

3. NUMBER NAMES FOR SETS IN A HYPOTHETICAL SYSTEM

The schemes of number names used differ widely and all are arbitrary in nature. A society invents its own sequence of number names as the need arises. Imagine a society which invents the number names shown in Fig. 4–4 for the model sets shown.

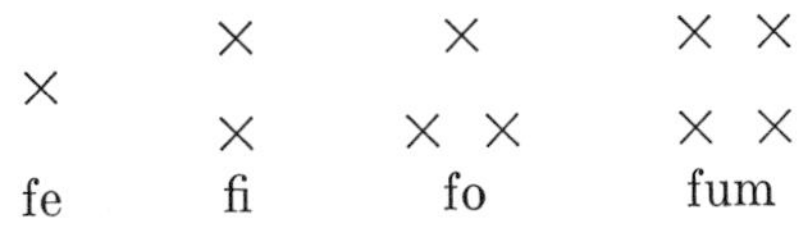

	×	×	× ×
×			
	×	× ×	× ×
fe	fi	fo	fum

FIGURE 4–4

A member of such a society would have "fe" head, "fi" hands, and "fi" eyes. However, with only "fe, fi, fo, and fum" as number names, the society is limited in the sets it can number. To describe a set of more than "fum" members, subsets have to be formed and used in the description. For example, these people would say that one person has "fum and fe" fingers on "fe" hand. To number the set of fingers on "fi" hands, the fingers would be placed in subsets of "fum" and named in the following manner:

Set $F = \{////\}$ $\{////\}$ $\{//\}$
$n(F) =$ fum   and   fum   and   fi

or

$n(F) =$ fi fums   and   fi

As the sets become larger, the use of only four names becomes inconvenient, as you can see below, where we name the number of the set L of letters of the English alphabet. Note how this inconvenience is overcome.

(1) Set L = {a, b, c, d, e, f, g, h, i, j, k, l, m, n, o, p, q, r, s, t, u, v, w, x, y, z}

(2) $n(L)$ =   fum and fum and fum and fum and fum and fum and fum and fi

or

(3) Set L = {a, b, c, d, e, f, g, h, i, j, k, l, m, n, o, p, q, r, s, t, u, v, w, x, y, z}

(4) $n(L)$ =   fum fums   and   fi fums   and   fi

or

(5) $n(L)$ =   gum   and   fi fums   and   fi

From the above, note that the numbering of L is made easier in two ways. First, the long number name of step 2 is shortened by forming a subset of "fum and fum and fum and fum" letters and naming it "fum fums." The first "fum" in "fum fums" is an adjective describing the number of subsets of "fum" letters. Similarly, "fi fums" is used to shorten "fum and fum." Second, since "fum" is the basic number set of the society and all sets are organized into sets and subsets of that number, a special name, "gum," is given to the number "fum fums" in step 5.

The ordered set of number names used for counting in this hypothetical fum system is:

> (fe, fi, fo, fum; fum and fe, fum and fi, fum and fo, fi fums; fi fums
> and fe, fi fums and fi, fi fums and fo, fo fums; fo fums and fe, fo fums
> and fi, fo fums and fo, gum; gum and fe, gum and fi, gum and fo,
> gum and fum; . . .).

The compounding points, i.e., the points at which there are fum sets of the last subset in the names listed above, are "fum" and "gum." The next compounding point will be "fum gums," which will be renamed "hum." The set could continue to grow following this pattern.

With this system of numeration, the months of July and August have "fe" fewer than "hum" days, the number of cents one gets in exchange for a dollar is "hum, fi gums and fum," and a gross of pencils is "fi hums and gum" pencils.

4. NUMBER NAMES FOR SETS IN THE DECIMAL SYSTEM

The development of the names of the counting numbers in the decimal system followed a pattern similar to that of the fum system. Historically, the first ten number names which identify the counting sets were assigned arbitrarily. They are "one, two, three, . . . , ten." These names are used with others to describe the number of sets with ten as the number of the basic organizing set.

The set to be numbered is organized into subsets of ten, as shown in Fig. 4–5.

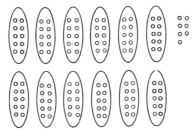

FIGURE 4–5

Whenever possible, these subsets are in turn further organized into subsets of ten tens, as shown in Fig. 4–6. When the organizing into subsets of tens is complete, the names from the existing system are used to describe the number of the set. At one time the set pictured in Fig. 4–6 may have been numbered ten tens, two tens and seven instead of one hundred twenty-seven.

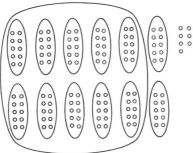

FIGURE 4–6

Actually, as the organizing process was extended to sets consisting of more and more members, the need for new number names became evident, and they were invented. Just as the "fum society" renamed "fum fum" as "gum," the "ten tens" of the decimal system became "hundred." The names of some other compounding points in the decimal system are thousand, ten thousand, and hundred thousand.

The decimal-number names used for sets of more than ten and less than twenty do not follow the pattern described for the "fum society." History gave us the special name "eleven" for "ten and one" and "twelve" for "ten and two." The names "thirteen, fourteen, ..., nineteen" would follow the pattern more closely if they were named "teenthree, teen-four, ..., teennine."

Today, the numbering of any set greater than ten is carried out by arranging the members of the set into subsets of ten or powers of ten and ones; the names of these subsets combined form the number name. For example, two gross of pencils are arranged into subsets of two ten tens, eight tens, and eight and named "two hundred eighty-eight."

The sequence of decimal-number names through "hundred million" is standard throughout the English-speaking world. The names for succeeding compounding points are not standard.

5.   NUMBER SYMBOLS

Once the number of a set was identified and given a name, men also represented it by a mark or written symbol. For example, the number of fingers on one hand was assigned the symbol "| | | | |" by many peoples, including the ancient Egyptians, "ϵ" by the ancient Greeks, and "V" by the Romans. Each group of people invented its own written symbols for number.

Egyptian system. The Egyptians invented symbols for the numbers of seven basic sets as they were needed. Table 4–1 lists the symbols which are part of the picture writing or hieroglyphics of the ancient Egyptians.

TABLE 4–1

EGYPTIAN NUMBER SYMBOLS

Decimal symbols	Egyptian symbols
1	/
10	∩
100	၅
1,000	⚡
10,000	⌡
100,000	⌒
1,000,000	⚯

The Egyptians separated a set which they wished to number into subsets for which they had number symbols. The number symbol of the set consisted then of the combined symbols for the series of arranged subsets. For example, a dozen objects were arranged into subsets of ten, one, and one; the result was symbolized by ∩ | | . A symbol was repeated as many times as it was needed. To interpret the symbol

$$\chi\chi \; \chi\chi \; {}^{\cap\,|||}_{\cap\,|||}$$

the numbers represented by the symbols were added to find the number of the set, i.e.,

$$1000 + 1000 + 1000 + 1000 + 10 + 10 + 10 + 1 + 1 + 1 + 1 + 1 + 1.$$

The Egyptian system is characterized by the principles of addition and repetition.

Roman system. With their earliest symbols, I, X, C, and M, the Romans also used the principles of addition and repetition. The symbols V, L, and D were invented later to avoid the repetition of symbols. Table 4–2 lists the Roman number symbols.

In a later Roman system, the principle of subtraction allowed further economy of notation. Subtraction is implied if the symbol I is placed before V or X, the symbol X before L or C, and the symbol C before D or M. In each case the number value of the first symbol is subtracted from the second.

To write numbers larger than M, the Romans used the principle of multiplication. A line is drawn over a number symbol to indicate a number one thousand times as great. The symbol for 50,000 is written $\overline{\text{L}}$ and 24,145 is written $\overline{\text{XXIV}}\text{CXLV}$.

TABLE 4–2

ROMAN NUMBER SYMBOLS

Decimal symbols	Roman symbols
1	I
5	V
10	X
50	L
100	C
500	D
1,000	M

TABLE 4–3

CHINESE-JAPANESE NUMBER SYMBOLS

Decimal symbols	Chinese-Japanese symbols
1	一
2	二
3	三
4	四
5	五
6	六
7	七
8	八
9	九
10	十
100	百
1,000	千

Chinese-Japanese system.   The Chinese-Japanese system of notation
is an additive-multiplicative system with symbols written in a vertical
rather than a horizontal pattern. The use of the principle of multiplication
avoids the inconvenience of repetition. Special symbols are used for one
through ten, for one hundred, and for one thousand, as shown in Table 4–3.

Multiplication is indicated when a symbol for one through nine is written
above a symbol for one ten, one hundred, or one thousand. For example,
the symbol for twenty is formed by writing the symbol for two above

TABLE 4–4

SPECIFIC CHINESE-JAPANESE NUMBER SYMBOLS

Decimal-number symbols	20	700	4720	5832
Chinese-Japanese number symbols	二 十	七 百	四 千 七 百 二 十	五 千 八 百 三 十 二

the symbol for ten; the symbol for seven hundred is formed by writing the symbol for seven above the symbol for hundred (see Table 4–4). The symbol for four thousand seven hundred twenty is composed of the symbol for four thousand written above the symbol for seven hundred, which in turn is written above the symbol for twenty.

Hindu-Arabic system. As societies became more complex, some systems of notation proved to be inadequate or inconvenient and were discarded. However, the system invented by the Hindus and adopted by the Arabs, who carried it into Europe, has been universally adopted because of its conciseness and adaptability. This system uses as base the set whose number is ten and arranges objects of a set into subsets of "powers of ten." The system is called the *decimal system*. The word decimal is derived from *decem*, the Latin word for ten.

The basic number symbols, 0, 1, 2, 3, 4, 5, 6, 7, 8, and 9, are called digits. Each digit is a number symbol itself or may be used in combination with other digits to form still other symbols. Each digit has a distinguishing value of its own, called *face value*. The face value of "2" is derived from the number of your eyes and of all sets equivalent to that set. The face value of 2 is the same in each of the following number symbols: 2580; 320; 202; and 12. Each digit of a number symbol also has a *place value* determined by its position in the symbol. The number ten is thought of as one ten and is symbolized by 10. In the symbol, 10, the digit 1 is in the base or tens' place and indicates one group of the base, ten; the digit 0 is in the units' place and indicates no units.

The place values of the digits of a decimal number symbol are consecutive powers of the base, ten. Each place value is ten times as great as the place

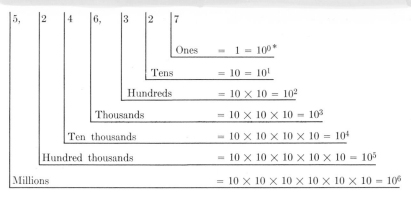

FIGURE 4–7

* It is a convention universally followed in algebra that any counting number raised to the zero power is one ($10^0 = 1$, $3^0 = 1$, $x^0 = 1$).

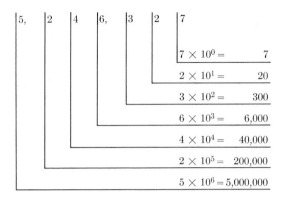

$$7 \times 10^0 = 7$$
$$2 \times 10^1 = 20$$
$$3 \times 10^2 = 300$$
$$6 \times 10^3 = 6{,}000$$
$$4 \times 10^4 = 40{,}000$$
$$2 \times 10^5 = 200{,}000$$
$$5 \times 10^6 = 5{,}000{,}000$$

FIGURE 4–8

value immediately to its right. Figure 4–7 shows the place value of the digits in the decimal number symbol 5,246,327.

The digit 4 in the number symbol 5,246,327 has face value four and place value 10^4, or 10,000. The "4" denotes 40,000, the product of the face value and the place value. Figure 4–8 shows the number symbolized by each of the digits in the decimal number symbol 5,246,327. All of these together indicate the number 5,246,327.

For convenience in reading a number symbol, the people of the United States separate the digits of a number symbol into groups of threes* by means of commas, counting from the units' place to the left; e.g.,

$$7{,}256{,}234{,}205{,}640{,}231.$$

These groups are called *periods*. The names of the first six periods are given in Fig. 4–9.

Quadrillions	Trillions	Billions	Millions	Thousands	Units
7,	256,	234,	205,	640,	231

FIGURE 4–9

The number symbol 7,256,234,205,640,231 is read 7 quadrillion, 256 trillion, 234 billion, 205 million, 640 thousand, 231.

---

* Since the eye can scan and the brain retains a sequence of five digits easily, it has been found convenient to separate the digits of the large numbers produced by computers into groups of five digits. Thus, for example, 725,623,420,564,023 appears as 72562 34205 64023.

The decimal system is economical and concise. It uses a few symbols in an infinite number of possible place values to express the number of any set. The system could not have developed, however, had not the ingenious Hindus invented a symbol for zero, the number of the empty set. A symbol for zero makes possible the use of the principle of place value, the key to the conciseness of a place-value system.

EXERCISE SET 4–1

1. List the counting set needed to find the number of the sets below.
   (a) Cents equal in value to a nickel
   (b) Fingers on your hand
   (c) Pages in this chapter
2. Write the sequence of number names used in the fum system to count the letters of the English alphabet by "fes."
3. State the number of each of the following sets using the number names of the fum system.
   (a) Eggs in a dozen   (b) Letters used in this line of type
   (c) Lines of print on this page   (d) Letters used in all of Exercise 3
4. Draw a diagram to show how a set of members of four regulation football teams are arranged into subsets for numbering:
   (a) in the fum system;   (b) in the decimal system.
5. Write the Hindu-Arabic number symbol for each of the following Egyptian number symbols.

(a) $\begin{array}{l} \text{((9 |} \\ \text{∩∩ |} \end{array}$

(b) ⌐⌐99 |||||

(c) $\begin{array}{l} \text{∩∩ ||||} \\ \text{⌐ ((∩∩ ||||} \end{array}$

(d) $\begin{array}{l} \text{99999∩∩||} \\ \text{9999 ∩∩∩||} \end{array}$

6. Write the Hindu-Arabic number symbol for each of the following Roman number symbols.
   (a) $\overline{\text{X}}$DCLXXVIII   (b) MCMLXIII
   (c) MLXVI   (d) MDCCLXXVI
7. Write the Hindu-Arabic number symbol for each of the following Chinese-Japanese number symbols.

(a)
七
十

(b)
二
百
四
十

(c)
六
千
八
十

(d)
一
千
九

8. Write the number symbol for each of the following in the Egyptian, Roman, and Chinese-Japanese systems.
   (a) 49   (b) 528   (c) 1974   (d) 1492

9. Which system of numeration, Roman, Egyptian, Chinese-Japanese, and Hindu-Arabic, used each of the following?
   (a) Place value   (b) Addition   (c) Subtraction
   (d) Multiplication   (e) Repetition
10. Write seven different symbols for the idea "three."
11. What is the value denoted by each of the digits in the number 205,428?
12. What place-value name is associated with each of the following?
   (a) 10^4 (b) 10^9 (c) 10^1 (d) 10^0
13. Explain how the Egyptians and Romans expressed the idea of zero in writing.
14. What number name do the English give to the number represented by the symbol 7256234205640231? (Consult an encyclopedia.)

6. THE ABACUS

The abacus is the oldest computing machine known to man and is even now used by more people than is the paper-and-pencil method of calculation. Operators of abaci may be very rapid and efficient. The abacus has taken many forms. Each, however, consists of movable objects placed in columns. A common type of abacus has beads on wires: each wire is assigned a place value just as the places of a decimal number symbol have place value, and each bead represents "one" of the particular place value of its wire. For example, a bead on a wire assigned the place value 10^2 will represent 1×10^2.

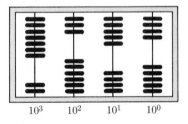

FIGURE 4–10

The wires of the abacus of Fig. 4–10 have been assigned the place values of the decimal system. The decimal number indicated is $2(10)^3 + 6(10)^2 + 4(10)^1 + 5(10)^0 = 2645$.

7. NONDECIMAL SYSTEMS OF NUMERATION

The decimal system is a base-ten place-value system. The use of ten as a base is thought to be a biological accident. If human beings had six fingers on each hand, the system used would probably be one having a base of twelve, a duodecimal system. The base ten, then, is not essential to a place-value system.

The symbol 10 is used in the decimal system to indicate one ten; it could be used in another system to indicate "one" of the chosen base. For example, in a base-four system, 10 is the symbol for "four"; in a base-nine system, 10 is the symbol for "nine"; and in a base-twenty-three system, 10 is the symbol for "twenty-three."

The base used for number symbols of a system other than the decimal system will be indicated as follows: $10_{(four)}$; $10_{(three)}$; etc. The symbol $10_{(four)}$ is read "one, zero, base four." It is never called "ten." "Ten" is a name reserved for the number of all sets equivalent to the set of your fingers. The number denoted by $10_{(four)}$ numbers the legs of a dog, not your fingers: $10_{(four)} \neq 10_{(ten)}$.

Base-four system. In a base-four system, the digits 0, 1, 2, 3 are needed. The symbols for "four" and for any set whose number is greater than four are formed by a combination of digits in a manner similar to that of the decimal system. Thus the counting numbers used to count thirty-two objects by 1's to $200_{(four)}$ have the following symbols:

1	11	21	31	101	111	121	131
2	12	22	32	102	112	122	132
3	13	23	33	103	113	123	133
10	20	30	100	110	120	130	200

The place value of each digit in the number symbol $20,322_{(four)}$ is shown in Fig. 4–11.

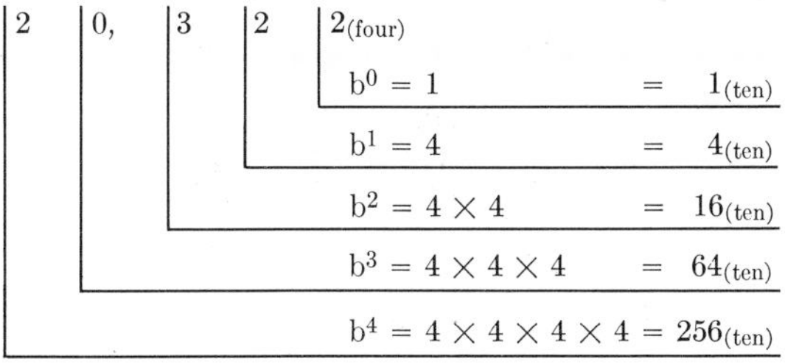

$$2 \quad 0, \quad 3 \quad 2 \quad 2_{(four)}$$

$$b^0 = 1 \qquad\qquad = \quad 1_{(ten)}$$
$$b^1 = 4 \qquad\qquad = \quad 4_{(ten)}$$
$$b^2 = 4 \times 4 \qquad = \quad 16_{(ten)}$$
$$b^3 = 4 \times 4 \times 4 \qquad = \quad 64_{(ten)}$$
$$b^4 = 4 \times 4 \times 4 \times 4 = 256_{(ten)}$$

FIGURE 4–11

The number symbols of a base-four system may be shown on an abacus which has place values of powers of four assigned to the specific wires as shown in Fig. 4–12. Note that the abacus needs only three beads on

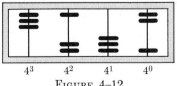

$$4^3 \qquad 4^2 \qquad 4^1 \qquad 4^0$$

FIGURE 4–12

each wire. The number indicated on the abacus in Fig. 4–12 is

$$2(4)^2 + 3(4)^1 + 1(4)^0 \quad \text{or} \quad 231_{(four)}.$$

The number names of the imaginary fum society described in Section 3 which consisted of "fe, fi, fo, fum; ... gum; ... hum; ..." may be used for the number symbols of the base-four system. In the number $231_{(four)}$ shown on the abacus in Fig. 4–12, 2 or "fi" is in the "gum" place, 3 or "fo" is in the "fum" place, and 1 or "fe" is in the "fe" place.

2	3	1	would be named "fi gum, fo fum and fe"
gum	fum	fe	by the fum society.

2	0	3	2	2	would be named "fi fum-hum,
fum-hum	hum	gum	fum	fe	fo gum, fi fum and fi."

The number symbol $20322_{(four)}$ and other number symbols of a base-four system may be changed to number symbols of the decimal system in this manner:

$$
\begin{aligned}
\text{(a)} \quad 20322_{(four)} &= 2(4)^4 + 0(4)^3 + 3(4)^2 + 2(4)^1 + 2(4)^0 \\
&= 2(256) + 0(64) + 3(16) + 2(4) + 2(1) = 570_{(ten)}
\end{aligned}
$$

$$
\begin{aligned}
\text{(b)} \quad 231_{(four)} &= 2(4)^2 + 3(4)^1 + 1(4)^0 \\
&= 2(16) + 3(4) + 1(1) = 45_{(ten)}
\end{aligned}
$$

Number symbols of the decimal system may be changed to number symbols of the base-four system as follows:

$$
\text{(c)} \quad 43_{(ten)} = \underset{\substack{4^3 \\ 64}}{\underline{\quad}} \; \underset{\substack{4^2 \\ 16}}{\underline{\quad}} \; \underset{\substack{4^1 \\ 4}}{\underline{\quad}} \; \underset{\substack{4^0 \\ 1}}{\underline{\quad}}_{(four)};
$$

$$2(16) + 2(4) + 3(1) = 43_{(ten)}$$

$$\downarrow \qquad\quad \downarrow \qquad\quad \downarrow$$

$$
43_{(ten)} = \underset{\substack{4^3 \\ 64}}{\underline{\quad}} \; \underset{\substack{4^2 \\ 16}}{\underline{2}} \; \underset{\substack{4^1 \\ 4}}{\underline{2}} \; \underset{\substack{4^0 \\ 1}}{\underline{3}}_{(four)}
$$

To express $43_{(ten)}$ in a base-four number symbol, 43 may be regrouped into subsets of 64's, 16's, 4's, and 1's, as indicated in (c). The largest subsets possible should be formed first and then the others until all of 43 is arranged into subsets, as shown above.

Another example is:

(d) $126_{(ten)}$ = $\underline{}$ $\underline{}$ $\underline{}$ $\underline{}$ $\underline{}$(four);

$$
\begin{array}{ccccc}
4^4{}_{(ten)} & 4^3{}_{(ten)} & 4^2{}_{(ten)} & 4^1{}_{(ten)} & 4^0{}_{(ten)} \\
256_{(ten)} & 64_{(ten)} & 16_{(ten)} & 4_{(ten)} & 1_{(ten)}
\end{array}
$$

$$1(64) + 3(16) + 3(4) + 2(1) = 126_{(ten)}$$
$$\downarrow \qquad \downarrow \qquad \downarrow \qquad \downarrow$$

$126_{(ten)}$ = $\underline{}$ 1 $\quad$ 3 $\quad$ 3 $\quad$ 2 $\underline{}$(four)

$$
\begin{array}{ccccc}
4^4{}_{(ten)} & 4^3{}_{(ten)} & 4^2{}_{(ten)} & 4^1{}_{(ten)} & 4^0{}_{(ten)} \\
256_{(ten)} & 64_{(ten)} & 16_{(ten)} & 4_{(ten)} & 1_{(ten)}
\end{array}
$$

Duodecimal system. If the base of a place-value system is greater than ten, additional digits are needed. In a base-twelve system, single-digit symbols for ten and eleven are needed. Here "t" will symbolize ten and "e" will symbolize eleven. Twelve is written $10_{(twelve)}$, with "1" in the base place and "0" in the units' place. The symbols for numbers from 1 to $100_{(twelve)}$ are given in Table 4–5.

TABLE 4–5

DUODECIMAL NUMERALS 1 TO 100

1	11	21	31	41	51	61	71	81	91	t1	e1
2	12	22	32	42	52	62	72	82	92	t2	e2
3	13	23	33	43	53	63	73	83	93	t3	e3
4	14	24	34	44	54	64	74	84	94	t4	e4
5	15	25	35	45	55	65	75	85	95	t5	e5
6	16	26	36	46	56	66	76	86	96	t6	e6
7	17	27	37	47	57	67	77	87	97	t7	e7
8	18	28	38	48	58	68	78	88	98	t8	e8
9	19	29	39	49	59	69	79	89	99	t9	e9
t	1t	2t	3t	4t	5t	6t	7t	8t	9t	tt	et
e	1e	2e	3e	4e	5e	6e	7e	8e	9e	te	ee
10	20	30	40	50	60	70	80	90	t0	e0	100

Figure 4–13 shows an abacus which has place values of powers of twelve assigned to specific wires. The number indicated here is $1(12)^3 + t(12)^2 + 5(12)^1 + 6(12)^0$, or $1t56_{(twelve)}$.

Duodecimal number symbols are changed to base-ten number symbols and base-ten number symbols are changed to base twelve as was

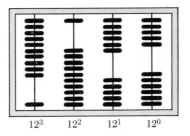

12^3	12^2	12^1	12^0

FIGURE 4–13

described in the previous section. Examples of each of these changes are:

(e) $23t4_{(twelve)} = 2(12)^3 + 3(12)^2 + t(12)^1 + 4(12)^0$
$= 3456_{(ten)} + 432_{(ten)} + 120_{(ten)} + 4_{(ten)}$
$= 4012_{(ten)}$

(f) $3234_{(ten)} = $ ___ ___ ___ ___ $_{(twelve)};$

$$\underset{1728_{(ten)}}{12^3_{(ten)}} \quad \underset{144_{(ten)}}{12^2_{(ten)}} \quad \underset{12_{(ten)}}{12^1_{(ten)}} \quad \underset{1_{(ten)}}{12^0_{(ten)}}$$

$$1(1728) + t(144) + 5(12) + 6(12)^0 = 3234_{(ten)}$$
$$\downarrow \qquad \downarrow \qquad \downarrow \qquad \downarrow$$

$3234_{(ten)} = $ 1 $\qquad$ t $\qquad$ 5 $\qquad$ 6 $_{(twelve)}.$

$$\underset{1728_{(ten)}}{12^3_{(ten)}} \quad \underset{144_{(ten)}}{12^2_{(ten)}} \quad \underset{12_{(ten)}}{12^1_{(ten)}} \quad \underset{1_{(ten)}}{12^0_{(ten)}}$$

Base twelve has been suggested as a replacement for the base ten of our system because twelve has more factors than ten. The advocates of the duodecimal system claim that its use would make operations with fractions simpler. You may wish to study the system and formulate an opinion.

Binary system. A place-value system with a binary base, or base two, uses two digits, 0 and 1. The number symbol for two is $10_{(two)}$, for four is $100_{(two)}$, for a dozen $1100_{(two)}$, for a gross $10,010,000_{(two)}$. $10,010,000_{(two)} = 1(2)^7 + 1(2)^4 = 144_{(ten)}$.

The symbols for the numbers from 1 to $100_{(two)}$ in the binary system are:

$$1, \ 10, \ 11, \ 100.$$

Modern calculating machines use base-two number symbols for their operations. Since an electric current is either on or off, the presence of an electric current for a specific time interval indicates "one," and its absence indicates "zero." A hole punched in a record which the machine makes indicates "one," and no hole represents "zero." For people working with this system, the binary symbols are very cumbersome because of the many digits required even for the number of a small set. The machines do not, however, find this a disadvantage because of the great speed with which they work. People who work with computers also use the octal system, a base-eight system.

8. NUMBERS OF FINITE SYSTEMS

Some counting patterns are not infinite as are those of the place-value systems described. The counting set of a clock uses the numbers one through twelve and then repeats them over and over. It could be specified in this way: $(1, 2, 3, \ldots, 12; 1, 2, 3, \ldots, 12; 1, 2, 3, \ldots, 12; \ldots)$.

It is true that a distinction is made between 1 a.m. and 1 p.m., so that one might say twenty-four symbols are used. The armed forces of the United States avoid the use of a.m. and p.m. by using a 24-hour clock and 24 number symbols.

If the hypothetical fum society invented a clock which counted time intervals in groups of "fums," instead of "twelve" as our conventional clock does, the counting set used on the clock would be (fe, fi, fo, fum; fe, fi, fo, fum; . . .). If the number of time intervals equal to the number of fingers on "fi" hands had elapsed since the clock read "fe" (Fig. 4–14a), the clock would show "fo" (Fig. 4–14b).

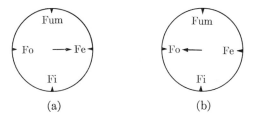

(a)   (b)

FIGURE 4–14

Finite number systems have many interesting properties which will be considered later. The arithmetic of finite number systems is often referred to as *modular arithmetic.*

9. RENAMING NUMBERS

The expression $5 \times 7 = 30 + 5$ is read, "five sevens equal thirty plus five." In this mathematical sentence the symbol "=" means "names the same number." The sentence might be read, "five sevens names the same number as thirty plus five."

When 48 is read "forty-eight," its name indicates that the number is thought of as "four tens and 8." It is often useful to think of 48 in different ways, e.g., a merchant may think of 48 as 4 dozen or as 8 half-dozen; a child who wishes to buy a half-dollar item thinks of 48 as two less than fifty; or, you may think of 48 as 3 tens and 18 when you subtract in the exercise, $48 - 29$. In each of these examples, 48 is said to be "renamed." 48 may be renamed in other ways:

$$48 = 2 \text{ tens } 28 \text{ ones} \qquad 48 = 60 - 12$$
$$= 1 \text{ ten } 38 \text{ ones} \qquad = \tfrac{1}{2} \text{ of } 96$$
$$= 3 \times 16 \qquad = 25 + 23$$
$$= 3 \times 2 \times 8 \qquad = 10 + 10 + 28$$
$$= 3 \times 2 \times 2 \times 2 \times 2 \qquad = 7^2 - 1$$

It is true that $7 + 1$, $16 \div 2$, and 4×2 all rename 8, but the name 8 is the simplest and most easily recognized. The name $574 + 948$ may be renamed $40 \times 190 - 6078$, or $1813 - 291$, or $30{,}440 \div 20$, etc., but the simplest name is 1522. Although renaming is arbitrary, it is done with a purpose. Unless there exists a purpose other than simplicity, a number should always be named in its simplest and most easily recognized form.

The techniques which are used for performing the operations of arithmetic depend on the renaming of numbers. These ideas will be developed further in Chapter 6.

EXERCISE SET 4–2

1. Express the place value of each digit in the following in powers of the base.
   - (a) $523_{(six)}$
   - (b) $1203_{(four)}$
   - (c) $1101_{(two)}$
   - (d) $5236_{(twelve)}$
   - (e) $30t21_{(twenty)}$
   - (f) $524_{(n)}$
2. Express each of the following by means of a decimal number symbol.
   - (a) $2213_{(four)}$
   - (b) $12430_{(five)}$
   - (c) $10110_{(two)}$
   - (d) $375_{(eight)}$
   - (e) $6te_{(twelve)}$
   - (f) $235_{(twenty)}$
3. (a) How many digits are needed in a place-value numeration system with base thirteen?
   (b) Write these digits using the conventional symbols for digits and inventing any new ones needed.
   (c) Write the number symbol in base thirteen for each of the following sets of eggs: one dozen; two dozen; three dozen; four dozen.
4. Change each of the following decimal number symbols to a number symbol in base four.
   - (a) 35
   - (b) 64
   - (c) 312
   - (d) 1000
5. Change each of the following decimal number symbols to a number symbol in base twelve.
   - (a) 22
   - (b) 59
   - (c) 285
   - (d) 3235
6. Change each of the following decimal number symbols to a number symbol in base two.
   - (a) 9
   - (b) 17
   - (c) 41
   - (d) 50
7. Change each of the following decimal number symbols to a number symbol in base twenty.
   - (a) 22
   - (b) 484
   - (c) 9761
   - (d) 55
8. Indicate by the use of a simple sketch of an abacus the number represented by each of the following.
   - (a) $1011_{(two)}$
   - (b) $312_{(four)}$
   - (c) $123t_{(twelve)}$
   - (d) $e52_{(twenty)}$
   - (e) $6e4t_{(n)}$
9. Choose the largest number from each of the following.
   - (a) $5_{(six)}$; $5_{(ten)}$; $100_{(three)}$
   - (b) $122_{(three)}$; $122_{(four)}$
   - (c) $325_{(twelve)}$; $462_{(ten)}$
   - (d) $45_{(eight)}$; $32_{(twelve)}$; $100100_{(two)}$
10. Rename each of the following in at least ten ways. Attempt to vary the names.
    - (a) $36_{(ten)}$
    - (b) $100_{(ten)}$

11. Write the number symbols used to count by one-hour intervals from 12 a.m. today to 5 p.m. tomorrow.

12. The face of a quarter-hour clock is shown below. Draw a series of sketches to show the clock face at the following times:

(a) Three quarter-hours after time indicated in figure;

(b) two quarter-hours after time indicated in (a);

(c) five quarter-hours after time indicated in (b);

(d) two hours after time indicated in (c).

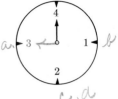

13. For each number in the left column, choose an expression or expressions from the right column which also name the number. (Each symbol is written in base ten.)

(a) 42

(b) 125

(c) 236

(d) 36

(e) 720

(f) 43

(1) $23 \times 10 + 6$ = 236

(2) $2 \times 2 \times 3 \times 3$ = 36

(3) $100 + 120 + 16$ = 236

(4) $30 + 10 + 3$ = 43

(5) $100 + 20 + 5$ = 125

(6) $7 \times 7 - 7$ = 42

(7) $(512 + 928) \div 2$ = 720

(8) $5 + 20 + 100$ = 125

(9) $6^2 + 6$ = 42

(10) $375 \div 3$ = 125

10. DISTINGUISHED SUBSETS OF WHOLE NUMBERS

In review, the set of natural numbers and the number zero form a set called the *whole numbers*. It is the universal set for this chapter and also for Chapters 5 and 6. The whole numbers are referred to as the set W:

$$W = \{0, 1, 2, \ldots\}.$$

The set of whole numbers has many subsets which are distinguished or interesting because of their special role in mathematics. Some of those used later in this text will be defined and discussed.

Multiples. If a whole number b can be renamed as a product of two other whole numbers c and d so that $b = c \times d$, b is called a multiple of c and a multiple of d. For example, since 18 can be renamed as 2×9, 18 is both a multiple of 2 and a multiple of 9. There are many other multiples of 2 and multiples of 9. In fact, the set of multiples of 2 and the set of multiples of 9 are members of a family of distinguished subsets of set W.

If b is any whole number, the set of all multiples of b is denoted by M_b. For example,

$$M_2 = \{0, 2, 4, 6, \ldots\}, \qquad \text{and} \qquad M_9 = \{0, 9, 18, 27, \ldots\}.$$

By using the language of variables introduced in Chapter 2, Section 8, the set M_b may be defined mathematically as follows:

$$M_b = \{b \times n \mid n \text{ any whole number}\}$$

Some systems of number names have the advantage that the structure of the name is related to the properties of the number. For example, the name "twelve," an arbitrarily selected name, gives no clue about the nature of the number twelve; but, the name "12," based on the structure of a place-value system, gives many clues. There are simple ways of testing a number for membership in M_2, M_{10}, and certain other sets of multiples, by examining its number symbol.

The multiples of two are commonly called even numbers. They are each exactly divisible by their common factor, 2. The whole numbers which do not belong to this set do not have a factor of two and are called odd numbers. Any number of tens is a multiple of two such as the 20 tens in 206, the 594 tens in 5940, and the 1249 tens in 12492. Therefore, it is only necessary to examine the part of the number represented by the digit in the units' place to determine whether the number is a multiple of two. The number represented by the 6 in 206, the 0 in 5940, and the 2 in 12492, respectively, is a multiple of two; consequently, 206 is a multiple of two, and so are 5940 and 12492. The number 8125 is not a member of the set of multiples of two because even though 812 tens is a multiple of two, 5 is not a multiple of two.

Multiples of ten form the set $\{0, 10, 20, 30, \ldots, 480, \ldots, 7250, \ldots\}$. The members of this set must number only "tens," and no more, and hence any number whose symbol has a "zero" in the units' place is a member of the set. 7250 is a multiple of 10; 7257 is not a multiple of ten.

Multiples of five form the set $\{0, 5, 10, \ldots, 25, \ldots, 835, \ldots, 7290, \ldots\}$. A number of this set may also be identified by its number symbol. Since any number of tens is a multiple of five, only the number represented by the digit in the units' place needs to be examined to determine whether it is a multiple of five. The numbers 835 and 7290 are multiples of five because the numbers which the "5" and "0" represent are multiples of five. The numbers 836 and 7291 are not multiples of five because 6 and 1 are not multiples of five.

Multiples of four form the set $\{0, 4, 8, \ldots, 124, \ldots, 2152, \ldots, 19732, \ldots\}$. Any number of hundreds is a multiple of four such as the 100 of 124, the 2100 of 2152 and the 19700 of 19732. Therefore, it is only necessary to examine the part of the number represented by the digits of the tens' and the units' places to determine whether it, and therefore the total number, has a factor four. The 24 in 124, the 52 in 2152, and the 32 in 19732 are multiples of four; consequently, 124, 2152, and 19732 are multiples of four. The 25 in 625 and the 37 in 529137 are not multiples of four; consequently, 625 and 529137 are not multiples of four.

Multiples of eight form the set $\{0, 8, 16, \ldots, 424, \ldots, 7576, \ldots, 92784, \ldots\}$. Any number of thousands is a multiple of eight such as the 7000 in 7576 and the 92000 in 92784. It is only necessary, therefore, to examine the part of the number represented by the digits in the hundreds', tens', and units' places to determine whether it, and therefore the total number, is a multiple of eight. The 576 of 7576 and the 784 of 92784 are multiples of eight; consequently, 7576 and 92784 are multiples of eight. The 125 of 9125 and the 41 of 12041 are not multiples of eight; consequently, 9125 and 12041 are not multiples of eight.

Multiples of nine form the set $\{0, 9, 18, 27, 36, 45, 54, \ldots, 99, 108, 117, \ldots 189, 198, 207, \ldots 999, 1008, \ldots 1575, \ldots 59877, \ldots\}$. The multiples of nine have the common property that the sum of the face value of the digits of the number symbol is itself a multiple of nine. For example, from the multiples enumerated above,

$$
\begin{array}{rl}
45: & 4 + 5 = 9; \\
99: & 9 + 9 = 18; \\
207: & 2 + 0 + 7 = 9; \\
999: & 9 + 9 + 9 = 27; \\
1575: & 1 + 5 + 7 + 5 = 18; \\
59877: & 5 + 9 + 8 + 7 + 7 = 36.
\end{array}
$$

This property is due to the fact that the powers of 10, as shown below, are equal to 1 more than a multiple of nine. If each is divided by 9, there is a remainder of 1.

$$
\begin{array}{rll}
10^0 = & 1 = & 0 + 1 \\
10^1 = & 10 = & 9 + 1 \\
10^2 = & 100 = & 99 + 1 \\
10^3 = & 1000 = & 999 + 1 \\
10^4 = & 10000 = & 9999 + 1 \\
\vdots & \vdots & \vdots
\end{array}
$$

Consequently, if 40 or 4×10; or 400 or 4×100; or 4000 or 4×1000 is divided by 9, there is a remainder of 4. If 7, or 700, or 70,000 is divided by 9, there is a remainder of 7.

If 45 is renamed $40 + 5$, and 40 and 5 are each divided by nine, there are remainders of 4 from $40 \div 9$ and 5 from $5 \div 9$. The sum of the remainders 4 and 5 is 9, which is itself a multiple of nine. The remainders 4 and 5 may be represented by the digits of 45.

If 1575 is renamed $1000 + 500 + 70 + 5$ and each of these addends is divided by 9, there are remainders of 1 from $1000 \div 9$, 5 from $500 \div 9$, 7 from $70 \div 9$, and 5 from $5 \div 9$. These remainders may be represented by the digits of the number 1575. The sum of the remainders, 18, is a multiple of nine; consequently, the number 1575 is a multiple of nine.

The number 4879 is not a multiple of nine because the sum of the digits of its number symbol is 28. Twenty-eight is the sum of the remainders when 4000, 800, 70, and 9 are each divided by 9. If nines are then divided out of 28 renamed $20 + 8$, the remainders are $2 + 8$, or 10. If nines are then divided out of 10, there is a remainder of 1. One, then, is the remainder for $4879 \div 9$. This result may be accomplished by a series of addition of digits.

$$4879 \rightarrow 4 + 8 + 7 + 9 = 28 \quad \text{(remainder)},$$
$$28 \rightarrow 2 + 8 = 10 \quad \text{(remainder)},$$
$$10 \rightarrow 1 + 0 = 1 \quad \text{(remainder)}.$$

In summary, to decide whether a number has nine as a factor, you need only add the digits of the number. If this sum is itself a multiple of nine, the number is a multiple of nine.

Multiples of three form the set $\{0, 3, 6, \ldots, 27, 30, \ldots, 447, \ldots, 3258, \ldots\}$. This set has as a subset the set of multiples of nine. The numbers of the set which are not multiples of nine have remainders when divided by nine which are multiples of three. To test for divisibility by three use the test for divisibility by nine; if the remainder is divisible by three, so is the original number.

The number 447 is not a multiple of nine since $4 + 4 + 7 = 15$. It is, however, a multiple of three since the remainder 15 is a multiple of three. The number 628 is not a multiple of three since $6 + 2 + 8 = 16$, and 16 does not have three as a factor.

Numbers of special form. Multiples form the basis for the description of other important subsets of whole numbers. For example, an even number may be described as $2n$ or twice any whole number; and an odd number may be described as $2n + 1$ or one more than twice any whole number. An odd number may also be described as a whole number which when divided by 2 has a remainder of 1.

Other sets may be described in a similar way. The members of the ordered set $(1, 5, 9, 13, \ldots)$ may be determined by the expression $4n + 1$. In like manner, the set $(3, 7, 11, 15, \ldots)$ consists of whole numbers of the form $4n + 3$, and the set $(2, 6, 10, 14, \ldots)$ consists of whole numbers of the form $4n + 2$. You will note that all multiples of four may be thought of as whole numbers of the form $4n + 0$.

EXERCISE SET 4-3

1. List the ten smallest numbers in each of the following sets.
   (a) M_2 (b) M_5 (c) M_9
   (d) M_{12} (e) M_0 (f) M_1

2. Show that a number which is not a multiple of 2 cannot be a multiple of 4, or 6, or 8.

3. Test each of the numbers (a) through (i) and find whether it is a multiple of 2, 3, 4, 5, 8, 9, or 10.
   (a) 43   (b) 1243   (c) 133
   (d) 24,345   (e) 2438   (f) 737
   (g) 990   (h) 3473   (i) 1000

4. (a) List the first fifteen members of the set of digits in the units' place of the symbols of the numbers of the ordered set M_9.
   (b) Describe the set listed in (a).
   (c) Explain why it has its chief characteristic.
   (d) If the list made in (a) were extended indefinitely would your answers to (b) and (c) hold true?

5. Identify and describe M_0 and M_1.

6. (a) Define the complement of M_2 in W.
   (b) What are the sets M_2 and its complement in W usually called to distinguish them from other subsets of W?

7. (a) Is the proposition, "Every set M_b is an infinite set," true or false?
   (b) If the proposition is false, modify it so that it becomes a true proposition.

8. (a) Four is an element of M_2 and $M_2 \supseteq M_4$. Six is an element of M_2 and $M_2 \supseteq M_6$. Make a general statement regarding M_2 of which these two statements are special cases.
   (b) If a is an element of M_b, what is the relation between M_b and M_a?
   (c) If $M_c \supseteq M_d$, what is the relation between d and c?
   (d) Test the answers to exercises (b) and (c) with numerical examples.

9. (a) Define the set intersection $M_2 \cap M_3$ in an English sentence.
   (b) Rename this same set in M_b symbolism.

10. (a) The number 18 is an element of M_2 and of M_9. Find all the sets M_b of which 18 is a member.
    (b) What is the relation of the number 18 to b if 18 is an element of M_b?

11. (a) The number 24 is an element of M_2 and M_4. Find all the sets M_b of which 24 is a member.
    (b) What is the relation of 24 to b if 24 is an element of M_b?

12. What is the relation of 11 to b if 11 is an element of M_b?

13. (a) Define the set intersection $M_2 \cap M_3$.
    (b) Define the set intersection $M_2 \cap M_6$.
    (c) Define the set intersection $M_2 \cap M_b$.
    [*Caution:* There are three main cases depending on the choice of b.]

14. (a) Show that $M_6 \cap M_5 = M_{30}$.
    (b) Find all sets M_b such that $M_6 \cap M_b = M_{30}$.
    (c) Find all sets M_b such that $M_2 \cap M_b = M_{24}$.

15. (a) Show with examples that it is not possible to decide whether a number is a multiple of 8 merely by examining the last two digits of the number.
    (b) How do you explain this fact?

16. To decide whether a number is divisible by 2, the number formed by the last digit is examined. To decide whether a number is divisible by 4 ($2 \times 2 = 4$), the number formed by the last two digits is examined. To decide whether a number is divisible by 8 ($2 \times 2 \times 2 = 8$), the number formed by the last three digits is examined.

    How may one decide which of the following numbers is divisible by 16? 214,272; 216,272.

17. Describe the form of the numbers of each of the following sets.
    (a) {0, 3, 6, 9, 12, . . .}
    (b) {1, 4, 7, 10, 13, . . .}
    (c) {2, 5, 8, 11, 14, . . .}

18. (a) Write several members of the set of numbers of the form $6n + 3$.
    (b) What is the relation of numbers of this form to numbers which are multiples of 3?

10. DISTINGUISHED SUBSETS OF WHOLE NUMBERS (continued)

Squares. A whole number n is called a perfect square or simply a square if there exists another whole number m such that $n = m^2$. Here m^2 is the usual algebraic abbreviation for $m \times m$. For example, 25 and 121 are squares because $25 = 5 \times 5$ and $121 = 11 \times 11$, but 26 and 120 are not perfect squares. $n = m^2$ is read, "n equals m squared" or "n is the square of m." Thus $36 = 6^2$ because $36 = 6 \times 6$. Note that 0 and 1 are both squares. The first ten squares are

$$0, 1, 4, 9, 16, 25, 36, 49, 64, 81.$$

The set of squares is an important distinguished subset of the set W of whole numbers. It will be denoted by S. Thus

$$S = \{m^2 \mid m \text{ any whole number}\}.$$

Square roots. If $n = m^2$, m is called the square root of n. Thus the square root of 4 is 2 because $4 = 2^2$, and the square root of 324 is 18 because $324 = 18^2$. This relationship is shown by the symbol $\sqrt{324} = 18$, read, "The square root of 324 equals 18."

Most whole numbers do not have whole-number square roots because few of them have a pair of equal factors. The square root of the square nearest to a given number c may be easily found from a list of squares. This number is called the approximate whole-number square root of c. For example, since 4 is the nearest square to 5, 2 is the approximate square root of 5. Two is also the approximate square root of 6, but 3 is the approximate square root of 7.

Factors and divisors. If a whole number b can be renamed as a product of two whole numbers c and d, both c and d are called factors of b. For example, since 18 can be renamed as 2×9, both 2 and 9 are factors of 18. It follows from the definition of multiple that b is a multiple of c if and only if c is a factor of b. Thus, every multiple of two has two as a factor, every multiple of three has three as a factor, etc. In the discussion of sets of multiples, convenient tests were developed for deciding whether a number has the factors 2, 3, 4, 5, 8, 9, and 10. There was no test for the factor 1 since for any whole number n, $1 \times n = n$; every whole number n has the factors 1 and n. It may also be observed that every whole number greater than 1 has at least two distinct factors.

The factors of a number are identified in pairs as is indicated by the definition of a factor. For example,

$$18 = 1 \times 18, \qquad 18 = 2 \times 9, \qquad 18 = 3 \times 6,$$

so that the six factors 1, 2, 3, 6, 9, and 18 of 18 occur in three pairs. It is often important to determine whether a given number, e.g. 143, has factors other than itself and 1. No general way of finding such factors is known other than by trial.*

To identify the factors of 143, several observations and trials are made. It is observed that the number is odd and that neither 3 nor 5 is a factor. And, since $7 \times 20 = 140$, 7 is not a factor of 143. You may verify that 11 divides 143 exactly, in fact, $11 \times 13 = 143$. Hence 11 and 13 are factors of 143. It may also be verified that 1, 11, 13, and 143 are the only factors of 143.

It will be noted in the example above that although 11 and 13 are paired, the division procedure by which these factors were found was tentative. To allow for this frequently occurring situation, the following general definition is used. A whole number d is said to be a *divisor* of a whole number b if it divides b exactly; that is, if there exists a whole number c such that

$$b = c \times d,$$

d is called a divisor of b. It may be possible to show that d is a divisor of b without finding the other factor c in the product $b = c \times d$. For example, 9 is a divisor of 473,301 because the sum of its digits is divisible by 9. To discover the other factor c such that $9 \times c = 473{,}301$, a division must be performed. Note that here factor and divisor are synonymous.

---

* The number of trials necessary decreases with increasing experience with factoring.

If b is any whole number, the set of all divisors of b is denoted by D_b. For example,

$$D_2 = \{1, 2\}, \qquad D_{18} = \{1, 2, 3, 6, 9, 18\},$$

and

$$D_{143} = \{1, 11, 13, 143\}.$$

Because of the tentative nature of the process by which the divisors of b are found, it is not usually possible to produce a simple formula for the elements of D_b.

Prime and composite numbers. It has already been observed that every whole number greater than one has at least two distinct factors. A whole number with exactly two distinct factors is called a *prime number* or simply a *prime*. The ten smallest primes are

$$2, 3, 5, 7, 11, 13, 17, 19, 23, \text{ and } 29.$$

The importance of the set of prime numbers in arithmetic arises from the following fact, called "The Fundamental Theorem of Arithmetic":

Every number greater than one is expressible as a prime number or as the product of prime numbers in essentially one way only.

For example,

$$36 = 2 \times 2 \times 3 \times 3, \qquad 60 = 2 \times 2 \times 3 \times 5, \qquad 1001 = 7 \times 11 \times 13.$$

How these expression may be found and in what sense they are unique will be discussed presently.

The set of prime numbers will be denoted by

$$P = \{2, 3, 5, 7, 11, 13, 17, 19, 23, \ldots\}.$$

The number of primes less than any given number, say less than one hundred or one thousand, is finite, so that tables of the primes less than a chosen number may be compiled. Indeed, there exists a table,* prepared in 1909, listing all primes less than ten million. There is no simple mathematical formula for determining the elements of the set P. Today mathematicians determine primes by algorithms using computing machines. Observe that this is in marked contrast with the behavior of other distinguished subsets of W which have been discussed. Consider, for example,

---

* Lehmer, D. N., *List of Primes from 1 to 10,006,721*. Carnegie Institution of Washington, Publication 165, 1909, 478 pp.

the set M_2 of multiples of two. The definition,

$$M_2 = \{2 \times n \mid n \text{ a variable over } W\},$$

defines each element of M_2 explicitly. Furthermore, it is easy to decide whether any given number, no matter how large it may be, is or is not a member of M_2.

In contrast, the larger a number is, the more difficult it is to decide in general whether it has two or more than two distinct factors; that is, to decide whether it is, *or is not*, a prime number.

Numbers with more than two distinct factors are called *composite numbers*. The first ten composite numbers are

$$4, 6, 8, 9, 10, 12, 14, 15, 16, \text{ and } 18.$$

Note that if b is greater than one, all multiples of b, except perhaps b itself, are composite and that all squares greater than one are composite.

This discussion results in the classification of the set W of whole numbers into four subsets; the set $\{0\}$; the set $\{1\}$; the set of prime numbers; and the set of composite numbers. Note that this classification is both exclusive and exhaustive.

It is important to be able to identify prime numbers. The primeness of any number n may be decided by determining whether it has factors other than 1 and n. To determine whether 83 is a prime it must be decided whether it has a factor of 2 or 3 or 4 or ... 80. However, it is not necessary to try each of the whole numbers; for if all are tried which are equal to or less than the approximate square root, the others need not be. The multiples of prime numbers may also be eliminated from the trial set, e.g., if 83 does not have 2 as a factor, then it cannot have 4, 6, 8, ... as factors. And, since the approximate square root of 83 is 9, it is only necessary to determine whether the prime numbers 2, 3, 5 and 7 are factors. The number 83 does not have 2, 3, 5, or 7 as factors; therefore, it is a prime number.

To determine whether 527 is prime, it is necessary to find out whether any prime number less than its approximate square root, 23, is a factor. The prime numbers less than 23 are

$$2, 3, 5, 7, 11, 13, 17, \text{ and } 19.$$

By observation, 527 is not an even number. By the tests of divisibility, neither 3 nor 5 is a factor. The other primes, 7, 11, 13, 17, and 19, are tested as factors by the process of division in the order in which they are written. It is found by this procedure that 7, 11, and 13 are not factors and that 17 is because $17 \times 31 = 527$. The fact that 17 is a factor determines that 527 is not prime but is a composite number.

	2	3	4	5	6	7	8	9	10
11	12	13	14	15	16	17	18	19	20
21	22	23	24	25	26	27	28	29	30
31	32	33	34	35	36	37	38	39	40
41	42	43	44	45	46	47	48	49	50
51	52	53	54	55	56	57	58	59	60
61	62	63	64	65	66	67	68	69	70
71	72	73	74	75	76	77	78	79	80
81	82	83	84	85	86	87	88	89	90

Figure 4–15

As early as 194 B.C. the Greek scholar, Eratosthenes, used a sieve method for finding the prime numbers less than a given number, e.g., 90. All the numbers from 2 through 90 were first written, as in Fig. 4–15. From these numbers all the multiples of two that follow 2 were marked out or punched out, as were all the multiples of three that follow 3, all the multiples of five that follow 5, and all the multiples of seven that follow 7.

The numbers not marked or punched out of the "sieve" are the prime numbers less than 90. The method which Eratosthenes used is well adapted to mechanical procedures and is used today to compile extensive tables of prime numbers.

Factorization. Any renaming of 24 such as

$$1 \times 24, \quad 2 \times 12, \quad 8 \times 3,$$
$$2 \times 2 \times 6, \quad \text{or} \quad 2 \times 3 \times 2 \times 2$$

is called a factorization of 24. Each of the numbers that appears in one or more factorization of 24 is a factor of 24. The first factorization 1×24 is said to be trivial. Any number has a trivial factorization. A factorization in which only prime numbers appear is called a *prime factorization*. Of the four factorizations of 24 given, only the last is a prime factorization.

Each of the other factorizations may give rise to a prime factorization by replacement of the composite numbers which appear by their factorizations. Consider, for example, the first factorization, 2×12. Since 3×4 is a factorization of 12, $2 \times 3 \times 4$ is another factorization of 24. It is not a prime factorization because the composite number 4 appears in it. On replacing 4 by 2×2, you obtain the prime factorization $2 \times 3 \times 2 \times 2$. Similarly, the factorization 3×8 leads to a prime factorization $3 \times 2 \times 2 \times 2$, and the factorization $2 \times 2 \times 6$ leads to a prime factorization $2 \times 2 \times 2 \times 3$.

Note that all four of the prime factorizations of 24 are identical except for the order in which the prime factors appear. That this will always be the case, whatever number is factored, is the meaning of the fundamental theorem of arithmetic.

A prime number such as 23, has only the trivial factorization 1×23. Since the number one is not considered as a factor in a prime factorization, the prime factorization of 23 is 23.

The problem of finding the prime factorizations of numbers like 24, 30, 36, 60, 72, or 108 did not present any difficulties because in each case a factor of the number could be recognized by the procedures discussed in the previous section on multiples. For example, since the sum of the digits 108 is 9, 108 has the divisor 9. By division, $108 = 9 \times 12$. The problem of obtaining the prime factorization of 108 is reduced to obtaining the prime factorizations of 9 and 12.

If a factor of a number cannot be immediately recognized, obtaining the prime factorization becomes more laborious. Consider the factorization of 931. This number is odd and is not divisible by 3 or 5. It is found by division that $931 = 7 \times 133$. Hence the problem is reduced to one of factoring 133. Since $12 \times 12 = 144$ and $11 \times 11 = 121$, the approximate square root of 133 is 12 and either 133 is a prime number or it has a prime factor no greater than 12. It is already known that 2, 3, and 5 cannot be divisors of 133. By trial, 7 and 11 are not divisors. Consequently, 133 is a prime number, and 7×133 is the prime factorization of the number 931.

The greatest common divisor (GCD). The sets D_{12} and D_{30} of the divisors of 12 and 30 are

$$D_{12} = \{1, 2, 3, 4, 6, 12\},$$
$$D_{30} = \{1, 2, 3, 5, 6, 10, 15, 30\}.$$

The set intersection of these two sets is the set $\{1, 2, 3, 6\}$. But this set may be described simply as D_6. Thus

$$D_6 = D_{12} \cap D_{30}.$$

The number 6 so obtained is called the greatest common divisor or greatest common factor of 12 and 30. Note that it has two properties: first, 6 is a divisor of both 12 and 30; second, every common divisor of 12 and 30 is also a divisor of 6.

The greatest common divisor or factor of a set of numbers is useful when a fraction is renamed, e.g., $\frac{24}{56} = \frac{3}{7}$. The greatest common factor of 24 and 56 is 8, the factor which is divided out of the numerator and the denominator of $\frac{24}{56}$ to rename it $\frac{3}{7}$.

The least common multiple (LCM). The LCM of 12 and 30 may be found by examining the sets M_{12} and M_{30} of the multiples of 12 and 30.

$$M_{12} = \{0, 12, 24, 36, 48, 60, \ldots\},$$
$$M_{30} = \{0, 30, 60, 90, 120, 150, \ldots\}.$$

The set intersection of these two sets is the set $\{0, 60, 120, \ldots\}$. But on examination this set may be described simply as M_{60}. The number 60 obtained in this manner is called the least common multiple of 12 and 30. Note that zero as a multiple is not considered because it is a multiple of all whole numbers. A least common multiple has two properties: first, 60 is a multiple of both 12 and 30; second, every common multiple of 12 and 30 is a multiple of 60.

The common multiples and least common multiples of numbers are useful when two or more common fractions are renamed as fractions with a common denominator, e.g.,

$$\tfrac{11}{30} + \tfrac{7}{12} = \tfrac{22}{60} + \tfrac{35}{60} = \tfrac{57}{60}.$$

It is not necessary to enumerate the sets of multiples of two or more numbers and then examine these sets to find the least common multiple. The least common multiple may be found from the prime factorization of the numbers, e.g., 15, 4, and 56.

$$15 = 3 \times 5,$$
$$4 = 2 \times 2,$$
$$56 = 2 \times 2 \times 2 \times 7.$$

The least common multiple is the product of all the distinct prime factors in the prime factorization of 15, 4, and 56; and each factor is used the maximum number of times it occurs in any one of the prime factorizations.

$$\text{LCM of 15, 4, and 56} = 3 \times 5 \times 2 \times 2 \times 2 \times 7$$
$$= 840.$$

In summary, the least common multiple of two or more numbers has a factorization that contains the prime factorization of each of the numbers. The least common multiple of several numbers may also be found in the manner shown in Fig. 4–16. The method requires the finding of prime factors of one or more of the numbers by a series of divisions, as shown. The divisions continue until the divisors and the quotients are all prime numbers. The least common multiple is the product of these prime factors. From Fig. 4–16, the LCM of 24, 15, 8 and 2 is $2 \times 2 \times 2 \times 3 \times 5$, or 120.

2	24	15	8	2	(2 is a prime factor of 24, 8, and 2)
2	12	15	4	1	(2 is a prime factor of 12 and 4)
2	6	15	2	1	(2 is a prime factor of 6 and 2)
3	3	15	1	1	(3 is a prime factor of 3 and 15)
	1	5	1	1	

FIGURE 4–16

A similar procedure may be used to compute the greatest common divisor of two or more numbers from their prime factorizations. Consider, for example, 12 and 90. Let d denote their greatest common divisor. Each prime divisor of d appears in the prime factorization of d the minimum number of times it occurs in the prime factorizations of 12, $2 \times 2 \times 3$, and of 90, $2 \times 3 \times 3 \times 5$. The prime factor 2 appears once in $2 \times 3 \times 3 \times 5$ and twice in $2 \times 2 \times 3$ so that it appears once as a factor of d. Similarly, the prime factor 3 appears once as a factor of d. The prime factor 5 of 90 is not a prime factor of 12; consequently, it is not a factor of d. The greatest common divisor d of 12 and 90 is 2×3 or 6.

Powers of a number. The powers of a number, b, form a useful distinguished subset of the set of whole numbers. The set of powers of two is a particularly important subset,

$$\{2^0, 2^1, 2^2, 2^3, \ldots\}$$

or

$$\{1, 2, 4, 8, \ldots\}.$$

The set of powers of the number 10 is especially important in the decimal system of notation. The set of powers of ten is

$$\{10^0, 10^1, 10^2, 10^3, \ldots\}$$

or

$$\{1, 10, 100, 1000, \ldots\}.$$

The members of this subset are the denominations of decimal numbers and form the basis for the decimal system of numeration (Chapter 9, Section 7).

Tables of interesting subsets. Certain distinguished subsets of the set of whole numbers are so useful that tables of these subsets have been prepared for reference. You have made some tables of multiples. The sieve of Eratosthenes provides a table of prime numbers. Tables of squares and square roots may be found in dictionaries and encyclopedias and in special books of tables. They may also be found in Appendix I. Others, e.g., extensive tables of factors and prime numbers, are produced by electronic computers.

11. ORDERING WHOLE NUMBERS

The set of whole numbers is usually thought of as an ordered set, $(0, 1, 2, 3, \ldots)$. It is ordered when any whole number b of the set is to the left of all numbers greater than b and to the right of all numbers less than b.

The number 7 occurs between 4 and 13 in the natural ordering. It follows that 7 is greater than 4. In symbols, this fact is indicated by the notation $7 > 4$ and read, "7 is greater than 4." Seven precedes 13 and is less than 13. In symbols, this is written $7 < 13$ and read, "7 is less than 13." The statements may be combined thus:

$$4 < 7 < 13.$$

If the set of whole numbers is arranged in its natural order any non-empty subset is ordered and has a first element. For example, examine some of the subsets of the set of whole numbers. The set of multiples of two, $(0, 2, 4, 6, \ldots)$, is ordered and has a first element, zero. The set of powers of ten, $(1, 10, 100, 1000, \ldots)$, is ordered and has one as a first element. The set of common multiples of 8 and 12 that are greater than 129 is non-empty, ordered, and has a first element.

EXERCISE SET 4–4

1. Compile a table of all the whole numbers less than 33 and their squares, arranging the table so that it may also be used as a table of all the whole numbers less than 1000 having whole-number square roots.
2. List the sets of numbers between 100 and 300 that have whole-number square roots. Use the table prepared for Exercise 1.
3. Which of the following numbers are squares?

$$961;\ 725;\ 625;\ 529;\ 400;\ 342;\ 136;\ 81;\ 5$$

Use the table prepared for Exercise 1.
4. Which of the following have whole-number square roots? State the square root. Use the table prepared for Exercise 1.
   (a) 421   (b) 729   (c) 861
   (d) 399   (e) 756   (f) 576
5. Find the approximate whole-number square root of
   (a) 360   (b) 361   (c) 362   (d) 648
6. List the set of whole numbers that have 3 as their approximate square root.
7. List the members of each of the following sets.
   (a) D_{45} (b) D_{144} (c) D_{315}
   (d) D_2 (e) D_1 (f) D_0

8. Define the complement of each of the following with W as the universal set.

    (a) D_2 (b) D_1 (c) D_0

9. (a) Is the proposition, "every divisor set D_b is finite," true or false?

    (b) If the proposition is false, modify it so that it becomes a true proposition.

10. Given: Two is a factor of 4 and $D_4 \supseteq D_2$; two is a factor of 6 and $D_6 \supseteq D_2$.

    (a) What general statement regarding 2 as a factor can you make so that these two statements are special cases?

    (b) If a is an element of D_b, what is the relation between D_b and D_a?

    (c) If $D_c \supseteq D_d$, what is the relation between c and d? between M_c and M_d?

    (d) Test the answers to (b) and (c) with numerical examples.

11. Find all the pairs of factors for each of the following.

    (a) 42   (b) 64   (c) 100

    (d) 144   (e) 173   (f) 201

12. From the results of Exercise 11, list the set of divisors of each of the numbers.

13. Identify each of the following whole numbers as prime or composite. If it is composite, state the pair of factors that you found to prove it composite.

    (a) 7286   (b) 5247   (c) 231

    (d) 421   (e) 4235   (f) 471

14. Determine in several different ways the prime factorization of each of the following. In each case, verify the fundamental theorem of arithmetic.

    (a) 36   (b) 30   (c) 60   (d) 108

15. Find the prime factorization of each of the following numbers.

    (a) 3618   (b) 299   (c) 301

16. Find the greatest common divisor of each of the following pairs of numbers. In each case, verify that the divisor has the two properties of a greatest common divisor.

    (a) 24; 36   (b) 24; 56

17. Find the least common multiple for the following pairs of numbers and verify that it has the two properties of a least common multiple.

    (a) 24; 36   (b) 24; 56

18. Find the product of each of the following pairs of numbers; determine the product of the greatest common divisor and the least common multiple of each pair.

    (a) 12; 30   (b) 24; 36   (c) 24; 56

19. (a) What did you observe about the results in Exercise 18?

    (b) What general statement is suggested by your observations?

20. (a) Verify that the greatest common divisor of 200 and 205 is 5.

    (b) Compute the least common multiple of 200 and 205.

21. (a) Considering the results of Exercise 20, state under what circumstances the least common multiple of two numbers is equal to their product.

    (b) Illustrate your answer to (a) by several numerical examples.

22. Find the greatest common divisor of the following groups of numbers from the prime factorization of the numbers.

    (a) 24; 56   (b) 65; 91   (c) 4; 14; 696

23. List the first five members of the set of powers of 3 in two ways.

REFERENCES

ANDREWS, F. EMERSON, *New Numbers; How Acceptance of a Duodecimal (12) Base Would Simplify Mathematics*. New York: Essential Books, 1944, 168 pp.

BANKS, J. HOUSTON, *Elements of Mathematics*. Boston: Allyn and Bacon, Inc., 1961, pp. 47–116.

BOYER, LEE EMERSON, *An Introduction to Mathematics*. New York: Henry Holt and Company, 1955, pp. 1–36.

BRUMFIEL, CHARLES F., ROBERT E. EICHOLZ, and MERRILL E. SHANKS, *Fundamental Concepts of Elementary Mathematics*. Reading, Mass.: Addison-Wesley Publishing Company, Inc., 1962, pp. 14–62, 87–95.

JOHNSON, DONOVAN A., and WILLIAM H. GLENN, *Exploring Mathematics on Your Own*. Garden City, N. Y.: Doubleday and Company, Inc., 1961, pp. 1–53.

LAY, L. CLARK, *Arithmetic: An Introduction to Mathematics*. New York: The Macmillan Company, 1961, pp. 47–62.

MUELLER, FRANCIS J., *Arithmetic, Its Structure and Concepts*. Englewood Cliffs, N. J.: Prentice-Hall, Inc., 1956, pp. 1–47.

School Mathematics Study Group, "Number Systems," in *Studies in Mathematics*, Volume VI. New Haven, Conn.: Yale University, 1961, pp. 17–89.

SWAIN, ROBERT L., *Understanding Arithmetic*. New York: Rinehart and Company, Inc., 1957, pp. 1–26, 113–134.

CHAPTER FIVE

INDUCTION

---

1. DEFINITION AND IMPORTANCE

We learn from experience by formulating what is observed in general terms. The process of going from particular experiences with flames and kittens to the general statements, "Fire burns" and "Cats scratch," is called inductive reasoning. You use it informally and almost unconsciously every day; it is used formally and consciously by scientists in their development of new knowledge. In fact, "scientific method," the principal contributor to our present-day civilization, consists largely of the skillful, persistent use of inductive reasoning.

Basing general statements on particular cases is accompanied by an unavoidable uncertainty; as is known only too well, the conclusions may be wrong. Nevertheless, inductive reasoning is a significant method for developing new knowledge. To verify that conclusions are right, they are used with the risk that they may be wrong. If found wrong, they can be modified.

Induction is the systematization of those methods of inductive reasoning which experience has shown best minimize the risk of drawing wrong conclusions. Looking at the subject in a more positive way, we may say that *induction is the logic of discovery.*

2. ITS HISTORY

Induction is much younger than its companion subject, deductive logic. It arose from the efforts of philosophers with scientific curiosity and scientists with philosophic interests to understand the phenomenal development of science. Science as it is understood today is barely three centuries old, while induction has been studied formally for only a century. Among the important contributors to the development of induction are John Stuart Mill (1806–1873), John Dewey (1859–1952), and George Polya (1887–   ).

3. INDUCTION IN MATHEMATICS

Deduction begins with premises, and reasons from them to the conclusions to be established. In mathematics, conclusions are usually general statements, such as

> For all whole numbers x and y, $x \times y = y \times x$.
>
> The medians of any triangle meet in a common point.

The source of these statements is irrelevant to deductive logic; all that is important is whether or not they can be proved. However, before a statement can be proved, it must first be formulated as a result of discovery. If the statement is more than idle conjecture, its proof should be attempted.

A proof follows a plan, a plan which itself must be discovered. Otherwise, you would simply wander about in a maze of implications with small chance of arriving at the conclusion.

Deduction then requires the discovery of a conclusion to be proved, and the discovery of a plan of proof.

Induction in mathematics is concerned with the processes of discovery. It would like to answer the questions: "How are new mathematical results discovered?" "How are the proofs of mathematical results discovered?" From this standpoint, induction is an indispensable complement to deductive logic. Both are necessary, both are used in mathematics, and both should be used in the study of mathematics. The discussion which follows is concerned with the first question: How are new mathematical results discovered?

4. ILLUSTRATIONS OF DISCOVERY BY INDUCTION

ILLUSTRATION I. In his study of elementary school arithmetic a student observes that

$$2 \times 3 = 3 \times 2, \qquad 4 \times 2 = 2 \times 4,$$
$$4 \times 5 = 5 \times 4, \qquad 3 \times 6 = 6 \times 3.$$

These four observations and possibly others may result in the formulation of a verbal or nonverbal equivalent of the statement, "A product is unaffected by changing the order of its factors." He may further test this generalization by finding that 19×21 and 21×19 both equal 399. These products and the products of other pairs of whole numbers strengthen his belief. He has not proved the generalization, but has made a mathematical discovery, an important property of multiplication, which he may later prove. He is using induction.

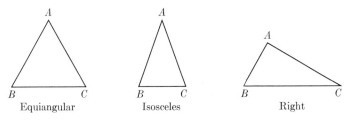

FIGURE 5–1

ILLUSTRATION II. In his study of geometry a student observes the results of experiments on several triangles beginning with the special triangles of Fig. 5–1. He first performs the following construction.

Step 1: The mid-points P, Q, and R of the three sides $\overline{BC}$, $\overline{AC}$, and $\overline{AB}$ of the equiangular triangle ABC are located as shown in Fig. 5–2. (The points may be located by folding a piece of paper having the length AB or by judging the length.)

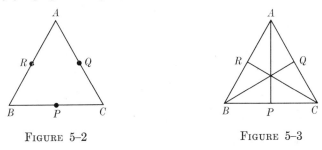

FIGURE 5–2   FIGURE 5–3

Step 2: Line segments are drawn from A to P, B to Q, and C to R. These line segments, called medians, are shown in Fig. 5–3. This step completes the construction for this triangle.

Similar constructions are performed on other equiangular triangles and on isosceles and right triangles. As the constructions are carried out, the observation is made that in every case the three lines drawn in step 2 meet in a point. The student may formulate the following generalization: "In any triangle, the medians meet in a common point." The generaliza-

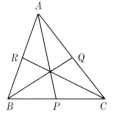

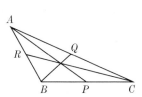

FIGURE 5–4

tion appears to be true for all the triangles, equiangular, isosceles, and right, which have been considered. The more general triangles of Fig. 5–4 are tested next to find whether the generalization is true for any triangle. The outcome of the test on the triangles shown in Fig. 5–4 and on other triangles strengthens the student's belief in the generalization. He has made a mathematical discovery which he may prove many years later by deduction. He is using induction.

5. THE THREE MAIN STEPS IN INDUCTION

The examples just given illustrate the three main steps in any inductive procedure: *observation, generalization,* and *testing.* The students first made observations, generalized from their observations, and finally tested their generalization by further observation.

The inductive procedure is not peculiar to mathematics. Observation plays an important role in discovery in all the sciences. Usually scientific observations either lead to a generalization, or they are deliberately made to test some hypothesis which the scientist has tentatively accepted. When the generalization has been formulated or the hypothesis has been confirmed by the observations immediately at hand, the scientist performs further tests to determine whether the hypothesis correctly predicts the results of future observations. The power of accurate prediction is the most crucial criterion. If the hypothesis makes an incorrect prediction, it is rejected. If it appears always to predict correctly, it is provisionally accepted.

The distinctive feature of mathematics is that the generalizations initially found by induction can be subjected to a decisive test, deductive proof. If a generalization can be proved, it is unconditionally accepted. If it can be disproved, it is rejected without need of further testing.

Prior to a more detailed discussion of the relationship between inductive reasoning and deductive proof, it will be well to describe more fully the main steps in inductive reasoning, and to give you the opportunity to make some discoveries of your own.

6. OBSERVATION

Some discoveries are lucky guesses, but discoveries based on observation require that the observations be well organized, and extensive enough to suggest a reasonable hypothesis. Above all, the observations should be accurate. In experimental science, where observation is all-important, accuracy of observation requires elaborate precautions. It may involve learning special techniques for using properly the complicated experimental apparatus, e.g., electron microscopes or particle accelerators, that are used in making the observations.

The mathematician's apparatus is seldom more complicated than a pencil, a pad of paper, and perhaps a straightedge and compass. Accuracy of observation is aided by neatness, the avoidance of errors in arithmetic, and the systematic arrangement of the data.

In Illustration I observations were made on a sufficient number of examples that the student was reasonably certain that changing the order of the factors could not change the product. In Illustration II constructions were performed on enough triangles to convince the student that the three medians meet in a common point. The number of observations that need to be made before a conclusion is arrived at may vary with the individual. In each of the illustrations the observer was accurate in his work so that he was not led to false generalizations.

7. PERCEIVING GENERALIZATIONS

The most difficult step in inductive reasoning is perceiving generalizations. Making a correct generalization depends first on careful observation. But this is not enough. The ability to make a generalization depends both on the ability to recognize a pattern revealed by observation and on the ability to *link this pattern to a possible cause*. The last-mentioned ability increases with experience. But luck, persistence, and interest also play important roles.

TABLE 5–1

TABLE OF MULTIPLES

×	0	1	2	3	4	5
0	0	0	0	0	0	0
1	0	1	2	3	4	5
2	0	2	4	6	8	10
3	0	3	6	9	12	15
4	0	4	8	12	16	20
5	0	5	10	15	20	25

For example, a student observes a table of multiples, Table 5–1, prepared by a friend and folding it on the diagonal sketched in the figure, finds that the table is symmetrical with respect to the fold. An 8 falls on an 8, a 20 on a 20, etc. He observes a pattern and immediately asks, "Why?"

To answer this question, he seeks the cause of the pattern. Studying the table, he finds that the 8 to the left of the diagonal is the product of 4 and 2 and the 8 to the right is the product of 2 and 4. He finds also that 5×4 and 4×5 are the sources of the 20's. The pairs of products that reflect into each other are the products of the same factors with the order changed. He has found a cause to link to the pattern; he can generalize, "If the order of two whole-number factors is changed, there is no change in the product." The generalization of Illustration I has been perceived.

In Illustration II a pattern was observed as more and more constructions were made. The student recognized that the pattern resulted because the lines drawn were medians. He could see that a line which was not a median did not meet the other two medians in one point. The cause was linked to the pattern to formulate the generalization perceived, "If the medians of a triangle are drawn, they meet in a point."

Larger patterns are often suggested by smaller ones. The pattern of Illustration I involving whole numbers should raise the question of whether the pattern which led to the generalization is a part of a larger pattern; that is, whether the generalization is true for all numbers. Questions to be answered are: Is the product changed when there is a change in the order of two factors that are fractional numbers? Is the product changed when there is a change in the order of two factors that are integers? Does the generalization apply to all numbers?

The procedure illustrated here of asking whether an observation or generalization originally made in a smaller setting may be true in a larger setting is a fruitful method of mathematical discovery.

Seeing patterns is partly a matter of innate ability, but it also depends on interest and on knowing kinds of patterns to look for. Most people find it easy to see geometrical patterns, but difficult to see patterns in arithmetic. Such people usually respond to the symmetry and beauty of geometrical ornaments in architecture and design, but are less responsive to the less obvious symmetry and beauty in number relationships. The feeling for pattern and form is in part aesthetic. Like other aesthetic feelings, it is usually stronger in some areas than others. But even in an abstract subject like arithmetic the feeling can be cultivated and refined by experience.

A person with a complete lack of experience or interest in discovering patterns in mathematics will have difficulty perceiving them. It is also probable that he will not be a very successful mathematics teacher until his experiences are broadened. Teachers find that most children are interested in number patterns, and can discover them for themselves. Teachers also find that experience with discovery results in an increased interest in the discovery of patterns.

Knowing what kind of pattern to look for is helpful. Observations may suggest several generalizations, some true, some false, some relevant, some irrelevant. The experiences of others are valuable, but your own experience with actual discovery is even more valuable. Exercise Set 5–1 offers opportunities for you to find patterns, establish links, and formulate generalizations.

EXERCISE SET 5–1

1. What generalizations are suggested from each of the following?
   (a) The numbers 5, 15, and 25 are divisible by 5.
   (b) The numbers 3, 13, 23, 43, 53, and 73 are prime numbers.
   (c) The numbers 9, 39, 49, 69, and 169 are not prime numbers.
2. (a) Have enough observations been made in each of the situations in Exercise 1 to convince you that the generalizations made are correct?
   (b) Can you prove or disprove any of your generalizations?
3. Are any generalizations suggested by the following observations?
   (a) The first four whole numbers whose number symbols have a units' digit of "2" are 2, 12, 22 and 32. None of these numbers are squares.
   (b) The first four whole numbers whose number symbols have a units' digit of "6" are 6, 16, 26 and 36. Two of these numbers are squares.
4. Make some other observations and determine whether the generalizations suggested by parts (a) and (b) of Exercise 3 are also true for your own observations.
5. (a) The whole numbers greater than zero can be classified into two sets: set E which has as elements the numbers which have an even number of divisors; and set O which has as elements the numbers which have an odd number of divisors. List all the divisors of the numbers 1 through 10; find some numbers of set O.
   (b) Does your study of the numbers of set O suggest any generalization? You may need to find other elements of O.
6. Observe the ordered set M, (9, 19, 29, 39, 49, 59, 69, . . .), of all the whole numbers with symbols having a units' digit of "9." The two consecutive numbers 19 and 29 are prime; the two consecutive numbers 39 and 49 are composite.
   (a) Consider ordered sets of three consecutive numbers of set M, such as

$$(9, 19, 29) \quad \text{or} \quad (29, 39, 49).$$

   In neither of these ordered sets are all three members of the set prime, nor are all three composite. Examine other sets of three consecutive numbers of set M and see whether a generalization can be made about the existence of sets which consist of three consecutive primes.
   (b) Repeat (a) and see whether there is a generalization which can be made about the existence of sets which consist of three consecutive composite numbers.

7. The set of whole numbers which has exactly one divisor is the set {1}.
   (a) Determine some elements of set P, the set of whole numbers with exactly two divisors.
   (b) What kind of numbers form set P?
   (c) Determine some elements of set T, the set of whole numbers with exactly three divisors.
   (d) What generalization is suggested as set T is observed?
   (e) What generalization is suggested regarding the relationship of set P and set T?

8. Let F denote the set of whole numbers that has exactly four divisors.
   (a) Are the numbers below all elements of F?

$$6, 10, 14, 15, 21, 32, 33, 35, 55, 77.$$

   (b) Do they suggest a generalization about the elements of F?
   (c) Does the fact that 26 and 39 are also elements of F confirm your generalization?
   (d) Are you sure your generalization is correct? Why?

9. (a) Study sets T and P of Exercise 7. Define T by means of P.
   (b) Does your definition suggest a pattern by which other sets, for example, F of Exercise 8, may be defined by means of P?

10. (a) Do the numbers 8, 27, 125, and 343 bear a relationship to the numbers in P?
    (b) How many divisors does each of these numbers have?
    (c) Do your observations make it necessary for you to reconsider your generalization in Exercise 8?

11. The numbers 26, 126, 226, and 326 have "26" as the last two digits of their symbols, and none of them are squares. Is this just an accident? Examine other numbers with the same property. Make a generalization as a result of your observations.

12. A mathematician has found that no number which has 26 as the last two digits of its symbol is a square and further that no number which has 34, 10, 46, or 14 as the last two digits of its symbol is a square. (For example, 134, 210, 146, and 314 are not squares.)
    (a) Can you find a property common to 26, 34, 10, 46 and 14? If so, state it as a generalization.
    (b) If 62, 06, 38, 18, and 02 were added to the set, would the numbers then have a common property? If so, state it. (Note that the mathematician appears to be right since 162, 206, 138, 118, and 402 are not squares.)

13. Classify all the number symbols from 0 to 100 into two sets: those which can be terminal digits of symbols of squares, and those which cannot. (Classify first the digits from 0 to 10, and then reclassify them with the number symbols from 10 to 100 by writing them 00, 01, 02, 03, etc., to represent the possible last two digits of a number greater than 99.)

14. From your observations in Exercise 13, decide which of the following are not squares:

$$147,931; \quad 1,543,799; \quad 65,536; \quad 131,072; \quad 194,184,174,164,154.$$

15. Observe the first few odd squares, 1, 9, 25, 49, 81, and 121, and make a generalization which will enable you to conclude that

No number of the form $100n + 31$ can be a square.

16. Can the number symbol for an odd number which is also a square end with the digits 55 or 59?

8. TESTING GENERALIZATIONS

The most frequent test of a generalization which results from induction is *further observation*. It has been pointed out that one example to the contrary is sufficient to disprove a tentative generalization. On the other hand, no finite number of observations of special cases can prove a generalization which is a statement about an infinite number of cases.

Since beyond a certain point, the mere accumulation of more observational evidence does little to strengthen confidence in a generalization, it is important that one be able to recognize the kind of generalization whose truth can be established by means of a few observations. The student in Illustration II must be certain that in his careful constructions he has tested all types of triangles. If he has, he need test no further. However, in Illustration I the student must test more and more pairs of factors which have products that are not immediately recognized. The question could be raised among others,

Does $57,983 \times 257,305 = 257,305 \times 57,983$?

In geometry, what appears to be true from a well-drawn figure can frequently be proved to be true; that is, proved by deduction. The situation in arithmetic is not parallel. Few people have arithmetic intuitions that are as trustworthy as their geometric intuitions are. Hence experience is invaluable in that it helps one to recognize the amount of testing which is necessary before an arithmetic generalization may be made with confidence.

9. CONJECTURES IN MATHEMATICS

The hypotheses and inductive generalizations of mathematics may be subjected to the test of deductive proof as was pointed out in Section 5. Those that can be proved are accepted; those that can be disproved are rejected. There remain generalizations for which some inductive evidence is available, but for which neither proof nor disproof has been discovered. On these, the mathematician suspends judgment. They are conjectures. Naturally the conjectures of interest are those with some inherent plausibility and some relation to existing knowledge.

An example of a famous conjecture is that made by the mathematician Goldbach in 1745:

Every even number greater than two is the sum of two prime numbers.

For example,

$$4 = 2 + 2, \qquad 6 = 3 + 3, \qquad 8 = 5 + 3, \qquad 10 = 7 + 3,$$

etc. This conjecture has been tested for hundreds of thousands of cases, and no exception has been found. Neither has a proof been found— despite great efforts.

It may seem strange not to accept as true a generalization supported by such an overwhelming amount of numerical evidence. But the mere number of observations supporting a generalization is of little significance, as the following example demonstrates.

Let g be the total number of even numbers for which Goldbach's conjecture has been tested and found to be true (up to January 1964). Then the conjecture,

Every whole number x is less than g^2,

though supported by far more observational evidence than Goldbach's conjecture, is false. The amount of observational evidence supporting a generalization is not as important as the inherent reasonableness of the generalization.

Mathematicians have learned from the history of mathematics to be wary of plausible conjectures unsupported by proof. Even the greatest mathematicians have been wrong. An example is found in the history of the Fermat (pronounced Fur mah$'$) numbers.

The seventeenth-century French jurist, Pierre Fermat (1601–1665), was a brilliant amateur mathematician. Among other achievements, he anticipated Newton in the discovery of calculus, but his greatest discoveries were made in arithmetic. He was particularly interested in the prime numbers as well as the relationship of the set of prime numbers to other sets of numbers. He proved that each of the prime numbers 5, 13, 17, 29, ... of the form $4n + 1$ may be represented as a sum of two squares. For example,

$$5 = 1 + 4, \qquad 13 = 4 + 9, \qquad 17 = 1 + 16, \qquad \text{and} \qquad 29 = 4 + 25.$$

Fermat conjectured that for any whole number n, the number $2^{2^n} + 1$ is always a prime number. These numbers are called Fermat numbers and are denoted by F_n. Thus

$$F_0 = 2^{2^0} + 1 = 3, \qquad F_1 = 2^{2^1} + 1 = 5,$$
$$F_2 = 2^{2^2} + 1 = 17, \qquad F_3 = 2^{2^3} + 1 = 257.$$

All four of these numbers are primes, in accordance with Fermat's generalization. Fermat next tested his generalization by computing $F_4 = 2^{16} + 1 = 65,537$. It too is a prime. But years later, the Swiss mathematician, Leonard Euler (1707–1783), tested $F_5 = 2^{32} + 1 = 4,294,967,297$. He found that this number was divisible by 641; so Fermat's conjecture was wrong.

Since that time, many other Fermat numbers have been examined. The most recent work was done in 1957 by the American mathematician, R. M. Robinson, who used a high-speed computer. Without exception, all the numbers examined have been found to be composite. For example, it is now known that F_n is a composite for $n = 5; 6; 7; 8; 9; 10; 11; 12$ and for numerous other values, including $n = 284; 316; 452,$ and 1945.

If observational evidence is to be trusted, F_n is never prime for n greater than 4, but a single new observation could disprove this conjecture. It is because of experiences like this that mathematicians insist on deductive proof wherever it is possible and have little faith in unproved conjectures.

10. PERCEIVING ANALOGIES AND PATTERNS

As you worked through Exercise Set 5–1 you made several successful generalizations and discoveries based on observation. Nevertheless, what you observed in these exercises was not of your own choosing. In many, you were directed to make a particular kind of arithmetical observation. It is natural to ask what led mathematicians like Fermat and Euler, who first studied the questions of Exercise Set 5–1, to choose these portions of arithmetic for observation. The question may be asked more generally: how does one determine the kinds of observation that have a good chance of leading to successful generalizations?

The mathematician is guided in part by an innate interest in number patterns and is helped by luck and persistence in his choice of the right observations. But if this were all that could be said about mathematical discovery, it would be on a par with the chance discovery of a gold mine by a prospector and his burro who accidentally stumbled upon some rich outcropping. But mathematical discovery is not the result of pure chance. If it were, it would not warrant serious discussion.

There is indeed more that can be said about the process of mathematical discovery. Usually the kind of observations worth making and the kind of questions worth answering are those that bear an analogy to successful observation and interesting questions already answered. The pattern for discovery is often determined by analogy with what has already been discovered. A few examples should make the importance of analogy clear.

A student observing that $5 + 2 = 2 + 5, 7 + 15 = 15 + 7$, etc., may conclude that the conjecture,

A sum is unaffected by the order of two whole-number addends,

is true. The fact that it is true may lead him by analogy to the conjecture that

A product is unaffected by the order of two whole-number factors,

which he tests and also finds true. The pattern thus established leads by analogy to similar conjectures about subtraction and division and to observation and testing to find whether the conjectures are true.

Fermat's discovery that certain primes may be represented as the sum of two squares was referred to in Section 9. By analogy, it might seem profitable to study numbers which are the sum of three squares, and in particular prime numbers which are the sum of three squares. The question arises, does this set of numbers include all the primes? Here analogy guides us to the observation of the set of numbers which are the sums of three squares, and its intersection with the set of primes.

11. THE ROLE OF CONJECTURE IN MATHEMATICAL DISCOVERY

The deliberate search for analogies and similarities of pattern is an important aid to mathematical discovery. A second aid of a more subjective character is the use of conjecture without immediately attempting deductive proof.

From the point of view of deductive logic, the one usually adopted by the mathematician, a conjecture which can neither be proved nor disproved is valueless. But from the point of view of induction, such a conjecture may be extremely valuable. As experience has shown, a conjecture, even though it turns out later to be wrong, often leads to observations that would not otherwise be made, and thus serves as a stimulus to discovery. Besides, it is difficult to avoid making conjectures about any subject in which one is interested.

In the actual course of discovery, it is neither necessary nor desirable to stop to formulate all conjectures with great verbal precision. Some of the most valuable ones may emerge as vague intuitions to be made more precise in the course of observation and testing.

The use of conjecture in mathematical discovery is analogous to the use of hypotheses in experimental science. As further facts are discovered, the experimental scientist modifies and changes his hypotheses accordingly. The mathematician modifies his conjectures in the same way. The exercises in this chapter have been chosen to give you first-hand experiences both with making your own conjectures and with modifying them as the observations demanded.

It is essential for both the discoverer in the field of mathematics and the teacher of mathematics to distinguish clearly between what is conjecture and what has been proved. It is equally essential for both discoverer and teacher to recognize relevant conjectures and to insist on the modification of the conjecture as further experience is gained. The goal of both discoverer and teacher, who may well be one and the same person, is to make and to help others make true conjectures, that is, generalizations ultimately capable of deductive proof.

12. CHANGE IN SCIENCE AND MATHEMATICS

Since to formulate a generalization is to go beyond the observations, there is an unavoidable uncertainty about the generalization. Because of this, the hypotheses and theories of science keep changing as significant new facts are observed.

Obtaining new facts is often the result of the invention of new instruments of observation. The changing theories of astrophysicists about stellar evolution and cosmology are examples. The particle accelerators of the nuclear physicists and the radio telescopes of the astronomers keep revealing new facts about the constitution of matter and the distribution of the stars which compel the astrophysicists to revise their theories almost continually.

In new branches of mathematics, there is also rapid change; conjectures change as new results are discovered. In older branches of mathematics, such as the arithmetic and geometry taught in schools, change is much less rapid. The subject matter has long been known and is capable of deductive proof. Although there is room for change and improvement in the choice of both mathematical subject matter and techniques, the period of discovery of the actual content often lies thousands of years in the past. This does not mean that the beginner to whom most of the results are new should be deprived of the pleasure and benefit of discovering some of the results for himself.

Some of the changes which occur in what appears to be completely developed branches of mathematics result from the discovery that branches previously considered separate may be connected. For example, algebra and geometry are connected in analytic geometry. But the really far-reaching changes are due to the introduction of new ways of thinking about mathematics.

The introduction of an important new idea in mathematics has somewhat the same effect as the introduction of a new instrument of observation in physics or astronomy. It not only leads to new discoveries, but it gives a deeper insight into older mathematical theories allowing the subject matter to be organized in simpler and more natural ways, and reveals connections which had previously been unrecognized. For example, Vièta's (1540–1603) idea of using variables in algebra changed the mathematician's way of thinking about arithmetic.

The concept of a set and the idea of formulating a theory of sets are important recent examples. This idea was introduced into mathematics in the late nineteenth century by the mathematician Georg Cantor (1845–1918). Since then his ideas have not only resulted in the development of entirely new branches of mathematics, but they have been used with great success to simplify older branches of mathematics and gain deeper insight into the nature of mathematical thought in general. The importance and usefulness of set ideas in arithmetic should now be clear to you. The concepts are equally useful in geometry, as will be shown in Chapters 8 and 13.

Although mathematics is often described and presented as though it were a purely deductive science, its development depends on the continual introduction of new methods and new ideas. These are not discovered deductively, but by skillful use of both inductive and deductive reasoning.

The inductive aspect of mathematics should therefore not be slighted. Indeed, you should use the inductive methods of formulating hypotheses and testing them both experimentally and deductively in order to participate in some way in the creative aspect of mathematics, the phase of mathematics on which all further progress depends.

EXERCISE SET 5–2

1. Observe that the prime numbers 2 and 5 may be represented as the sum of two squares,

$$2 = 1 + 1 \quad \text{and} \quad 5 = 1 + 4,$$

but the prime number 3 cannot be so represented.
   (a) Find at least five other primes which cannot be renamed as the sum of two squares.
   (b) Make a generalization as a result of your observations.
   (c) Try to prove your generalization.
2. Fermat proved that if a prime could be represented as the sum of two squares, there was only one way to do so. Discover and list the 25 numbers less than 51 which can be so represented. Do this by systematically adding

a pair of the first seven squares. For example, since

$$9 = 0^2 + 3^2 \qquad \text{and} \qquad 10 = 1^2 + 3^2,$$

both 9 and 10 should appear on your list.

(a) Do your data confirm Fermat's result?

(b) Is Fermat's result true for composite numbers as well as prime numbers?

3. (a) From the data of Exercise 2, list the 26 numbers less than 51 which cannot be represented as the sum of two squares.

  (b) Do your observations suggest a generalization? If so, state it. If not, compile more data and continue to study them until a generalization is suggested.

  (c) There are four numbers less than 101 which may be represented as a sum of two squares in more than one way. Find them. Is a generalization suggested? State.

4. Any square may be trivially represented as the sum of two squares. For example,

$$49 = 7^2 + 0^2, \qquad \text{or} \qquad n^2 = n^2 + 0^2.$$

(a) Find some squares which can be nontrivially represented as the sum of two squares.

(b) If you can find one, you can find an infinite number. Why?

5. The number zero has the property that $0 + n = n + 0 = n$ for any whole number n. What is the analogous number and property for multiplication?

6. (a) State another property of addition.

  (b) Guided by analogy, formulate a corresponding property for multiplication.

7. To double a number, the number is added to itself; to square a number, the number is multiplied by itself. There is an analogy between doubling and squaring.

(a) State an analogy to tripling a number.

(b) State an analogy between $n \times a$ and a^n.

8. Any number that is the sum of two squares may be trivially renamed as the sum of three squares. For example,

$$5 = 1^2 + 2^2 \qquad \text{and} \qquad 5 = 1^2 + 2^2 + 0^2;$$
$$49 = 7^2, \qquad 49 = 7^2 + 0^2, \qquad \text{and} \qquad 49 = 7^2 + 0^2 + 0^2.$$

(a) Has 49 any nontrivial representation as the sum of two squares?

(b) Has 49 any nontrivial representation as the sum of three squares?

(c) Has 5 any nontrivial representation as the sum of three squares?

(d) Guided by analogy with the results of your observations, state what worthwhile generalization can be made regarding the members of set T, which may be represented as the sum of two squares, and the members of set S, which may be represented as the sum of three squares.

9. Given the sets of Exercise 8 and the generalization $S \supseteq T$, answer the following questions.

(a) Does $S = T$?

(b) There are six odd numbers less than 50 which cannot be represented as the sum of three squares. Find them.

(c) Is any generalization suggested?

10. Review definitions of classification of sets into finite sets and infinite sets in Chapter 2 and answer the questions below.

(a) Classify some of the subsets of the set of whole numbers defined and discussed in this chapter as finite and infinite.

(b) Which of these sets appear to be interesting in this connection?

11. Given: A and B denote sets, and $A \supseteq B$; $A \supseteq B$ will be interpreted for the purpose of the analogy to be made to mean: "A is a superset of B." If A is the set of multiples of a, B is the set of multiples of b, and $a \mid b$ (a divides b), then

$$a \mid b \Leftrightarrow A \supseteq B.$$

(a) Guided by analogy with what you know about set inclusion, develop as many properties as you can of the relation of division of whole numbers.

(b) Can you find analogs for the universal set and the empty set? (Test each discovery with numerical examples.)

12. (a) Reasoning by analogy with Fermat's discovery about the set of whole numbers which are sums of two squares, define some other distinguished sets of whole numbers whose examination might be of interest.

(b) For each set defined, formulate a question whose investigation might be interesting.

REFERENCES

POLYA, G., *Mathematical Discovery*, Volume I. New York: John Wiley and Sons, Inc., 1962, 216 pp.

POLYA, G., *How to Solve It*. Garden City, N. Y.: Doubleday and Company, Inc., 1957, 253 pp.

SMITH, EUGENE P., and KENNETH B. HENDERSON, "Proof," in *The Growth of Mathematical Ideas*, Twenty-fourth Yearbook of the National Council of Teachers of Mathematics. Washington, D. C.: The Council, 1959, pp. 111–181.

CHAPTER SIX

OPERATIONS — THE FUNDAMENTAL OPERATIONS OF ARITHMETIC

1. OPERATIONS ON TWO WHOLE NUMBERS

A common procedure in arithmetic is to select two whole numbers and decide upon some *process* to be performed on them which determines a third whole number. For example, if one selects the numbers 24 and 6, then

(1) by adding them, you determine the number 30;
(2) by finding their greatest common divisor, you determine the number 6;
(3) by finding the sum of two times 24 and three times 6, you determine the number 66;
(4) by subtracting the given numbers, you determine the number 18; and
(5) by finding the arithmetic average of 24 and 6, you determine the number 15.

In each of these illustrations, the process is *performable* on 24 and 6, and the *result is unique*. A process which has these two properties is called an *operation* on whole numbers, and the unique third number determined is said to be obtained by operating on 24 and 6 in that order.

The five operations used as illustrations are called *binary operations* because in each case the operation is performed on two numbers. The operations of doubling, halving, and squaring are not binary operations because the operation is performed on only one number. They are called *unary* operations. All operations considered in this chapter are binary.

Performability. A characteristic of any binary operation is that it can be performed on the whole numbers selected in the order selected. Performability of a given operation may depend on the numbers selected. As shown in each of the illustrations, if the numbers selected are 24 and 6 in that order, the operations can be performed. However, if the numbers selected are 23 and 6, the operation of averaging cannot be performed. There is no whole number which is the average of 23 and 6.

111

Performability depends not only on the numbers selected but also on the order in which they are selected. If 24 and 6 are selected, then subtraction can be performed, i.e., $24 - 6 = 18$. If 6 and 24 are selected, subtraction cannot be performed, for there is no whole number that can be used as the result for the subtraction $6 - 24$. The order of the two numbers selected is indicated by the order in which they are mentioned or written. This order must be respected.

Uniqueness of the result. A second characteristic common to binary operations is that if two numbers are selected in a given order, then the resulting number is uniquely determined.

Whenever 24 and 6 are added, the result is 30; whenever the greatest common divisor of 24 and 6 is found, it is 6; whenever the sum of two times 24 and three times 6 is found, it is 66; etc. However, if the process chosen is that of finding a common factor for 24 and 6, the result may be 1, 2, 3, or 6. In this process, there is no certainty of always getting the same result. The process of finding a common factor is not an operation.

The result may depend on the order in which the numbers are selected. The operation of finding the sum of two times the first number and three times the second number gives a unique result if the two numbers are operated on in the specified order. But note that

$$(2 \times 6) + (3 \times 24) \neq (2 \times 24) + (3 \times 6)$$

and

$$(2 \times 0) + (3 \times 1) \neq (2 \times 1) + (3 \times 0).$$

On the other hand, the operations of addition, finding the greatest common divisor, and averaging give a unique whole number regardless of the order in which the numbers are selected.

2. ILLUSTRATIONS OF OPERATIONS

Addition. If the process performed on a and b to determine c is adding, the mathematical sentence that describes this process is

$$a + b = c. \tag{1}$$

Note that in this sentence, the operation of addition is indicated by the plus sign, "$+$," while the expressions $a + b$ and c both denote the result of applying the operation of addition to the whole numbers a and b.

Finding the greatest common divisor. To describe the operation of finding the greatest common divisor in a compact mathematical sentence, it is necessary to choose a symbol to indicate the operation, analogous to the plus sign for the operation of addition. The symbol "$*$" (star) will be used for this purpose. The mathematical sentence indicating the operation of finding the greatest common divisor of a and b is

$$a * b = d. \tag{2}$$

Note that $*$ indicates the operation of finding the greatest common divisor, and both $a * b$ and d denote the number which results from performing the operation $*$ on the numbers a and b. Thus

$$24 * 6 = 6, \qquad 6 * 21 = 3, \qquad \text{and} \qquad 12 * 38 = 2.$$

The expression $24 * 6 = 6$ may be read "24 star 6 equals 6" just as $24 + 6 = 30$ is read "24 plus 6 equals 30."

The actual method by which the operation $*$ is performed on any two numbers is immaterial. Two possible methods have been developed in Chapter 4, Section 10, and a third method is indicated in Exercise Set 5–1, Exercise 17.

Finding the sum of two times the first number and three times the second number. To describe this operation in a compact mathematical sentence, a symbol to indicate the operation is chosen analogous to the plus sign for the operation of addition. The symbol "ξ" (wiggle) will be used for this purpose. The mathematical sentence indicating the operation ξ on a and b is

$$a \, \xi \, b = e. \tag{3}$$

The symbol ξ in the mathematical sentence indicates the operation of finding the sum of two times a and three times b, and both $a \, \xi \, b$ and e denote the numbers which result from performing the operation ξ on the numbers a and b. Thus,

$$24 \, \xi \, 6 = 66; \qquad 6 \, \xi \, 24 = 84; \qquad \text{and} \qquad 2 \, \xi \, 3 = 13.$$

The expression $24 \, \xi \, 6 = 66$ may be read "24 wiggle 6 equals 66." Observe that $a \, \xi \, b = 2a + 3b$.

The actual method by which the operation ξ is performed on any two numbers is immaterial. However, the order in which the numbers are operated on is important since $24 \, \xi \, 6 \neq 6 \, \xi \, 24$.

The operations $+$, $*$, and ξ can be performed on any two whole numbers. Other mathematical operations are frequently encountered for which this is not true. The result of an operation is not always a whole number, as is shown in the two operations to be discussed below.

Subtraction. The operation of subtraction within the set of whole numbers has a limitation; the operation cannot always be performed. For example, it can be performed on 5 and 3, 5 — 3, and on 4 and 0, 4 — 0, but it cannot be performed on 3 and 5, 3 — 5, and on 0 and 4, 0 — 4. This limitation may be overcome in one of two ways.

(a) The set of whole numbers may be replaced by a more inclusive set in which subtraction is always possible.

(b) The choice of two numbers may be restricted in such a manner that subtraction may always be performed.

The first of these alternatives is used in Chapter 11. The more inclusive set, the set of integers, has 3 — 5 and 0 — 4 as members.

The second of these alternatives is the one used in this chapter. If the whole numbers selected for the operation of subtraction are a and b, $a - b$ has no meaning unless a is greater than or equal to b.* With this condition met, "$a - b$" always names a unique whole number. For example,

$$7 - 7 = 0, \quad 7 - 6 = 1, \quad 7 - 5 = 2, \ldots, \quad 7 - 0 = 7.$$

Subtraction is called an operation on whole numbers even though it does not always result in a whole number. A compact mathematical sentence which describes this operation is

$$a - b = f \quad \text{if} \quad a \geq b. \tag{4}$$

In the sentence, the minus symbol, "—," is the symbol for the operation, while $a - b$ and f each denotes the result of applying the operation to a and b in that order.

Averaging. The "average" of two numbers is defined as one-half their sum. The resulting third number is not a whole number if one of the numbers selected is odd and the other is even. If the process of finding the average of two numbers is to be considered an operation, one of two alternatives analogous to those described for subtractions must be followed.

In this chapter, the second alternative will be adopted. The two numbers to be averaged will be chosen so that the averaging operation may always be performed. This requires that the numbers be both odd or both even.

The symbol "$\triangle$" will be used to denote the averaging operation. Thus

$$3 \triangle 15 = 9 \quad \text{and} \quad 10 \triangle 10 = 10.$$
$$9 \triangle 13 = 11 \quad \text{because} \quad \tfrac{1}{2}(9 + 13) = 11.$$

---

*$a \geq b$ is used to symbolize "a is greater than or equal to b."

A mathematical sentence describing the operation is

$$a \triangle b = g \qquad \text{if} \quad a \text{ and } b \text{ are both odd or both even.} \qquad (5)$$

average

In this sentence, $\triangle$ denotes the operation of averaging, and both $a \triangle b$ and g name the result of applying the operation $\triangle$ to the whole numbers a and b. Observe that $a \triangle b = \frac{1}{2}(a + b)$.

3. DETERMINING THE RESULT OF AN OPERATION

In operating on any two numbers a and b, it is immaterial how the resulting third number is actually obtained. For example, in $a + b = c$, it is immaterial how c is obtained provided c correctly renames $a + b$. If $a = 2$ and $b = 3$, it is immediately recognized that c is 5. But if $a = 26,879$ and $b = 28,676$ one may have to perform the addition before he recognizes that c is 55,555.

It is of no consequence whether the result of an addition or any other operation required in a given mathematical sentence is known immediately or requires thought, whether it is performed with or without pencil and paper, by consulting tables, or by using a computing machine. What is important is that the third number renames "$a + b$."

The mathematical considerations which underlie the development of an effective method for adding, subtracting, multiplying, and dividing with the help of pencil and paper are the subject of Chapter 7.

4. COMPARING BINARY OPERATIONS

Operations differ. How they differ may best be explained by illustrations. For example,

$$5 + 2 = 2 + 5 \qquad \text{but} \qquad 5 - 2 \neq 2 - 5;$$

and

$$(15 + 9) + 3 = 15 + (9 + 3) \qquad \text{but} \qquad (15 - 9) - 3 \neq 15 - (9 - 3).$$

In general, the manner in which numbers are ordered and grouped for adding may be changed without a change in the result, but the order and grouping for subtraction may not be changed without a change in the result. The examples above indicate the importance of considering the properties of operations.

Operations are performed on different kinds of numbers. For example, the four operations of addition, subtraction, multiplication, and division may be performed not only on whole numbers, but also on fractions (rationals) and integers. Operations on all these numbers are considered in this book. Operations on real numbers and complex numbers are discussed in more advanced mathematics.

To discuss a general binary operation, a symbol is needed to denote the operation. The symbol ○, which we shall call "circle," will be used for this purpose.

The fundamental mathematical sentence which describes a binary operation in a set N of numbers is

$$a \circ b = c. \tag{6}$$

Here a and b denote members of set N, and ○ denotes the operation being performed on a and b. Both $a \circ b$ and c denote the result of performing the operation ○ on a and b in that order.

For example, let N denote the set of common fractions and ○ denote the operation $\times$ of multiplication. Then, if $a = \frac{1}{2}$ and $b = \frac{1}{3}$, sentence (6) becomes

$$\tfrac{1}{2} \times \tfrac{1}{3} = \tfrac{1}{6}.$$

Again, let N denote the set of even numbers and let ○ denote the operation $\triangle$ of averaging discussed in Section 2. Then if $a = 4$ and $b = 8$, sentence (6) becomes

$$4 \triangle 8 = 6.$$

As each new set of numbers is studied, a comparison and classification of the properties of the basic operations give a deeper insight both into the nature of the operations and into the nature of the set of numbers. Section 5 below identifies and describes important general properties which an operation in a well-defined set N of numbers may have (N is not necessarily the set of whole numbers). Section 6 and subsequent sections describe these properties for the four basic operations in the set of whole numbers.

5. PROPERTIES OF BINARY OPERATIONS

The closure property. If, for any two numbers a and b of a set N, the result $a \circ b$ of operating on a and b is always an element of N, the set N is said to be closed with respect to the operation ○. If, in this case, set N is the universal set, the operation ○ is said to have the closure property.

The closure property depends both on the operation and the set. For example, the set of even numbers is closed with respect to addition, but the set of odd numbers is not closed with respect to addition. Neither the set of even numbers nor the set of odd numbers is closed with respect to $\triangle$, the averaging operation, for although $4 \triangle 8$ is even and $3 \triangle 7$ is odd, $4 \triangle 6$ is odd and $3 \triangle 5$ is even.

The essential requirement for closure is that the operation shall apply to every pair of numbers a and b in the set N under discussion, and that the result also shall be in N.

It is often desirable to replace set N over which some operation $\circ$ is being considered by a more inclusive set of numbers closed with respect to $\circ$. For example, the set of counting numbers is not closed with respect to the operation of division. But if the set of counting numbers is replaced by the set of fractions, this new set is closed with respect to division.

The reverse procedure is sometimes possible; that is, if a set N is closed with respect to $\circ$, a proper subset of N may also be closed with respect to $\circ$. Usually the most interesting subset of this kind is the smallest one that has this property. For example, the set of fractions is closed with respect to the averaging operation $\triangle$. The smallest subset of fractions closed with respect to $\triangle$ is the set of all fractions whose denominators are powers of 2.

The associative property. If for any three elements of set N for which the indicated operations may be performed the following sentence is true, then the operation $\circ$ is said to be associative, or to have the associative property:

$$(a \circ b) \circ c = a \circ (b \circ c). \tag{7}$$

The operation $+$ of addition and the operation $*$ of finding the greatest common divisor are associative in the set of whole numbers. For example, since

$$(12 * 20) * 18 = 4 * 18 = 2 \qquad \text{and} \qquad 12 * (20 * 18) = 12 * 2 = 2,$$

then

$$(12 * 20) * 18 = 12 * (20 * 18).$$

Neither the operation $-$ of subtraction nor the operation $\triangle$ of averaging is associative within the set of whole numbers. For example,

$$(18 - 7) - 5 = 11 - 5 = 6$$

but

$$18 - (7 - 5) = 18 - 2 = 16;$$

since $6 \neq 16$, the operation $-$ of subtraction is not associative. Since

$$(5 \triangle 13) \triangle 21 = 9 \triangle 21 = 15$$

but

$$5 \triangle (13 \triangle 21) = 5 \triangle 17 = 11,$$

the operation $\triangle$ of averaging is not associative.

The commutative property. The operation ○ is said to be commutative in set N or to have the commutative property if for any two elements a and b of N,

$$a \circ b = b \circ a. \tag{8}$$

a.c.o.

The operations $+$, $*$, and $\triangle$ are commutative in the set of whole numbers. For example,

$$5 + 2 = 2 + 5, \qquad 9 * 12 = 12 * 9, \qquad \text{and} \qquad 5 \triangle 11 = 11 \triangle 5.$$

The operation ξ of finding the sum of twice the first number and three times the second is not commutative in the set of whole numbers. For example, since $0 \; \xi \; 1 = 3$ and $1 \; \xi \; 0 = 2$,

$$0 \; \xi \; 1 \neq 1 \; \xi \; 0;$$

2a + 3b

and since $2 \; \xi \; 5 = 19$ and $5 \; \xi \; 2 = 16$,

$$2 \; \xi \; 5 \neq 5 \; \xi \; 2.$$

This is only one example of many noncommutative operations.

The cancellation property. The operation of addition of whole numbers has a property which is so obvious in its applications that it is rarely identified. If a, b, and c are whole numbers and $b = c$, then $a + b = a + c$. Conversely, if $a + b = a + c$, then $b = c$. This converse statement is called the cancellation property of addition because the number a may be said to cancel out of the mathematical sentence $a + b = a + c$, and thus $b = c$.

More generally, the operation ○ is said to have the cancellation property if

$$a \circ b = a \circ c \qquad \text{implies that} \qquad b = c,$$

and

$$\tag{9}$$

$$b \circ a = c \circ a \qquad \text{implies that} \qquad b = c.$$

The letters a, b, and c denote any elements of set N for which the indicated operations can be performed.

The importance of the cancellation property will become apparent later. Of the five illustrative operations of Section 2, all have the cancellation property except the operation $*$ of finding the greatest common divisor. For example, $10 * 15 = 5$ and $10 * 25 = 5$. Therefore, $10 * 15 = 10 * 25$. But $15 \neq 25$.

The existence of an identity. Observation shows that when any number n is multiplied by 1, the product is n. For example, $5 \times 1 = 5$ and $798 \times 1 = 798$. Also, when any number n is added to 0, the result is n. For example, $6 + 0 = 6$ and $492 + 0 = 492$. The number 1 is called an identity element for multiplication; and zero is called an identity element for addition.

For a general operation $\circ$, a number i of set N is said to be an identity element for the operation $\circ$ if for any number a of set N both of the following are true:

$$a \circ i = a \quad \text{and} \quad i \circ a = a.$$

There are few operations which have identity elements. For example, there is no identity element for division, for even though $8 \div 1 = 8$, $1 \div 8 \neq 8$.

6. A GENERAL PROPERTY OF ASSOCIATIVE AND COMMUTATIVE OPERATIONS

If a set N is closed with respect to a commutative and an associative operation, there is an important general property that the operation possesses. Before stating this property, we shall examine some special cases. Let N denote the set of whole numbers, and assume that N is closed with respect to an operation $\circ$. In the discussion which follows, the operation $\circ$ is not, at first, assumed to be either commutative or associative.

If two different numbers are chosen, for example 4 and 5, there are two ways of operating on them with $\circ$: $4 \circ 5$ and $5 \circ 4$. But if three different numbers are chosen, for example 4, 5, and 11, there are twelve ways of operating on them with $\circ$. (See Table 6–1.) Each differs in the manner of grouping and ordering the numbers 4, 5, and 11.

TABLE 6–1

OPERATIONS ON THREE NUMBERS

(i) $4 \circ (5 \circ 11)$	(vii) $(4 \circ 5) \circ 11$	
(ii) $4 \circ (11 \circ 5)$	(viii) $(4 \circ 11) \circ 5$	
(iii) $5 \circ (4 \circ 11)$	(ix) $(5 \circ 4) \circ 11$	
(iv) $5 \circ (11 \circ 4)$	(x) $(5 \circ 11) \circ 4$	
(v) $11 \circ (4 \circ 5)$	(xi) $(11 \circ 4) \circ 5$	
(vi) $11 \circ (5 \circ 4)$	(xii) $(11 \circ 5) \circ 4$	

All 12 of these numbers may be different if the operation $\circ$ is neither commutative nor associative. For example, if the operation $\circ$ is ξ, then the operation is neither commutative nor associative. It may be shown that all twelve numbers in Table 6–1 are different for this choice of $\circ$. For example,

$2a + 3b$

$4 \xi (5 \xi 11) = 137, \quad 4 \xi (11 \xi 5) = 119, \quad \text{and} \quad (4 \xi 5) \xi 11 = 79.$

$10 + 33$

$4 \xi 43$

$8 + 129 = 137$

However, if the operation ○ is both associative and commutative, the 12 numbers of Table 6–1 have a different characteristic. For example, suppose ○ is the operation of addition which is both associative and commutative. Then

$$4 \circ (5 \circ 11) = 4 + (5 + 11) = 20.$$

But by associativity

$$(4 + 5) + 11 = 20.$$

By commutativity

$$4 + (11 + 5) = 20, \qquad (5 + 4) + 11 = 20, \qquad (5 + 11) + 4 = 20,$$

and

$$11 + (4 + 5) = 20.$$

By reasoning in the manner shown, all the numbers in Table 6–1 may be proved to be equal to 20. In fact, whenever the operation ○ is both commutative and associative, the numbers listed in Table 6–1 will always be equal.

Consequently, the result of the operation may be denoted by 4 ○ 5 ○ 11, for, no matter how one groups and arranges numbers in performing the operations, the result is the same. The reasoning below applies to operations on any finite set of numbers chosen from N:

IMPORTANT

> If the operation ○ is associative and commutative, the result of using the operation ○ on any finite set of numbers chosen from set N depends only on those numbers, and not on the manner in which they are grouped and ordered for performing the operation.

EXERCISE SET 6–1

1. A process β (beta) which may be performed on two whole numbers is defined as doubling the first number and subtracting the second: $a \beta b = 2a - b$. Can the process be performed on each of the pairs of numbers below? If so, give the results.
    (a) 5; 2   (b) 2; 5   (c) 0; 8   (d) 50; 12
2. (a) Is the process β performable on any pair of whole numbers?
    (b) Does the process give a unique result with any pair of whole numbers on which it can be performed?
    (c) May the process be called an operation on whole numbers?
    (d) If it is an operation, is it commutative? Illustrate your answer.
    (e) If it is an operation, is it associative? Illustrate your answer.

3. A process # (cross) which may be performed on two whole numbers is defined as finding a common prime factor. Is the result unique when this process is performed with the following number pairs? If so, give the results.
   (a) 6; 18   (b) 8; 32   (c) 54; 36   (d) 5; 13

4. (a) Does the process # give a unique result with any pair of whole numbers on which it can be performed?
   (b) Is the process # always performable with any two whole numbers?
   (c) Is the process # an operation? Why?

5. From the four examples given in each of parts (a) through (d), define an operation which might have been performed. (More than one definition may be possible.)

   (a) $2 \ominus 7 = 15$; $0 \ominus 6 = 12$; $6 \ominus 1 = 13$; $7 \ominus 8 = 21$

   (b) $3 \mathbin{\mathrm{g}} 2 = 11$; $0 \mathbin{\mathrm{g}} 2 = 2$; $4 \mathbin{\mathrm{g}} 3 = 19$; $1 \mathbin{\mathrm{g}} 2 = 3$

   (c) $6 \vee 9 = 3$; $25 \vee 25 = 10$; $13 \vee 52 = 13$; $0 \vee 5 = 1$

   (d) $12 \wedge 3 = 12$; $5 \wedge 2 = 5$; $5 \wedge 5 = 5$; $9 \wedge 0 = 9$

6. Is each of the operations defined in Exercise 5 commutative? Illustrate.

7. Is each of the operations defined in Exercise 5 associative? Illustrate.

8. Do any of the operations defined in Exercise 5 have an identity element? If so, illustrate.

9. Is the set of whole numbers closed under each of the operations defined in Exercise 5? Illustrate.

10. Show that in the set of whole numbers, zero is the identity element for the operation * of finding the greatest common divisor. [*Hint:* Show that if a is any whole number, a is a divisor of 0 and also a divisor of a.]

11. (a) Does the process of finding the least common divisor of two numbers define a mathematical operation in the set of whole numbers? Why?
    (b) If it does, define a symbol for the operation and determine the closure property for the set of whole numbers with respect to the operation.
    (c) If it is an operation, identify two other properties of the operation.

12. Does the process of finding the largest odd number less than the sum of two whole numbers define a mathematical operation in the set of whole numbers? Why?

13. Does the process of finding the largest fraction less than the sum of two fractions define a mathematical operation on the set of fractions? Why?

14. Define an operation on the set of whole numbers so that the result of the operation is a whole number if one number is odd and the other number is even, but is not a whole number if both numbers are odd or both are even. [*Hint:* Examine the operations illustrated in Section 2.]

15. An operation ○ is defined over the set W of whole numbers by the formula $a \circ b = \frac{1}{2}(a^2 + b^2)$. Find the largest subsets of W which are closed with respect to the operation ○.

16. (a) An operation ○ is defined over the set of whole numbers by the formula $a \circ b = \frac{1}{3}(a + b)$. Under what circumstances will the result of this operation be a whole number?
    (b) What restrictions must be placed on a and b for the operation to be performed?

17. An easy method of finding the greatest common divisor of two numbers is dependent on the following principle:

> If a, b, and c are whole numbers and c is a factor of both a and b, then c is a factor of both $a + b$ and $a - b$, provided a is greater than b.

For example, the factors of 70 and 21 are also factors of $70 + 21 = 91$ and $70 - 21 = 49$. Since 49 has factors of 49, 7, and 1, and 7 is also a factor of 91, then 7 is the greatest common divisor of 70 and 21.

Using this principle, find the greatest common divisor of each of the pairs below.

(a) 60; 24　　　　(b) 16; 40　　　　(c) 27; 36　　　　(d) 133; 209

18. Using the principle stated in Exercise 17 prove:
    (a) Each common factor of 91 and 105 is a common factor of 91 and 14.
    (b) Each common factor of 91 and 14 is a common factor of 91 and 105.
    (c) $105 * 91 = 14 * 91$.

7. FUNDAMENTAL OPERATIONS OF ARITHMETIC

The operations of addition, subtraction, multiplication, and division of whole numbers are called the fundamental operations of arithmetic because all other operations in arithmetic ultimately reduce to adding, subtracting, multiplying, and dividing whole numbers. Of the four operations, addition and multiplication are the most important. Subtraction may be defined by its relation to addition and division by its relation to multiplication.

Both addition and multiplication can be performed by counting. The sum, $19 + 15$, can be found by counting by ones, and the product, 6×5, can be found by counting by fives. Any addition can be performed by counting by ones and any multiplication can be performed by counting by groups or by ones. Indeed, the beginning concepts of these processes are usually developed through counting experiences in the home and at school.

A sharp distinction should be made, however, between the various processes for performing addition and multiplication and the operations of addition and multiplication. The following discussion is concerned with the concept of operation.

The addition and subtraction of whole numbers will be defined in terms of set concepts. It was shown in Chapter 2, Section 14, that the number of a finite set is always a whole number. The property of finiteness can also be defined without reference to counting: a finite set is one which cannot be put into a one-to-one correspondence with one of its proper subsets.

The set union, set intersection, or Cartesian product of any two finite sets is also a finite set. This property will be used to define and develop the operations of addition and multiplication of whole numbers. In the discussion that follows all sets considered are finite.

8. ADDITION

Addition is the operation of finding the sum of two numbers. A sum of two numbers may best be defined in terms of operations on finite sets. For example, the sum of 5 and 7 can be found by choosing two disjoint sets, a set F of five objects and a set S of seven objects, and finding their union. The sum of 5 and 7 is the number of the set union of sets F and S:

$$5 + 7 = n(F \cup S).$$

Figure 6–1 shows at a glance that the number of the set union is 12 and that the definition must ensure that $5 + 7 = 12$. However, $5 + 7$ is defined entirely by set ideas.

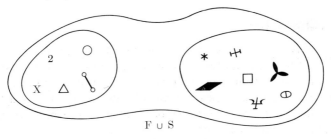

F ∪ S

FIGURE 6–1

The definition of the sum $a + b$ follows the same pattern as that for $5 + 7$.

If A and B are disjoint finite sets and if $n(A) = a$, and $n(B) = b$, then the sum of a and b is the number of the union of sets A and B,

$$a + b = n(A \cup B). \tag{10}$$

This definition ensures that addition is an operation, for $a + b$ is uniquely determined by a and b. The sum, $a + b$, is independent of the nature of the elements in the sets A and B.

Properties. Certain properties of the operation of addition follow directly from its definition. For example, if A and B are finite sets, $A \cup B$ is a finite set. Since the number of a finite set is always a whole number, it follows that

The set of whole numbers is closed under the operation of addition.

Also, since $A \cup B = B \cup A$, $a + b = b + a$. Therefore

Addition is a commutative operation.

It may be proved in a similar way that the operation of addition has the following other properties.

Addition is an associative operation:

$$(a + b) + c = a + (b + c).$$

Addition has the cancellation property:

If $a + b = a + c$,   then $b = c$.

The identity element for addition is zero:

$$a + 0 = a \quad \text{and} \quad 0 + a = a.$$

9. MULTIPLICATION

Multiplication is the operation of finding the product of two numbers. The product of two numbers is also defined in terms of operations on sets. For example, the product of 3 and 2 can be found by choosing two sets, a set A of three objects and a set B of two objects, and finding their Cartesian product. The product of 3 and 2 is the number of the Cartesian product of sets A and B (Chapter 2, Section 15),

$$3 \times 2 = n(A \otimes B).$$

To illustrate, let set A be the set $\{\triangle, \bigcirc, \square\}$ and set B the set $\{\wedge, \vee\}$. Then the elements of the Cartesian product $A \otimes B$ are the set of ordered pairs,

$$\{(\triangle, \wedge), (\triangle, \vee), (\bigcirc, \wedge), (\bigcirc, \vee), (\square, \wedge), (\square, \vee)\}.$$

An examination of this set shows that $n(A \otimes B) = 6$ and that the definition must ensure that $3 \times 2 = 6$.

Note that the product of 3×2 is defined in terms of operations on sets. The definition of the product $a \times b$ may be made in a similar manner:

If A and B are sets and if $n(A) = a$, and $n(B) = b$, then the product of a and b is the number of the Cartesian product of A and B,

$$a \times b = n(A \otimes B). \tag{11}$$

This definition ensures that multiplication is an operation, for $a \times b$ is uniquely determined by a and b. The product, $a \times b$, is independent of the nature of the elements in the sets A and B.

Properties. Certain properties of the operation of multiplication follow directly from its definition. For example, if A and B are finite sets, $A \otimes B$

is a finite set. Since the number of a finite set is always a whole number, it follows that

The set of whole numbers is closed under the operation of multiplication.

Also, since $A \otimes B$ may be put into a one-to-one correspondence with $B \otimes A$, then

$$n(A \otimes B) = n(B \otimes A) \quad \text{and} \quad a \times b = b \times a.$$

Therefore,

Multiplication is a commutative operation.

It may be proved similarly that the operation of multiplication also has the following properties.

Multiplication is an associative operation:
$$(a \times b) \times c = a \times (b \times c).$$

Multiplication has the cancellation property:

If $a \neq 0$ and $a \times b = a \times c,$ then $b = c.$

The identity element for multiplication is one:

$$a \times 1 = a \quad \text{and} \quad 1 \times a = a.$$

10. THE LANGUAGE OF ADDITION AND MULTIPLICATION

Addition. In the mathematical sentence expressing addition, $a + b = c$, a and b are called the *addends,* and both $a + b$ and c are called the *sum.* If $a = 49$ and $b = 51$ then $49 + 51 = s$; and $s = 100$ is determined by the performance of the operation that renames $49 + 51$ in the simplest manner. In these sentences s is not a variable. It is a number that is uniquely determined by a and b.

Multiplication. In the mathematical sentence expressing multiplication, $a \times b = c$, *a* and *b* are called *factors,* * and both $a \times b$ and c are called the *product.* If $a = 12$ and $b = 9$, then $12 \times 9 = p$; and p is determined by the performance of the operation which renames 12×9 in the simplest

---

*The first of two factors of a product is sometimes called the multiplier and the second the multiplicand; e.g., in the sentence, $12 \times 9 = p$, the 12 is called the multiplier and the 9 the multiplicand.

manner. In these sentences, p is not a variable. It is a number which is uniquely determined by a and b.

For purposes of simplification $a \times b$ is also written $a \cdot b$ or simply ab. In each of these expressions the symbols indicate that the operation of multiplication is performed on a and b in that order.

11. INVERSE OPERATIONS

Another binary operation, $\square$, may sometimes be defined in terms of the operation $\circ$ in the mathematical sentence $a \circ n = c$ if a and c are known; or, if $a \circ n = c$, then $c \square a = n$.

In determining the number n in this sentence, one may encounter several situations depending on the choice of a and c and on the operation $\circ$. (For the sake of simplicity the operation $\circ$ is assumed to be commutative.) For example, given that $a = 10$ and $c = 5$, then in the sentence $10 \circ n = 5$,

(1) there is no whole number n if $\circ$ is the operation of addition:

$$10 + n = 5;$$

(2) there is a unique whole number n if $\circ$ is the operation of averaging:

$$10 \triangle n = 5, n = 0;$$

or

(3) there is an infinite number of whole numbers n if the operation is that of finding the greatest common divisor:

$$10 * n = 5, n = 5 \quad \text{or} \quad 15 \quad \text{or} \quad 25, \ldots$$

In situation (1), n does not exist and in situation (2), n exists and is unique. This result is not dependent on the choice of the numbers 10 and 5, but on the fact that the operations of addition and averaging have the property of cancellation. In situation (3) the operation does not have the cancellation property, and n is undetermined in the sentence $10 * n = 5$.

If the operation $\circ$ is a commutative operation on whole numbers with the cancellation property, then for any choice of a and c, there is no more than one whole number b such that $a \circ b = c$.

By this general principle, if there is one whole number b determined by $a \circ b = c$, then b is unique and an operation $\square$ may be said to be performed on c and a. If, however, there exists no whole number b such that $a \circ b = c$, the operation $\square$ is not performable on c and a.

A new binary operation $\square$ may now be defined, for, if any two whole numbers c and a are selected in that order and there exists a whole number n such that $a \circ n = c$, then n is unique and may be defined by the mathematical sentence

$$c \square a = n. \tag{12}$$

Note that the operation $\square$ is defined in terms of the operation $\circ$. The operation $\circ$ is the primary operation; the operation $\square$ is secondary and dependent on the operation $\circ$.

For example, let $a = 4$, $c = 7$, and let the operation $\circ$ be addition. Then $4 + n = 7$ and $n = 3$. In terms of the definition of $\square$ and these conditions, the operation $\square$ is subtraction, since $7 - 4 = 3$.

As a further example, let $a = 2$, $c = 12$, and let the operation $\circ$ be multiplication. Then $2 \times n = 12$ and $n = 6$. In terms of the definition of $\square$ and these conditions, the operation $\square$ is division, since $12 \div 2 = 6$.

Two operations are said to be *inverse* if they are related as the operations $\circ$ and $\square$ are related. For just as operation $\circ$ defines operation $\square$, the operation $\square$ may define the operation $\circ$. Addition and subtraction are a pair of inverse operations, and so are multiplication and division.

12. SUBTRACTION AND DIVISION

Subtraction. The operation of subtraction is the inverse of the operation of addition. If a and c are known in $a + b = c$, then they uniquely determine b, and this operation, if performable, is called subtraction. It is the operation of *finding a missing addend* when the sum and one addend are known.

$$c - a = b. \tag{13}$$

If one addend is 25 and the sum is 49, then $25 + n = 49$, $n = 49 - 25$, and $n = 24$. However, if one addend is 49 and the sum is 25, then $49 + n = 25$, $n = 25 - 49$, and n is not a whole number. It is evident that subtraction is not always performable, and that its performance is dependent on the order of the number selected. If 49 and 25 are selected, subtraction can be performed; but if 25 and 49 are selected, subtraction cannot be performed.

The set of whole numbers is not closed under the operation of subtraction.

The two numbers operated on are the *sum* and *known addend*, in that order. The result is called the *missing addend*.* In $c - a = b$, c is the sum, a is the known addend, and b is the missing addend.

---

*The missing addend is also called the difference or remainder.

Division. The operation of division is the inverse of the operation of multiplication. If a and c are known in $a \times b = c$ and if they uniquely determine b, then this operation is performable and is called division. It is the operation of *finding a missing factor* when the product and one factor are known.

$$c \div a = b. \tag{14}$$

If one factor is 3 and the product is 27, then

$$3 \times n = 27, \qquad n = 27 \div 3,$$

and $n = 9$. However, if one factor is 27 and the product is 3, then $27 \times n = 3$, $n = 3 \div 27$, and n is not a whole number. It is evident that division is not always performable, and that its performance is dependent on the order of the numbers selected. If 27 and 3 are selected, division can be performed; but if 3 and 27 are selected, division cannot be performed.

The set of whole numbers is not closed under the operation of division.

The two numbers operated on are the *product* and *known factor*, in that order. The result is called the *missing factor*.* In $c \div a = b$, c is the product, a is the known factor, and b is the missing factor.

13. DISTRIBUTIVE PROPERTY OF MULTIPLICATION AND DIVISION WITH RESPECT TO ADDITION AND SUBTRACTION

The distributive property of multiplication with respect to addition allows either factor to be renamed as the sum of two numbers, and the other factor distributed over these addends. For example,

$$3 \times 47 = 3 \times (40 + 7)$$
$$= (3 \times 40) + (3 \times 7) = 120 + 21 = 141.$$

The factor 47 was renamed $40 + 7$ and the other factor 3 distributed over the addends 40 and 7. This property may be expressed for any whole numbers a, b, and c as

$$a \times (b + c) = (a \times b) + (a \times c),$$

or $$\tag{15a}$$

$$(b + c) \times a = (b \times a) + (c \times a).$$

---

*The missing factor is also called the quotient; the product, the dividend; and the known factor, the divisor.

There is also a distributive property for multiplication with respect to subtraction which follows from (15a). If $b \geq c$ and $c + n = b$, then $n = b - c$. From (15a),

$$a \times (c + n) = (a \times c) + (a \times n),$$

or

$$a \times n = a \times (c + n) - (a \times c). \qquad \text{Definition of subtraction.}$$

Therefore

$$a \times (b - c) = (a \times b) - (a \times c). \qquad \begin{array}{l} n \text{ renamed as } b - c; \\ c + n \text{ renamed as } b. \end{array} \qquad \text{(15b)}$$

Similarly

$$(b - c) \times a = (b \times a) - (c \times a).$$

There is a corresponding distributive property of division, which allows the product to be renamed as the sum of two numbers and the known factor distributed over the addends. For example,

$$135 \div 3 = (120 + 15) \div 3 = (120 \div 3) + (15 \div 3) = 40 + 5 = 45.$$

The product 135 was renamed $120 + 15$, and the known factor 3 was distributed over the addends 120 and 15. When the whole numbers a, b, and c are selected so that the indicated divisions are performable in the set of whole numbers, the distributive property of division may be expressed as

$$(a + b) \div c = (a \div c) + (b \div c). \qquad \text{(16a)}$$

There is also a distributive property for division with respect to subtraction. Following a development similar to that for the distributive property with respect to subtraction, it may be shown that if $a \geq b$, then

$$(a - b) \div c = (a \div c) - (b \div c). \qquad \text{(16b)}$$

Wide use is made of the distributive property of multiplication and division with respect to addition. The property and others will be considered further in Chapter 7 as the algorithms for operations on whole numbers are developed.

14. ZERO AND ONE IN MULTIPLICATION AND DIVISION

Zero and one play a special role in multiplication and division. One is a factor of every whole number and also a divisor of every whole number, since

$$1 \times a = a \times 1 = a. \qquad \text{(17)}$$

Zero is neither a factor nor a divisor of any whole number other than itself, since

$$0 \times a = a \times 0 = 0. \tag{18}$$

It is therefore impossible to find n in $c \div a = n$ if a is zero and c is not zero. If both a and c are zero, then the operation of division does not apply, since $0 \div 0$ may be any whole number. Consequently *division by zero is impossible*.

15. FINITE ARITHMETICS AND THEIR PROPERTIES

A finite arithmetic, called *modular arithmetic*, results from the use of a numeration scheme similar to that of the hours on a clock face. These numbers form a finite set. When compared with the arithmetic of whole numbers, modular arithmetic exhibits some interesting properties which shall be examined. For simplicity, the example used in this section is the arithmetic of a six-hour clock (Fig. 6–2). It will be called modulo-six arithmetic.

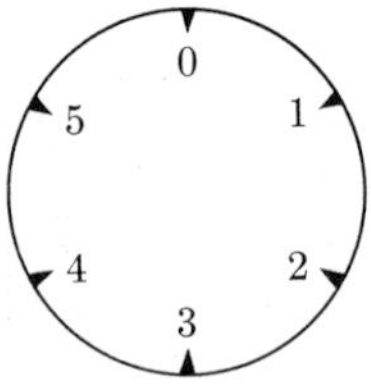

FIGURE 6–2

The numbers in this scheme are 0, 1, 2, 3, 4, and 5. Counting proceeds as follows: 1, 2, 3, 4, 5, 0, 1, 2, 3, 4, 5, ..., with the same series of numbers repeated over and over again. Using these numbers as counting numbers, you will find that you have five fingers on one hand, four fingers on two hands, and two fingers and toes on two hands and feet. Operating with the numbers, you will obtain the following results:

$$2 + 3 = 5; \quad 2 + 4 = 0; \quad 3 - 2 = 1; \quad 3 - 4 = 5; \quad 2 \times 3 = 0;$$

and

$$2 \times 5 = 4.$$

It is apparent that the number symbol "3" has many meanings, as does, for example, the "3" in "3 o'clock."

A study of the addition chart for modulo-six arithmetic of Table 6–2 shows that the operation of addition is commutative since for any number a and b, $a + b = b + a$; zero is the identity element; the set of num-

TABLE 6–2

ADDITION CHART

+	0	1	2	3	4	5
0	0	1	2	3	4	5
1	1	2	3	4	5	0
2	2	3	4	5	0	1
3	3	4	5	0	1	2
4	4	5	0	1	2	3
5	5	0	1	2	3	4

TABLE 6–3

MULTIPLICATION CHART

×	0	1	2	3	4	5
0	0	0	0	0	0	0
1	0	1	2	3	4	5
2	0	2	4	0	2	4
3	0	3	0	3	0	3
4	0	4	2	0	4	2
5	0	5	4	3	2	1

1, 3 not possible

closure

$3 \times 4 = 0$

bers is closed under addition; and addition has the cancellation property. It is less obvious but may be proved that addition is also associative.

Using Table 6–2 as a subtraction chart, we observe an interesting property of subtraction. Unlike the set of whole numbers, the numbers of modulo-six arithmetic are closed under the operation of subtraction. Any pair of numbers may be subtracted in the order selected, for example,

$$3 - 2 = 1; \quad 2 - 3 = 5; \quad \text{and} \quad 4 - 5 = 5.$$

The study of the multiplication chart of Table 6–3 shows that the operation of multiplication is commutative, since for any number a and b, $ab = ba$; one is the identity element; and the set of numbers is closed under multiplication. It is less obvious but can be proved that multiplication is also associative. However, the cancellation property does not apply. Note from the table that $3 \times 3 = 3$ and $3 \times 5 = 3$. Therefore, $3 \times 3 = 3 \times 5$ but $3 \neq 5$.

Using Table 6–3 as a division chart, note that not only does $3 \div 3 = 1$, but $3 \div 3 = 3$ and $3 \div 3 = 5$. Thus, division by 3 is not an operation since the result is not unique. Observation will also show that division by 2, 4, and 0 is not an operation within this set. The set of numbers of modulo-six arithmetic is not closed under division, and there is no possible way of extending the system to make division always possible as it is with the natural numbers.

EXERCISE SET 6–2

1. Let operation ⊛ be the operation of finding the least common divisor of two whole numbers, a ⊛ $b = c$.
   (a) Define the operation in words.
   (b) Is the operation associative?
2. Let operation ◎ be the operation of finding the least common multiple of two whole numbers, a ◎ $b = c$.
   (a) Discover four properties of the operation ◎ .
   (b) Do these properties also apply to operation ⊛ ?
3. An operation ϕ is defined as finding the larger of two whole numbers if they are unequal, or one of the numbers if they are equal.
   (a) Make an operation-ϕ chart for all a and b less than six.
   (b) Is the operation commutative?
   (c) Does it have the cancellation property?
   (d) Does it have an identity element?
4. An operation ⊠ is defined as finding the smaller of two whole numbers if they are unequal, or one of the numbers if they are equal.
   (a) Make an operation-⊠ chart for all a and b less than six.
   (b) Do the properties of operation ϕ hold for operation ⊠ ?
5. Given the set of multiples of five, state whether the set is closed under (a) addition; (b) multiplication; (c) subtraction; (d) division.
6. Let ℱ be the family of all the subsets of the whole numbers and let A, B, and C be three of these subsets.
   (a) Show that set union, $A \cup B = C$, is an operation on two sets A and B. [*Hint:* Test by examining whether set union has the two characteristics of an operation.]
   (b) Is the operation commutative? Illustrate.
   (c) Is the operation associative? Illustrate.
   (d) Is ℱ closed under the operation?
   (e) Does the operation have an identity element? Explain.
   (f) Does the operation have an inverse? Explain.
   (g) For what sets A is $A \cup A = A$?
7. Let ℱ be the family of all the subsets of the whole numbers and let A, B, and C be three of these subsets.
   (a) Show that set intersection, $A \cap B = C$, is an operation on two sets A and B.
   (b) Is the operation commutative? Illustrate.
   (c) Is the operation associative? Illustrate.
   (d) Is ℱ closed under the operation?
   (e) Does the operation have an identity element? Explain.

(f) Does the operation have an inverse? Explain.

(g) For what sets A is $A \cap A = A$?

8. An operation ⊛ on whole numbers is defined as follows:

$$a \circledast b = a + b + (a \times b) + 1.$$

(a) Make an operation-⊛ chart for the whole numbers 1 through 9 (see addition chart, Table 6–2).

(b) Discover three properties of the operation ⊛ .

(c) Does the operation have an inverse? Why?

(d) Does the operation have an identity element? Illustrate.

9. The operation △ is the operation of finding one-half the sum of two numbers (averaging), $a \triangle b = c$.

(a) Describe its inverse operation, ▽.

(b) The operation $a \triangle b$ is defined by $a \triangle b = \frac{1}{2}(a + b)$. Define $c \triangledown a$ in a similar way.

10. Complete the following charts for $a \triangle b$ and $c \triangledown a$. $\frac{a+b}{2}$ $2c - a$

(a)

△	0	2	4	6	8
0	0	1			
2			3		
4					
6			5	6	
8					

(b)

▽	0	1	2	3	4	5
0	0					
1	2	1	0			
2				1		
3						
4						
5						

11. (a) Show that ▽ is not commutative.

(b) Show that ▽ is not associative.

12. The operation ξ may be defined as $a \xi b = 3a + 2b$. Show that the operation has the cancellation property.

13. Under what condition will the operation ξ have an inverse? Note that the operation is noncommutative.

14. If $3a + 2b$ defines $a \xi b$, which of the following defines its inverse, $c \xi a$?

(a) $c - 3a$ (b) $2a - 3c$ (c) $\frac{1}{2}(3a - c)$

(d) $\frac{1}{3}(c - 2a)$ (e) $\frac{1}{2}(c - 3a)$ (f) $\frac{1}{2}(a - c)$

15. Show why the sum $a + b = n(A \cup B)$ is independent of the nature of the elements of the sets A and B. Use as examples the sets $A = \{a, b, c\}$ and $B = \{p, q\}$; and $A' = \{\triangle, \circ, \square\}$ and $B' = \{\varnothing, \triangledown\}$.

16. Why is it necessary that any pair of sets A and B of Exercise 15 be disjoint?

17. Show by the distributive property for multiplication that $40 + 50 = 90$.

18. Show by the distributive property for multiplication that $40 \times 60 = 2400$.

19. Consult the multiplication chart for modulo-six arithmetic and verify the following as correct or incorrect. If incorrect, tell why.

(a) Since $5 \div 1 = 5$ and $1 \div 5 = 5$, $5 \div 1 = 1 \div 5$.

(b) Since $4 \div 2 = 2$ and $2 \div 4 = 2$, $4 \div 2 = 2 \div 4$.

20. In modulo-twelve arithmetic,

$$6 \div 2 = 3, \qquad 6 \div 6 = 3, \qquad \text{and} \qquad 6 \div 10 = 3.$$

What conclusion regarding division do these examples suggest?

21. (a) Make a multiplication chart for modulo-five arithmetic.
    (b) The set of nonzero numbers of modulo-six arithmetic is not closed under the operation of division. Does this property apply to modulo-five arithmetic? State the reason for your answer.

REFERENCES

BANKS, J. HOUSTON, *Learning and Teaching Arithmetic*. Boston: Allyn and Bacon, Inc., 1959, pp. 73–232.

BRUMFIEL, CHARLES F., ROBERT E. EICHOLZ, and MERRILL E. SHANKS, *Fundamental Concepts of Elementary Mathematics*. Reading, Mass.: Addison-Wesley Publishing Company, Inc., 1962, pp. 63–95.

KEEDY, MERVIN L., *A Modern Introduction to Mathematics*. Reading, Mass.: Addison-Wesley Publishing Company, Inc, 1963, pp. 15–26, 49–58.

MUELLER, FRANCIS J., *Arithmetic, Its Structure and Concepts*. Englewood Cliffs, N. J.: Prentice-Hall, Inc., 1956, pp. 48–149.

OSBORN, ROGER, M. VERE DeVAULT, and W. ROBERT HOUSTON, *Extending Mathematical Understanding*. Columbus, Ohio: Charles E. Merrill Books, Inc., 1961, pp. 115–128.

PETERSON, JOHN A., and JOSEPH HASHISAKI, *The Theory of Arithmetic*. New York: John Wiley and Sons, 1963, pp. 86–112, 142–151.

School Mathematics Study Group, " Number Systems," in *Studies in Mathematics*, Volume VI. New Haven, Conn.: Yale University, 1961, pp. 51–94, 281–319.

SWAIN, ROBERT L., *Understanding Arithmetic*. New York: Rinehart and Company, Inc., 1957, pp. 46–96.

WILLIAMS, SAMMIE M., H. GARLAND READ, JR., and FRANK L. WILLIAMS, *Modern Mathematics in the Elementary and Junior High Schools*. Syracuse, N. Y.: The L. W. Singer Company, Inc., 1961, pp. 41–73.

CHAPTER SEVEN

THE FUNDAMENTAL ALGORITHMS OF ARITHMETIC

1. EXAMPLES AND USE OF ALGORITHMS

A systematic procedure for performing a mathematical operation is called an algorithm. For example, there are algorithms for dividing whole numbers, for finding the square and cube roots of a whole number, and for finding the greatest common factor of two whole numbers. Pattern 1 forms the basis for an algorithm; so does Pattern 2. Each has all the elements necessary to the process of finding the product of 527 and 32. However, the written Pattern 1 is a commonly recognized and accepted form for the process of multiplication; Pattern 2 is not immediately recognized as the process of multiplication. The algorithms considered in this chapter are mainly those which are generally accepted.

$$
\begin{array}{r}
527 \\
32 \\
\hline
1054 \\
1581 \\
\hline
16864
\end{array}
$$

FIG. 7–1. Pattern 1.

$$
\begin{array}{r|r|l}
32 & 15810 & 16864 \\
527 & 1054 &
\end{array}
$$

FIG. 7–2. Pattern 2.

The basic algorithms of arithmetic are those involving whole numbers. Algorithms are used to reduce the processes of addition, subtraction, multiplication, and division of numbers greater than ten to simpler processes in a systematic way. For example, by application of the properties of multiplication, the multiplication of 32 and 527 in Pattern 1 is reduced to a series of multiplications of numbers less than ten. The complicated becomes simple through the use of an algorithm. Its use reduces 32×527 to

$$2 \times 7, \quad 2 \times 2, \quad 2 \times 5, \quad 3 \times 7, \quad 3 \times 2, \quad \text{and} \quad 3 \times 5.$$

All computations of arithmetic, e.g., those with fractions and integers, may be reduced to the basic operations on whole numbers by the use of algorithms. This places great importance on the algorithms, for they are shortcuts to longer complete developments.

The purpose of this chapter is to derive the basic algorithms of arithmetic through the application of the properties of the operations. For clarity, each algorithm recommended will be referred to as *the* algorithm although many other algorithms exist.

2. THE ADDITION ALGORITHM

The derivation of the addition algorithm. The addition algorithm is dependent on the renaming of numbers, and on the commutative and associative properties for addition.

If a and b in the mathematical sentence $a + b = n$ are each numbers less than ten, n is known immediately; but if a and b are each greater than ten, n may not be known immediately. For example, if $a = 40$ and $b = 50$, the steps below are followed to determine n. A justification for each step is given.

EXAMPLE 1
$$n = 40 + 50$$

(a) $n = (4 \times 10) + (5 \times 10)$ Two addends renamed.

(b) $n = (4 + 5) \times 10$ Distributive property for multiplication.

(c) $n = 9 \times 10$ Addition performed.

(d) $n = 90$ Multiplication performed.

In Example 1, the addends were multiples of ten. In the examples which follow, the addends are not multiples of ten but the processes used are dependent on that used in Example 1.

EXAMPLE 2
$$n = 45 + 53$$

(a) $n = (40 + 5) + (50 + 3)$ Two addends renamed.
$a \circ b = b \circ a$ $(a \circ b) \circ c = a \circ (b \circ c$

(b) $n = (40 + 50) + (5 + 3)$ Commutative and associative properties for addition applied.

(c) $n = 90 + 8$ Addition performed.

(d) $n = 98$ Addition performed.

In Example 2 and in similar examples, the result in step (c) can be expressed directly as a single decimal number. In other examples, it cannot be. The result must be renamed and the commutative and associative properties used. For example, if $a = 48$ and $b = 77$, additional steps are necessary after step (c).

EXAMPLE 3
$$n = 48 + 77$$

(a)	$n = (40 + 8) + (70 + 7)$	Two addends renamed.
(b)	$n = (40 + 70) + (8 + 7)$	Commutative and associative properties for addition applied.
(c)	$n = 110 + 15$	Addition performed.
(d)	$n = (100 + 10) + (10 + 5)$	110 and 15 renamed.
(e)	$n = 100 + (10 + 10) + 5$	Associative property for addition applied.
(f)	$n = 100 + 20 + 5$	Addition performed.
(g)	$n = 125$	Addition performed.

In each of the previous examples there were two addends. A similar process is applied, however, to examples which have more than two addends. The process may be performed by operating on the numbers in pairs. It may be shortened, however, by an algorithm which allows for renaming and the application of the associative and commutative properties. Given the addends 77, 25, 39, and 23, the following steps are followed to derive the algorithm.

EXAMPLE 4
$$n = 77 + 25 + 39 + 23$$

(a)	$n = (70 + 7) + (20 + 5)$ $+ (30 + 9) + (20 + 3)$	Each addend renamed.
(b)	$n = (70 + 20 + 30 + 20)$ $+ (7 + 5 + 9 + 3)$	Commutative and associative properties for addition applied.
(c)	$n = 140 + 24$	Addition performed.
(d)	$n = (100 + 40) + (20 + 4)$	Each addend renamed.
(e)	$n = 100 + (40 + 20) + 4$	Associative property for addition applied.
(f)	$n = 100 + 60 + 4$	$(40 + 20)$ renamed.
(g)	$n = 164$	Addition performed.

The algorithm. The writing of addends in columns abbreviates the process used in Examples 1 through 4. For example, the addends of Example 4 are written in columnar form below.

EXAMPLE 4.
$$\begin{array}{r} 77 \\ 25 \\ 39 \\ 23 \\ \underline{24} \\ 140 \\ \hline 164 \end{array}$$

Observe the similarity between the procedure described in the previous paragraph and that of the columnar form. Each groups the number of units together and the number of tens together; each records the sums indicating the number of ones and the number of tens; and each renames these partial sums as a single decimal number.

In the columnar form of Example 4 the partial sums are also recorded to illustrate the application of the commutative and associative properties for addition; the partial sums are not recorded in the algorithms for addition. See Example 5 below. The addition algorithm through its columnar form provides a pattern which makes the commutative and associative properties for addition easy to apply.

In the algorithm for addition the sums of the units, tens, hundreds, etc., are determined in that order; and each of these partial sums is immediately renamed. In the example below,

EXAMPLE 5.
$$\begin{array}{r} 5728 \\ 2483 \\ \underline{8346} \\ \hline 16557 \end{array}$$

the sum of the units, 17, is renamed 1 ten and 7. The 7 is recorded and the 1 ten is added with the other tens immediately to obtain the partial sum 15 tens. The 15 tens is renamed 1 hundred and 5 tens. The 5 tens is recorded and the 1 hundred is added with the other hundreds immediately to obtain the partial sum 15 hundreds. The 15 hundreds is renamed 1 thousand and 5 hundreds. The 5 hundreds is recorded and the 1 thousand is added with the other thousands immediately to obtain the partial sum, 16 thousands. This partial sum is recorded. The sum of the three addends is 16,557.

The term "rename" is used rather than the more common terminology which contains the word "carry" because "rename" is more descriptive of the process and has a broader application in mathematics.

Illustration of the algorithm with an abacus. A loop abacus with at least 18 beads on each wire is a useful device for demonstrating the application of renaming, as well as the commutative and associative properties for addition in the algorithm for addition. Each step in the use of an addition algorithm is illustrated below.

EXAMPLE 6.

(a)   258
      385
      ———

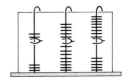

Sets of beads are chosen and separated to show the two addends.

(b)   258
      385
      ———

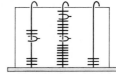

Add: 8 + 5 = 13

Remove the separator on the units' wire to combine 8 and 5 to show 13.

(c)   258
      385
      ———
        3

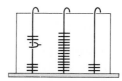

Rename 13 as 1 ten and 3. Record 3 and remember 1 ten.

Separate 13 units into 10 units and 3. Exchange 10 units for 1 ten.

(d)   258
      385
      ———
        3

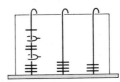

Add: 1 ten + 5 tens + 8 tens = 14 tens

Remove the separators on the tens' wire to combine 1 ten, 5 tens, and 8 tens into 14 tens.

(e)   258
      385
      ———
       43

Rename 14 tens as 1 hundred and 4 tens. Record 4 tens and remember 1 hundred.

Separate 14 tens into 10 tens and 4 tens. Exchange 10 tens for 1 hundred.

EXAMPLE 6 (*cont.*)

(f)   258
       385
       643

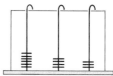

Add: 1 hundred + 2 hundreds +   Remove the separators on the
     3 hundreds = 6 hundreds.   hundreds' wire to combine 1 hundred,
                                    2 hundreds, and 3 hundreds into
     Record 6 hundreds.   6 hundreds.

Note that the abacus in step (a) shows the two addends 258 and 385 and that the abacus in step (f) shows the sum 643. Both the algorithm and the abacus illustrate how the properties of numbers and operations are applied to find the sum of two numbers greater than ten.

3.   THE SUBTRACTION ALGORITHM

The derivation of the subtraction algorithm. The derivation of the subtraction algorithm is similar in meaning to the derivation of the addition algorithm: each is dependent on the renaming of numbers and on the commutative and associative properties for addition.

In the mathematical sentence $a + n = c$ or $n = c - a$, if c is 18 or less and a is less than 10, then n is known immediately; but, if a is greater than 18 and c is greater than 9, n may not be known immediately. For example, if $c = 547$ and $a = 235$, the steps below are followed to determine n. A justification for each step is given.

EXAMPLE 7

$$n = 547 - 235$$

(a) $n = (500 + 40 + 7)$ Sum and known addend renamed.
          $- (200 + 35 + 5)$

(b) $n = (500 - 200)$ Commutative and associative
          $+ (40 - 30) + (7 - 5)$ properties for addition applied.

(c) $n = 300 + 10 + 2$ Subtraction performed.

(d) $n = 312$ Addition performed.

The manner in which 547 is named in step (a), Example 7, makes it easy to find the missing addend. This is not always the case. Consider Example 8 below. If 547 is renamed 5 hundreds, 4 tens, and 7, it is not convenient to subtract 179. To subtract 1 hundred, 7 tens, and 9 from 547, the 547 is renamed so that it names at least as many as 7 tens in the tens' place, and 9 in the units' place. To meet this condition the sum 547 may be re-named 4 hundreds, 13 tens, and 17.

EXAMPLE 8

$n = 547 - 179$

(a) $n = (400 + 130 + 17)$ Sum and known addend renamed.
     $- (100 + 70 + 9)$

(b) $n = (400 - 100)$ Commutative and associative
     $+ (130 - 70) + (17 - 9)$ properties for addition applied.

(c) $n = 300 + 60 + 8$ Subtraction performed.

(d) $n = 368$ Addition performed.

The algorithm. The algorithm for subtraction shortens the process shown in the derivation by using a columnar form with the known addend written under the sum in a manner which groups the units, tens, etc., to-gether. The derivation illustrated in Example 7 is shortened by the use of the following algorithm.

EXAMPLE 7'.   547
                  235
                  ———
                  312

In the algorithm the sum 547 is renamed 5 hundreds, 4 tens, and 7, and 235 is renamed 2 hundreds, 3 tens, and 5, just as in the derivation. The missing addend is determined by finding and recording partial missing addends in this order: $7 - 5 = 2$; 4 tens $- 3$ tens $= 1$ ten; and 5 hundreds $- 2$ hundreds $= 3$ hundreds. The missing addend recorded is 312.

The algorithm for Example 8 and similar examples requires a considera-tion of the known addend for the renaming of the sum, as was shown in the derivation. The sum in Example 8 is renamed 4 hundreds, 13 tens, and 17 so that one may conveniently subtract 1 hundred, 7 tens, and 9.

EXAMPLE 8'.   547
                  179
                  ———
                  368

The missing addend in Example 8 is now determined by finding and re-cording partial missing addends in this order:

$$17 - 9 = 8; \qquad 13 \text{ tens} - 7 \text{ tens} = 6 \text{ tens};$$

and

$$4 \text{ hundreds} - 1 \text{ hundred} = 3 \text{ hundreds}.$$

The missing addend recorded is 368.

As the algorithm for subtraction is commonly used, the renaming of the sum is done in steps. The renaming begins by a renaming of part of the sum so that the units of the known addend may be subtracted, and proceeds to the left. In Example 8, to subtract 9, the 47 of the sum is renamed 3 tens and 17 (17 − 9 = 8). To subtract 7 tens, the 53 tens is renamed 4 hundreds and 13 tens (13 tens − 7 tens = 6 tens). The 1 hundred is subtracted from 4 hundreds (4 hundreds − 1 hundred = 3 hundreds) to complete the operation.

Observe the similarity between the processes followed in the derivations and in the algorithm. Each applies the commutative and associative properties for addition by grouping the number of units together, the number of tens together, etc.; each renames the sum and known addend for convenience in subtracting; and each finds partial missing addends and records them to form the missing addend.

The term "rename" is also used in the subtraction algorithm rather than the more common terminology which contains the word "borrow," because "rename" is more descriptive of the process and has a broader application in mathematics.

Illustration of the algorithm with an abacus. The same loop abacus used to illustrate addition demonstrates the application of renaming as well as the commutative and associative properties for addition in the algorithm for subtraction. Each step in the use of an algorithm to find the missing addend is illustrated below.

EXAMPLE 9.   (a)   625
                     477
                     ———

Sum is shown on abacus.

(b)   625
       477
       ———

The 25 of the sum 625 is renamed 1 ten and 15.

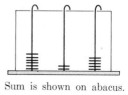

Beads are rearranged to represent 2 tens and 5 as 1 ten and 15.

(c)   625
       477
       ———
         8

Subtract: 15 − 7 = 8

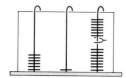

The separator shows 15 as 7 and the partial missing addend 8.

Example 9 (*cont.*)

(d) 625
     477
     ———
       8

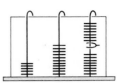

61 tens is renamed 5
hundreds and 11 tens.

Beads are rearranged to represent
6 hundreds and 1 ten as 5 hundreds
and 11 tens.

(e) 625
     477
     ———
      48

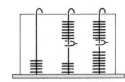

Subtract: 11 tens −
7 tens = 4 tens.

The separator shows 11 tens as
7 tens and the partial missing
addend 4 tens.

(f) 625
     477
     ———
     148

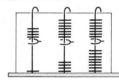

Subtract: 5 hundreds −
4 hundreds = 1 hundred.

The separator shows 5 hundreds
as 4 hundreds and the partial missing
addend 1 hundred.

Note that the abacus in step (a) shows the sum 625 and that in step (f)
it shows the sum as the known addend 477 and the missing addend 148.
Both the algorithm and the abacus illustrate how the properties of number
and operations are applied to subtract numbers greater than 10.

EXERCISE SET 7-1

1. Write a statement which justifies each step below.
   $n = 728 + 934$
   (a) $n = (700 + 20 + 8) + (900 + 30 + 4)$ *renaming*
   (b) $n = (700 + 900) + (20 + 30) + (8 + 4)$
   (c) $n = 1600 + 50 + 12$
   (d) $n = 1600 + (50 + 10) + 2$
   (e) $n = 1600 + 60 + 2$
   (f) $n = 1662$
2. Write a statement which justifies each step below.
   $n = 547 - 126$
   (a) $n = (500 + 40 + 7) - (100 + 20 + 6)$
   (b) $n = (500 - 100) + (40 - 20) + (7 - 6)$
   (c) $n = 400 + 20 + 1$
   (d) $n = 421$

3. Write a statement which justifies each step in the following subtraction.

$n = 941 - 78$

(a) $n = 900 + 41 - (70 + 8)$
(b) $n = 900 + 30 + 11 - (70 + 8)$
(c) $n = 900 + 30 - 70 + (11 - 8)$
(d) $n = 900 + 30 - 70 + 3$
(e) $n = (800 + 100) + 30 - 70 + 3$
(f) $n = 800 + (130 - 70) + 3$
(g) $n = 800 + 60 + 3$
(h) $n = 863$

4. Write a statement which justifies each step in the following addition exercise.

$n = 7205 + 9907 + 8063$

(a) $n = (7000 + 200 + 5) + (9000 + 900 + 7) + (8000 + 60 + 3)$
(b) $n = (7000 + 9000 + 8000) + (200 + 900 + 60) + (5 + 7 + 3)$
(c) $n = 24000 + 1100 + 60 + 15$
(d) $n = 20000 + (4000 + 1000) + 100 + (60 + 10) + 5$
(e) $n = 20000 + 5000 + 100 + 70 + 5$
(f) $n = 25,175$

5. Find n in each of the following by applying the properties of number and of operations. Follow the plan of Exercises 1 through 4.

(a) $n = 232 + 145 + 520$ (b) $n = 579 - 328$
(c) $n = 728 + 436$ (d) $n = 748 - 39$

6. (a) Invent another algorithm for addition.
   (b) What are the advantages and disadvantages of your algorithm as compared with the accepted algorithm for addition?

7. (a) Use an algorithm to determine the sum of 343 and 478.
   (b) Illustrate the steps of (a) by sketching a series of abaci.

8. (a) Use an algorithm to find n in

$$n = 821 - 343.$$

   (b) Illustrate the steps of (a) by sketching a series of abaci.

9. (a) What relation exists between the steps of Exercises 7(a) and 8(a)?
   (b) Explain why this relation exists.

10. (a) What relation is there between the illustrations sketched for Exercises 7(b) and 8(b)?
    (b) Explain why this relation exists.

11. Rename the sum in each of the following as it is renamed in the subtraction algorithm.

(a) $n = 528 - 119$ (b) $n = 528 - 389$
(c) $1248 + n = 4139$ (d) $2005 + n = 3422$
(e) $427 + n = 1005$ (f) $n = 240 - 157$

12. What is the advantage of writing numbers which are to be added or subtracted in columnar rather than in horizontal form?

Note: If you need practice in performing the basic operations of arithmetic, see Appendix II, "Skill Tests."

4. THE MULTIPLICATION ALGORITHM.

The derivation of the multiplication algorithm. The multiplication algorithm is dependent on the following: the renaming of numbers, the commutative and associative properties for addition and multiplication, and the distributive property for multiplication.

If the numbers a and b in the mathematical sentence $n = a \times b$ are each less than 10, n is known immediately; but if a and b are greater than 10, then the product n may not be known immediately. In such examples, a and b are renamed and one is distributed over the other to find the product n.

For example, if $a = 30$ and $b = 20$, the steps below are needed to determine the product n in $n = 30 \times 20$. The justification for each step is given.

EXAMPLE 10

$\qquad n = 30 \times 20$

(a) $n = (3 \times 10) \times (2 \times 10)$ Factors renamed.

(b) $n = (3 \times 2) \times (10 \times 10)$ Associative and commutative property for multiplication.

(c) $n = 6 \times 100$ Multiplication performed.

(d) $n = 600$ Multiplication performed.

In Example 10 the factors are multiples of ten. In the examples which follow, the factors are not multiples of ten, but the processes used are dependent on those used in Example 10.

EXAMPLE 11

$\qquad n = 32 \times 23$

(a) $n = (2 + 30) \times (3 + 20)$ Factors renamed.

(b) $n = 2(3 + 20) + 30(3 + 20)$ 2 and 30 are each distributed over $(3 + 20)$.

(c) $n = (2 \times 3) + (2 \times 20)$ $+ (30 \times 3) + (30 \times 20)$ 2 distributed over 3 and 20; 30 distributed over 3 and 20.

(d) $n = (6 + 40) + (90 + 600)$ Multiplication performed.

(e) $n = 46 + 690$ Addition performed.

(f) $n = 736$ Addition performed.

In Example 11 and in similar examples, the result in step (d) requires no renaming to determine the partial products of step (e). However, if $a = 34$ and $b = 46$, several additional steps are needed as in Example 12.

EXAMPLE 12

$n = 34 \times 46$

(a) $n = (4 + 30) \times (6 + 40)$ Factors renamed.

(b) $n = 4(6 + 40) + 30(6 + 40)$ 4 and 30 are each distributed over $(6 + 40)$.

(c) $n = (4 \times 6) + (4 \times 40)$ 4 distributed over 6 and 40;
      $+ (30 \times 6) + (30 \times 40)$ 30 distributed over 6 and 40.

(d) $n = (24 + 160)$ Operation of multiplication ap-
      $+ (180 + 1200)$ plied.

(e) $n = (4 + 20 + 60 + 100)$ Addends renamed.
      $+ (80 + 100 + 1200)$

(f) $n = (4 + 80 + 100)$ Addition performed.
      $+ (80 + 1300)$

(g) $n = 184 + 1380$ Addition performed.

(h) $n = 1564$ Addition performed.

The algorithm. The algorithm for multiplication abbreviates the derivation illustrated in Examples 11 and 12. A written pattern like that shown in Example 11′ makes it easy to follow these steps: rename 23 as $20 + 3$ and 32 as $30 + 2$, distribute 2 over the 3 and 20 of 23 to determine the partial product $6 + 40$, or 46; distribute 30 over the 3 and 20 of 23 to determine the partial product $90 + 600$, or 690; and add the partial products to determine the product, 736.

EXAMPLE 11′.

$$
\begin{array}{r}
23 \\
32 \\
\hline
46 \\
690 \\
\hline
736
\end{array}
$$

Example 12 requires a few more steps both in its derivation and in the algorithm. The algorithm of Example 12′(b) is a refinement of the form to the left.

EXAMPLE 12′. (a)   (b)

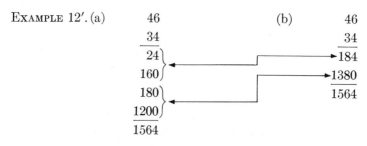

In each of the forms at 12', the distributive property for multiplication is applied as it was in the algorithm for Example 11. In this algorithm as in its derivation the elements of the partial products require renaming for purposes of addition. For example, form (a) records the product of $4(6 + 40)$ as 24 and 160; in form (b) the sum of 24 and 160 is determined mentally and recorded as 184.

Comparing the derivation of the product for Example 12 with the algorithm given, note that each of the steps of the derivation is carried out in the algorithm. However, the algorithm permits one to perform these steps with greater ease: the writing of the factors in columns makes it convenient to distribute one factor over the addends of the other; and the placing of the partial products in columns makes it convenient to add them to determine the product. The algorithm for multiplication is a pattern for the effective application of the properties of numbers and operations.

Illustration of the algorithm with an array. An array is an orderly rectangular arrangement of objects into rows and columns. In mathematics, it may be used as a diagram of all the matchings of the elements of two finite sets. (See Chapter 2, Section 12.)

Any objects may be used to represent pairs of matched elements, e.g., the asterisks of Fig. 7–3, the circles of Fig. 7–4, or the squares of Fig. 7–5.

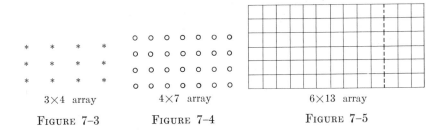

3×4 array	4×7 array	6×13 array
Figure 7–3	Figure 7–4	Figure 7–5

Figure 7–3 is a 3 × 4 array. The asterisks represent all the couples which may be formed by matching the cups of a set of 3 cups with the saucers of a set of 4 saucers. They also represent the pairs formed by matching a set of 3 pillows with a set of 4 sofas or the elements of any set of 3 with the elements of any set of 4. Note that in describing an array, the number of rows is mentioned first.

An array may be chosen to illustrate the Cartesian product, $A \otimes B$, of any two finite sets A and B, or the product ab, of any two numbers a and b. Figure 7–3 illustrates that 3 × 4 = 12. The array of Fig. 7–4 shows that 4 × 7 = 28, and Fig. 7–5 shows that 6 × 13 = 78.

The algorithm for multiplication and its use of the distributive property for multiplication are well illustrated by an array. The 6×13 array of Fig. 7–5 illustrates the distributive property in the product 6×13. A dashed line separates the array into two arrays, one 6×10 and the other 6×3, just as the distributive property permits 6×13 to be expressed as $6 \times 10 + 6 \times 3$.

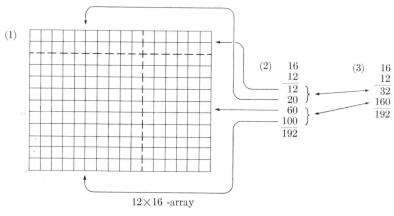

12×16 -array

FIGURE 7–6

Figure 7–6 shows an algorithm for multiplying 12×16 and a 12×16 array chosen to illustrate it. Dashed lines are drawn in the array to separate it into parts corresponding to those of the algorithm. Arrows are drawn to point out the relation between the parts of the algorithm and the parts of the array.

More complicated algorithms for multiplication, e.g., 276×148, may be illustrated by omitting the detailed lines forming the small squares in

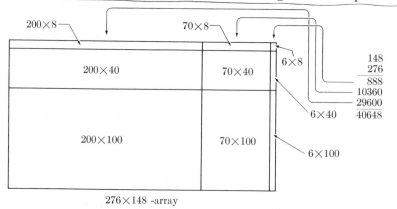

276×148 -array

FIGURE 7–7

Fig. 7–6. The array of Fig. 7–7 pictures the distribution of the 6, 70, and 200 of 276 over the 8, 40, and 100 of 148 in 276 × 148.

5.   THE DIVISION ALGORITHM

The derivation of the division algorithm.   Division is the operation of determining the missing factor if the product and a factor are known.   In the sentences,

$$an = b \quad \text{and} \quad n = b \div a,$$

n is the missing factor.   Any algorithm for division is based on this inverse relationship of multiplication and division.   The multiplication algorithm uses the distributive property for multiplication; the division algorithm uses the distributive property for division.

If b is a multiple of any of the numbers 0 through 9 and is less than 81 and if a is known (and not zero), then n is known immediately; but if b is a multiple of any other whole number or is greater than 81, then the missing factor may not be identified immediately.   In such examples, the product b is renamed and the known factor is distributed over the addends.

In the example below, the known factor 21 is distributed over addends of 504 renamed.   You choose those addends which make it easy to identify partial missing factors.

(a) $\quad \frac{504}{21} = \frac{210}{21} + \frac{210}{21} + \frac{42}{21} + \frac{42}{21} = 10 + 10 + 2 + 2 = 24,$

(b) $\quad \frac{504}{21} = \frac{420}{21} + \frac{42}{21} + \frac{21}{21} + \frac{21}{21} = 20 + 2 + 1 + 1 = 24,$

(c) $\quad \frac{504}{21} = \frac{420}{21} + \frac{84}{21} = 20 + 4 = 24.$

Note that 504 may be renamed in many other ways to facilitate division of the addends by 21.   It could be named as the sum of 24 twenty-ones or of 12 forty-twos.   In an algorithm, the most convenient way of renaming is chosen.   In the example above, the renaming in (c) is the most convenient.

If the known factor of 504 is not 21 but 12, 504 is renamed differently; i.e. in this case, the addends chosen are multiples of 12.   Following are some of the ways in which 504 may be renamed if 12 is the known factor.

(a) $\quad \frac{504}{12} = \frac{240}{12} + \frac{240}{12} + \frac{24}{12} = 20 + 20 + 2 = 42,$

(b) $\quad \frac{504}{12} = \frac{360}{12} + \frac{120}{21} + \frac{24}{12} = 30 + 10 + 2 = 42,$

(c) $\quad \frac{504}{12} = \frac{480}{12} + \frac{24}{12} = 40 + 2 = 42.$

The algorithm. An algorithm for each of the ways in which 504 was just renamed for division by 12 is shown below:

(a)		(b)		(c)	
	42		42		42
	2*		2*		2*
	20*		10*		40*
	20*		30*	12)504	
12)504		12)504		480˙	
	240˙		360˙		24˙
	264		144		
	240˙		120˙		
	24˙		24*		

The numbers which have a dot to their right are the addends of 504 over which 12 has been distributed. The numbers which have an asterisk to their right are the partial missing factors obtained by dividing the addends of 504 by 12. The sum of the partial missing factors is 42 and appears at the top. Note the similarity of method used in the three algorithms above and in the development of the algorithm in the preceding paragraph.

The algorithm in common use today is a modification of (c). For example, the 0 in the units' place of the partial missing factor 40 is omitted, and the other partial missing factor is placed in the units' place to show 40 + 2 or 42. It is also customary to omit the terminal zero in the addend 480; however, this omission is not recommended for those who are interested in understanding the algorithm.

EXAMPLE 13.
$$\begin{array}{r} 123 \\ 37\overline{)4551} \\ 3700 \\ \hline 851 \\ 740 \\ \hline 111 \end{array}$$

The form used today is, in essence, illustrated by Example 13, which deviates from common practice only in that it includes all the terminal zeros of the number symbols. The algorithm (zeros included) is the form recommended to you and used in this material. Its application ensures that all numbers used are properly identified, e.g., that 3700 is not assumed to be 37.

The efficient use of the algorithm for division depends both on knowing multiples so they may be used in renaming the product and on the choice of the addends of the new name. The solution of examples like $n =$

$4551 \div 37$ is perfomed with greater ease if you can rename 4551 into addends which are multiples of 37 for use of the distributive property for division.

The 4551 in Example 13 is renamed $3700 + 740 + 111$, and the 37 is distributed over each addend. Each of the addends of 4551 is chosen so that the largest partial missing factor for any single place value is found in one step. The efficient execution of the division algorithm requires that the product be renamed in this way. However, as the process is learned, this renaming ability is developed through algorithms of the form (a), (b), and (c).

In general, the division of whole numbers, $n = a \div b$, is performed with greater efficiency if you know multiples of the known factor b and can easily rename the product a as a sum of those multiples so that a maximum partial factor is obtained for each place value in one step.

Illustration of the algorithm with an array. A $b \times n$ array of a elements illustrates the sentence $n = a \div b$. If $a = 276$ and $b = 12$, the array needed will have 276 elements arranged in 12 rows of n columns. (See Fig. 7–8)

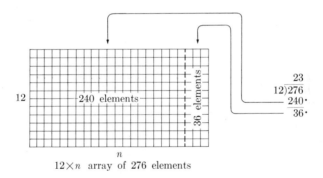

$12 \times n$ array of 276 elements

FIGURE 7–8

Figure 7–8 shows the relation between the 276-element array and the algorithm for $276 \div 12$. The 276 elements of the array and the 276 in the algorithm are each thought of as $240 + 36$. Each shows that

$$276 = 240 + 36,$$
$$276 = 12 \times \underline{20} + 12 \times \underline{3},$$
$$276 = 12 \times \underline{23},$$

and

$$n = 23.$$

6. THE DIVISION PROCESS

The process. The operation of division is defined as finding the missing factor n given the product and one factor in the sentence $a = b \times n$ or $n = a \div b$. If the sentence to be solved is $70 = 6 \times n$ and the universal set is the set of whole numbers, the operation of division cannot be performed. Nevertheless $70 = 6 \times 11 + 4$. In this sentence an operation has *not* been performed since from the two numbers 70 and 6 there resulted not one number but two, 11 and 4.

Finding the factor q and the remainder r for sentences similar to $70 = 6 \times q + r$ will be referred to as the division process and not as division. "Division" will be reserved for use in the operational sense. Given any two whole numbers a and b with $b \neq 0$, the mathematical sentence describing the division process is

$$a = b \times q + r.$$

The process determines q and r uniquely, since it is required that the remainder r be less than b. It is only when $r = 0$ that the division process may be called an operation. In such a case,

$$a = b \times q + 0 \qquad \text{and} \qquad q = a \div b.$$

Note that if a and b are large, the process has to be completed before it can be known whether or not it is an operation because r is the last number determined.

In the mathematical sentence $b = a \times q + r$, q is called the quotient and r is the remainder obtained when a is divided by b. If r is zero, an operation has been performed and the process is exact division; if r is greater than zero, an operation has not been performed and the process is division with remainder.

The algorithm. The algorithm for the division process is similar to that for exact division. It requires the renaming of the product into addends which may be divided conveniently. The form used is illustrated by Algorithm 13. Note that the product 1739 is renamed $1200 + 480 + 48 + 11$. Each of the addends is marked with a dot in the illustration below.

$$
\begin{array}{r}
144 \\
12\overline{)1739} \\
1200^{\textstyle\cdot} \\
\hline
539 \\
480^{\textstyle\cdot} \\
\hline
59 \\
48^{\textstyle\cdot} \\
\hline
11^{\textstyle\cdot}
\end{array}
$$

EXAMPLE 14.

By the distributive property of division, each addend of 1739 is divided by 12 if the division is possible within the set of whole numbers, and the results are added.

In Example 14 the result of the division process is

$$1739 = 12 \times 144 + 11,$$

with $q = 144$, and $r = 11$.

The set of numbers used in this chapter is the set of whole numbers. If it were the set of fractional numbers, then the result of distributing 12 over $1200 + 480 + 48 + 11$ would be

$$100 + 40 + 4 + \tfrac{11}{12}, \qquad \text{or} \qquad 144\tfrac{11}{12}.$$

Illustration of the algorithm with an array. The sentence, $176 = 12q + r$, where $r \neq 0$ and $r < 12$, is illustrated by the largest possible $12 \times q$ array that can be made from 176 elements. There are r additional elements to make 176. (See Fig. 7-9.)

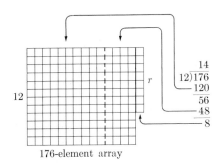

176-element array

FIGURE 7-9

Figure 7-9 shows the relationship between the array and 8 additional elements, and the algorithm showing the process for dividing 176 by 12. Note from the figure that

$$176 = 12 \times \underline{10} + 12 \times \underline{4} + 8 \qquad \text{or} \qquad 176 = 12 \times 14 \times 8,$$

with $q = 14$ and $r = 8$.

EXERCISE SET 7-2

1. Using the form for the derivation of the multiplication algorithm of Section 4 determine the products given below.
   (a) 72×61 (b) 87×49
   (c) 124×32 (d) 253×46

2. Solve each part of Exercise 1 by using the algorithm for multiplication of Section 4.

3. Illustrate the commutative property for multiplication with an array.

4. Illustrate the distributive property for multiplication with an array.

5. Show at least six alternatives of renaming for the purpose of performing the multiplications in (a) and (b). Use an asterisk to mark the most convenient way of renaming 72 in (a) and in (b).
   (a) $n = 8 \times 72$ (b) $n = 68 \times 72$

6. Find n in each of the following by using an array and an algorithm. Use arrows to connect the related parts of each solution.
   (a) $18 \times n = 134$ (b) $n = 335 \times 28$

7. Many people omit the terminal zeros in the number symbols for some partial products in the multiplication algorithm, as shown below in (i). In this chapter the terminal zeros have been used consistently as in (ii).

(i)	1246	(ii)	1246
	3008		3008
	9968		9968
3738		3738000	
3747968		3747968	

   (a) What are the advantages of omitting the terminal zeros as in (i)?
   (b) What are the advantages of not omitting the terminal zeros as in (ii)?
   (c) The product is determined by the addition of partial products. Do you know of any other example of the addition of numbers which omits the terminal zeros?

8. Using the form for the derivation of the division algorithm of Section 5, perform the divisions below.
   (a) $625 \div 25$ (b) $1728 \div 24$
   (c) $728 \div 13$ (d) $1632 \div 12$

9. Solve each part of Exercise 8 by using the algorithm for division of Section 5.

10. Illustrate the distributive property for division with an array.

11. In (a) through (d) show at least six ways of renaming 144 for the purpose of division. Using an asterisk, mark the most convenient way of renaming 144 in each part.
   (a) $n = 144 \div 6$ (c) $144 \div 9$
   (b) $n = 144 \div 12$ (d) $144 \div 24$

12. Express the results of the following indicated divisions in the form $a = bq + r$.
   (a) $25 \div 3$ (b) $24 \div 3$ (c) $233 \div 2$
   (d) $368 \div 12$ (e) $4280 \div 25$ (f) $3250 \div 50$

13. Rename 760 in each of the following in the most convenient way for the purpose of performing the divisions indicated.
   (a) $760 \div 6$ (b) $760 \div 12$ (c) $760 \div 25$
   (d) $760 \div 36$ (e) $760 \div 48$ (f) $760 \div 50$

14. Find n in each of the following by using an array and an algorithm. Use arrows to connect the related parts of each solution.
    (a) $n = 210 \div 15$ (b) $n = 145 \div 11$

15. Many people omit the terminal zeros in the number symbols of the partial products in the division algorithm, as shown in (i) below. In this chapter the terminal zeros have been used consistently, as shown in (ii).

(i)
```
        145
   12)1740
       12
       54
       48
       60
```

(ii)
```
        145
   12)1740
     1200
      540
      480
       60
```

(a) What are the advantages of omitting the terminal zeros as in (i)?
(b) What are the advantages of not omitting the terminal zeros as in (ii)?
(c) The process is dependent on the subtraction of numbers. Do you know of any other example of subtraction of numbers which omits the terminal zeros?

16. Solve each of these:
    (a) Multiply: (b) Divide:

```
   196
    14
```
                                         $196)\overline{2744}$

17. (a) Was there any relation between the processes you used in Exercise 16(a) and (b)?
    (b) Explain what this relationship is, if any. (Use the algorithms and connect related parts by arrows.)

7. AN HISTORIC NOTE

The algorithms used today are refined versions of the work of generations of people, which has been passed down to us through the centuries on various types of materials, ranging from clay tablets and sand tables to slate and paper. The evolution of the algorithms was, however, greatly influenced by procedures used in nonwritten solutions.

Algorithms of the scratch method. When solutions do involve writing, the most economical procedure is to consider parts of the numbers which are expressed by the digits to the left and to consider these one at a time. The scratch method follows this procedure, working from left to right. Partial results are recorded and are then scratched out if future thought requires a change.

Below are examples of one of the algorithms of the scratch method for each of the four basic operations.

A. Addition	B. Subtraction	C. Multiplication	D. Division
749	3427	643	~~141~~
376	1848	34	~~214~~
783	~~2689~~	~~18000~~	~~4368~~)273
~~1798~~	157	~~11292~~	1666
~~11~~		~~2946~~	11
~~80~~		~~263~~	
~~1~~		~~111~~	
9		~~76~~	
		8	

In Example A, the sum of the hundreds, 17, is first recorded and then the sum of the tens, 19, is written down. The 7 and 1 in the hundreds' place of the sum are added immediately, each is then scratched out, as shown in the algorithm, and their sum, 8, placed below them. This plan is continued to the units' place.

Subtraction by the scratch method is more complicated than is addition. You will understand the following description more easily if you use pencil and paper and perform each step as it is described.

In Example B, the part of the known addend represented by a digit in the thousands' place is subtracted first,

$$3 \text{ thousands} - 1 \text{ thousand} = 2 \text{ thousands},$$

and the 2 thousands is recorded. It is next necessary to subtract 8 hundreds. This requires that the 2 thousands of the missing addend and the 4 hundreds of the sum be renamed as 1 thousand and 14 hundreds. The 2 thousands is scratched and replaced by 1 thousand. The 8 hundreds is subtracted,

$$14 \text{ hundreds} - 8 \text{ hundreds} = 6 \text{ hundreds},$$

and the 6 hundreds recorded. This plan is continued to the tens' and units' places.

The scratch method for multiplication also proceeds from left to right. In Example C, the product of 3 tens and 6 hundreds, 18 thousands, is recorded first and then the product of 3 tens and 4 tens, 12 hundreds, is recorded. The 8 and 1 of the thousands' place are added immediately, each is scratched, and their sum, 9, is written beneath the 1 thousand. The plan of recording products and determining sums of columns immediately is followed until the product 21,862 is determined.

The algorithm for the scratch method for division in Example D shows the known factor written each time that an addend of 4368 is divided by 16. Note that the last two times the known factor appears, the digits 1 and 6 are not on the same horizontal line. The 16 is first written under 43 hundreds. The 2 of the partial quotient is multiplied by 10, then 6, and each product is immediately subtracted. After the product 2 thousands is subtracted from 4 thousands, the 4 is scratched and 2 placed above it. The product 12 hundreds is then subtracted from 23 hundreds, the 2 and 3 are scratched, and each is replaced by 1's. The first step in division is complete. Again the divisor 16 is placed under an addend of the given product, 36 tens. The plan continues. Note that in this example the remainder is zero.

Multiplication algorithms. The arrangement of the number symbols in the addition and subtraction algorithms used in the past differs little from that of the algorithm currently used. This is not true, however, for the multiplication algorithms. Below are some forms which were used for finding the product of 276 and 634 in fifteenth-century Europe.

E. 216
    34
    ——
    68
    34
    204
    ——
    7344

F. 216
    34
    ——
    648
    864
    ——
    7344

G. 216
    34
    ——
    864
    648
    ——
    7344

H. 2
    1
    6
    34
    ——
    24
    4
    8
    18
    3
    6
    ——
    7344

I. 216
    864/4
    648/3
    ——
    7344

J.

(Lattice method)

Out of these emerged the algorithm which we use today. The factors of the modern algorithm are arranged similarly to those of E, F, and G; the partial products are determined in the same order as those of F, C, and I; and the partial products are arranged for adding as in I.

Division algorithms. There have been fewer division algorithms developed than algorithms for other operations because the division process was considered difficult. In the fifteenth century only the well-educated were able to perform division. For most people, knowledge was limited to factors or divisors of less than 10 and to processes involving no writing.

Below are four examples of division algorithms of the past. They, together with the scratch method illustrated in Example D, influenced the algorithm used today, which was not well established until the end of the seventeenth century.

```
                                                          67
  K. 804 − 12       L. 12)804     M. 12)804(67     N. 12)804
     067                  67            60              84
                          80            ──             ─
     80                   72            20             0
     72                   ──            12
     ──                   84            ──
     84                   84            84
     84                                 70
     ──                                 ──
                                        14
                                        14
```

Note the different locations of the divisor 12 and the quotient 67. Forms M and N are similar to the algorithm you use. However, the partial products of form M are broken down in parts, e.g., the partial product of 60×12 is expressed as 60 tens and 12 tens rather than as 72 tens. In form N the partial products are omitted entirely in the algorithm and only the remainders are recorded.

8. SHORTCUTS

Shortcuts for algorithms are achieved by omitting some or all the steps of a process or by finding techniques for special cases. Shortcuts are helpful for those who understand the operations and use the algorithms for the operation effectively. A few examples follow. You may try to devise other shortcuts and find many described in reference material.

The lightning method. This method of multiplication requires that partial products be added without recording. In fact, only the product is recorded. To multiply 43×75, you compute partial products as usual. They are, however, added mentally and only the product is recorded, as in the following example:

```
      (i)   75        (ii)  75       (iii)  75
            ↑               ⋈              ↑
            ↓                              ↓
            43              43             43
            ──              ──             ──
            5               25             3225
```

In step (i), the product 15 is renamed 1 ten and 5. The 5 is recorded. In step (ii), the 1 ten is immediately added to the products, 21 tens and 20 tens. The sum, 42 tens, is renamed 4 hundreds and 2 tens. The 2 tens is recorded. In step (iii), the 4 hundreds is immediately added to the product 28 hundred. The sum, 32 hundred, is recorded. The multiplication is complete.

The method may be extended to larger numbers. The multiplication of 435×728 is shown below in steps.

$$
\begin{array}{lllll}
\text{(i)} \quad 435 & \text{(ii)} \quad 435 & \text{(iii)} \quad 435 & \text{(iv)} \quad 435 & \text{(v)} \quad 435 \\
\quad\quad 728 & \quad\quad 728 & \quad\quad 728 & \quad\quad 728 & \quad\quad 728 \\
\quad\quad\quad 0 & \quad\quad\quad 80 & \quad\quad 680 & \quad\quad 6680 & \quad 316{,}680
\end{array}
$$

The lightning method is a very efficient procedure for those who spend a little time developing the technique. It is a real shortcut.

The square of a number. Squaring 72 requires the addition of four products. For example,

$$
\begin{aligned}
72^2 &= (70 + 2)(70 + 2) \\
&= 70(70 + 2) + 2(70 + 2) \\
&= (70 \times 70) + (70 \times 2) + (2 \times 70) + (2 \times 2) \\
&= 70^2 + 2(70 \times 2) + 2^2.
\end{aligned}
$$

As shown above, two of the products are the same. Thus, finding 72^2 is finding the sum of 70^2, 2^2, and twice the product of 70 and 2. The square of any number renamed as the sum of two numbers may be found in this same way, since

$$
\begin{aligned}
(a + b)^2 &= (a + b)(a + b) \\
&= a(a + b) + b(a + b) \\
&= a^2 + ab + ab + b^2 \\
&= a^2 + 2ab + b^2.
\end{aligned}
$$

For example,

$$
95^2 = 90^2 + 5^2 + 2 \times 90 \times 5
$$

and

$$
730^2 = 700^2 + 30^2 + 2 \times 70 \times 30.
$$

The product of numbers which differ by two. The product of $(n + 1)$ and $(n - 1)$ may be easily determined if n^2 is known. Note the two arrangements of the objects in Figs. 7–10 and 7–11.

6×8 -array   (7×7) − 1 elements

FIGURE 7–10   FIGURE 7–11

Figure 7–10 shows a 6 × 8 array of 48 elements. Figure 7–11 shows a rearrangement of the 6 × 8 array with one column moved to make part of a row in an attempt to make a 7 × 7 array. There is one element too few, however. The two arrangements of the elements show that

$$6 \times 8 = (7 \times 7) - 1 \quad \text{or} \quad 6 \times 8 = 7^2 - 1.$$

If a 16 × 14 array is rearranged into 15 rows, there is one element too few to make a 15 × 15 array:

$$16 \times 14 = 15^2 - 1.$$

If a 178 × 176 array is rearranged into 177 rows, there is one element too few to make a 177 × 177 array:

$$178 \times 176 = 177^2 - 1.$$

These and similar products justify the formula

$$(n + 1)(n - 1) = n^2 - 1.$$

This formula may be used as a shortcut to find the product of any two numbers which differ by two, e.g.,

$$14 \times 16 = 15^2 - 1 = 225 - 1 = 224.$$

9. ALGORITHMS FOR NUMBERS EXPRESSED IN A NONDECIMAL BASE

Addition and subtraction. All the whole numbers used in this chapter have been expressed in symbols of the decimal system. The basic form of the algorithm may be used with number symbols expressed in other bases.

TABLE 7–1

ADDITION CHART

(BASE-SIX NUMBER SYMBOLS)

+	0	1	2	3	4	5
0	0	1	2	3	4	5
1	1	2	3	4	5	10
2	2	3	4	5	10	11
3	3	4	5	10	11	12
4	4	5	10	11	12	13
5	5	10	11	12	13	14

For number symbols in base six, Table 7–1 summarizes the basic addition facts.

The algorithms for the addition and subtraction of numbers expressed in base six use the basic addition facts, renaming of partial sums, and the commutative and associative properties for addition just as the algorithms for decimal numbers do.

EXAMPLE 15.   32   EXAMPLE 16.   423
               45   145
               40   234
              201

In Example 15, the sum of the units' column is $11_{(six)}$. The 11 is renamed $10 + 1$. The 1 is recorded. The 10 or 1 six is immediately added with the other numbers recorded in the base place ($1 + 3 + 4 + 4 = 20$). This sum is recorded as shown.

In Example 16, the subtraction of $145_{(six)}$ from $423_{(six)}$ is accomplished by renaming the 423 as $300 + 110 + 13$. Then the partial missing addends are determined from the addition chart, Table 7–1:

$$13 - 5 = 4,$$
$$110 - 40 = 30,$$

and

$$300 - 100 = 200.$$

These results are recorded in the proper places.

Multiplication and division. The algorithms for multiplication and division with number symbols in any base are similar to those for base-ten number symbols. A multiplication chart for base five is given in Table 7–2.

TABLE 7–2

MULTIPLICATION CHART

(BASE-FIVE NUMBER SYMBOLS)

×	0	1	2	3	4
0	0	0	0	0	0
1	0	1	2	3	4
2	0	2	4	11	13
3	0	3	11	14	22
4	0	4	13	22	31

EXAMPLE 17.
$$
\begin{array}{r}
234 \\
32 \\
\hline
1023 \\
13120 \\
\hline
14143
\end{array}
$$

EXAMPLE 18.
$$
\begin{array}{r}
143 \\
4)\overline{1232} \\
400^{\bullet} \\
\hline
332 \\
310^{\bullet} \\
\hline
22 \\
22^{\bullet} \\
\hline
\end{array}
$$

In Algorithm 17 each of the addends of $(30 + 2)$ is distributed over 200, 30, and 4. From the multiplication chart (Table 7–2), $2 \times 4 = 13$. The 13 is renamed into 1 five and 3. The 3 is recorded and the 1 five is immediately added to the product of 2×3 fives, 11 fives. The sum, 11 fives + 1 five = 12 fives, is renamed 1 twenty-five + 2 fives. The 2 fives is recorded. The process continues as in the multiplication of decimal numbers.

In Algorithm 18, the product 1232 is renamed $400 + 310 + 22$, and each of these addends is divided by 4. From the multiplication chart,

$$400 \div 4 = 100, \quad 310 \div 4 = 40, \quad \text{and} \quad 22 \div 4 = 3.$$

These missing factors are recorded to show a result of 143.

EXERCISE SET 7–3

1. Solve each of the following by the scratch method.
   (a) $456 + 398 + 465$ (b) $7246 - 2569$
   (c) 1348×43 (d) $3456 \div 24$
2. (a) Try to devise a more efficient algorithm than the one you use for the multiplication process.
   (b) Explain your best invention and tell why it is or is not more efficient than the algorithm currently used.

3. (a) Try to devise a more efficient algorithm than the one you use for the division process.

   (b) Explain your best invention and tell why it is or is not more efficient than the algorithm currently used.

4. Use the lightning method to find the products below.

   (a) 48×37 (b) 39×44 (c) 324×436 (d) 832×725

5. Give the squares of the numbers below by using a shortcut method.

   (a) 25   (b) 32   (c) 44

   (d) 91   (e) 48   (f) 56

6. Give the products indicated by using a shortcut method.

   (a) 19×21 (b) 13×11 (c) 41×39

   (d) 99×101 (e) 1001×999 (f) 26×24

7. Show how the array which illustrates 10^2 is related to a 9×11 array.

8. Show how the array which illustrates n^2 is related to an $(n+1)(n-1)$ array.

9. (a) Show that $427 - 148 = 479 - 200$.

   (b) Show that $a - b = (a + k) - (b + k)$.

   (c) Study the description of the equal-addition process of subtraction in a reference book and show how it relates to (b).

10. What is a shortcut for multiplying by each of the following?

    (a) 10, 100, or any power of 10.   (b) 25   (c) 11

11. What is a shortcut for dividing by each of the following?

    (a) 10, 100, or any power of 10.   (b) 25

12. Consult a reference book for information about Napier's Bones. Show by a sketch how they are used to find the product of 243 and 148.

13. Algorithm J of Section 7 illustrates the lattice method of multiplication. Use this method to multiply the following:

    (a) 264×326 (b) 48×547 (c) 298×742 (d) 497×366

14. Algorithm N of Section 7 suggests a shortcut to the division algorithm. Use this method to solve the following:

    (a) $5205 \div 15$ (b) $26064 \div 36$ (c) $8190 \div 42$

15. In what base are the numbers in each of the following expressions?

    (a) $6 + 6 = 10$ (b) $10 - 4 = 4$ (c) $3 \times 3 = 11$

    (d) $10 \div 2 = 6$ (e) $3 + 4 = 12$ (f) $6 \times 6 = 30$

    (g) $12 \div 3 = 3$ (h) $11 - 3 = 5$ (i) $5 \times 5 = 21$

    (j) $12 - 4 = 4$ (k) $9 + 1 = t$ (l) $15 \div 2 = 6$

16. In what base are the numbers for each of the following addition algorithms?

(a)	5	(b)	22	(c)	22	(d)	23	(e)	134
	3		33		33		131		34
	12		33		33		231		34
			23		23		425		202
			303		133				

17. In what base are the number symbols for each of the subtraction algorithms below?

(a)	12	(b)	135	(c)	201	(d)	2445	(e)	4032
	3		42		144		1235		487
	4		63		79		1210		3t9t

18. In what base are the number symbols for each of the following multiplication algorithms?

(a)	6	(b)	5	(c)	56	(d)	151	(e)	123
	4		3		4		4		2
	20		21		270		624		246

19. In what base are the number symbols for each of the division algorithms below?

(a) $10 \div 2 = 4$

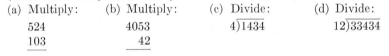

$$
\begin{array}{llll}
\text{(b)} \quad 51 & \text{(c)} \quad 33 & \text{(d)} \quad 11 & \text{(e)} \quad 48 \\
3\overline{)163} & 2\overline{)132} & 12\overline{)132} & 7\overline{)288} \\
& \underline{120} & \underline{120} & \underline{240} \\
& 12 & 12 & 48
\end{array}
$$

20. Prepare an addition chart with numbers expressed in base-five number symbols.

21. Use the chart prepared in Exercise 20 and solve each of the following. All the numbers symbols are expressed in base five.

(a) Add:	(b) Add:	(c) Subtract:	(d) Subtract:
324	12423	43021	20031
433	10232	14234	2342
232	13234		
433			
204			

22. Prepare an addition and multiplication chart with numbers expressed in base-six number symbols.

23. Use the charts prepared in Exercise 22 and solve each of the following. (All the number symbols are expressed in base six.)

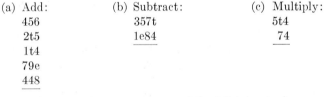

(a) Multiply:	(b) Multiply:	(c) Divide:	(d) Divide:
524	4053	4$\overline{)1434}$	12$\overline{)33434}$
103	42		

24. Make charts if necessary and solve each of the following. (All the number symbols are expressed in the base twelve.)

(a) Add:	(b) Subtract:	(c) Multiply:
456	357t	5t4
2t5	1e84	74
1t4		
79e		
448		

25. Prepare a class report on one or more of the following topics:
    (a) Austrian method of subtraction
    (b) Complementary method of subtraction
    (c) Finger multiplication
    (d) Napier's bones
    (e) Lattice multiplication (Gelosia multiplication)
    (f) Egyptian multiplication, a doubling process
    (g) Russian multiplication

(h) History of the multiplication tables
(i) Short division
(j) Galley method of division
(k) Division by duplation and mediation
(l) The first Arithmetic Book
(m) The literal meaning of the words "addition," "subtraction," "multiplication," and "division"
(n) The history of the symbols for addition, subtraction, multiplication, and division
(o) The mathematician, Al-Khowarizmi (*ca.* 825 A.D.)

REFERENCES

BALL, W. W. ROUSE, *A Short Account of the History of Mathematics.* New York: The Macmillan Company, 1924, 522 pp.

CAJORI, FLORIAN, *A History of Mathematics.* New York: The Macmillan Company, 1938, 516 pp.

KARPINSKI, LOUIS CHARLES, *A History of Arithmetic.* New York: Rand McNally and Company, 1925, 200 pp.

PETERSON, JOHN A., and JOSEPH HASHISAKI, *The Theory of Arithmetic.* New York: John Wiley and Sons, 1963, pp. 69–80, 100–107.

SANFORD, VERA, *A Short History of Mathematics.* Boston: Houghton Mifflin Company, 1930, 402 pp.

SMITH, DAVID EUGENE, *History of Mathematics,* Volume II. Boston: Ginn and Company, 1925, 725 pp.

CHAPTER EIGHT

GEOMETRY

1. HISTORY

Geometry has many aspects that can be understood only in the light of its past. It is necessary, therefore, to know something of its history and its commanding place in western culture in order to realize its importance in education and to understand why it is now being introduced in the elementary school curriculum.

Geometry is as venerable a subject as arithmetic. Geometric ornamentation appears on neolithic pottery made in the Nile valley nearly six thousand years ago, and effective geometric designs have been devised from prehistoric times to the present by artists of tribes living in a Stone Age culture, e.g., some South American Indians.

Ancient geometry. The beginnings of both plane and solid geometry are believed to have occurred in the civilizations which flourished in the Nile and Euphrates valleys over four thousand years ago. Greek tradition ascribed the invention of geometry to the Egyptians. But recently deciphered inscriptions on clay tablets unearthed in Mesopotamia during the last hundred years reveal that the Babylonians of 1700 B.C. knew a considerable number of geometric facts.

The etymological meaning of the word "geometry" is "land measurement." Some of the Babylonian clay tablets contain instructions for computing the area of triangular and quadrilateral plots of land. Other tablets show that the Babylonians utilized the theorem of Pythagoras and properties of similar triangles in their computations. Still other tablets give rules for computing the volumes of trapezoidal dikes and other simple solid bodies. These rules are not all correct. Papyrus scrolls show that the Egyptians of this period had about the same degree of knowledge as the Babylonians. But there is no evidence that either of these people organized their geometric knowledge into an orderly pattern. This was not done until over a thousand years later when the Greeks created the science of geometry.

Greek geometry and mathematics. In the period from 600 B.C. to 300 B.C. the Greeks transformed geometry from a haphazard collection of isolated results and mechanical rules to a highly developed mathematical science. In the course of doing so, they discovered many new geometric concepts. Their great contribution, however, was the demonstration that important and useful knowledge can be obtained by reasoning deductively from explicitly stated premises. By adopting this approach the Greeks invented pure mathematics.

Although we are almost totally ignorant of the actual beginnings of Greek mathematics, we know that it developed in close connection with philosophy. No writings of the traditional founders, Thales (686 B.C.) and Pythagoras (550 B.C.), have survived. Geometry was highly esteemed by the Greeks as a revelation of the harmony and order of the universe. So great was the success of their geometry, that all their mathematics, even arithmetic and algebra, was given a geometric cast.

The famous Academy of Plato in Athens attracted many mathematicians; one of the greatest was Eudoxus (370 B.C.), who was both mathematician and astronomer. The achievements of the Platonic Mathematicians and their Pythagorean predecessors were compiled about seventy years later in Alexandria by the mathematician Euclid (300 B.C.). He was eminently successful in this undertaking, and produced one of the most famous textbooks of all times, the *Elements*.

Euclid's *Elements*. The thirteen books of Euclid's *Elements* are intended to give a strictly logical development of plane geometry and solid geometry. All theorems are proved from a small number of explicitly stated definitions and postulates which form the premises of the work. The treatment throughout is strictly deductive. There is no motivation, no discussion of how constructions are to be performed, and no applications of the theorems other than to prove other theorems.

The historical importance of Euclid's *Elements* is indicated by the following quotation:

> The *Elements* form, next to the Bible, probably the book most reproduced and studied in the history of the Western world. More than a thousand editions have appeared since the invention of printing and before that time manuscript copies dominated much of the teaching of geometry. Most of our school geometry is taken, often literally, from (the first) six of the thirteen books; and the Euclidean tradition still weighs heavily on our elementary instruction. . . .*

---

* Struik, D. J., *A Concise History of Mathematics*, Volume II. New York: Dover Publications, Inc., 1948, pp. 58–59.

During the early Middle Ages, the *Elements* were assiduously studied by the Arabs, but known in Europe only to a handful of learned monks. By the end of the Middle Ages, the plane geometry of the first six books, which is now taught in some form in every high school in the United States, had become a university subject in Europe. Lectures were given on the *Elements* at the Universities of Prague (founded in 1348), Vienna (1365), Heidelberg (1386), and Leipzig (1409) almost from the date of founding. The first printed edition of the book was a Latin version printed in Venice in 1486.

Euclid has not been popular with all students. At the venerable University of Paris (founded about 1160), Master of Art's candidates in the early sixteenth century had to swear a solemn oath that they had faithfully attended lectures on the first six books. A similar oath was required at the University of Heidelberg.

By the nineteenth century, plane geometry had become a school subject in Western Europe and North America. The remarkable thing is that in England and the United States the subject was presented to boys and girls in almost exactly the same way that it was presented to mature specialists in mathematics in Alexandria over two thousand years previously.

To this day, plane geometry and solid geometry are referred to collectively as Euclidean geometry, partly to distinguish them from other more recently discovered kinds of geometry, but principally as a tribute to Euclid's genius as a teacher and expositor.

2. PRESENT-DAY IMPORTANCE

From a practical standpoint, geometry is an idealization and systematization of our ordinary space experiences, experiences which every human being has almost from the moment of birth. As a science of space, geometry has two aspects: a logical aspect such as that shown in Euclid's *Elements*, and a physical aspect represented by its applicability to our actual space experiences.

These dual aspects should be clearly understood. Thus, for example, from the standpoint of logic, the theorems of Euclidean geometry would still be true in the sense that they necessarily follow from the postulates of that geometry, even if rigid bodies could not be moved around freely in space, and if the angles of carefully drawn triangles did not always form an angle of hundred and eighty degrees. However, the importance of Euclidean geometry would be slight in this case since it would then merely be one of the many mathematical systems which have been deductively elaborated by mathematicians without consideration of any physical application.

As a matter of fact, Euclidean geometry does agree extremely well with our ordinary space experiences. This agreement is the primary reason for its continued importance. Furthermore, the basic *concepts* of Euclidean geometry, that is, the ideas of a point, a line, a plane, and a geometric figure, are consonant with our space intuitions. Finally, because these concepts are abstract and yet can be visualized, they furnish us with powerful ways of thinking in geometric imagery about situations not directly concerned with physical space. The development of a child's geometric imagination is one of the important objectives that educators had in mind when they included geometry in the elementary-school curriculum.

3. EUCLIDEAN GEOMETRY AS A PHYSICAL SCIENCE

The first men to understand the dual physical and logical aspects of geometry were the great nineteenth-century mathematicians, Gauss (1777–1855), Lobachevski (1793–1856), and Riemann (1826–1866).   Prior to their discoveries, it was widely believed that any concept of space other than Euclid's was impossible.

Little attention was paid to the geometries developed by these mathematicians until the twentieth century, when the insight of Albert Einstein (1879–1955) and the revolution in physics brought about by his theory of relativity led to the general recognition of the dual nature of geometry. It is now well understood that Euclidean geometry may be regarded as a branch of theoretical physics. Since this fact has a direct bearing on the geometry of the schools, it will be discussed further.

Any science has two aspects, theoretical and experimental, as was pointed out in Chapter 4.   In a well-developed science such as physics, the theoretical side consists of various mathematical models chosen to agree with experimental observation and capable of mathematical elaboration so that the predictions made on the basis of the model may be tested by experimentation.   From this standpoint, Euclidean geometry as a mathematical model is a portion of theoretical physics. It predicts what will happen when certain simple experiments are performed in a portion of space remote from material bodies and rapidly changing fields of force. Ideally, this portion of space should be empty, i.e. free of all matter or energy.   In such a situation, rigid measuring rods may be moved around slowly without any detectable change in their size and shape, light signals travel along straight-line paths, and if a triangle is laid out on a flat surface and its interior angles carefully measured in degrees, the sum of the angles will be about one hundred and eighty degrees.

The conditions presupposed here are not met in our ordinary surroundings.   But the distortions of size and shape which occur are usually too slight to be detectable. The excellent agreement of geometric theory with physical experiment, for most events, is shown by the fact that the great branch of theoretical physics founded by Newton and now known as classical mechanics presupposes Euclidean geometry as the theoretical description of space.

With the advent of the theory of relativity, it became possible to understand hitherto unexplained contradictions between experimental facts and the theoretical predictions based on classical mechanics and its underlying geometry. As a result, scientists developed new mathematical models of space based on the theory of relativity and hence on non-Euclidean geometries.

The geometry which applies in the world of the rapidly moving elementary particles studied by nuclear physicists is still unknown. It is quite certain that it is not Euclidean. Nevertheless, Euclidean geometry is extremely important to applied science since all the engineering sciences ultimately rest upon classical mechanics, and hence on Euclidean geometry.

4. EXPERIMENTAL GEOMETRY

The apparatus traditionally used in experimental plane geometry is available in any classroom. It consists of a sheet of paper, a sharp pencil, a compass, and a straightedge. With this simple apparatus, one can perform a great variety of experiments whose outcome may be predicted in advance by theoretical geometry; that is, by the mathematical model elaborated in Euclid's *Elements*.

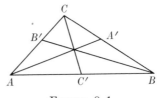

FIGURE 8–1

For example, suppose that we wish to perform the experiment illustrated in Fig. 8–1. We proceed as follows.

Step 1. A triangle is drawn, and its vertices are lettered A, B, and C.

Step 2. The mid-points of the sides of the triangle are located and lettered A', B', and C'.

Step 3. The line segments $\overline{AA'}$, $\overline{BB'}$, and $\overline{CC'}$ are drawn, joining the vertices of the triangle to the mid-points of the opposite sides.

Step 4. The intersection of the segments drawn in step 3 is observed.

Euclidean geometry predicts that the three line segments drawn in step 3 will meet in a single point. The closeness of agreement in step 4 of the experiment with the theoretical prediction will depend upon the quality of the experimental instruments and the skill and care of the experimenter. Naturally, if the experiment is performed by an experienced draftsman using fine drawing instruments, its outcome will be better than if done by a child at his desk in school. However, even an elementary-school student who uses some care in carrying out the steps will be able to draw a figure which is in agreement with the theoretical prediction.

Note that nothing is proved by this experiment no matter how often it is repeated and how carefully it is carried out. Nevertheless the experimental procedure provides inductive evidence to support a theorem of Euclidean geometry:

> *The lines joining the vertices of any triangle to the mid-points of the opposite sides meet in a point.*

The experiment just described has probably been performed thousands of times. Similar experiments may suggest the truth of other geometric theorems even in those situations where deductive proof is unknown or is incomprehensible to the experimenter. Such carefully performed experiments are examples of the process of discovery by induction. Since the theoretical side of geometry is very highly developed, it is not likely, as it is in less advanced sciences, that experiments will lead to results previously unknown. Nevertheless they may be of considerable value to the beginner in geometry if he does not confuse them with deductive proof.

5. DEFINITIONS IN GEOMETRY

Verbal definitions. Basic terms, such as "point," "line," and "plane," which are used in Euclidean geometry are familiar to nearly everyone; but from the very beginning of geometry, defining the ideas which these terms are meant to convey has been found a difficult and even controversial endeavor. About twenty-five hundred years ago, the Pythagoreans defined a point as "unity in position." More recently, similar definitions have been proposed, such as:

> A point is an object having position but no magnitude,

or

> A point is a location in space.

The same types of definitions have been attempted for line and plane.

In each of the cited definitions, other, less simple, terms appear. Consider the definition, "a point is an object having position but no magnitude." If this statement is to convey the meaning of a point, the meaning of the terms "position" and "magnitude" must also be understood. Presumably the terms refer to ideas which are simpler than the idea of a point. But a little reflection will convince you that the ideas of position and magnitude are as hard to understand and define as the idea of a point. A good definition should use only terms that are more easily understood than the term being defined.

There are two ways of meeting the difficulty of conveying the meaning of terms, one informal and intuitive, the other formal and logical. Neither makes an attempt to define a point or line in terms of any simpler idea.

Intuitive definitions. The informal method of developing the meaning of concepts is to appeal to geometric experience and intuition. For example, the meaning of a point is suggested by a dot made with a piece of chalk on the chalkboard or, better yet, by a dot made with a sharp pencil on a piece of paper. A free-hand chalk line suggests what is meant by a line; and a line drawn with a sharp pencil and a straightedge provides an even better picture of a line.

A point, a line, and a plane are abstract ideas, even though their meaning may be understood to a certain extent by an act of imagination suggested by geometric pictures. This informal method has no logical justification, but experience has shown that it often results in an understanding of geometric ideas. It consists basically in demonstrating the kind of situations that led to the ideas of point and line in the first place.

Mathematical definitions. The second method of meeting the difficulty of developing the meaning of concepts is now universally adopted in mathematics. Basic terms such as point and line are allowed to have any meaning, provided they satisfy the conditions which the postulates of the geometry impose on them. This manner of thinking about geometry is best explained by an example. Consider the following rudimentary geometry.

Given the following:

ASSUMPTION 1.   A nonempty set S of objects called "points."

ASSUMPTION 2.   A nonempty family of distinguished subsets of S called "lines."

Furthermore, the points and lines of S satisfy the following:

ASSUMPTION 3.   If A and B are distinct points, there exists one and only one line l containing both A and B.

ASSUMPTION 4.   If a and b are distinct lines, there exists at most one point L contained in both a and b.

DEFINITION 1.   If l is a line and A is a point which is an element of l, A is called a point of l. Also l is said to pass through A.

DEFINITION 2.   If a and b have only one common point, they are said to intersect. Otherwise, they are said to be parallel.

ASSUMPTION 5.   Every line of S contains at least three points.

ASSUMPTION 6.   If l is any line of S, and A is any point of S, there exists at most one line containing A which is parallel to l.

ASSUMPTION 7.   There exist at least two lines in S.

DEFINITION 3.   S is called a plane.

If you interpret the terms, point and line, in the way you are accustomed to in Euclidean geometry, all the assumptions and definitions given are intelligible statements. Further, if you understand the set concepts of Chapter 2, then Assumptions 1 through 7 and Definitions 1 through 3 convey meaning although the precise nature of S, the elements of S, and the family of lines of S is unspecified. Assumptions 1 through 7 are the premises for the geometry being considered.

Further properties of this geometry are given in Exercise Set 8–1.

6. MODELS IN EXPERIMENTAL GEOMETRY

The usefulness of well-drawn figures and visual analogies in demonstrating the meaning of fundamental geometric concepts has been discussed in Section 4. Many such models are used in the teaching of geometry. They may be very simple, such as a piece of cardboard and stick used to illustrate the intersection of a point and a plane, or quite elaborate, such as a complicated geometric figure illustrating each step of a rigorous deductive proof. An important part of experimental geometry consists of the use of such figures or models to enable a student to intuitively grasp the meaning of geometric concepts and theorems.

The detailed description of the nature and use of figures properly belongs to the methodology of teaching geometry. But an example is needed now to clarify further the distinction between experimental geometry and theoretical geometry; it will also be needed later to demonstrate how inductive and deductive reasoning are combined in geometry. The example chosen is an easily constructed model illustrating an important geometric theorem.

Generally speaking, models which illustrate geometric definitions and theorems may be thought of as auxiliaries to the traditional apparatus, pencil, compass, and straightedge, of experimental geometry. Indeed, auxiliary experimental equipment is used at all levels of learning in the sciences both to illustrate and to discover the workings of scientific laws.

Such apparatus should help illustrate important principles and yet be simple enough so the student can perform his own experiment. The geometric model to be described meets all these requirements. The only material needed is a sheet of stiff cardboard.

THEOREM. The geometric sum of the three interior angles of a triangle is a straight angle.

This theorem was discovered and proved by the Pythagorean mathematicians about 500 B.C. Its truth may be shown intuitively by a simple model (Fig. 8–2).

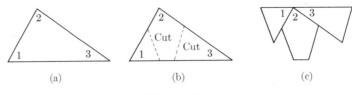

(a)   (b)   (c)

FIGURE 8–2

Figure 8–2 illustrates the steps taken to demonstrate the theorem experimentally. Figure 8–2(a) is a representation of a triangle with its angles numbered 1, 2, and 3. In Fig. 8–2(b), the triangle is cut into three pieces along the dashed lines. In Fig. 8–2(c), the lozenge-shaped piece containing angle 2 is left in position, and the two triangular pieces containing angles 1 and 2 are turned and fitted to the left and right of the lozenge, as shown. Note that the three angles 1, 2, and 3 of the triangle fit together to form a straight angle. Demonstration thus suggests that the sum of the three interior angles of any triangle is a straight angle.

The experimental nature of this demonstration should be recognized. The experiment consists of fitting the pieces of a particular model together in another way. If the model is carefully made, the experiment will probably convince you of the truth of the theorem. But it is inductive evidence for the truth of the theorem, not logical proof. This fact, however, in no way detracts from the value of such models as devices capable of making you aware of the meaning of a geometric theorem.

EXERCISE SET 8–1

1. The Pythagorean mathematicians represented certain numbers geometrically by a regular pattern of dots. They represented the squares 1, 4, 9, ... as shown below:

                                        . . .
                            . .   . . .
                  . ,   . . ,   . . . ,   etc.

Other numbers, called triangular numbers, were represented as follows:

$$\cdot \; , \qquad \cdot \atop \cdot \; , \qquad \cdot \; \cdot \atop \cdot \; , \qquad \text{etc.}$$

(a) List the first ten square numbers.

(b) List the first ten triangular numbers.

2. The Pythagoreans discovered that the sums

$$1, \qquad 1 + 2, \qquad 1 + 2 + 3, \qquad 1 + 2 + 3 + 4, \ldots$$

resulted in triangular numbers. Show how this fact may have been discovered geometrically.

3. The Pythagoreans also found a way of representing square numbers as the sum of consecutive odd numbers. Show how this may have been discovered geometrically.

4. Write a brief report on the contribution of one of these early geometers: Eudoxus, Thales, Pythagoras, Archimedes.

5. Write a brief report on the contribution to non-Euclidean geometry made by one of these mathematicians: Saccheri, Bolyai, Lobachevsky, Gauss, Riemann.

6. Use a straightedge and draw a series of quadrilaterals. Be sure to include each of the following: square, rhombus, rectangle, parallelogram, trapezoid, and several with noncongruent sides. Draw in all the diagonals of the quadrilaterals. (Diagonals are line segments connecting nonconsecutive vertices.) Can you make any intuitive prediction about the following?

(a) How many diagonals does a quadrilateral have?

(b) Are the diagonals of any of the quadrilaterals perpendicular?

(c) Do the diagonals of any of the quadrilaterals bisect each other?

7. Were the statements you made in Exercise 6 (a), (b), and (c) proved by your experimentation? Why?

8. Write a brief report on one of the following observations:

The many ways a point has been defined,

or

The many ways a line has been defined.

9. Identify three objects in a classroom which may be used as a model for each of the following. Identify with an asterisk the object which makes the best model for each.

(a) Point   (b) Line   (c) Surface

10. Using the rudimentary geometry of Section 5 answer the following questions.

(a) If a and c are lines in the plane S in what three ways may they be related?

(b) Expand the geometry to include assumptions and definitions regarding planes by writing assumptions and definitions analogous to Assumptions 3–7 and Definition 1 for planes. One assumption needed is: there exists a family of distinguished subsets of S, called planes.

11. Show by the following demonstration
that the theorem of Pythagoras is
intuitively evident.

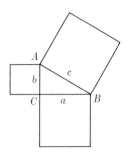

> THEOREM. The square con-
> structed on the hypotenuse of
> the right triangle ABC has an
> area equal to the sum of the
> areas of the squares constructed
> on the legs (Fig. 8–3).

FIGURE 8–3

Step 1. Prepare seven pieces of cardboard with the measurements shown in Fig. 8–4. Label each carefully as shown in the figure.

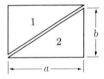 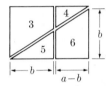

FIGURE 8–4

Step 2. Fit all the pieces of step 1 together to make a square whose dimensions are c (Fig. 8–5).

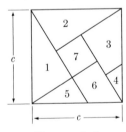

FIGURE 8–5

Step 3. Fit pieces 1, 2, 4, 6, and 7 together to form a square whose dimensions are a.

Step 4. Fit pieces 3 and 5 together to form a square whose dimensions are b.

Explain how these steps give inductive evidence of the truth of the Pythagorean theorem. Use a more detailed form of Fig. 8–3 for your discussion.

7. GEOMETRIC OBJECTS CONSIDERED AS POINT SETS

As a mathematical idea, Euclidean space is a universal set of elements called "points." Geometric objects such as straight lines, curves, planes, surfaces, and solids, the topics of elementary geometry, are families of distinguished subsets belonging to this universal set.

The modern treatment of geometry makes continual use of the set concepts discussed in Chapter 2, but some change of notation is necessary since it is customary, in elementary geometry, to denote points by capital italic letters, $A, B, \ldots, Z$, and lines, or portions of lines, by lower-case italic letters, $a, b, \ldots, z$.

Accordingly the capital Greek letters Γ (gamma) and Δ (delta) will be used in this chapter to denote sets of points in space or in the plane. A set of points will be frequently called a "point set." A point P which is an element of a point set Γ will be said to belong to Γ. Broadly speaking, any set of points in space may be thought of as a geometric object. The simplest sets are those consisting of a finite number of points. The sets next in order of simplicity are those associated with the straight lines of space. For brevity, the term "line" is used to mean a straight line.

Lines, line segments, and rays. The set of points called a *line* in Euclidean geometry is conceived to extend indefinitely in either direction. A line is determined by any two points of the set. A portion of a line joining any two of its points is called a *segment* (Fig. 8–6).

The two points P and Q are called the *end points* of the segment joining P and Q, and the segment is said to join its end points. Note that these end points are points of the segment. Any line contains an infinite number of segments, but any segment is contained in only one line. This line is said to be obtained by extending the segment in both directions.

The segment joining the points P and Q is denoted in elementary geometry either by $\overline{PQ}$ or by $\overline{QP}$. Read "segment PQ" and "segment QP." Sometimes a segment such as $\overline{PQ}$ in Fig. 8–6 is denoted by a single lower-case letter, say as c. If $\overline{PQ}$ is thought of as a point set, its elements are its two end points P and Q and all points X of the line that are between P and Q.

Any point P on a line separates the line into two parts called *rays* (Fig. 8–7). These extend in opposite direction from the point, which

FIG. 8–6. A line and a segment of the line.

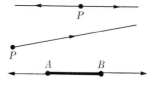

FIG. 8–7. Rays.

belongs to both rays. It is called the end point of either ray. Their directions are indicated by the arrowheads in the figure.

If $\overline{AB}$ of Fig. 8–7 is extended in the direction from A to B, a ray is obtained with end point A. If the segment is extended in the direction from B to A, a second ray is obtained with end point B. The set intersection of these two rays is $\overline{AB}$, and their set union is the line determined by A and B.

Angles. The point set formed by two distinct rays with a common end point is called an *angle*. The common end point is called the *vertex* of the angle, and the two rays are called the *sides* of the angle (Fig. 8–8). When the union of the two sides of the angle is a line, the angle is called a *straight angle* (Fig. 8–8b).

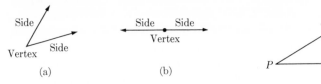

FIG. 8–8. Angles formed by two rays.   FIG. 8–9. Angle determined by two segments with common end point.

Two segments $\overline{PQ}$ and $\overline{PR}$ with a common end point determine an angle with vertex P provided that R is not on the ray determined by $\overline{PQ}$ (Fig. 8–9). The sides of the angle are the rays obtained by extending $\overline{PQ}$ and $\overline{PR}$ in the directions from P to Q and P to R.

The angle of Fig. 8–9 is denoted by the symbol "$\angle RPQ$," "$\angle QPR$," or simply by "$\angle P$." These expressions are read respectively "angle RPQ," "angle QPR," and "angle P." Note that the point which is the vertex occupies the central position in the name or is the name of the angle.

Vectors. A direction is naturally associated with a ray. A line segment which is directed is called a *vector*. Several vectors are shown in Fig. 8–10 with their direction indicated by arrowheads. Note that a line segment may be assigned one of two directions.

Vectors are extensively used in mathematics, science, and engineering to help illustrate complicated physical ideas geometrically. Their study is now a part of elementary and high-school mathematics. The addition and subtraction of integers by the use of vectors is illustrated in Chapter 11.

FIG. 8–10. Vectors.

FIG. 8–11. Euclidean plane figures.

Euclidean plane figures. In Euclid's development of geometry, the first geometric objects studied are plane figures made up of a finite number of lines, rays, and segments. Several such objects are shown in Fig. 8–11. One of the most familiar of these figures is the triangle. A *Euclidean triangle* is a point set consisting of three distinct points not on the same straight line, called the vertices of the triangle, and the three line segments joining these points. The line segments are called the sides of the triangle. Triangles are named by their vertices.

In Chapter 3 it was stated that Euclid's development of plane geometry is logically defective in that he did not state explicitly all the postulates used in proving his theorems; that is, he appealed implicitly to properties of figures which could not be proved on the basis of his postulates. Figure 8–12 illustrates one of these hidden assumptions.

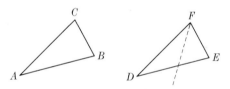

FIG. 8–12. Euclidean triangles.

It seems obvious that if a ray is drawn through one of the vertices of the triangle so as to intersect the interior of the triangle, it must intersect the opposite side of the triangle. Such a ray is shown by the dashed line in $\triangle DEF$ of Fig. 8–12. This fact cannot be proved on the basis of Euclid's postulates, and in a rigorous treatment of geometry, it must be assumed. It is for reasons such as this that mathematicians make a sharp distinction between deductive proof and inductive reasoning based on experimental geometry.

It is not the objective of this chapter to give a deductive treatment of Euclidean geometry; our aim is to make geometry intuitively simpler. The Euclidean triangle and other plane figures, such as rectangles, squares, and circles, are redefined so that their interior points are considered as part of the figure. We have chosen this approach because it is intuitively simpler to conceive of a triangle as a surface consisting not only of its sides and vertices, but also of all the points in its interior. If it is necessary

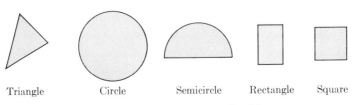

Triangle   Circle   Semicircle   Rectangle   Square

FIG. 8–13. Common geometric objects.

to distinguish this geometric object from the Euclidean triangle, the Euclidean triangle will be referred to as the *boundary*, and the interior will be called a *triangular region*. In the figures in this book, surfaces are usually indicated by shading. A number of these common geometric objects are pictured in Fig. 8–13. Each is obtained from the identically named Euclidean figure by forming the union of it and all the points in the interior of the figure.

Set operations on point sets. The operations of finding the complement of a set and the set union and set intersection of two or more sets may be applied to point sets in the plane or in space. These operations often allow you to visualize the fact that complicated sets are geometrically related to much simpler sets. The complement of a plane point set is defined as all the points of the plane which do not belong to the set.

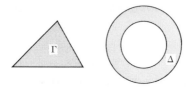

FIG. 8–14. Complements of plane point sets.

For example, the complement of the triangle Γ of Fig. 8–14 consists of all of the plane which is outside of the triangle. This set is usually called the *exterior* of the triangle. The complement of a set may be more complicated. For example, if point set Δ is the shaded ring shown in Fig. 8–14, the complement of point set Δ is the union of two disjoint sets.

Bounded and unbounded sets. A point set in the plane is said to be bounded if it may be completely enclosed in a circle. Otherwise, the point set is said to be unbounded. For example, a triangle is a bounded point set, but the exterior of a triangle is an unbounded point set. Every finite point set is bounded. Other examples of unbounded point sets are lines, rays, angles, and the entire plane.

(a)   (b)

FIG. 8–15. (a) The circle of the imagination. (b) The circle as a point set.

Geometric objects in general. There is an intuitive difficulty in conceiving of geometric objects as sets of points. This difficulty exists because points are discrete and space appears to be continuous. To the intuition, points present themselves as tiny isolated dots, all exactly alike. Yet the most striking intuitive characteristic of a geometric object such as a circle is that it appears to the imagination to be a single connected whole, and not just a vast assemblage of tiny dots. Note the illustrations in Fig. 8–15.

From the study of geometry and the applications of geometry to other parts of mathematics, methods of thinking about geometric objects have been developed which help the intuition bridge the gap between the discrete and the continuous. These new ways of thinking about geometry have enabled mathematicians to define other intuitive ideas so that these may be understood more easily. The new ideas apply to space as well as to the plane. They will be described here only as they apply to the plane, for ease of illustration and visualization. These new ideas are the *neighborhood of a point*, the *boundary of a set*, *closed sets*, *convex sets*, and *half-planes*.

Neighborhoods. Let P be any point of the plane, for example, P of Fig. 8–16. Then the set of points interior to a Euclidean circle whose center is P is called a neighborhood of P. The bounding circle is not a part of the neighborhood. A given point, for example, Q, has an infinite number of neighborhoods, for the radius of the bounding circle of the neighborhood may be chosen arbitrarily. If Q of Fig. 8–16 is any point of the plane distinct from P, there exist neighborhoods of P which contain Q. There also exist neighborhoods of P and Q which are disjoint. Note that a point, say P, belongs to all of its neighborhoods.

A triangle and three points, P, Q, and R, are shown in Fig. 8–17. The point P is a point of the interior of the triangle. It is evident that there

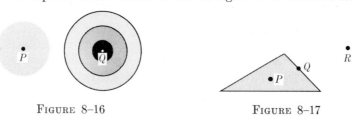

FIGURE 8–16   FIGURE 8–17

exist neighborhoods of P consisting entirely of points in the interior of the triangle. Similarly the point R which is exterior to the triangle has neighborhoods consisting entirely of points in the exterior of the triangle. The situation is quite different for the point Q which lies on the side of the triangle. Every neighborhood of Q contains both points belonging to the triangle and points not belonging to the triangle. This fact is independent of the position of Q on the boundary. Thus the boundary of the triangle may be characterized by a property of the neighborhoods of the points belonging to the boundary.

Boundary of a set. In general, if Γ is any point set in a plane (Fig. 8–18) the boundary of Γ is the set of all points Q such that in every neighborhood of Q, there is a point belonging to Γ, and a point belonging to the complement of Γ.

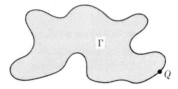

FIGURE 8–18

A set may consist exclusively of boundary points; for example, a line segment or a Euclidean triangle is made up entirely of boundary points. The boundary points of a set may or may not belong to the set. For example, a triangle is a set which contains all its boundary points; the interior of a triangle contains none of its boundary points. A point set Γ which contains all its boundary points is said to be closed. For example, a line segment is a closed set.

Convex figures. An obvious difference between the interior and the exterior of a triangle is that one set is bounded, and the other is unbounded. But there is a more subtle difference.

In Fig. 8–19(a), the triangle Γ is shaded, and in Fig. 8–19(b), its exterior is shaded. For brevity, the exterior of Γ will be referred to as Γ'; Γ and Γ' are complementary sets with no points in common.

Inspection of Fig. 8–19(a) makes it clear that if the triangle Γ contains both end points of a segment, it contains all points of the segment. The exterior Γ' does not possess this property. Figure 8–19(b) shows two segments, $\overline{PQ}$ and $\overline{RS}$, both of which have their end points in Γ'. The set Γ' contains all points of $\overline{PQ}$, but it does not contain all points of $\overline{RS}$. This difference between the triangle Γ and its exterior Γ' is expressed by the statement that Γ is a convex set, but Γ' is not a convex set.

More generally, a set of points either in the plane or in space is said to be convex if, whenever two distinct points belong to the set, the set con-

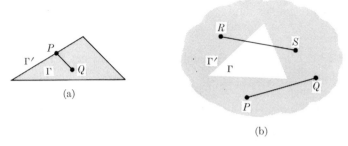

FIGURE 8–19

tains all the points of the segment joining them. If, in addition, the convex set is closed, that is, includes all of its boundary points, it is called a *convex figure*. Only convex figures will be discussed in this book.

Thus a convex figure always includes its boundary. A convex set need not include its boundary. For example, the interior of a triangle and the neighborhood of a point are convex sets, but not convex figures. Convex figures are common in plane geometry. For example, all the geometric objects pictured in Fig. 8–13 are convex figures. Convex figures constitute an interesting and important family of distinguished subsets of the plane. Plane convex figures have analogues in space. They are convex solids and will be discussed later.

A line, a ray, and a line segment are all convex figures, for each of these geometric objects satisfies the definition of a convex figure. For example, the ray Γ is a convex figure because (1) if P and Q are any two distinct points of Γ, then $\Gamma \supseteq \overline{PQ}$, and Γ is convex; (2) since every boundary point of Γ belongs to Γ, Γ is a closed set. It is convenient to consider a single point and the empty set as convex figures. They meet the conditions of the definition of a convex figure vacuously.

You will find the following proposition very useful while studying convex figures.

The set intersection of any two convex figures is also a convex figure.

The previous discussion shows that this proposition is evident if the two convex figures are disjoint or meet in a single point. If point sets Γ and Δ

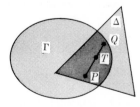

FIG. 8–20. The set intersection of convex figures.

of Fig. 8–20 are convex figures with at least two distinct points in common, then $\Gamma \cap \Delta$ may be shown to be an infinite convex set. The argument follows.

Let P and Q be any two distinct points of point set $\Gamma \cap \Delta$, and let T be any point of the segment $\overline{PQ}$. It is sufficient to show that T belongs to $\Gamma \cap \Delta$. Since $\Gamma \supseteq \Gamma \cap \Delta$, both P and Q belong to Γ. Therefore T belongs to Γ. Since $\Delta \supseteq \Gamma \cap \Delta$, both P and Q belong to Δ. Therefore T belongs to Δ. Since T belongs to both Γ and Δ, it belongs to $\Gamma \cap \Delta$. Therefore $\Gamma \cap \Delta$ is a convex set by definition, and contains an infinite number of points, since it contains the line segment $\overline{PQ}$.

In addition, it may be shown by a more involved argument that the boundary of $\Gamma \cap \Delta$ also belongs to $\Gamma \cap \Delta$. Consequently $\Gamma \cap \Delta$ is a convex figure. A more general proposition which has been proved is that:

The set intersection of any number of convex figures is also a convex figure.

Half-planes. The complement of a line in the plane is the set union of two disjoint convex sets. The geometric object consisting of the line and one of these sets is called a half-plane. Next to a line and a ray, a half-plane is the simplest unbounded convex figure. Line l of Fig. 8–21 is the set intersection of two half-planes. So is line m.

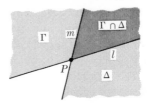

FIG. 8–21. Half-planes and angles.

Two half-planes, Γ and Δ, are indicated by shading in Fig. 8–21. Their set intersection, $\Gamma \cap \Delta$, has for its boundary a Euclidean angle with vertex at P. Many other important convex figures are the set intersections of half-planes or of half-planes and circles. Several figures of this kind are shown in Fig. 8–22. Examine each figure, and indicate how it may be thought of as a set intersection of half-planes and circles.

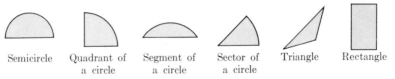

Semicircle   Quadrant of   Segment of   Sector of   Triangle   Rectangle
                a circle   a circle   a circle

FIG. 8–22. Convex figures obtainable from half-planes and circles.

The set intersection of two half-planes whose boundary lines meet in at least one point will be called an angle if there is no danger of confusion with the Euclidean angle previously defined, which is the boundary of the convex figure.

8. SOME IMPORTANT GEOMETRIC RELATIONS

Congruence. The most important relation which can exist between the geometric objects of Euclidean geometry is congruence. In a deductive development of Euclidean geometry, the term "congruence," like the terms "point" and "line," is undefined. Intuitively, two geometric objects are *congruent* if they have the *same size* and *shape*. In this case, if one object is imagined to be superposed on the other, the objects coincide point for point.

The customary symbolism for indicating that two geometric objects Γ and Δ are congruent is to write $\Gamma \cong \Delta$, read "Γ is congruent to Δ." The pairs of lines, triangles, and circles shown in Fig. 8–23 are congruent Euclidean figures. Using the symbolism of congruency, you may write:

$$\overline{AB} \cong \overline{CD},$$
$$\triangle EFG \cong \triangle HIJ,$$
$$\text{circle } M \cong \text{circle } N.$$

All points in space are congruent, all lines are congruent, all rays are congruent, and all planes are congruent. A compass or divider may be used as a device for deciding experimentally whether or not two line segments are congruent. If the points of a divider are separated and made to cover the end points of the first segment and then, on being transferred to the second segment, cover the end points of the second segment, the two segments are considered to be congruent. In Euclidean geometry, it is assumed that such a comparison of segments can always be made.

A famous proposition of Euclid states that two triangles are congruent if and only if the pairs of their sides are congruent. A similar proposition is not true, however, for Euclidean figures with more than three sides.

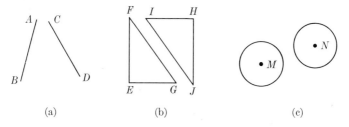

Fig. 8–23. Congruent figures.

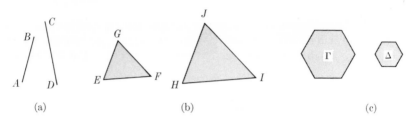

FIG. 8-24. Similar figures.

Similarity. Another important relation which can hold between geometric objects is *similarity*. Two geometric objects are *similar* if they have the same shape. Thus all line segments are similar, and all equilateral triangles are similar. The pairs of lines, triangles, and hexagons in Fig. 8-24 are similar figures. Similar figures may be of different sizes, but they must have the same shape. Consequently, all circles are similar, and all spheres are similar. Similarity, like congruence, is an equivalence relation over the set of all geometric figures, and congruent figures are necessarily similar. Euclid proved that two triangles are similar if and only if the pairs of their angles are congruent. A similar proposition is untrue for Euclidean figures with more than three sides.

Size. Qualitative relations of size between geometric objects may be expressed by set concepts. Let Γ and Δ be any two closed point sets in space or in the plane. If Δ is congruent to a proper subset of Γ, one says that "Γ is larger than Δ," or "Δ is smaller than Γ." In particular, if $\Gamma \supset \Delta$, Γ is larger than Δ. Thus a circle is larger than any circle contained in its interior. The two important special cases when the sets are line segments and angles are illustrated in Fig. 8-25.

In both (a) and (b) of Fig. 8-25, point set Δ' is a proper subset of Γ, and Δ is congruent to Δ'. Observe that the comparisons of size described here are purely qualitative. Quantative comparisons of size of line segments and angles are developed in later chapters.

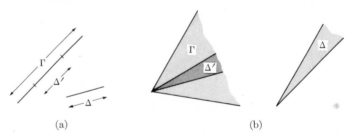

FIG. 8-25. Size of segments and angles.

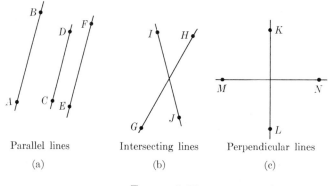

Parallel lines	Intersecting lines	Perpendicular lines
(a)	(b)	(c)

FIGURE 8–26

Relations between lines. Two lines in a plane either coincide, do not intersect at all, or intersect in exactly one point (Fig. 8–26). In the first two cases, the lines are said to be *parallel* (Fig. 8–26a). Thus a line is always parallel to itself. It may be shown that parallelism is an equivalence relation over the family of all the lines in the plane. Furthermore, if l is a line and P any point, there is only one line through P parallel to l.

In the last case, the lines are said to intersect (Fig. 8–26b and c). Two intersecting lines form four angles with a common vertex. If all four of these angles are congruent, the two lines are said to be *perpendicular* to each other, and the angles they form with each other are called *right angles*. All right angles are congruent to one another. Lines KL and MN of Fig. 8–26 are perpendicular; lines IJ and GH are not.

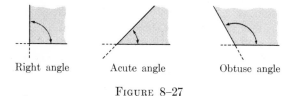

Right angle	Acute angle	Obtuse angle

FIGURE 8–27

An angle is said to be *acute* if it is smaller than a right angle, and *obtuse* if it is larger than a right angle but smaller than a straight angle. See Fig. 8–27.

In space, if two lines intersect or are parallel to each other, they lie in a plane. Two lines in space may neither intersect nor be parallel.

Congruence of vectors. Two vectors are said to be congruent if and only if they have the same direction and the segments determined by

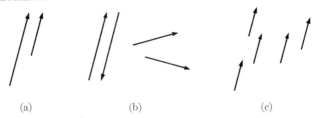

(a)   (b)   (c)

FIG. 8–28. Incongruent and congruent vectors.

them are congruent.   Various possibilities are illustrated in Fig. 8–28.
Congruence is an equivalence relation over the set of all vectors in space.
In most applications to problems in science and engineering, vectors are
freely replaced by congruent vectors.

EXERCISE SET 8–2

1. Are the following statements true or false? If a statement is false rewrite it,
   making it true.
   (a) Line AB is a point set.
   (b) Point B separates line AB into two rays.
   (c) Line AB is determined by point A.
   (d) Each of line segments $\overline{AB}$, $\overline{BC}$, and $\overline{AC}$ is
   a line segment of BC.
   (e) A is an end point of ray AC and $\overline{AC}$.

   FIGURE 8–29

2. Draw figures to show that the set intersection of two given rays may be
   any of the following.
   (a) The empty set   (b) A point
   (c) A line segment   (d) One of the given rays
3. Repeat Exercise 2 using two line segments instead of rays.
4. Why does a point have no next point?
5. Distinguish between a triangle as defined in this book and a Euclidean
   triangle.
6. Recall the manner in which "triangle" was defined in this text and by analogy
   define the following so that they may be distinguished from objects of the
   same name in Euclidean geometry.
   (a) Square   (b) Rectangle
   (c) Quadrilateral   (d) Circle
7. Consider the definition of a line segment in relation to the definition of the
   line of which it is a subset, and define an arc of a circle in a similar way.
8. Define the following sets of a plane. Illustrate each with a figure.
   (a) The complement of a circle
   (b) The complement of a Euclidean circle
   (c) The set intersection of a circle and a square, given that the center of
   the circle is a vertex of the square and the radius of the circle is less
   than a side of the square

(d) The set union of a triangle and a circle inscribed in the triangle

(e) The set union of a triangle and a circle circumscribed about the triangle

9. Which of the following point sets are bounded and which are unbounded?

(a) Circle   (b) Euclidean circle   (c) Exterior of a circle

(d) Line   (e) Line segment   (f) Ray

(g) Square   (h) Exterior of a square   (i) Euclidean triangle

10. Are the following sets closed? (Do they contain all their boundary points?)

(a) Triangle   (b) Ray   (c) Line segment

(d) Circle   (e) Exterior of a circle   (f) Complement of a triangle

11. Decide whether or not each of the following figures is convex (Fig. 8-30). Make a drawing for each to show how your answer is derived.

    (a)   (b)   (c)   (d)

FIGURE 8-30

12. Show that the family of all plane convex figures is closed with respect to the operation of set intersection. Draw at least five different figures to demonstrate this result.

13. Using sheets of paper as models of half-planes, make three or more of the models intersect so as to form the following figures. Make drawings to illustrate each.

(a) Triangle   (b) Quadrilateral   (c) Pentagon

14. Using sheets of paper as models of half-planes and circles, let three or more of the models intersect so as to form the following figures. Make drawings to illustrate each.

(a) Semicircle   (b) Segment of a circle   (c) Sector of a circle

15. (a) Show that four half-planes need not intersect in a bounded figure.

(b) If they do intersect in a bounded figure, is it always a quadrilateral? Illustrate your answer with a diagram.

16. Sketch congruent pairs of:

(a) triangles,   (b) rectangles,   (c) hexagons.

17. Sketch similar pairs of:

(a) triangles,   (b) quadrilaterals,   (c) pentagons.

18. Identify five pairs of congruent figures in your classroom.

19. Identify five pairs of similar figures in your classroom.

20. Demonstrate that the relation of congruency is an equivalence relation by showing that it is symmetric, reflexive, and transitive.

21. Prove that the relation of similarity is an equivalence relation by showing that it is symmetric, reflexive, and transitive.

22. Which of the relations below are equivalence relations? Give reasons for each answer.

(a) Parallel (lines)   (b) Perpendicular (lines)   (c) Intersection (lines)

23. Order the following pairs of sets.
   (a) A triangle Γ and its boundary Δ (b) A triangle Γ and its interior Δ
24. Identify (a) the right angles, (b) the acute angles, and (c) the obtuse angles
   in Fig. 8–31.

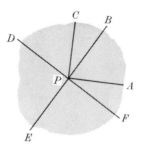

FIGURE 8–31

25. Identify pairs of lines in your classroom which are models for:
   (a) parallel lines,   (b) intersecting lines,   (c) skew lines.

9.   GEOMETRIC FIGURES AND THEIR SPECIALIZATIONS

Specialization. In the study of various kinds of numbers, e.g. whole
numbers, it is useful to examine subsets which are distinguished by some
special property, such as evenness or primeness. The same procedure is
of advantage when you study kinds of geometric objects, for example
triangles. The selection of some particular kind of triangle for consideration is called a specialization.

Specialization is a device of deductive logic, which enables you to
clarify a general idea by illustrating its meaning in various simpler cases.
For example, the definition of a triangle is arrived at inductively by examining many triangles. The meaning of the definition is then made clear
by showing how it applies to particular cases. When specialization is used,
a general property does not have to be proved over and over again.

Special triangles. Since the most striking intuitive difference among
triangles is their shape, we consider here those specializations which
simplify the shape of a triangle. Simplification can be achieved in three
ways, namely:

   (1) by requiring that two or more sides be congruent;   *isosceles*
                                                            equilateral

   (2) by requiring that two or more angles be congruent;

   (3) by imposing some other restriction on one or more angles.

Specializations of type (1) lead to the identification of *isosceles* triangles,
i.e., triangles with two sides congruent, and *equilateral* triangles, i.e., tri-

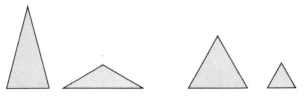

Fig. 8–32. Isosceles and equilateral triangles.

angles which have three sides congruent. All equilateral triangles have the same shape, but isosceles triangles may be of many shapes, as shown in Fig. 8–32.

A famous result of Euclid implies that no new kind of triangle results from specializations of type (2). Indeed, Euclid proved the following propositions:

> *A triangle is isosceles if and only if two of its angles are congruent; and a triangle is equilateral if and only if all three of its angles are congruent.*

The most interesting specialization of type (3) is that based on the requirement that one angle of the triangle be a right angle. Such a triangle is called a *right-angled triangle* or a right triangle. The other two angles of a right triangle are called its acute angles. The side opposite the right angle is called the *hypotenuse* of the right triangle, and the other two sides are called the *legs* of the right triangle.

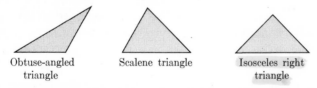

Obtuse-angled
triangle

Scalene triangle

Isosceles right
triangle

Fig. 8–33. Specialization of angles.

If an angle of the triangle is required to be obtuse, the triangle is called an *obtuse-angled triangle*. If all three angles are required to be acute, the triangle is called an *acute-angled triangle*. Isosceles triangles may be either obtuse-angled or acute-angled. An interesting special case is the isosceles right triangle which is neither obtuse-angled nor acute-angled (Fig. 8–33).

Quadrilaterals and their specializations. A convex figure bounded by four distinct line segments is called a *convex quadrilateral*. It is the set intersection of four half-planes. A convex quadrilateral and the Euclidean

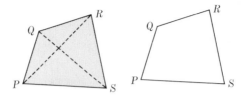

FIG. 8–34. The quadrilateral.

quadrilateral which is its boundary are shown in Fig. 8–34. The points P, Q, R, and S are the vertices of the quadrilateral, and the segments $\overline{PQ}$, $\overline{QR}$, $\overline{RS}$, $\overline{SP}$ are the sides of the quadrilateral. The dashed segments $\overline{PR}$ and $\overline{QS}$ are called the diagonals of the quadrilateral.

Quadrilaterals may be specialized in the three ways given for triangles, as well as in a fourth way, namely:

(4) by requiring that one or more pairs of opposite sides be parallel.

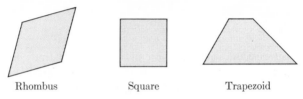

Rhombus   Square   Trapezoid

FIG. 8–35. Some special quadrilaterals.

Three of the many possible specializations of the quadrilateral are shown in Fig. 8–35. A *rhombus* is a quadrilateral with all four sides congruent. The simplest rhombus is the *square* whose four angles are congruent as well. A *trapezoid* is a quadrilateral with one pair of opposite sides parallel. These sides are often called the bases of the trapezoid. Other specializations are left for you to examine in the exercises.

Polygonal paths and polygons. Suppose that $k + 1$ points are chosen in the plane, not necessarily all distinct, but in a definite order:

$$P_1, P_2, P_3, \ldots, P_{k-1}, P_k, P_{k+1}.$$

Then the set union of

$$\overline{P_1P_2}, \overline{P_2P_3}, \ldots, \overline{P_{k-1}P_k}, \overline{P_kP_{k+1}}$$

is a *polygonal path* joining P_1 and P_{k+1}. Two such paths are illustrated for $k = 6$ in Fig. 8–36(a) and (b).

The points $P_1, \ldots, P_{k+1}$ are called the vertices of the path, and the segments are called the sides of the path. The adjective "polygonal" is derived from a Greek word meaning "many-sided." The path may be

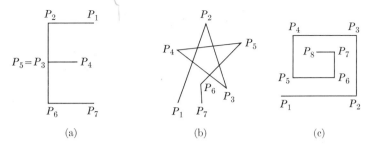

FIG. 8–36. Polygonal paths.

quite complicated unless the choice of the vertices is restricted. If the first k vertices are distinct and no two sides meet unless they are adjacent sides like $\overline{P_1P_2}$ and $\overline{P_2P_3}$ with a common vertex P_2, the path is said to be *simple*. A simple polygonal path with eight vertices is shown in Fig. 8–36(c). Only simple paths will be considered in this chapter.

A simple path for which $P_1 = P_{k+1}$ is called a *simple closed path*. Thus the boundary of a triangle or a quadrilateral is a simple closed path. The geometric figure consisting of a simple closed path and its interior is called a *polygon*. The boundary is often called its *perimeter*. A polygon may or may not be a convex figure. Four simple closed paths which are polygons of ten sides are shown in Fig. 8–37. Figures (a), (b), and (c) are nonconvex polygons, and (d) is a convex polygon.

A segment joining two nonadjacent vertices of a polygon is called a *diagonal* of the polygon. Two five-sided polygons, one of which is convex, are shown in Fig. 8–38. Their diagonals are indicated by dashed lines.

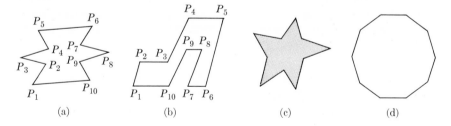

FIG. 8–37. Simple closed paths and polygons.

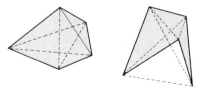

FIGURE 8–38

TABLE 8–1

Common name of polygon	Number of vertices	Number of sides	Number of diagonals
Triangle	3	3	None
Quadrilateral	4	4	2
Pentagon	5	5	5
Hexagon	6	6	9
Heptagon	7	7	14
Octagon	8	8	20

Table 8–1 lists the polygons with eight or fewer sides and the number of diagonals for each.

If all the sides of a polygon are congruent and all the angles are also congruent, the polygon is said to be *regular*. A regular polygon is always convex. The equilateral triangle and the square are regular polygons of three and four sides. Regular pentagons and the regular hexagons are probably also familiar to you. Every regular polygon may be inscribed in a circle. Hence a hexagon is easily constructed by first drawing a circle, locating two points, A and B, on the boundary such that they are the end point of a line segment congruent to the radius. Locate point C from point B in a similar way. Continue until six points are located.

Curves.   It is impossible to give both an elementary and a logically precise definition of what is meant by a curve, but the demonstrative meaning is familiar enough. Figure 8–39 illustrates seven curves. Curves (a), (c), (e), and (g) are simple curves since they do not intersect themselves, but curves (b), (d), and (f) are not simple. Curves (c), (e), and (g) are simple closed curves.

Models of curves may be made by laying a piece of fine string or thread on a table and moving it around. If the string does not overlap, the curve formed is simple, and if the string is a loop, a closed curve results. The meaning of a simple curve and a simple closed curve is the same as

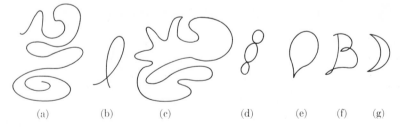

(a)   (b)   (c)   (d)   (e)   (f)   (g)

FIGURE 8–39

that of a polygonal path. Indeed, a polygonal path is considered to be a special kind of curve.

In general, any simple closed curve separates the plane into two disjoint sets, its interior, which is bounded, and its exterior, which is unbounded. But this fact which appears so evident to geometrical intuition is difficult to prove. The first correct proof was given in 1905 by the American mathematician, Oswald Veblen (1880–1960).

Circles. A circle is a bounded convex figure with the following property. There exists a point C interior to the circle such that all segments joining points of the boundary of the circle to C are congruent. C is called the *center* of the circle, and any segment joining a boundary point to C is called a *radius* of the circle. A line joining two boundary points of the circle and passing through the center of the circle is called a *diameter*. The boundary of a circle is called its *circumference*. If two points are chosen on the circumference, they separate it into two parts called *arcs*. These are analogues of line segments.

10. SOME USEFUL EUCLIDEAN CONSTRUCTIONS

The compass and straightedge are employed to develop four theoretically exact constructions from Euclidean geometry. These are presented here because of their usefulness.

CONSTRUCTION I. To construct an angle congruent to a given angle.

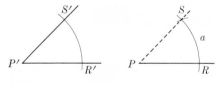

FIGURE 8–40

To construct an angle congruent to the angle with vertex P' in Fig. 8–40, proceed as follows. Draw ray PR. With any convenient radius, draw an arc with center at P', meeting the sides of the given angle at R' and S'. With the same radius draw an arc with center at P meeting the given ray at R. Call this arc a. With R as a center and with a radius equal to the distance from R' to S', draw an arc meeting the arc a at the point S. Draw the ray from P through S to complete the construction.

CONSTRUCTION II. To construct a perpendicular to a line at a given point or to construct a right angle at a given point on a line.

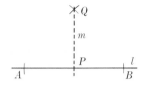

FIGURE 8-41

Given line l and point P (Fig. 8-41). Draw an arc centered at P with any convenient radius, cutting line l at A and B. With A and B as centers and a radius greater than the distance from A to P, draw two arcs meeting at Q. The dashed line m through P and Q completes the construction. Line m is perpendicular to l at P, and the four angles formed by m and l at P are right angles.

CONSTRUCTION III.   To draw a line through a given point parallel to a given line.

FIGURE 8-42

Two lines a and b (Fig. 8-42) are cut by a third line c. The pair of angles formed by c with a and b, labeled 1 and 2 in the figure, are called alternate interior angles. Angles 3 and 4 are also alternate interior angles.
A simple criterion for parallel lines is given by Euclid.

The lines a and b (Fig. 8-43) are parallel if and only if the alternate interior angles formed by any transversal c are congruent.

Using this criterion as a basis for the construction in Fig. 8-44 of a line through a given point P parallel to a given line b, one proceeds as follows.

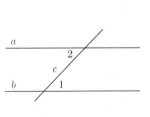

FIGURE 8-43

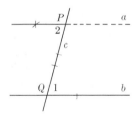

FIGURE 8-44

If P is not on the line b, draw any line c through P, intersecting the line b at Q. Angle 1 in the figure is one of the angles with vertex Q. Now construct, by Construction I, a ray at P forming the alternate interior angle 2, congruent to angle 1. By extending this ray to the right through P, one obtains the required parallel line.

Note that if the given point P were on the given line b, Construction III of Fig. 8–44 would be trivial.

CONSTRUCTION IV.   To divide a line segment into any number of congruent parts.

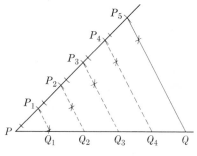

FIGURE 8–45

The construction in Fig. 8–45, which divides the line segment $\overline{PQ}$ into five congruent parts, is carried out as follows. Let PQ be the given segment. Draw a ray through P making an acute angle at P. On this ray lay off with a compass five congruent segments, $\overline{PP_1}$, $\overline{P_1P_2}$, $\overline{P_2P_3}$, $\overline{P_3P_4}$, $\overline{P_4P_5}$. Join P_5 and Q. Construct lines parallel to segment $\overline{P_5Q}$ through P_1, P_2, P_3, and P_4, meeting the segment $\overline{PQ}$ at Q_1, Q_2, Q_3, Q_4. These four points now divide segment $\overline{PQ}$ into five congruent parts.

Characteristics of constructions. None of the four constructions given make any use of measurement. They merely compare line segments with a compass. All four constructions are theoretically exact. If a construction like Construction IV is needed for the purposes of experimental geometry, the parallel lines shown in Fig. 8–45 can usually be drawn accurately enough by aligning the straightedge parallel to $\overline{P_5Q}$ by eye.

There does not exist an exact straightedge-and-compass construction for dividing an arbitrarily chosen angle into k congruent parts unless k is a power of two. In particular, an arbitrarily chosen angle cannot be divided into three congruent parts by straightedge and compass alone. This does not mean that a special angle such as a right angle or a straight angle cannot be divided into three congruent parts by straightedge and compass. Such constructions are left for you in the exercises.

You should distinguish clearly between exact constructions such as those described here and constructions based on measurement. An exact construction is a mathematical process and is not subject to error. A construction based on measurement is a physical process subject to the errors inherent in measurement (Chapter 14). Indeed, any angle may be divided approximately into a number of congruent parts by using a device such as a protractor for measuring angles, just as a line segment may be divided approximately into a number of congruent parts by using a device such as a graduated ruler. These distinctions will be discussed further in Chapters 13 and 14, when you understand the connection between number and geometry.

11. SOLID GEOMETRY

Space. If the basic set of points which Euclidean geometry presupposes does not lie entirely in a line or a plane, the geometry is called solid geometry, and the basic set is called *Euclidean space* or, simply, *space*. Important distinguished subsets of space are lines, line segments, rays, and planes.

The concepts of a point set, of its interior, of its exterior, and its boundary may all be extended to space.

A neighborhood of a point P of space is defined to be the set of all points within a Euclidean sphere whose center is at P.

Closed sets, convex sets, and convex figures are defined as in the plane.

The geometric objects of space are more varied and complex than those in the plane. Only a few of the many possible kinds of geometric objects in space will be discussed here.

Planes and lines in space. Just as a line is determined by any two distinct points, a *plane* is determined by any three distinct points. The flatness of a plane as contrasted with other surfaces, such as the surface of a sphere or of a cylinder, is shown by the fact that it is the only surface in space such that every line which has two points in common with it lies entirely within the surface. Consequently, two *intersecting lines* always determine a plane in which both lines lie. For example, you may choose for the three points determining the plane, the point of intersection of two lines and one other point on each line. It may also be shown that if l is a line in space and P a fixed point on l, the set of all the lines in space which are perpendicular to the line l at P lie in a plane Λ (Fig. 8–46a).

Two lines may lie in the same plane but need not intersect (Fig. 8–46b). In this case, they are parallel in that plane and, by definition, *parallel* in space. In space, as in the plane, a line is considered to be parallel to

(a)   (b)

FIG. 8–46. (a) Plane determined by perpendiculars to a line. (b) Plane determined by two parallel lines.

itself. If the lines neither intersect nor are parallel they are called *skew lines*. Skew lines never lie in the same plane.

A line and a plane in space may intersect in one point. If they intersect in more than one point, the line lies entirely in the plane. If they do not intersect, the line and the plane are said to be parallel. In this case, every plane through the line, except one, cuts the given plane in a line parallel to the given line. The plane which is the exception does not meet the given plane at all, and is said to be parallel to it.

Two distinct planes are either parallel and do not meet at all, or they intersect in a line called their line of intersection. Three planes usually meet in one point, and the line of intersection of two of the planes meets the third plane in a single point. The exceptions which may occur are left for you to discover.

Convex solids in space. The analogue of a square in space is a *cube*, and the analogue of a circle in space is a *sphere*. These geometric objects are solids, and each consists of a boundary surface and its interior, and each is convex. The analogue of a triangle is not so well known. It is a convex solid called a *tetrahedron*. (Some convex solids are illustrated in Fig. 8–47.) A tetrahedron has four vertices, six edges, and four triangular faces which constitute its boundary surface. The specialization analogous to the equilateral triangle is the *regular tetrahedron* with six congruent edges. Each face of a regular tetrahedron is an equilateral triangle.

Many interesting convex solids may be thought of as obtained by one of the following two methods.

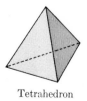

Tetrahedron

Cone

Square pyramid

FIG. 8–47. Convex solids.

First method. Choose a convex figure Γ in a plane and select a point P not in the plane of Γ. Imagine that line segments are drawn from P to every point in Γ. The convex body made up of all the points on all these line segments is called a *conical solid*. All the convex bodies in Fig. 8–47 are conical solids.

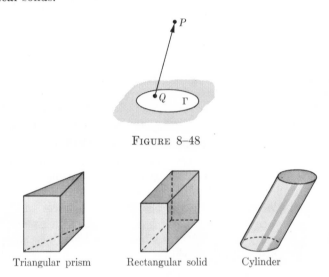

FIGURE 8–48

Triangular prism   Rectangular solid   Cylinder

FIG. 8–49. Cylindrical solids.

Second method. Choose a convex figure Γ in a plane and select (a) a point P not in the plane of Γ, and (b) a point Q in the plane of Γ (Fig. 8–48). You thus determine a vector QP which does not lie in the plane of Γ. Then draw a vector from every point of Γ, parallel and congruent to the vector QP. The convex body made up of all the points on all these vectors is called a *cylindrical solid*. Three cylindrical solids are illustrated in Fig. 8–49. Other solids obtainable by these methods are left for you to examine in the exercises.

12. THE PLACE OF EUCLIDEAN GEOMETRY IN MODERN MATHEMATICS

There are many geometries beside Euclidean geometry that are useful in present-day science and technology. These new geometries were developed and studied by mathematicians in the eighteenth and nineteenth centuries, often with no thought of immediate application. One of the most important of them is topology, whose ideas and methods pervade nearly all of modern mathematics.

The critical movement in nineteenth-century mathematics produced the first adequate postulate systems for Euclidean geometry. Some modern texts of high-school geometry are based on these new systems. Unfortunately, these systems are complicated. The viewpoint of many mathematicians today is that neither Euclidean geometry as conceived by the Greeks nor the detailed study of the geometric methods used by them to prove theorems is particularly important as a branch of pure mathematics. These methods cannot be used to advantage in other parts of mathematics. What is important is something slighted in Euclid's *Elements:* the connection between geometry and number. This connection is developed in Chapter 13 and is the key to the applications of Euclidean geometry to science and engineering. A similar connection with number has been found for the more recently developed geometries. The use of coordinates, which establish the connection between points and numbers, pervades nearly all of present-day geometry. Coordinate geometry is now introduced in high-school mathematics since it is a prerequisite to the understanding of the calculus and all higher mathematics.

EXERCISE SET 8–3

1. Apply the following specialization to quadrilaterals and describe the resulting special quadrilateral.
   (a) Opposite sides are required to be parallel.
   (b) Opposite sides are required to be congruent.
   (c) All sides are required to be congruent.
   (d) All angles are to be congruent.
   (e) All sides and all angles are to be congruent.
2. Apply the following specialization to quadrilaterals and describe the resulting special quadrilateral.
   (a) Diagonals must be congruent.
   (b) Diagonals must be perpendicular.
   (c) Diagonals must be both congruent and perpendicular.
3. Describe the geometric figure for which a kite could be used as a model.
4. Show that every triangle is the set union of two right triangles.
5. Show that every square is the set union of four isosceles right triangles.
6. What is the maximum number of obtuse angles that a triangle may have? Why?
7. What is the maximum number of obtuse angles that a quadrilateral may have? Why?
8. Identify models for each of the following from your immediate surroundings.
   (a) Equilateral triangle   (b) Isosceles triangle   (c) Acute triangle
   (d) Scalene triangle   (e) Obtuse triangle   (f) Right triangle
9. Identify models for each of the following from your immediate surroundings.
   (a) Parallelogram   (b) Rectangle   (c) Square
   (d) Trapezoid   (e) Rhombus   (f) Quadrilateral

10. (a) Sketch examples of five simple closed polygonal paths.
    (b) Sketch examples of five simple closed curves.
11. (a) Sketch two hexagons, making only one of them convex.
    (b) Show in the figures how you decide whether a figure is convex.
12. Is a Euclidean triangle or a triangular region a type of polygon? Why?
13. Verify that the number of diagonals listed in Table 8–1 for different types of polygons is correct by making a sketch for each.
14. Extend the table to include information about nonagons and decagons.
15. (a) Can you predict the number of diagonals in a polygon of twenty sides?
    (b) How many diagonals does a polygon of n sides have?
16. (a) Is the family of simple closed curves closed with respect to set intersection?
    (b) Make a sketch to illustrate your answer to (a).
17. Identify five examples of simple closed curves found in nature.
18. (a) Use a straightedge and draw an obtuse angle.
    (b) Using only a straightedge and compass, construct an angle equal to the angle drawn in (a).
19. (a) Draw three line segments which are noncongruent. Label them a, b, and c.
    (b) Using only compass and straightedge, construct line segments a', b', and c' congruent to the lines of (a).
20. (a) Draw a line and locate two points off the line, one in each half-plane formed by the line.
    (b) Construct a perpendicular to the given line from each of the points.
    (c) What is the relation of the two lines you constructed?
    (d) Do you think that relation will always be true for the conditions of the construction? If your answer is yes, state the appropriate generalization.
    (e) Does your experimentation prove the generalization of (d)? Explain.
    (f) If the generalization of (d) is not proved, should it be discarded as a mathematical idea? Explain.
21. (a) Draw a line and locate two points off the line.
    (b) Construct a parallel to the given line through each of the points.
    (c) What is the relation of the two lines you constructed?
    (d) Do you think that this relation will always be true for the conditions of the construction? If your answer is yes, state the appropriate generalization.
    (e) Does your experimentation prove the generalization of (d)? Explain.
    (f) If the generalization of (d) is not proved, should it be discarded as a mathematical idea? Explain.
22. A simple method of separating a given line segment AB into a given number of congruent segments, say five, consists of the following steps. A sketch of the method is shown in Fig. 8–50.
    (a) On a piece of lined theme paper, draw a line segment perpendicular to the lines of the paper, of just the proper length to be separated into five congruent segments by the lines of the paper. Label the line segment PQ. Fold along $\overline{PQ}$.

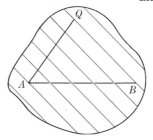

FIGURE 8–50

(b) Superimpose the lined paper over the paper on which the given segment AB is drawn so that point P is superimposed on point A.

(c) Keeping point P superimposed on point P, move the lined paper so the line of the paper which contains point Q intersects point B.

(d) The lines of the lined paper now intersect AB in a manner which separates it into five congruent segments.

Note that in the figure the theme paper is represented by the region enclosed by a curved line, and the line AB is assumed to be on the page of your book.

(i) Draw three line segments. Using the method just described, separate one of them into three congruent segments, one into four congruent segments, and the other into seven congruent segments.

(ii) Using one of the figures from (i), explain why this construction is the same as Construction IV of Section 10.

23. (a) Devise a construction for bisecting a given line segment.

(b) Devise a construction for bisecting a given angle.

(c) Devise a construction for dividing a right angle into three congruent angles.

(d) Devise a construction for dividing a straight angle into three congruent angles.

24. (a) Define a bounded set in space.

(b) Give three examples of a bounded set in space.

(c) Give three examples of an unbounded set in space.

25. Describe the difference between the interior, the exterior, and the boundary of a cube in space by means of the idea of the neighborhood of a point.

26. Cubes and spheres are classed as convex solids.

(a) Explain how you may determine whether a solid is convex.

(b) Give three other examples of convex solids.

(c) Give three examples of solids which are not convex.

27. Is a doughnut a convex solid? Explain. (Doughnuts may have different shapes.)

28. (a) Define what is meant by parallel lines in space.

(b) Develop as many analogies as you can between parallel lines in the plane and parallel planes in space.

29. (a) What are all the relations which may exist between a line and a plane in space?

(b) What are all the relations which may exist between two planes in space?

(c) What are all the relations which may exist among three planes in space?

30. Give a model from your immediate surroundings for the relationships you described in Exercise 29(a), (b), and (c).

31. Define the following convex solids as point sets.

    (a) Sphere   (b) Cube   (c) Tetrahedron

32. Define the following sets of space.

    (a) The complement of a sphere

    (b) The complement of a Euclidean sphere

    (c) The set intersection of a cube and a sphere which intersect in such a way that the eight vertices of the cube are in the boundary of the sphere.

33. Determine whether there exists a tetrahedron each of whose faces is an isosceles triangle. (Use paper models for the surfaces.)

34. In Section 11, we described methods of obtaining convex solids in space. Using these methods, describe the solid resulting in each of the following situations.

    (a) Given: a rectangle and a point not of the rectangle.

    (b) Given: a circle and a fixed line.

    (c) Given: a pentagon and a point not of the pentagon.

    (d) Given: a pentagon and a fixed line.

REFERENCES

BALL, W. W. ROUSE, *A Short Account of the History of Mathematics*. New York: The MacMillan Company, 1924, 522 pp.

BANKS, J. HOUSTON, *Elements of Mathematics*. Boston: Allyn and Bacon, Inc., 1961, pp. 347–390.

BRUMFIEL, CHARLES F., ROBERT E. EICHOLZ, and MERRILL E. SHANKS, *Fundamental Concepts of Elementary Mathematics*. Reading, Mass.: Addison-Wesley Publishing Company, Inc., 1962, pp. 237–312.

CAJORI, FLORIAN, *A History of Mathematics*. New York: The Macmillan Company, 1938, 516 pp.

MESERVE, BRUCE E., and MAX A. SOBEL, *Mathematics for Secondary School Teachers*. Englewood Cliffs, N. J.: Prentice-Hall, Inc., 1962, pp. 177–357.

SANFORD, VERA, *A Short History of Mathematics*. Boston: Houghton Mifflin Company, 1930, 402 pp.

SCHAAF, WILLIAM L., *Basic Concepts of Elementary Mathematics*. New York: John Wiley and Sons, Inc., 1960, pp. 59–97.

School Mathematics Study Group, "Concepts of Informal Geometry," in *Studies in Mathematics*, Volume V. New Haven, Conn.: Yale University, 1960, 270 pp.

School Mathematics Study Group, "Intuitive Geometry," in *Studies in Mathematics*, Volume VII. New Haven, Conn.: Yale University, 1961, 227 pp.

SMITH, DAVID EUGENE, *History of Mathematics*, Volume II. Boston: Ginn and Company, 1925, 725 pp.

STRUIK, DIRK J., *A Concise History of Mathematics*, Volume II. New York: Dover Publications, Inc., 1948, 299 pp.

CHAPTER NINE

FRACTIONS

1. ORIGIN AND DEFINITION OF FRACTIONS

The idea of a fractional number arises in counting situations where a unit is divided into a number of congruent subunits and where a method is needed to count both with the subunit and with the original, or primary, unit.

For example, if the primary unit, one foot, on a yardstick is divided into twelve congruent subunits called inches, the fraction $\frac{1}{12}$ expresses the relationship of the subunit to the primary unit.

If the inch is the primary unit, the inches on a yardstick are counted as $1, 2, 3, \ldots, 36$ inches. But if the foot is the primary unit, the inches are counted as $\frac{1}{12}, \frac{2}{12}, \frac{3}{12}, \ldots, \frac{36}{12}$ feet.

In general, if a primary unit is divided into d congruent subunits, the fraction $\frac{1}{d}$ expresses the relationship of the subunit to the primary unit. The subunits are counted as $1, 2, 3, \ldots$ subunits or they are counted in primary units as

$$\frac{1}{d}, \; \frac{2}{d}, \; \frac{3}{d}, \ldots, \frac{c}{d}, \ldots$$

The fraction $\frac{7}{12}$ indicates a count of 7 subunits each of which is $\frac{1}{12}$ of the primary unit, and the fraction $\frac{c}{d}$ indicates a count of c subunits each of which is $\frac{1}{d}$ of the primary unit. The numbers 7 and c are called the *numerators* of the fractions $\frac{7}{12}$ and $\frac{c}{d}$ and 12 and d are called the *denominators*.

If congruent segments of a yardstick are counted using the subunit $\frac{1}{12}$ foot, the same number of subunits is obtained each time. If noncongruent segments of a yardstick are counted, using the subunit $\frac{1}{12}$ foot, a different number of subunits is obtained each time. In the first instance the fractions which indicate the result of the counts are equal, and in the second instance they are not equal.

The above interpretation of a fraction as the result of a counting procedure leads to the following principle.

Principle I. Two fractions with the same denominator are equal if and only if their numerators are the same.

Fractional numbers. If a yard is chosen as the primary unit and then divided into twelve equal subunits, the fraction $\frac{1}{12}$ expresses the relation between the subunit and the yard unit. But the inch unit is $\frac{1}{36}$ of the yard unit, and there are three inches in the new subunit. Therefore, the fractions $\frac{3}{36}$ and $\frac{1}{12}$ both express the same relationship, the relationship of the new subunit to the yard unit. The question which naturally arises is, In what sense may the fractions $\frac{1}{12}$ and $\frac{3}{36}$ be considered the same?

Various answers have been given to this question in the past. It has been said, "The fractions $\frac{1}{12}$ and $\frac{3}{36}$ have the same value" or "The fractions $\frac{1}{12}$ and $\frac{3}{36}$ are equivalent." Since in both these cases the notation $\frac{1}{12} = \frac{3}{36}$ was used, the symbol $=$ was given a meaning different from that which it ordinarily has in mathematics and in this book.

The equality sign in a mathematical sentence of the form $A = B$ has only one meaning: the symbols A and B both denote or name the same object. *Equality means renaming.* For example, the mathematical sentence $1 + 3 = 2 + 2$ means that both

$$1 + 3 \qquad \text{and} \qquad 2 + 2$$

name the same whole number. This number has an infinite number of other names:

$$12 \div 3, \quad 16 \div 4, \quad 20 \div 5, \ldots, 5 - 1, \quad 6 - 2, \quad 7 - 3, \ldots$$

Its simplest name is the number symbol 4.

From this interpretation of equality, it follows that the symbols $\frac{1}{12}$ and $\frac{3}{36}$ are names, and each names the same fractional number. The mathematical sentence $\frac{1}{12} = \frac{3}{36}$ expresses this fact.

Every fraction of the set A below names the same fractional number:

$$A = \left\{ \tfrac{1}{12}, \tfrac{2}{24}, \tfrac{3}{36}, \tfrac{4}{48}, \ldots \right\}.$$

The fractional number itself is an *idea.* It is an idea associated with each fraction in the set A which distinguishes it from every fraction in the set B:

$$B = \left\{ \tfrac{1}{2}, \tfrac{2}{4}, \tfrac{3}{6}, \tfrac{4}{8}, \ldots \right\}.$$

The fractions of set B are applicable to a different counting situation and consequently name a different fractional number.

The term "fraction" as commonly used is ambiguous. Sometimes it means "fractional symbol" and sometimes it means "fractional number." For example, in the statement, "3 is the numerator of the fraction $\frac{3}{36}$," the word "fraction" means "fractional symbol." In the statement, "The fraction $\frac{1}{2}$ is less than 1," the word "fraction" means "fractional number."

In the discussion in this and later chapters, common usage will be followed with respect to the word "fraction" when the context makes the meaning clear, as in the examples in the preceding paragraph. When it is necessary to emphasize the distinction between number and symbol, the term "fractional number" will be used.

The numerator and denominator of a fraction. The meanings of the numerator and denominator of a fraction have already been explained in a counting situation which the fraction describes. Now their meaning is considered from a different standpoint.

The symbol $\frac{3}{36}$ has three parts: the "3," the "36," and the horizontal bar separating them. Associated with the symbol $\frac{3}{36}$ is the ordered pair of numbers (3, 36). This ordered pair is different from the ordered pair associated with $\frac{5}{36}$ or with $\frac{36}{3}$. The numerator 3 of the symbol $\frac{3}{36}$ is the first member, and the denominator 36 is the second member of the ordered pair (3, 36).

The ordered pairs associated with a fractional number. Associated with the fractions of set A is an infinite set S of ordered pairs of whole numbers.

$$S = \{(1, 12), (2, 24), (3, 36), (4, 48), \ldots\}.$$

Each pair of S is the numerator and denominator of the corresponding fraction in the set A. The fractional number then is a property possessed by each ordered pair of the set S, which distinguishes it from every pair of the set T.

$$T = \{(1, 2), (2, 4), (3, 6), (4, 8), \ldots\}.$$

One property which every pair of the set S possesses is that it belongs to that set, and does not belong to any other such set. For example, (3, 36) is an element of S but not an element of T. The fractional number associated with S is sometimes defined in mathematics to *be* the set S. Each member of an ordered pair may therefore be thought of as a numerator or a denominator of some fractional number.

Note that the denominator is always a natural number, but the numerator may be either a natural number or zero.

2. RENAMING FRACTIONS

When fractions are to be compared or when operations with fractions are to be performed, it is often necessary to decide by renaming a given fractional number whether two fractions name the same fractional number. Two methods will be described which make use of diagrams to effect these renamings. The idea underlying both methods of renaming is geometric. The first method has already been used in describing the counting situation arising from the choice of different subunits on a yardstick. It is based on the measurement of line segments. The second method is based on the measurement of rectangular regions.

(a) Measurement of line segments. To measure line segments, a fixed segment is first chosen to serve as a primary unit of measure. The choice of this segment is arbitrary, but once chosen, its measure is $\frac{1}{1}$, or 1 unit. Other segments are measured by comparing them with the unit segment.

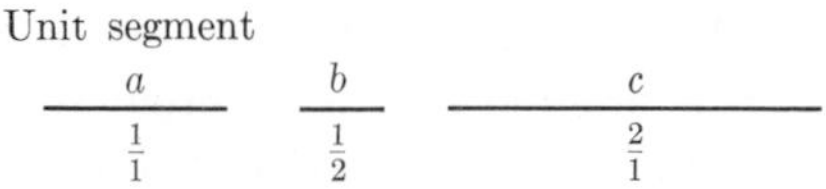

Unit segment

a	b	c
$\frac{1}{1}$	$\frac{1}{2}$	$\frac{2}{1}$

FIGURE 9–1

In Fig. 9–1, a is a unit segment of measure $\frac{1}{1}$, b is a segment of measure $\frac{1}{2}$, and c is a segment of measure $\frac{2}{1}$.

Application to renaming. The application of the above procedure to renaming rests on the principle that once the unit measure is chosen, the measure of any other segment is uniquely determined. Consequently, if the same segment can be measured with different subunits of the unit measure, the measures must be the same. The process by which $\frac{1}{2}$ is renamed $\frac{3}{6}$ is illustrated in Fig. 9–2.

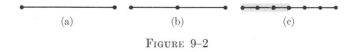

(a)   (b)   (c)

FIGURE 9–2

The unit segment is pictured in Fig. 9–2(a). In Fig. 9–2(b), the unit segment is divided into two congruent segments. Each of these segments is of measure $\frac{1}{2}$. In Fig. 9–2(c), each of the two segments of Fig. 9–2(b) is subdivided into three congruent segments, thus dividing the unit segment into six parts each of measure $\frac{1}{6}$. When one of these segments is used as a subunit, the shaded segment in Fig. 9–2(c) is of measure $\frac{3}{6}$. Since it also is of measure $\frac{1}{2}$, it follows that $\frac{1}{2} = \frac{3}{6}$, and $\frac{3}{6}$ renames $\frac{1}{2}$.

(b) Measurement of rectangular regions. To measure regions in the plane, a region of convenient shape and size is first selected as a unit. By definition, its measure is 1 or $\frac{1}{1}$, but its choice is arbitrary. The measure of any other region is found by comparing it with the unit measure. The customary unit is a square each of whose sides is assigned the

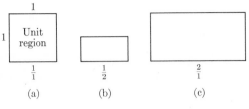

FIGURE 9–3

measure 1. Figure 9–3 shows a unit square and two rectangular regions of measures $\frac{1}{2}$ and $\frac{2}{1}$.

Application to renaming. The application of the procedure above to renaming rests on the principle that once the unit region is chosen, the measure of any other region is uniquely determined. Consequently, if the same rectangular region can be measured with different subunits of the unit region, the measures must be the same. The process by which $\frac{1}{2}$ is renamed $\frac{3}{6}$ is illustrated in Fig. 9–4.

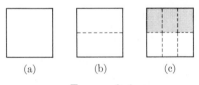

FIGURE 9–4

The square of Fig. 9–4(a) is the unit region of measure $\frac{1}{1}$. It will be referred to here and later as the "unit square." In Fig. 9–4(b), the unit square has been separated into two congruent parts each of measure $\frac{1}{2}$. In Fig. 9–4(c), each of the two regions of Fig. 9–4(b) has been divided into three congruent regions. The unit square is thus divided into six congruent parts, each of measure $\frac{1}{6}$. With one of these parts used as a subunit, the shaded region in Fig. 9–4(c) is of measure $\frac{3}{6}$. Since it also is of measure $\frac{1}{2}$, it follows that $\frac{1}{2} = \frac{3}{6}$, and $\frac{3}{6}$ renames $\frac{1}{2}$.

Process of renaming a fraction. Either of the geometric procedures just described will show that

$$\frac{1}{2} = \frac{2}{4} = \frac{3}{6} = \frac{4}{8} = \cdots.$$

Either may be employed to rename any fraction $\frac{a}{b}$ as

$$\frac{a \cdot c}{b \cdot c}$$

when c is a natural number. In general, then, the fraction obtained from a given fraction by multiplying its numerator and denominator by the same natural number denotes the same fractional number. This principle may be stated more briefly as follows.

Principle II.   Any fraction may be renamed by multiplying its numerator and denominator by the same natural number.

For example,

$$\tfrac{17}{3} = \tfrac{85}{15} = \tfrac{170}{30}.$$

Here the numerator and denominator of $\tfrac{17}{3}$ have been multiplied first by 5 and then by 10.

This principle may be thought of in another way when it is desirable to find a simpler name for a given fraction. Observe that in the equality

$$\frac{17}{3} = \frac{170}{30} = \frac{10 \cdot 17}{10 \cdot 3},$$

we could say that $\tfrac{170}{30}$ is renamed $\tfrac{17}{3}$ by dividing out the common factor 10 from the numerator and denominator of $\tfrac{170}{30}$. The general principle illustrated may be stated as follows.

Principle III.   Any fraction may be renamed by dividing out a common factor of its numerator and denominator.

For example, $\tfrac{15}{10} = \tfrac{3}{2}$ because

$$\frac{15}{10} = \frac{5 \cdot 3}{5 \cdot 2}$$

and 5 is a common factor which may be divided out.

The two principles, II and III, will be simplified in Section 5 of this chapter.

The simplest name of a fractional number.   A fractional number has many names. For example, all the fractions of the set

$$\left\{ \tfrac{1}{3}, \tfrac{2}{6}, \tfrac{3}{9}, \tfrac{4}{12}, \ldots \right\}$$

are names for the same fractional number. The simplest name for this number is $\tfrac{1}{3}$. It is the fraction of the set which has the smallest numerator and denominator. The numerators and denominators of all other fractions in this set have a common factor greater than one. Consequently, the simplest name may also be defined as the fraction whose numerator and denominator have no common factor greater than one.

If the fraction $\tfrac{a}{b}$ is the simplest name for a fractional number, $\tfrac{a}{b}$ is said to be in simplest form, and renaming $\tfrac{3}{12} = \tfrac{1}{4}$ is said to express $\tfrac{3}{12}$ in simplest form.

To decide whether a given fraction is the simplest name for some fractional number you must search for common factors of the numerator and denominator. This search may be laborious if the numerator and denominator are large numbers. (See Chapter 4, Section 10, "Factorization.") Renaming a fraction in simplest form usually consists of several steps. Consider, for example, the renaming of $\frac{546}{234}$. By the test for multiples given in Chapter 4, both 234 and 546 are multiples of 2 and of 3. Therefore $2 \cdot 3$, or 6, is a factor of both 546 and 234. In fact,

$$546 = 6 \cdot 91 \qquad \text{and} \qquad 234 = 6 \cdot 39.$$

Therefore, $\frac{546}{234} = \frac{91}{39}$ by Principle III. However,

$$39 = 3 \cdot 13 \qquad \text{and} \qquad 91 = 7 \cdot 13.$$

Therefore, $\frac{91}{39} = \frac{7}{3}$. The numbers 7 and 3 have no common factor; so the simplest name of $\frac{546}{234}$ is $\frac{7}{3}$.

Renaming is a matter of convenience. How a fraction shall be renamed depends upon the purpose for which it is to be used. The simplest names, however, often make operations with fractions easier to perform. For example, finding the sum of the fractions $\frac{546}{234}$ and $\frac{394}{591}$ is easier if it is recognized that

$$\frac{546}{234} = \frac{7}{3} \qquad \text{and} \qquad \frac{394}{591} = \frac{2}{3}.$$

Equality of fractions. Geometrical diagrams of the measure of line segments and of rectangular regions may be used to decide when two given fractions are equal. If they both measure congruent segments or congruent rectangular regions, they are equal. The procedure is illustrated in Fig. 9–5. There two regions of measure $\frac{9}{12}$ and $\frac{3}{4}$ are compared. Since the regions are congruent, the fractions are equal.

Figure 9–5(a) is the unit square. In Fig. 9–5(b), subunits of measure $\frac{1}{12}$ are indicated. The shaded region is of measure $\frac{9}{12}$. In Fig. 9–5(c), the two dashed vertical lines of Fig. 9–5(b) have been erased. The shaded region in (c) has measure $\frac{3}{4}$ and is congruent to the shaded region in (b). Therefore, $\frac{9}{12} = \frac{3}{4}$.

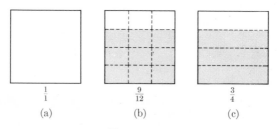

$\frac{1}{1}$

(a)

$\frac{9}{12}$

(b)

$\frac{3}{4}$

(c)

FIGURE 9–5

It is possible to use Principles I and II to obtain a convenient general test for the equality of two fractions. Consider, for example, $\frac{9}{12}$ and $\frac{15}{20}$. By Principle II,

$$\frac{9}{12} = \frac{9 \cdot 20}{12 \cdot 20} \quad \text{and} \quad \frac{15}{20} = \frac{12 \cdot 15}{12 \cdot 20}.$$

The two fractions have now been renamed as fractions with the same denominator, $12 \cdot 20$, or 240. By Principle I, these fractions are equal if and only if they also have the same numerator. Since

$$9 \cdot 20 = 180 \quad \text{and} \quad 12 \cdot 15 = 180,$$

the fractions have the same numerators, and therefore $\frac{9}{12} = \frac{15}{20}$.

This test for the equality of any two fractions may be stated as follows:

$$\frac{a}{b} = \frac{c}{d} \quad \text{if and only if} \quad a \cdot d = b \cdot c. \tag{1}$$

For example, $\frac{2}{3} = \frac{18}{27}$ because $2 \cdot 27 = 3 \cdot 18$, but $\frac{3}{5} \neq \frac{5}{8}$ because $3 \cdot 8 \neq 5 \cdot 5$.

3. ORDERING FRACTIONS

Fractional numbers with the same denominator present themselves in a definite order. For example, the following numbers are ordered by their numerators:

$$\frac{0}{12}, \quad \frac{1}{12}, \quad \frac{2}{12}, \quad \frac{3}{12}, \quad \frac{4}{12}, \quad \frac{5}{12}, \quad \cdots ;$$

$\frac{3}{12} < \frac{5}{12}$ because $3 < 5$; and $\frac{14}{12} > \frac{9}{12}$ because $14 > 9$. In general, the following principle holds for ordering fractional numbers written with the same denominator b.

$$\frac{a}{b} > \frac{c}{b} \quad \text{if} \quad a > c; \qquad \frac{a}{b} < \frac{c}{b} \quad \text{if} \quad a < c. \tag{2}$$

It is now possible to decide for any two fractions $\frac{a}{b}$ and $\frac{c}{d}$ whether

$$\frac{a}{b} = \frac{c}{d} \quad \text{or} \quad \frac{a}{b} > \frac{c}{d} \quad \text{or} \quad \frac{a}{b} < \frac{c}{d}.$$

All that is necessary is to rename the fractions $\frac{a}{b}$ and $\frac{c}{d}$ so that they have the same denominators and to apply Condition (2) if the numerators are not the same. If the numerators are the same, the fractions are equal.

Observe the following:

$$\frac{5}{2} > \frac{3}{2} \quad \text{and} \quad 5 \cdot 2 > 2 \cdot 3;$$
$$\frac{7}{2} > \frac{1}{3} \quad \text{and} \quad 7 \cdot 3 > 2 \cdot 1;$$
$$\frac{5}{2} = \frac{10}{4} \quad \text{and} \quad 5 \cdot 4 = 2 \cdot 10 \quad \text{[see (1) above]};$$
$$\frac{3}{2} < \frac{5}{2} \quad \text{and} \quad 3 \cdot 2 < 2 \cdot 5;$$
$$\frac{1}{3} < \frac{7}{2} \quad \text{and} \quad 1 \cdot 2 < 3 \cdot 7.$$

These observations may be summarized in the following statement.

Principle IV. If $\frac{a}{b}$ and $\frac{c}{d}$ are any two fractional numbers, then

$$\frac{a}{b} > \frac{c}{d} \quad \text{if} \quad a \cdot d > b \cdot c;$$

$$\frac{a}{b} = \frac{c}{d} \quad \text{if} \quad a \cdot d = b \cdot c;$$

and

$$\frac{a}{b} < \frac{c}{d} \quad \text{if} \quad a \cdot d < b \cdot c.$$

EXERCISE SET 9–1

1. (a) List ten fractions which name the fractional number one-third.
   (b) List the ordered pairs associated with the fractions listed in (a).
2. Distinguish between the fractional number $\frac{2}{3}$ and the fractional symbol $\frac{2}{3}$.
3. Does the word "fraction(s)" in each of the following mean the symbol(s) or fractional number(s)?
   (a) The fractions on this measuring cup are indistinct.
   (b) One-fourth is $\frac{1}{2}$ of the fraction $\frac{1}{2}$.
   (c) Write a fraction with a denominator of 7.
   (d) The fractions $\frac{2}{3}$ and $\frac{8}{12}$ are equal.
   (e) The sum of the fractions $\frac{1}{2}$ and $\frac{3}{4}$ is $\frac{5}{4}$.
4. Draw a line, select a primary unit and appropriate subunits, and illustrate each of the fractions below.
   (a) $\frac{3}{4}$ (b) $\frac{7}{8}$ (c) $\frac{1}{2}$ (d) $\frac{2}{4}$ (e) $\frac{4}{8}$
5. (a) Are any of the fractions of Exercise 4 equal?
   (b) Explain your answer to (a) in terms of the illustration you made in Exercise 4.
6. Illustrate each of the fractions below by using it as the measure of a region of unit square(s).
   (a) $\frac{1}{3}$ (b) $\frac{2}{3}$ (c) $\frac{4}{3}$ (d) $\frac{6}{3}$
7. Use a unit square to show that $\frac{1}{1} = \frac{2}{2} = \frac{3}{3} = \frac{4}{4}$.
8. Sketch six congruent unit squares and label them (a) through (f). Mark off and shade regions with the following measures.
   (a) $\frac{1}{2}$ (b) $\frac{1}{4}$ (c) $\frac{2}{8}$
   (d) $\frac{4}{16}$ (e) $\frac{2}{3}$ (f) $\frac{5}{6}$

9. (a) Which of the regions shaded in Exercise 8 are congruent?
   (b) Which of the fractions of Exercise 8 name the same fractional number?

10. What fractional number is associated with each of the following number pairs?
   (a) (2, 8)   (b) (0, 6)   (c) (2, 5)
   (d) (8, 2a)   (e) (15b, 25b)   (f) (a, b)
   [*Note:* a and b are natural numbers.]

11. What are some number pairs associated with each of these fractional numbers? (List three pairs for each.)
   (a) $\frac{3}{4}$ (b) $\frac{2a}{5a}$ (c) 5
   (d) $\frac{1}{10}$ (e) $\frac{1}{100}$ (f) $\frac{1}{1000}$

12. Rename each of these fractions, using three other names.
   (a) $\frac{100}{500}$ (b) $\frac{1}{2}$ (c) $\frac{0}{6}$
   (d) $\frac{9}{12}$ (e) $\frac{7}{3}$ (f) $\frac{9}{10}$

13. What principle did you use consciously or unconsciously in Exercises 12 each time you renamed a fraction?

14. What is the simplest name for each of the following fractional numbers?
   (a) $\frac{12}{148}$ (b) $\frac{8}{10}$ (c) $\frac{169}{221}$
   (d) $\frac{15}{19}$ (e) $\frac{216}{576}$

15. Which of these pairs of fractions name the same fractional number?
   (a) $\frac{5498}{10996}, \frac{72}{144}$ (b) $\frac{13}{23}, \frac{455}{815}$ (c) $\frac{1}{3}, \frac{3}{10}$

16. Decide for each of the following pairs of numbers whether the first is greater than, equal to, or less than the second by changing each to fractions with a common denominator. State answers as mathematical sentences.
   (a) $\frac{3}{8}, \frac{3}{4}$ (b) $\frac{13}{17}, \frac{169}{221}$ (c) $\frac{7}{9}, \frac{2}{3}$
   (d) $\frac{12}{144}, \frac{17}{204}$ (e) $\frac{12}{36}, \frac{13}{39}$ (f) $\frac{75}{100}, \frac{25}{75}$

17. Repeat Exercise 16, using Principle IV of Section 3.

18. How can you decide whether two fractions name the same fractional number? Illustrate.

19. How can you decide which of two fractions names the larger fractional number? Illustrate.

20. Decide for each of the following pairs of numbers whether the first member is greater than, equal to, or less than the second member. State answers as mathematical sentences.
   (a) $\frac{2}{3}, \frac{3}{4}$ (b) $\frac{1}{2}, \frac{29}{60}$ (c) $\frac{0}{3}, \frac{0}{2}$
   (d) $\frac{0}{2}, \frac{4}{1}$ (e) $\frac{10}{10}, \frac{4}{4}$ (f) $\frac{68}{92}, \frac{51}{69}$

21. Order the following sets of fractions from largest to smallest.
   (a) $A = \{\frac{0}{2}, \frac{1}{2}, \frac{3}{4}, \frac{5}{16}\}$ (b) $B = \{\frac{200}{300}, \frac{1}{2}, \frac{20}{24}, \frac{9}{12}\}$
   (c) $C = \{\frac{9}{9}, \frac{0}{9}, \frac{900}{100}, \frac{50}{150}\}$ (d) $D = \{\frac{4}{5}, \frac{7}{8}, \frac{19}{38}, \frac{34}{51}\}$

22. Order the following fractions beginning with the smallest.

$$\frac{3}{4}, \frac{1}{1}, \frac{1}{5}, \frac{1}{3}, \frac{1}{2}, \frac{1}{4}, \frac{2}{3}, \frac{3}{5}$$

23. (a) Name five fractions which are $< \frac{1}{2}$ and $> \frac{1}{4}$.
   (b) How many answers could be given to part (a)?

24. Decide whether each of the following are true or false. Give the reason for your answer.

(a) The fraction symbol $\frac{15}{35}$ is associated with the same number as (20, 28).

(b) The symbols $\frac{1}{2}$ and $\frac{12}{24}$ denote the same fractional number.

(c) The first member of an ordered pair is the denominator of the fraction associated with the ordered pair.

(d) Any natural number may be renamed as a fraction, and any fraction may be renamed as a natural number.

4. THE OPERATIONS OF ADDITION AND SUBTRACTION OF FRACTIONAL NUMBERS

Geometric meaning of the sum of two fractions. To show the sum of $\frac{15}{12}$ and $\frac{7}{12}$, two rectangular regions with these measures are drawn in Fig. 9–6. The region of Fig. 9–6(a) is a unit square; a region of measure $\frac{15}{12}$ is shown in Fig. 9–6(b); and a region of measure $\frac{7}{12}$ is shown in Fig. 9–6(c).

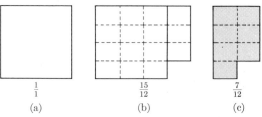

$\frac{1}{1}$

(a)

$\frac{15}{12}$

(b)

$\frac{7}{12}$

(c)

FIGURE 9–6

FIGURE 9–7

Figure 9–7 is a model of the sum of the two regions pictured in Fig. 9–6(b) and (c). It shows that

$$\tfrac{15}{12} + \tfrac{7}{12} = \tfrac{22}{12}.$$

Geometric meaning of the subtraction of two fractions. To perform the subtraction $\frac{15}{12} - \frac{7}{12}$ is to find the missing addend in the sentence

$$\tfrac{7}{12} + n = \tfrac{15}{12}.$$

Geometrically this requires that a region with the measure $\frac{15}{12}$ be sepa-

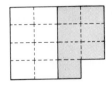

FIGURE 9–8

rated into two subregions, one of measure $\frac{7}{12}$. The separation is indicated by shading.

Figure 9–8 is the model of the sentence

$$\frac{7}{12} + n = \frac{15}{12} \quad \text{or} \quad \frac{15}{12} - \frac{7}{12} = n.$$

The region with a measure of $\frac{15}{12}$ consists of the shaded region of measure $\frac{7}{12}$ and the unshaded region of measure $\frac{8}{12}$. Therefore, $n = \frac{8}{12}$.

Fractions with the same denominators. Fractions such as $\frac{15}{12}$ and $\frac{7}{12}$ which have the same denominator may be added or subtracted geometrically as shown in Figs. 9–6 through 9–8. They may also be added or subtracted by adding or subtracting their numerators:

$$\frac{15}{12} + \frac{7}{12} = \frac{15 + 7}{12} = \frac{22}{12}, \qquad \frac{15}{12} - \frac{7}{12} = \frac{15 - 7}{12} = \frac{8}{12}.$$

If desired, the sum $\frac{22}{12}$ and the difference $\frac{8}{12}$ may be renamed in simpler form by using Principle III:

$$\frac{22}{12} = \frac{2 \cdot 11}{2 \cdot 6} = \frac{11}{6}, \qquad \frac{8}{12} = \frac{2 \cdot 4}{3 \cdot 4} = \frac{2}{3}.$$

Fractions with different denominators. If two fractional numbers with different denominators are to be added or subtracted, they are first renamed as fractional numbers with the same denominators, and then added or subtracted as shown above. For example, to add or subtract $\frac{3}{5}$ and $\frac{4}{7}$, rename $\frac{3}{5}$ and $\frac{4}{7}$:

$$\frac{3}{5} = \frac{3 \cdot 7}{5 \cdot 7} = \frac{21}{35} \quad \text{and} \quad \frac{4}{7} = \frac{4 \cdot 5}{7 \cdot 5} = \frac{20}{35}.$$

Then,

$$\frac{3}{5} + \frac{4}{7} = \frac{21}{35} + \frac{20}{35} = \frac{41}{35} \quad \text{and} \quad \frac{3}{5} - \frac{4}{7} = \frac{21}{35} - \frac{20}{35} = \frac{1}{35}.$$

The addition and subtraction of any two fractional numbers, $\frac{a}{b}$ and $\frac{c}{d}$, are performed similarly. First the fractions are renamed:

$$\frac{a}{b} = \frac{a \cdot d}{b \cdot d} \quad \text{and} \quad \frac{c}{d} = \frac{b \cdot c}{b \cdot d}.$$

The two fractions

$$\frac{a \cdot d}{b \cdot d} \quad \text{and} \quad \frac{b \cdot c}{b \cdot d}$$

have the same denominator $b \cdot d$. Therefore,

$$\frac{a}{b} + \frac{c}{d} = \frac{(a \cdot d) + (b \cdot c)}{b \cdot d}$$

and   (3)

$$\frac{a}{b} - \frac{c}{d} = \frac{(a \cdot d) - (b \cdot c)}{b \cdot d} \quad \text{if} \quad (a \cdot d) \geq (b \cdot c).$$

If $a \cdot d < b \cdot c$, the subtraction cannot be performed.

Properties of addition and subtraction of fractions. The operations of addition and subtraction of fractional numbers have the same properties as have the operations of addition and subtraction of whole numbers. The set of fractional numbers is *closed under the operation of addition,* and addition is an *associative* and *commutative* operation. The fraction $\frac{0}{1}$ is an *identity element for addition.*

Since addition has the cancellation property, subtraction and addition are inverse operations and

$$\left(\frac{a}{b} + \frac{c}{d}\right) - \frac{c}{d} = \frac{a}{b}.$$

Also, provided that $\frac{a}{b} \geq \frac{c}{d}$,

$$\left(\frac{a}{b} - \frac{c}{d}\right) + \frac{c}{d} = \frac{a}{b}.$$

Subtraction may thus be thought of as naming a missing addend in a mathematical sentence which indicates addition. If $\frac{a}{b} \geq \frac{c}{d}$, then the following sentences have the same mathematical meaning.

$$\frac{c}{d} + \frac{m}{n} = \frac{a}{b}, \qquad \frac{a}{b} - \frac{c}{d} = \frac{m}{n}.$$

To subtract the two fractions is to name the missing addend, $\frac{m}{n}$.

Addition and subtraction of fractions are actually carried out by performing suitable operations on their numerators and denominators in the set of whole numbers. These operations are concisely described in Formulas (3), which state how the sum and missing addend of any two fractions may be found. Renaming may be necessary to reduce the difficulty of performing the operation and to obtain the result in simplest form.

EXERCISE SET 9–2

1. Select a unit square and using regions of measures $\frac{5}{8}$ and $\frac{7}{8}$, draw a model for

$$\frac{5}{8} + \frac{7}{8} = \frac{12}{8}.$$

2. Draw a model to show that

$$\frac{7}{8} - \frac{5}{8} = \frac{2}{8}.$$

3. Draw a model to illustrate the operations below.
   (a) $\frac{2}{3} + \frac{3}{4}$ (b) $\frac{2}{3} - \frac{1}{2}$

4. Perform the following operations without models. Give the result its simplest name.
   (a) $\frac{1}{2} + \frac{3}{8}$ (b) $\frac{7}{9} - \frac{1}{3}$ (c) $\frac{3}{4} + \frac{4}{1} + \frac{3}{2}$
   (d) $\frac{5}{1} - \frac{2}{3}$ (e) $\frac{3}{2} - \frac{2}{3}$ (f) $\frac{5}{8} + \frac{360}{720}$
   (g) $\frac{24}{48} + \frac{5}{10} + \frac{4}{8}$ (h) $\frac{7}{8} - \frac{2}{3}$ (i) $\frac{5}{4} + \frac{2}{3} + \frac{5}{6}$

5. Use the fractional numbers $\frac{2}{5}$ and $\frac{3}{5}$ to show that the set of fractional numbers is not closed under subtraction.

6. Use the fractional numbers $\frac{2}{3}$ and $\frac{5}{3}$ to illustrate the commutative property for addition in the set of fractional numbers.

7. Use the fractional numbers $\frac{1}{2}$, $\frac{3}{4}$, and $\frac{1}{8}$ to illustrate the associative property for addition in the set of fractional numbers.

8. Use the fractional numbers $\frac{2}{3}$ and $\frac{5}{3}$ to prove that the operation of subtraction of fractions is not commutative.

9. (a) Define the set of common multiples of 3 and 4.
   (b) Define the set of common denominators for $\frac{1}{3}$ and $\frac{1}{4}$.
   (c) What is the least common multiple for 3 and 4 that can be used as a denominator?
   (d) What is the least common denominator for $\frac{1}{3}$ and $\frac{1}{4}$?

10. Consult Chapter 4, Section 10, and show three ways of finding the least common multiple of 36, 30, and 12, or the least common denominator of $\frac{1}{36}$, $\frac{1}{30}$, and $\frac{1}{12}$.

11. Which of the methods illustrated in Exercise 9 do you prefer using? Why?

12. (a) Do you ever know a common denominator for two or more fractions without using the methods of Exercise 11?
    (b) If your answer to (a) is "yes," list five pairs of fractions for which you know the common denominator.

13. Find a common denominator for each of the following. If you do not know it at once, use the method you chose in Exercise 11.
    (a) $\frac{7}{8}, \frac{1}{2}, \frac{13}{12}$ (b) $\frac{13}{24}, \frac{5}{6}, \frac{7}{8}$ (c) $\frac{1}{2}, \frac{1}{3}, \frac{1}{5}$
    (d) $\frac{1}{10}, \frac{1}{2}, \frac{1}{8}$ (e) $\frac{14}{25}, \frac{17}{10}, \frac{49}{50}$ (f) $\frac{1}{8}, \frac{1}{12}, \frac{1}{18}$

14. Perform the operations indicated. Express results in their simplest form.
    (a) $\frac{7}{8} + \frac{2}{3} + \frac{12}{24}$ (b) $\frac{3}{5} + \frac{3}{4} + \frac{3}{8}$ (c) $\frac{5}{36} + \frac{15}{24}$
    (d) $\frac{17}{12} - \frac{5}{8}$ (e) $\frac{7}{10} - \frac{3}{5}$ (f) $\frac{7}{8} + \frac{1}{4} + \frac{12}{24}$
    (g) $4 - \frac{5}{6}$ (h) $\frac{5}{12} + \frac{7}{8} + \frac{5}{10}$ (i) $\frac{1}{2} - \frac{3}{10}$
    (j) $\frac{7}{8} + \frac{11}{12} + \frac{17}{18}$ (k) $\frac{1}{2} + \frac{1}{3} + \frac{1}{4} + \frac{1}{6}$ (l) $\frac{14}{25} + \frac{17}{10} + \frac{49}{50}$

5. THE OPERATIONS OF MULTIPLICATION AND DIVISION OF FRACTIONAL NUMBERS

Definition of the product of two fractions. The product of the fractional numbers $\frac{a}{b}$ and $\frac{c}{d}$ is defined as follows:

$$\left(\frac{a}{b}\right) \times \left(\frac{c}{d}\right) = \frac{a \cdot c}{b \cdot d}. \qquad \frac{2}{4} = \frac{1}{2} \tag{4}$$

For example,

$$\frac{2}{4} \times \frac{3}{5} = \frac{6}{20}$$

$$4 = 4$$

since

$$2 \times 3 = 6 \quad \text{and} \quad 4 \times 5 = 20. \quad \frac{1}{3} \times \frac{1}{3} = \frac{1}{9}$$

The meaning of Formula (4) is best understood by using simultaneously the representation of fractions as measures of line segments and as measures of rectangular regions. When the same region is measured both with a unit of area and a subunit, the typical counting situation leading to fractions occurs. Formula (4) appears as a method of measuring a rectangular region for which the measures of adjacent sides are known.

Geometrical meaning of the product of two fractions. Figure 9–9(a) is a unit square. In Fig. 9–9(b), it has been divided by horizontal and vertical lines into 36 congruent squares. Any one of these squares, for example the shaded one, is chosen as a subunit for measuring regions. The measure of this subunit is $\frac{1}{36}$, and the measure of each of its sides is $\frac{1}{6}$.

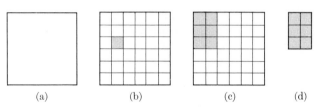

(a)   (b)   (c)   (d)

FIGURE 9–9

The measure of the shaded region in Fig. 9–9(c) may be found by counting the shaded subunits. It is composed of six subunits. Therefore, its measure is $\frac{6}{36}$.

The shaded rectangular region of Fig. 9–9(c) is shown for closer examination in Fig. 9–9(d). You may think of it as a 3 by 2 array made up of 3 × 2, or 6, subunits. The measures of its adjacent sides are $\frac{3}{6}$ and $\frac{2}{6}$.

From this model and by the definition of the product of two fractions, $\frac{3}{6} \times \frac{2}{6} = \frac{6}{36}$; that is, the measure of the shaded rectangular region is the product of the measures of its adjacent sides.

The principle illustrated here is very useful as a means of developing understanding of the meaning of multiplication of fractional numbers.

Principle V. If the fractional numbers $\frac{a}{b}$ and $\frac{c}{d}$ are the measures of the sides of a rectangle, then the measure of the rectangular region is the product

$$\frac{a}{b} \times \frac{c}{d} = \frac{a \cdot c}{b \cdot d}.$$

The identity fraction and reciprocal fractions.   Formula (4), which defines the product of two fractional numbers, has two important special cases.

If $c = d = 1$, the formula becomes

$$\frac{a}{b} \times \frac{1}{1} = \frac{a}{b}.$$

Similarly,

$$\frac{1}{1} \times \frac{a}{b} = \frac{a}{b}.$$

Therefore, the fraction $\frac{1}{1}$ is the identity element for the operation of multiplication of fractions, for

$$\frac{1}{1} \times \frac{a}{b} = \frac{a}{b} \times \frac{1}{1} = \frac{a}{b}. \tag{5}$$

The fraction $\frac{1}{1}$ will be referred to as the identity fraction or simply the identity element. *A fraction remains unchanged when multiplied by the identity element* (Chapter 6, Section 9).

If neither a nor c is zero, and $c = b$ and $d = a$, Formula (4) becomes

$$\frac{a}{b} \times \frac{b}{a} = \frac{1}{1}.$$

Similarly,

$$\frac{b}{a} \times \frac{a}{b} = \frac{1}{1}.$$

Therefore for any fraction $\frac{a}{b}$, with $a \neq 0$,

$$\frac{a}{b} \times \frac{b}{a} = \frac{b}{a} \times \frac{a}{b} = \frac{1}{1}. \tag{6}$$

The two fractions $\frac{a}{b}$ and $\frac{b}{a}$ are called *reciprocals* of each other. The reciprocal of $\frac{b}{a}$ is $\frac{a}{b}$ and the reciprocal of $\frac{a}{b}$ is $\frac{b}{a}$. The reciprocal of a number is also called its *multiplicative inverse.* The idea expressed by Formula (6) is:

> *The product of any fraction except zero and its reciprocal is the identity element or the product of any fraction and its multiplicative inverse is the identity element.*

The identity element $\frac{1}{1}$ has many names, e.g., $\frac{2}{2}$, $\frac{3}{3}$, ..., and may be used to simplify the statements of Principles II and III of Section 2. The statements, "Any fraction may be renamed by multiplying its numerator and denominator by the same natural number" and "Any fraction may be renamed by dividing out a common factor of its numerator and denominator," may be replaced with:

Principle VI. Any fraction may be renamed by multiplying it by the identity element.

For example,

$$\frac{5}{4} = \frac{5}{4} \times \frac{3}{3} = \frac{15}{12} \quad \text{or} \quad \frac{36}{42} = \frac{6 \times 6}{6 \times 7} = \frac{6}{6} \times \frac{6}{7} = \frac{6}{7}.$$

Properties of multiplication. The operation of multiplication of fractional numbers has the same properties as the operation of multiplication of whole numbers (Chapter 6, Section 9). Multiplication has the *closure property*, and is *associative* and *commutative*; the fraction $\frac{1}{1}$ is the *identity element for multiplication*, and multiplication has the *cancellation property*.

Consider the product $\frac{3}{4} \times (\frac{5}{7} + \frac{8}{7})$. Since $\frac{5}{7} + \frac{8}{7} = \frac{13}{7}$, the product is $\frac{3}{4} \times \frac{13}{7} = \frac{39}{28}$. But $\frac{3}{4} \times \frac{5}{7} = \frac{15}{28}$ and $\frac{3}{4} \times \frac{8}{7} = \frac{24}{28}$. Since $\frac{15}{28} + \frac{24}{28} = \frac{39}{28}$, it has been shown that

$$\tfrac{3}{4} \times (\tfrac{5}{7} + \tfrac{8}{7}) = \tfrac{3}{4} \times \tfrac{5}{7} + \tfrac{3}{4} \times \tfrac{8}{7}.$$

The principle illustrated here is the distributive property of multiplication with respect to addition.

The connection of the distributive property of multiplication of fractions with the distributive property of multiplication of whole numbers becomes clear if the product $\frac{3}{4} \times (\frac{5}{7} + \frac{8}{7})$ is written

$$\frac{3}{4} \times \frac{(5 + 8)}{7} .$$

For the numerator of the latter product is

$$3 \times (5 + 8) = (3 \times 5) + (3 \times 8).$$

The distributive property of multiplication may be expressed in a mathematical formula for any three fractions $\frac{a}{b}$, $\frac{c}{d}$, and $\frac{e}{f}$:

$$\frac{a}{b} \cdot \left(\frac{c}{d} + \frac{e}{f}\right) = \frac{a}{b} \cdot \frac{c}{d} + \frac{a}{b} \cdot \frac{e}{f}. \tag{7}$$

This formula may be proved by renaming $\frac{c}{d}$ and $\frac{e}{f}$ as

$$\frac{c}{d} \cdot \frac{f}{f} \quad \text{and} \quad \frac{d}{d} \cdot \frac{e}{f}$$

and then operating on them as in the illustrative example, $\frac{3}{4} \times \left(\frac{5}{7} + \frac{8}{7}\right)$.

Division of fractions. Since multiplication of fractions has the cancellation property, the inverse operation of division of fractions may be defined as renaming the missing factor $\frac{m}{n}$ in the mathematical sentence

$$\frac{m}{n} \cdot \frac{a}{b} = \frac{c}{d}, \tag{8}$$

or

$$\frac{m}{n} = \frac{c}{d} \div \frac{a}{b}. \tag{9}$$

It is assumed that $\frac{a}{b}$ is not zero.

Consider the special case of $\frac{2}{3} \div \frac{5}{4}$. From the mathematical sentence (9),

(a)
$$\frac{m}{n} = \frac{2}{3} \div \frac{5}{4}.$$

By the inverse relation of multiplication and division,

(b)
$$\frac{m}{n} \cdot \frac{5}{4} = \frac{2}{3}.$$

Since $\frac{2}{3} \cdot \frac{1}{1} = \frac{2}{3}$ and $\frac{1}{1}$ may be renamed $\frac{4}{5} \cdot \frac{5}{4}$, the mathematical sentence (b) may become

(c)
$$\frac{m}{n} \cdot \frac{5}{4} = \frac{2}{3} \cdot \left(\frac{4}{5} \cdot \frac{5}{4}\right).$$

By the associative property of multiplication,

(d)
$$\frac{m}{n} \cdot \frac{5}{4} = \left(\frac{2}{3} \cdot \frac{4}{5}\right) \cdot \frac{5}{4}.$$

By the cancellation property of multiplication,

(e)
$$\frac{m}{n} = \frac{2}{3} \cdot \frac{4}{5}.$$

Sentences (a) and (e) both name $\frac{m}{n}$. Therefore,

(f)
$$\frac{2}{3} \div \frac{5}{4} = \frac{2}{3} \cdot \frac{4}{5}.$$

The process by which $\frac{2}{3}$ is divided by $\frac{5}{4}$ is to multiply $\frac{2}{3}$ by the reciprocal of $\frac{5}{4}$.

The pattern of reasoning illustrated in this example may be applied to renaming $\frac{m}{n}$ in Sentence (8). It may be concluded that if $\frac{a}{b} \neq 0$, then

$$\frac{c}{d} \div \frac{a}{b} = \frac{c}{d} \cdot \frac{b}{a}. \tag{10}$$

The problem of how to divide one fraction by another is therefore answered by the following principle.

Principle VII. To divide a fractional number by a given nonzero fractional number, multiply the fractional number by the reciprocal of the given number.

For example,

$$\frac{2}{3} \div \frac{1}{2} = \frac{2}{3} \cdot \frac{2}{1} = \frac{4}{3} \quad \text{and} \quad \frac{5}{4} \div \frac{3}{4} = \frac{5}{4} \cdot \frac{4}{3} = \frac{5}{3}.$$

Observe that the operation of division may always be performed on two fractions $\frac{c}{d}$ and $\frac{a}{b}$ in that order provided that $\frac{a}{b}$ is not zero. *The set of fractional numbers is closed under the operation of division if division by zero is excepted.*

Finally, it may be shown that division is *distributive with respect to addition*; that is, if $\frac{a}{b} \neq 0$,

$$\left(\frac{c}{d} + \frac{e}{f}\right) \div \frac{a}{b} = \left(\frac{c}{d} \div \frac{a}{b}\right) + \left(\frac{e}{f} \div \frac{a}{b}\right). \tag{11}$$

For example, on performing the indicated operations in the following, note that the missing factors are equal:

$$(\tfrac{1}{2} + \tfrac{1}{3}) \div \tfrac{4}{5} = \tfrac{5}{6} \div \tfrac{4}{5} = \tfrac{25}{24},$$
$$(\tfrac{1}{2} \div \tfrac{4}{5}) + (\tfrac{1}{3} \div \tfrac{4}{5}) = \tfrac{5}{8} + \tfrac{5}{12} = \tfrac{25}{24}.$$

Therefore

$$(\tfrac{1}{2} + \tfrac{1}{3}) \div \tfrac{4}{5} = (\tfrac{1}{2} \div \tfrac{4}{5}) + (\tfrac{1}{3} \div \tfrac{4}{5}).$$

The distributivity of division with respect to addition has important applications. Some of these are discussed in the next section.

6. FRACTIONS AND DIVISION

It is customary to use the horizontal bar – as a symbol for the operation of division. In fact the formula for dividing a fraction by a fraction compels its use. Consider $6 \div 3$. Since $6 = \frac{6}{1}$ and $3 = \frac{3}{1}$,

$$6 \div 3 = \frac{6}{1} \div \frac{3}{1} = \frac{6}{1} \cdot \frac{1}{3} = \frac{6 \cdot 1}{1 \cdot 3} = \frac{6}{3} \qquad \text{or} \qquad 6 \div 3 = \frac{6}{3}.$$

Since

$$\frac{6}{3} = \frac{3 \cdot 2}{3 \cdot 1} = \frac{2}{1} = 2 \qquad \text{and} \qquad 6 \div 3 = 2,$$

the identification in this case is immediate. But the same identification can be made even when the division is not exact. For example, since $5 = \frac{5}{1}$ and $4 = \frac{4}{1}$,

$$5 \div 4 = \frac{5}{1} \div \frac{4}{1} = \frac{5}{1} \cdot \frac{1}{4} = \frac{5 \cdot 1}{1 \cdot 4} = \frac{5}{4} \qquad \text{or} \qquad 5 \div 4 = \frac{5}{4}.$$

Fractions in mixed form. Consider the fraction $\frac{189}{12} = 189 \div 12$. Applying the division process to 189 and 12 (Chapter 7, Section 6) gives

$$189 = 15 \cdot 12 + 9.$$

Division is distributive with respect to addition; therefore

$$(15 \cdot 12 + 9) \div 12 = (15 \cdot 12) \div 12 + 9 \div 12$$

$$= \frac{15 \cdot 12}{12} + \frac{9}{12}$$

$$= 15 + \frac{9}{12}.$$

It is customary to write the last sum as $15\frac{9}{12}$ and read it "fifteen and nine-twelfths." Thus

$$\frac{189}{12} = 15\frac{9}{12},$$

and the fraction $\frac{189}{12}$ is said to be expressed in mixed form; $15\frac{9}{12}$ is simply another name for the fractional number $\frac{189}{12}$; $\frac{189}{12}$ is said to be in *common fraction form*.

It is not necessary, although often convenient, to express a fraction in simplest form before expressing it in mixed form. The simplest form of $\frac{189}{12}$ is $\frac{63}{4}$. By the procedure just described, $\frac{63}{4} = 15\frac{3}{4}$, so that $\frac{189}{12} = 15\frac{3}{4}$. The identification of the second mixed form with the first is immediate since $\frac{9}{12} = \frac{3}{4}$.

A characteristic of the simplest name for a fraction in mixed form such as $15\frac{3}{4}$ is that the fractional part, in this case $\frac{3}{4}$, is always a fraction less than one.

Since a fraction in mixed form is the sum of two fractions, it may be changed to common fraction form when desired by performing the addition. For example,

$$7\frac{4}{5} = \frac{7}{1} + \frac{4}{5} = \frac{7 \cdot 5}{1 \cdot 5} + \frac{4}{5} = \frac{39}{5}, \quad \text{and} \quad 3\frac{4}{12} = \frac{3}{1} + \frac{4}{12} = \frac{36}{12} + \frac{4}{12} = \frac{40}{12}.$$

It is unnecessary to rename fractions in mixed form to common form in order to operate on them. The properties of the basic operations on fractions allow one to perform the operations regardless of how the fractions are named. Consider, for example, the sum $5\frac{1}{4} + 2\frac{1}{3}$.

$$5\frac{1}{4} = 5 + \frac{1}{4} = 5 + \frac{3}{12} \quad \text{and} \quad 2\frac{1}{3} = 2 + \frac{1}{3} = 2 + \frac{4}{12}.$$

Since addition is both associative and commutative,

$$5\frac{1}{4} + 2\frac{1}{3} = (5 + \frac{3}{12}) + (2 + \frac{4}{12}) = (5 + 2) + (\frac{3}{12} + \frac{4}{12}) = 7 + \frac{7}{12} = 7\frac{7}{12}.$$

Complex fractions. The division $\frac{5}{4} \div \frac{15}{8}$ may be expressed as

$$\frac{\frac{5}{4}}{\frac{15}{8}}.$$

Such an expression is called a complex fraction. It may be thought of as a fraction whose numerator and/or denominator are themselves fractions. These fractions may be in mixed form; for example,

$$\frac{\frac{5}{4}}{\frac{15}{8}} = \frac{1\frac{1}{4}}{1\frac{7}{8}}.$$

Any fraction may be thought of as a complex fraction. For example,

$$\frac{5}{4} = \frac{\frac{5}{1}}{\frac{4}{1}}.$$

Formula (10) for dividing a fraction by a fraction may be restated as a formula for simplifying a complex fraction; for since $\frac{c}{d} \div \frac{a}{b}$ equals both

$$\frac{\frac{c}{d}}{\frac{a}{b}} \quad \text{and} \quad \frac{c}{d} \cdot \frac{b}{a},$$

we have

$$\frac{c}{d} \div \frac{a}{b} = \frac{\dfrac{c}{d}}{\dfrac{a}{b}} = \frac{c \cdot b}{d \cdot a}. \tag{12}$$

This shows that *any complex fraction may be renamed as a simple fraction.* For example,

$$\frac{\dfrac{5}{4}}{\dfrac{15}{8}} = \frac{5}{4} \cdot \frac{8}{15} = \frac{2}{3}.$$

7. THE ALGORITHMS FOR OPERATIONS WITH FRACTIONS

The algorithms for addition and subtraction. The pattern for recording addition and subtraction of fractions shown in the previous section has been written in a horizontal form. This is a recommended algorithm because it saves time and because it is a method used in algebra.

The common algorithm places the fractions of common or mixed form in a column as in the addition of whole numbers. Columnar form is used to group together the symbols for numbers which have the same or similar denomination. For example,

(a) Add: $125\frac{7}{10}$ (b) Subtract: $125\frac{7}{10}$
$\phantom{\text{(a) Add: }}16\frac{2}{10}$ $\phantom{\text{(b) Subtract: }}16\frac{4}{10}$
$\phantom{\text{(a) Add: }}\overline{141\frac{9}{10}}$ $\phantom{\text{(b) Subtract: }}\overline{109\frac{3}{10}}$

If the fractions which are a part of the numbers to be added or subtracted have to be renamed for convenience as they do in the examples below, the necessary notes are made to the right of the numbers to be added, as shown in the following:

(c) Add: $13\frac{2}{3}$ $\frac{16}{24}$ (d) Subtract: $13\frac{2}{3}$ $\frac{16}{24}$ $12\frac{40}{24}$
$\phantom{\text{(c) Add: }}4\frac{7}{8}$ $\frac{21}{24}$ $\phantom{\text{(d) Subtract: }}4\frac{7}{8}$ $\frac{21}{24}$
$\phantom{\text{(c) Add: }}\overline{17}$ $\overline{\frac{37}{24}} = 18\frac{13}{24}$ $\phantom{\text{(d) Subtract: }}\overline{8}$ $\frac{19}{24}$

In Examples like (c) and (d) you are urged to do as little recording as possible.

The algorithm for multiplication and division. The common algorithm for multiplication of fractions has been presented. Examples follow for the multiplication of fractions in common-fraction and mixed-fraction form.

(e) $\dfrac{5}{8} \times \dfrac{24}{7} = \dfrac{120}{56} = \dfrac{15 \times 8}{7 \times 8} = \dfrac{15}{7}.$

In this example and in others similar to it, it is possible to divide out common factors before multiplying to find the product. For example,

$$\text{(e}')\qquad \frac{5}{\cancelto{1}{8}}\times\frac{\cancelto{3}{24}}{7}=\frac{15}{7},$$

$$\text{(f)}\qquad 3\frac{1}{2}\times 4\frac{2}{3}=\frac{7}{\cancelto{1}{2}}\times\frac{\cancelto{7}{14}}{3}=\frac{49}{3}.$$

The common algorithm for division is that which has been presented previously. Examples are:

$$\text{(g)}\qquad \frac{3}{4}\div\frac{2}{3}=\frac{3}{4}\cdot\frac{3}{2}=\frac{9}{8},$$

$$\text{(h)}\qquad 3\frac{1}{2}\div 1\frac{1}{6}=\frac{7}{2}\div\frac{7}{6}=\frac{\cancelto{1}{7}}{\cancelto{1}{2}}\cdot\frac{\cancelto{3}{6}}{\cancelto{1}{7}}=\frac{3}{1}=3.$$

EXERCISE SET 9–3

1. Sketch a unit square and separate it into four congruent regions by drawing in three horizontal lines. Separate each of these four congruent regions into four congruent regions by means of vertical lines.
   (a) What is the measure of one of the small regions of the unit square? Call each of these a subunit.
   (b) Shade a $\frac{3}{4}$ by $\frac{3}{4}$ region. Express the measure of this region in subunits.
2. Sketch a unit square and shade a region of the square whose adjacent sides measure $\frac{5}{8}$ and $\frac{2}{3}$.
   (a) With the unit square as the primary unit, what is the subunit formed when the lines for the $\frac{5}{8}$ by $\frac{2}{3}$ region are sketched?
   (b) Describe the shaded region by the measure of its sides.
   (c) Describe the shaded region by the number of subunits in its measure.
   (d) Are your answers to (b) and (c) equal?
3. Sketch a unit square and use it to find the product of $\frac{3}{4}$ and $\frac{5}{8}$.
4. Illustrate the meaning of

$$\frac{a}{b}\cdot\frac{c}{d}=\frac{a\cdot c}{b\cdot d}.$$

5. Perform these operations without geometric models. Express the product in its simplest name.
   (a) $\frac{3}{8}\cdot\frac{2}{3}$ (b) $\frac{4}{5}\cdot\frac{3}{4}$ (c) $\frac{7}{12}\cdot\frac{1}{2}$
   (d) $\frac{2}{3}\cdot\frac{4}{7}$ (e) $\frac{5}{9}\cdot\frac{7}{11}$ (f) $\frac{9}{10}\cdot\frac{3}{2}$
6. List five fractions which name the identity element for multiplication.

7. What name for the identity element was used in each of the following?

(a) $5 = \frac{10}{2}$ (b) $\frac{3}{4} = \frac{12}{16}$ (c) $\frac{1}{3} = \dfrac{33\frac{1}{3}}{100}$

(d) $\frac{10}{25} = \frac{2}{5}$ (e) $\frac{48}{72} = \frac{2}{3}$ (f) $\frac{10}{5} = \frac{2}{1}$

8. Use the fractional numbers $\frac{1}{2}$ and $\frac{3}{4}$ to illustrate the commutative property for multiplication of fractional numbers.

9. Use the fractional numbers $\frac{1}{2}$, $\frac{1}{4}$, and $\frac{1}{8}$ to illustrate the associative property for multiplication of fractional numbers.

10. (a) What property of the multiplication of fractional numbers does the following illustrate?

$$\tfrac{1}{2} \cdot \tfrac{178}{3} = (\tfrac{1}{2} \cdot \tfrac{160}{3}) + (\tfrac{1}{2} \cdot \tfrac{18}{3}) = \tfrac{80}{3} + \tfrac{9}{3} = \tfrac{89}{3}$$

(b) Illustrate the property with the fractions $\frac{2}{3}$ and $\frac{7}{4}$.

11. (a) What property of the multiplication of fractional numbers does the following illustrate?

$$\text{If} \quad \tfrac{1}{2} \cdot \tfrac{6}{8} = \tfrac{1}{2} \cdot \tfrac{15}{20}, \quad \text{then} \quad \tfrac{6}{8} = \tfrac{15}{20}.$$

(b) Give another illustration of the property named.

12. What is the reciprocal of each of the following?

(a) $\frac{2}{3}$ (b) 7 (c) $\frac{0}{3}$ (d) $\frac{1}{5}$ (e) $\dfrac{a}{b}$ (f) $\dfrac{b}{a}$

13. (a) Were there any fractions in Exercise 12 which did not have a reciprocal? Why?

(b) Should any restriction be placed on the numbers a and b in Exercises 12(e) and 12(f)?

14. What is the product of a fraction and its reciprocal? Illustrate your answer using each part of Exercise 12 whenever possible.

15. Study the following development.

$$(1) \quad 6 \div \frac{2}{3} = \frac{m}{n},$$

$$(2) \quad \frac{m}{n} \cdot \frac{2}{3} = 6,$$

$$(3) \quad \frac{m}{n} \cdot \frac{2}{3} = 6 \cdot \left(\frac{3}{2} \cdot \frac{2}{3}\right),$$

$$(4) \quad \frac{m}{n} \cdot \frac{2}{3} = \left(6 \cdot \frac{3}{2}\right) \cdot \frac{2}{3},$$

$$(5) \quad \text{Therefore} \ \frac{m}{n} = 6 \cdot \frac{3}{2}.$$

(a) Why can the mathematical sentence (1) be written in the form of Sentence (2)?

(b) Give a reason which makes it possible to derive Sentence (3) from Sentence (2).

(c) What property of multiplication is used to rewrite Sentence (3) as Sentence (4)?

(d) What property of multiplication is used to derive Sentence (5) from Sentence (4)?

16. Sentence (1) and Sentence (5) of Exercise 15 both name the fractional number m/n.

(a) Write a mathematical sentence which expresses the equality of these two expressions.

(b) Explain how your statement in (a) illustrates Principle VII.

17. State a general method for dividing fractions as illustrated in Exercises 15 and 16.

*18. Follow the procedure of Exercises 15, 16, and 17 to prove that

$$\frac{c}{d} \div \frac{a}{b} = \frac{c}{d} \cdot \frac{b}{a}.$$

19. Perform the operations below. Express results in simplest forms.

(a) $\frac{7}{8} \div \frac{3}{4}$ (b) $9 \div \frac{3}{5}$ (c) $1 \div \frac{2}{3}$

(d) $\frac{3}{4} \div \frac{1}{8}$ (e) $\frac{11}{12} \div \frac{1}{2}$ (f) $\frac{3}{5} \div \frac{4}{5}$

20. Perform the following operations.

(a) $1 \div \frac{3}{4}$ (b) $1 \div \frac{2}{3}$ (c) $1 \div \frac{1}{4}$

(d) $1 \div \frac{4}{5}$ (e) $1 \div \frac{2}{5}$ (f) $1 \div \frac{a}{b}$

21. (a) What is the relation of the results in Exercise 20 to the known factors?

(b) Will this relation always be true? If your answer is yes, state it as a generalization.

22. Derive your generalization of Exercise 21(b) from Sentence (6) of Section 5.

23. (a) What property of division of fractional numbers does the following illustrate?

$$\tfrac{1}{2} \div \tfrac{1}{8} = (\tfrac{1}{4} \div \tfrac{1}{8}) + (\tfrac{1}{4} \div \tfrac{1}{8}) = 2 + 2 = 4$$

(b) Give another illustration of the property named.

24. Change the following to mixed form.

(a) $\frac{7}{2}$ (b) $\frac{125}{3}$ (c) $\frac{41}{10}$ (d) $\frac{100}{3}$ (e) $\frac{175}{2}$ (f) $\frac{400}{6}$

25. Change the following to common-fraction form.

(a) $12\frac{1}{2}$ (b) $16\frac{2}{3}$ (c) $6\frac{1}{4}$ (d) $23\frac{2}{3}$ (e) $124\frac{3}{4}$ (f) $9\frac{5}{8}$

26. Change the following complex fractions to simple fractions.

(a) $\dfrac{\frac{1}{4}}{\frac{1}{2}}$ (b) $\dfrac{\frac{3}{4}}{\frac{2}{3}}$ (c) $\dfrac{3\frac{1}{3}}{\frac{1}{3}}$ (d) $\dfrac{12\frac{1}{2}}{100}$

27. Perform the following operations. Express the results in their simplest forms. (Solve all by using the horizontal form of the algorithm.)

(a) $\frac{5}{6} + \frac{2}{3}$ (b) $\frac{2}{3} - \frac{5}{8}$ (c) $\frac{7}{8} \cdot \frac{5}{14}$

(d) $\frac{7}{2} \div \frac{3}{2}$ (e) $\frac{5}{12} \cdot \frac{15}{18}$ (f) $5 - 4\frac{2}{3}$

(g) $4\frac{1}{2} + 2\frac{1}{4}$ (h) $7\frac{2}{5} - 5\frac{3}{10}$ (i) $5\frac{1}{6} - 4\frac{2}{3}$

(j) $6\frac{1}{2} \div \frac{3}{4}$ (k) $12\frac{1}{2} \div 6\frac{1}{4}$ (l) $12\frac{3}{5} + 19\frac{7}{10}$

28. Perform the following operations. Express the results in their simplest forms. Use either the horizontal or vertical form of the addition and subtraction algorithms.

(a) $12\frac{1}{2} + 3\frac{2}{3} + 6\frac{2}{3}$ (b) $12\frac{2}{3} - 6\frac{1}{4}$ (c) $1\frac{5}{6} \cdot 3\frac{3}{5}$

(d) $7\frac{1}{2} \div \frac{2}{5}$ (e) $12\frac{3}{10} - 4\frac{2}{5}$ (f) $87\frac{1}{2} \div 12\frac{1}{2}$

(g) $135 \cdot 33\frac{1}{3}$ (h) $100 \div 6\frac{1}{4}$ (i) $42\frac{2}{3} \div 2\frac{1}{2}$

(j) $4\frac{2}{3} + 5\frac{5}{6} + 3\frac{1}{2}$ (k) $178\frac{1}{2} - 46\frac{5}{6}$ (l) $\frac{1}{4} \cdot 3\frac{1}{2}$

(m) $4\frac{1}{2} \cdot 4\frac{1}{2}$ (n) $4\frac{1}{2} \cdot 4\frac{1}{2} \cdot 4\frac{1}{2}$ (o) $6\frac{2}{3} \div \frac{2}{3}$

(p) $12 \div \frac{3}{4}$ (q) $4\frac{1}{4} + 8\frac{1}{2} + 12\frac{3}{4}$ (r) $12\frac{1}{2} + 62\frac{1}{2} + 37\frac{1}{2}$

8. SOME DISTINGUISHED SUBSETS OF FRACTIONAL NUMBERS

The set B_b. A distinguished subset of the fractional numbers is associated with every natural number, b. This set will be denoted by B_b to call attention to the dependence of the set on the choice of b.

The set B_b is defined as the *set of all fractional numbers which may be denoted by fractions whose denominators are powers of b* (Chapter 4, Section 10). Thus the elements of B_b are fractional numbers which may be named as a/b^h when a and h are any whole numbers.

For example, let $b = 4$. Then the numbers 4^h are 1, 4, 16, 64, ... The identity $\frac{1}{1}$ is in set B_4 because $4^0 = 1$; $\frac{1}{2}$ is also an element because $\frac{1}{2} = \frac{2}{4}$; $\frac{1}{3}$ is not an element since no multiple of 3 is a power of 4.

Consider the fractions $\frac{5}{4}$ and $15/4^2$. Their sum is $35/4^2$; their difference is $5/4^2$; and their product is $75/4^3$. It may be concluded that the set B_4 is closed under addition and multiplication, and not closed under subtraction because subtraction is not always possible. And, although

is in the set B_4,

$$\frac{15}{4^2} \div \frac{5}{4} = \frac{15}{4^2} \times \frac{4}{5} = \frac{3}{4}$$

$$\frac{5}{4} \div \frac{15}{4^2} = \frac{5}{4} \times \frac{4^2}{15} = \frac{4}{3}$$

is not in the set B_4. Consequently, the set B_4 is not closed under division.

The same conclusions hold for any choice of b. The set B_b is closed under addition and multiplication and the identity $\frac{1}{1}$ is an element of B_b; B_b is not closed under subtraction or division.

The set B_1. The two most interesting choices for b are 1 and 10. For $b = 1$, the set B_1 is

$$B_1 = \{\tfrac{0}{1}, \tfrac{1}{1}, \tfrac{2}{1}, \tfrac{3}{1}, \ldots\}.$$

Let W be the set of whole numbers:

$$W = \{0, 1, 2, \ldots\}.$$

The matchings,

$$B_1 = \{\tfrac{0}{1}, \tfrac{1}{1}, \tfrac{2}{1}, \tfrac{3}{1}, \ldots\}$$

$$\updownarrow \ \ \updownarrow \ \ \updownarrow \ \ \updownarrow$$

$$W = \{0, 1, 2, 3, \ldots\},$$

define a one-to-one correspondence between B_1 and W. This correspondence preserves both order and the fundamental operations. For example, $\tfrac{5}{1} > \tfrac{3}{1}$ and $5 > 3$; $\tfrac{5}{1} + \tfrac{3}{1} = \tfrac{8}{1}$ and $5 + 3 = 8$; $\tfrac{5}{1} \cdot \tfrac{3}{1} = \tfrac{15}{1}$ and $5 \cdot 3 = 15$.

So far as their order and the performance of the operations are concerned, the fractions of B_1 and the whole numbers of W behave exactly alike.

Because of this similarity between B_1 and W, it is customary to use the same number symbols, "0," "1," "2," $\ldots$, to denote both the whole numbers of W and the fractional numbers of B_1. The symbols "0," "1," "2," $\ldots$ shall therefore be regarded as other names for $\tfrac{0}{1}, \tfrac{1}{1}, \tfrac{2}{1}, \ldots$ *The set W then may be replaced for all arithmetical purposes by the set B_1.* For example, the ordered set of fractions written below can be used as a counting set (Chapter 2, Section 14 and Chapter 4, Section 11):

$$N = (\tfrac{0}{1}, \tfrac{1}{1}, \tfrac{2}{1}, \ldots). \tag{13}$$

The objects pictured in Fig. 9–10 could be counted

$$\tfrac{1}{1}, \tfrac{2}{1}, \tfrac{3}{1}, \tfrac{4}{1}, \tfrac{5}{1} \qquad \text{instead of} \qquad 1, 2, 3, 4, 5.$$

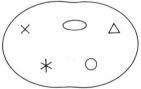

FIGURE 9–10

The replacement of the set W by the set B_1, along with the retention of the familiar number names for the corresponding fractions, allows the use of the set N as a counting set while eliminating the inconvenience of having to mention the denominator 1 each time the elements of a set are counted.

There is, however, a distinction in meaning between saying that a set has 5 objects in it and saying that a set has $\tfrac{5}{1}$ objects in it. In the latter case, the implication is that all the objects are alike in some respect. The renaming $5 = \tfrac{5}{1}$ allows the same number to be used for either kind of counting as circumstances may require.

The consequences of the renaming of the fractions of set B_1 for division were examined in Section 6.

It may be decided whether a fractional number is a member of a given set B_b by examining its simplest name. For example, $\frac{1007}{53}$ is an element of B_1 because 1007 is exactly divisible by 53:

$$1007 = 53 \cdot 19.$$

Consequently, the simplest name for $\frac{1007}{53}$ is $\frac{19}{1}$, or 19, and 19 is an element of B_1.

The set B_{10}. The members of B_{10} are numbers expressible as fractions whose denominators are powers of ten. However, they may have other names. For example,

$$\frac{5}{10} = \frac{1}{2}, \qquad \frac{8}{10^2} = \frac{2}{25} \quad \text{and} \quad \frac{50}{10^3} = \frac{1}{20}.$$

The question arises as to how you may decide whether a fraction is a member of B_{10}. Consider, for example, whether the following fractions are members of the set:

(a) $\dfrac{21}{28} = \dfrac{3}{4} = \dfrac{3}{2^2};$ $\dfrac{3}{2^2} \cdot \dfrac{5^2}{5^2} = \dfrac{75}{100}.$ (Yes)

(b) $\dfrac{39}{375} = \dfrac{13}{125} = \dfrac{13}{5^3};$ $\dfrac{13}{5^3} \cdot \dfrac{2^3}{2^3} = \dfrac{104}{1000}.$ (Yes)

(c) $\dfrac{40}{70} = \dfrac{4}{7}.$ (No)

(d) $\dfrac{5}{120} = \dfrac{5}{2^3 \cdot 3 \cdot 5}.$ (No)

The denominators of the simplest names of fractions (a) and (b) are multiplied by a whole number to obtain a product which is a power of ten. Each factor of 2 is paired with a 5, and each factor of 5 is paired with a 2. The numerator and denominator of the name of the identity element are determined in this way.

The denominator of the simplest names of fractions (c) and (d) have factors which cannot be paired with any whole number to obtain a product which is a power of ten. The factors of the denominator of $\frac{5}{120}$ may be partially paired as follows: $2^3 \cdot 5^3 = 1000$. However, there is no whole number to pair with the factor 3 to obtain a product of 10^n.

These examples illustrate the following generalization: A fractional number is an element of B_{10} if and only if the denominator of its simplest name has no prime factors other than 2 and 5.

$$B_{10} \supseteq B_1$$

The set B_{10} contains the set B_1. Because $10^0 = 1$, every element of B_1 may be named as $a/10^0$, where a is a whole number. For example, the number $\frac{1007}{53}$ is an element of B_{10} since its simplest name is 19 and $19 = 19/10^0 = \frac{19}{1}$.

The members of B_{10} are of importance in the applications of fractions to measurement and in other situations as well. Consequently, they will be given a special name and referred to as *decimal numbers*.

9. DECIMAL NUMBERS AND THEIR DECIMAL FRACTION FORM

The set B_{10} or the set of decimal numbers has been defined as the set of all fractional numbers which may be denoted by fractions whose denominators are powers of 10.

$$B_{10} = \{0, 1, 2, 3, \ldots; \tfrac{1}{10}, \tfrac{2}{10}, \tfrac{3}{10}, \ldots;$$

$$\tfrac{1}{100}, \tfrac{2}{100}, \tfrac{3}{100}, \ldots; \tfrac{1}{1000}, \tfrac{2}{1000}, \tfrac{3}{1000}, \ldots; \ldots\}.$$

Decimal numbers are either whole numbers or numbers which may be expressed in the common-fraction form with numerators and denominators written out and separated by a bar. For example, the symbol $\frac{3}{10}$ uses the symbol 3 to denote the numerator and the symbol 10 to denote the denominator, and the symbol $\frac{2}{1000}$ uses the symbol 2 to denote the numerator and the symbol 1000 to denote the denominator.

Decimal-fraction form of a decimal number. A form for expressing decimal numbers that is simpler than the common-fraction form follows the same scheme used for expressing the whole numbers which are themselves decimal numbers (Chapter 4, Section 5). The decimal number $\frac{1}{10}$ may be written in the form .1 and read "one-tenth." The decimal number $\frac{1}{100}$ may be written as .01 and read "one-hundredth." Fractions written following this scheme are said to be in *decimal-fraction form* and are called *decimal fractions*. Other examples of renaming decimal numbers in decimal fraction form are:

$$\tfrac{2}{10} = .2 \qquad\qquad \tfrac{45}{100} = .45$$
$$\tfrac{5}{100} = .05 \qquad\qquad \tfrac{345}{1000} = .345$$
$$\tfrac{72}{1000} = .072 \qquad\qquad \tfrac{75}{10000} = .0075$$

Each member of a pair of fractions above is read in the same way. For example, both $\frac{2}{10}$ and .2 are read "two-tenths," and both $\frac{45}{100}$ and .45 are read "forty-five hundredths." In both common and decimal form the numerator is expressed in the same way. For example, in the fraction $\frac{75}{10000}$ or .0075, the numerator 75 is expressed with the symbol for the whole number 75. It is the way in which the denominator is expressed which makes the two forms differ. In the common form the denominator is written as a whole number under the numerator. In the decimal-fraction form the denominator is determined by the place value of the numerator.

Extension of place value. The place value of the digits in a whole number are 10^0, 10^1, 10^2, 10^3, . . . , as shown below for 5296.

$$
\begin{array}{cccc}
5 & 2 & 9 & 6 \\
\updownarrow & \updownarrow & \updownarrow & \updownarrow \\
10^n \ldots 10^3 & 10^2 & 10^1 & 10^0
\end{array}
$$

If a point, commonly called a decimal point, is used to the right of the units' place so that the units' digit is always the point of reference, the place value scheme may be extended to the right of the units' place. Consider

$$
\begin{array}{ccccccc}
5 & 2 & 9 & 6 \ . \ 5 & 2 & 4 \\
\updownarrow & \updownarrow & \updownarrow & \updownarrow \ \updownarrow & \updownarrow & \updownarrow \\
10^n \ldots 10^3 & 10^2 & 10^1 & 10^0 \ 10^{-1} & 10^{-2} \ 10^{-3} \ldots 10^{-n}
\end{array}
$$

By definition,

$$
10^0 = 1, \quad 10^{-1} = \frac{1}{10^1}, \quad 10^{-2} = \frac{1}{10^2}, \quad 10^{-3} = \frac{1}{10^3}, \quad \text{and} \quad 10^{-n} = \frac{1}{10^n}.
$$

With these definitions, the place value of the digits of a decimal number may be shown as follows:

$$
\begin{array}{ccccccc}
5 & 2 & 9 & 6 \cdot 5 & 2 & 4 \\
\updownarrow & \updownarrow & \updownarrow & \updownarrow \ \updownarrow & \updownarrow & \updownarrow \\
10^n \ldots 10^3 & 10^2 & 10^1 & 10^0 \ 10^{-1} & 10^{-2} \ 10^{-3} \ldots 10^{-n} \\
\updownarrow & \updownarrow & \updownarrow & \updownarrow \ \updownarrow & \updownarrow & \updownarrow & \updownarrow \\
10^n \ldots 10^3 & 10^2 & 10^1 & 1 \quad \frac{1}{10^1} & \frac{1}{10^2} \ \frac{1}{10^3} \ldots \frac{1}{10^n}
\end{array}
$$

or

The 5296 is read "five thousand two hundred ninety-six." The .524 may be renamed $\frac{524}{1000}$ and is read "five hundred twenty-four thousandths." The number 5296.524 is then read "five thousand two hundred ninety-six and five hundred twenty-four thousandths."

Place value of numerators. The numerator of the fraction $\frac{3}{100}$ indicates that there are three parts of the measure $\frac{1}{100}$ being considered. In the decimal fraction .03, the three has the same meaning and may be said to have a place value of "hundredths." The measure $\frac{1}{100}$ or .01 is the denomination of the fraction; it is the unit measure.

In the fraction .045, the unit measure is .001 or "one-thousandths." The fraction has a numerator of 45 and a denomination of thousandths. The numerator, 45, numbers the thousandths and may be said to have a place value of thousandths.

Expressing a decimal number as a decimal fraction. There are two methods for expressing a decimal number as a decimal fraction. The first method is to rename the number, if necessary, so that its denominator is a power of ten. For example, consider the number $\frac{7}{8}$. Since $8 = 2^3$ and $5^3 = 125$, then

$$\tfrac{7}{8} = \tfrac{7}{8} \cdot \tfrac{125}{125} = \tfrac{875}{1000} = .875.$$

The second method is to interpret $\frac{7}{8}$ as meaning $7 \div 8$ and to perform the division. For example,

$$\frac{7}{8} = \frac{7.000}{8} = 7.000 \div 8 = .875.$$

For any decimal number the division will be exact.

However, if the second method is applied to a fraction such as $\frac{1}{3}$, which is not a decimal number, the division never terminates.

$$\tfrac{1}{3} = 1 \div 3 = .333 \ldots$$

The number $.333 \ldots$ is called a *nonterminating decimal.* Decimals of this type will be considered further in Chapter 13.

Renaming a decimal number. Just as a number in B_{10} named by a fraction in common-fraction form may be renamed as a decimal fraction, so a number in decimal-fraction form may be renamed in another decimal-fraction form or as a common fraction. For example,

$$.25 = \tfrac{25}{100} = \tfrac{250}{1000} = \tfrac{2500}{10000} = \tfrac{25000}{100000} = \cdots$$

or

$$.25 = .250 = .2500 = .25000 = \cdots$$

The latter form of renaming is useful when for purposes of ordering fractions or operating with fractions it is convenient to name them as decimal fractions with a common denomination. For example, .5 and .357 have common denominations when they are named .500 and .357.

Geometric representation of a fraction in decimal fraction form. The region in Fig. 9–11(a) is the unit square. In Fig. 9–11(b) the unit square has been separated into ten congruent regions each of measure $\frac{1}{10}$ or .1 and in Fig. 9–11(c) the unit square has been separated into one hundred congruent regions each of measure $\frac{1}{100}$ or .01.

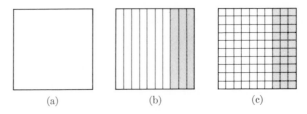

(a)   (b)   (c)

FIGURE 9–11

With the subunit .1 used as a unit of measure in Fig. 9–11(b), the shaded region has a measure of .3. Using a subunit of .01, we find that the shaded region in Fig. 9–11(c) has a measure of .30. These two regions are congruent. Therefore the diagrams show that .3 = .30. The unshaded region of Fig. 9–11(b) has a measure of .70. The diagram shows that the unshaded region is greater than the shaded region and therefore that .70 > .30.

Ordering decimal numbers.   Decimal numbers may be ordered by examining the decimal fractions naming them. If the fractions have the same denomination, the ordering may be done by examining their numerators. For example the numbers,

$$0, \quad .1, \quad .2, \quad .3, \quad .4, \quad .5, \quad \ldots$$

are ordered by their numerators. .3 < .7 because 3 < 7; and .9 > .2 because 9 > 2. In general, *two decimal fractions with common denominators are ordered as their numerators are ordered.*

To decide whether .52 > .4762 the decimal fractions should first be renamed so that they have common denominators, .5200 and .4762. By the principle above, they have the same order as their numerators, 5200 and 4762. Therefore, since 5200 > 4762,

$$.5200 > .4762.$$

10. OPERATIONS WITH DECIMAL NUMBERS

Since a decimal number is a particular kind of fraction, operations with decimal numbers are not special operations; they require only that operations be performed on whole numbers and the result interpreted in terms of the denominations of the fractions.

Addition and subtraction.   The principles for adding and subtracting fractions apply to all fractions including those written in decimal form. The fractions must first be expressed in the same unit measure or denomination, and then their numerators must be added or subtracted.

For example,

$$.5 + .17 = .50 + .17 = .67$$

or

$$.5 - .17 = .50 - .17 = .33.$$

When addition or subtraction exercises are of a more difficult nature than those above, the algorithm used is similar to that for whole numbers.

Addition algorithm	Subtraction algorithm
.78	.354
.09	.086
.54	.268
1.41	

Multiplication. The method for finding the product of two fractions (Section 5) may be applied to finding the product of fractions in decimal-fraction form. For example,

$$.5 \cdot .07 = \tfrac{5}{10} \cdot \tfrac{7}{100} = \tfrac{35}{1000} = .035.$$

In the previous example, the fractions to be multiplied were changed to common fractions and then the multiplication was performed. The product $\tfrac{35}{1000}$ in common-fraction form was renamed in decimal-fraction form, .035.

However, this procedure is unnecessary. The product of the numerators ($5 \times 7 = 35$) and the product of the denominations (tenths · hundredths) may be found, and the product of the fractions written as a decimal fraction directly.

The common algorithm for the multiplication of decimal fractions is shown below in two steps:

(i)	28	(ii)	.28
	79		.79
	252		252
	1960		1960
	2212		.2212

The product of the numerators of the fractions .28 and .79 being multiplied is found in Step (i), $28 \times 79 = 2212$. This number is the numerator of the product of the two fractions. The product of the denominations of the two fractions is determined ($\tfrac{1}{100} \times \tfrac{1}{100} = \tfrac{1}{10000}$) and indicates the denomination of the product of the two fractions. In Step (ii), the numerator, 2212, found in Step (i) is given the denomination ten thousandths ($\tfrac{1}{10000}$) by using the decimal point to locate the units' place.

Division. The operation of division is that of finding a missing factor. For example,

$$(a) \quad 1.25 \div .25 = n \qquad \text{means} \qquad .25 \times n = 1.25,$$
$$(b) \quad .125 \div 2.5 = n \qquad \text{means} \qquad 2.5 \times n = .125,$$
$$(c) \quad .125 \div .25 = n \qquad \text{means} \qquad .25 \times n = .125.$$

In each example above, it is clear that the numerator of n is 5 since $25 \times 5 = 125$ or $125 \div 25 = 5$. The denomination of n or 5 in each of the examples may be found by dividing the unit fractions of the two fractions being divided.

$$(a) \quad \tfrac{1}{100} \div \tfrac{1}{100} = 1; \qquad \text{so} \quad 1.25 \div .25 = 5,$$
$$(b) \quad \tfrac{1}{1000} \div \tfrac{1}{10} = \tfrac{1}{100}; \qquad \text{so} \quad .125 \div 2.5 = .05,$$
$$(c) \quad \tfrac{1}{1000} \div \tfrac{1}{100} = \tfrac{1}{10}; \qquad \text{so} \quad .125 \div .25 = .5.$$

An algorithm for the division of fractions in decimal-fraction form is shown below in two steps.

$$
\begin{array}{cc}
\text{(i)} & \text{(ii)} \\[2pt]
\begin{array}{r}
79 \\
28)\overline{2212} \\
1960 \\
\hline
252 \\
252 \\
\hline
\end{array}
&
\begin{array}{r}
.79 \\
.28)\overline{.2212} \\
1960 \\
\hline
252 \\
252 \\
\hline
\end{array}
\end{array}
$$

In Step (i) the numerators of the fractions .2212 and .28 are divided, $2212 \div 28 = 79$, to determine the numerator of the missing factor. Its denomination is found by dividing the denominations of the product, .2212, and the known factor, .28 $(\tfrac{1}{10000} \div \tfrac{1}{100} = \tfrac{1}{100})$. In Step (ii), the numerator 79 is given the denomination hundredths $(\tfrac{1}{100})$ by using the decimal point to locate the units' place.

Another method of dividing fractions in decimal form is to multiply both the known factor and the product by a power of ten selected such that the new known factor is a whole number. Note that this makes use of the identity element for multiplication. For example,

$$\frac{.35}{.2} = \frac{3.5}{2} \qquad \text{and} \qquad \frac{.736}{.08} = \frac{73.6}{8}.$$

Renaming two decimal fractions in this manner makes it easy to find the denominator of the missing factor. For example, in the three examples below,

$$(a) \quad 1.25 \div .25 = 125 \div 25,$$
$$(b) \quad .125 \div 2.5 = 1.25 \div 25,$$
$$(c) \quad .125 \div .25 = 12.5 \div 25,$$

the numerator of the missing factors is 5 and the denominations are the same as that of the products. Example (a) above becomes a division of whole numbers, and hence the missing factor is 5; in (b) the denomination of the product 1.25 is hundredths, so the missing factor is .05; and in (c) the denomination of the product is tenths, and so the missing factor is .5.

A division algorithm which applies this method of dividing decimal fractions is shown below in three steps:

$$
\text{(i)}\quad .28_\wedge\overline{)\,.22_\wedge 12} \qquad\qquad
\text{(ii)}\quad 28\overline{)2212}\;\;79 \qquad\qquad
\text{(iii)}\quad .28_\wedge\overline{)\,.22_\wedge 12}\;\;.79
$$

$$
\begin{array}{r}
19\ 60\\
252\\
\underline{252}
\end{array}
$$

The expression of the division

$$
\frac{.2212}{.28}
$$

is renamed in Step (i) by use of the identity element which is chosen such that the known factor (or divisor) of the new name is a whole number:

$$
\frac{.2212}{.28} \times \frac{100}{100} = \frac{22.12}{28} .
$$

The renaming is indicated by the use of carets. This symbolism means that $.2212 \div .28$ has the same missing factor as $22.12 \div 28$.

In Step (ii), $2212 \div 28 = 79$. In Step (iii), the numerator of the missing factor, 79, is given the same denomination as the product, 22.12. The missing factor is .79.

It should be noted again that the set B_{10} of decimal numbers is not closed under the operation of division. For example, $.25 \div .75$ is not a decimal number.

$$
.25 \div .75 = \tfrac{1}{3} \qquad \text{or} \qquad .333 \ldots
$$

EXERCISE SET 9–4

1. List ten members of the set B_3.
2. List ten members of the set B_1.
3. Why can the members of B_1 be used to rename the members of W, the set of whole numbers?
4. Show that set B_1 and W may be put in a one-to-one correspondence.
5. Do the fractions below belong to the set B_5?
   (a) $\frac{3}{75}$ (b) $\frac{45}{15}$ (c) $\frac{125}{5}$ (d) $\frac{25}{250}$ (e) $\frac{400}{800}$ (f) $\frac{400}{1250}$
6. Do the following fractions belong to the set B_{10}?
   (a) $\frac{45}{25}$ (b) $\frac{25}{45}$ (c) $\frac{2}{3}$ (d) $\frac{14}{16}$ (e) $\frac{121}{275}$ (f) $\frac{270}{360}$

7. (a) Why is the set B_1 important?
   (b) Why is the set B_{10} important?
8. (a) Show that set B_1 is a subset of B_{10}.
   (b) Show that set B_2 is a subset of B_{10}.
   (c) Name two other sets of the form B_b which are subsets of B_{10}.
9. What is the numerator of each of the following fractions?
   (a) $\frac{74}{100}$ (b) .74   (c) $\frac{3}{1000}$ (d) .003
   (e) $\frac{48}{10}$ (f) 4.8   (g) $\frac{238}{100}$ (h) 2.38
10. What is the denomination of each of the fractions of Exercise 9?
11. Write the following in common-fraction form.
    (a) .7   (b) .255   (c) .78   (d) 2.3
    (e) .04   (f) .025   (g) 2.75   (h) .365
12. Write the following in decimal-fraction form.
    (a) $\frac{6}{10}$ (b) $\frac{256}{1000}$ (c) $\frac{48}{100}$ (d) $\frac{5}{100}$
    (e) $\frac{235}{100}$ (f) $\frac{72}{10}$ (g) $\frac{1452}{1000}$ (h) $\frac{12}{1000}$
13. Write the following as a common fraction of the set B_{10} and then in decimal-fraction form.
    (a) $\frac{12}{24} = \frac{1}{2} = \frac{5}{10} = .5$ (b) $\frac{1}{4}$
    (c) $\frac{12}{75}$ (d) $\frac{21}{24}$
    (e) $\frac{144}{240}$ (f) $\frac{81}{750}$
    (g) $\frac{7}{20}$ (h) $\frac{490}{2800}$
14. Change the fractions of Exercise 13 to decimal-fraction form by interpreting fractions as expressions of division. (They may first be given their simplest name.)
15. With the decimal number 2596.325 and with the units' place as the point of reference, show with a diagram the symmetry of the place values of a decimal number.
16. Which of the following cannot be written as a decimal fraction? If a fraction is a decimal number, write it in decimal fraction form.
    (a) $\frac{2}{3}$ (b) $\frac{15}{20}$ (c) $\frac{21}{14}$ (d) $\frac{165}{440}$ (e) $\frac{2}{5}$ (f) $\frac{5}{7}$
17. Rename each of the following in decimal-fraction form in two different ways.
    (a) .7   (b) .43   (c) 5   (d) 2.3   (e) .02   (f) 20
18. Express the following pairs in a common denomination if they are not so expressed.
    (a) .5; .7   (b) .8; .07   (c) .75; .125
    (d) 4; .6   (e) .6253; .623   (f) .2; .257
19. Order each pair of fractional numbers of Exercise 18.
20. Solve each of the following both in common-fraction form and in decimal-fraction form.
    (a) $\frac{72}{100} - \frac{45}{100}$ (b) .125 + .75   (c) $\frac{3}{10} \times \frac{1}{2}$
    (d) .75 ÷ .125   (e) $\frac{1}{2} + \frac{1}{4} + \frac{375}{1000}$ (f) $\frac{1}{2} - \frac{3}{8}$
    (g) $\frac{8}{2} \div \frac{5}{4}$ (h) $\frac{5}{10} \times \frac{15}{10}$ (i) $\frac{255}{10} \times \frac{15}{10}$
21. Since 1.6 and .3 are members of the set of decimal numbers and $1.6 \div .3 = 5.33\ldots$, what can you conclude regarding the closure property under division of the set of decimal numbers?

22. (a) If $15 \times 15 = 225$ and $\frac{1}{10} \times \frac{1}{10} = \frac{1}{100}$, what is the numerator and denominator of the product of 1.5×1.5?

   (b) If $225 \div 15 = 15$ and $\frac{1}{100} \div \frac{1}{10} = \frac{1}{10}$, what is the numerator and denominator of the simplest name for $2.25 \div 1.5$?

23. Perform the following operations.

   (a) $12.2 - 6.75$ (b) $6.7 + 2.54 + 5.2$

   (c) 5.72×3.2 (d) $51.84 \div .36$

   (e) $1.728 \div 1.2$ (f) $34.56 \div .144$

   (g) $12 - 2.37$ (h) $12.32 - 5.2$

   (i) $7.2 + 9.3 + 18.4 + 8$ (j) 5.27×3.78

   (k) $.7 \times .5 \times .3$ (l) $9.438 \div 2.6$

24. Illustrate $.5 \times .7$ with a diagram.

REFERENCES

BRUMFIEL, CHARLES F., ROBERT E. EICHOLZ, and MERRILL E. SHANKS, *Fundamental Concepts of Elementary Mathematics.* Reading, Massachusetts: Addison-Wesley Publishing Company, Inc., 1962, pp. 96–140.

LAY, L. CLARK, *Arithmetic: An Introduction to Mathematics.* New York: The Macmillan Company, 1961, pp. 82–115, 125–151, 196–236.

School Mathematics Study Group, "Number Systems," in *Studies in Mathematics*, Volume VI. New Haven, Connecticut: Yale University, 1961, pp. 95–166.

CHAPTER TEN

PROBLEM SOLVING AND THE USE OF MATHEMATICAL MODELS

---

1. PROBLEM SOLVING, A LEARNED ACTIVITY

The thoughtful pursuit of the answers to questions is a basic human endeavor called problem solving. Each of you use it daily in many areas of your living; some more successfully than others. However, each could profit by the improvement of your problem-solving technique.

Problem solving has played an important role in the development of mathematics. The solution of specific problems suggested either by nature or by mathematics itself has resulted in the invention of new ideas and methods which are applicable to many other kinds of problems. Indeed mathematics is best learned and taught through a problem-solving and discovery approach.

Problem solving is a learned activity, learned as the result of experience with many problems. It is learned unconsciously and instinctively by a few, but for most the ability results from a deliberate and determined thoughtful consideration of problems and their solutions.

The purpose of this chapter is to help you improve your problem-solving ability first by learning some of the problem-solving techniques others have found helpful and second, by solving many problems and studying their solutions.

2. PROBLEMS OF THIS CHAPTER

Problems are used in mathematics classes for three purposes: first, to provide an opportunity for the use of known mathematical ideas; second, to provide an opportunity for the use and study of problem-solving methods; and third, to develop new mathematical ideas.

This chapter will concentrate on the first two uses of problems. The entire text, however, is concerned with the third purpose. The use of problems for the discovery of mathematical patterns is a method of studying and teaching which is one of the premises of this book.

3. THE METHOD OF PROBLEM SOLVING AND THE USE OF A MATHEMATICAL MODEL

Example of problem solving and the use of a model. In the application of mathematics to the problems of science and daily life, a successful technique has been developed which makes systematic use of mathematical models. How a mathematical model can be used in problem solving is best shown by an example. Consider the following very simple problem.

> Anne and Mary bought 15 pieces of candy. If Mary bought twice as many pieces as Anne, how many pieces did each child buy?

The solution of this problem may conveniently be divided into four steps.

Step (1): The problem is examined and the features that are relevant to its solution are isolated. These features are then restated in a single sentence. Sometimes a restatement is not necessary. In the example above you realize at once that the relevant features are: "One child bought twice as many pieces as the other, and together they bought 15 pieces." In other problems, the essential features may not be so obvious, and the restatement of the problem may require more thought.

Step (2): The essence of the problem situation is stated in mathematical language, and a mathematical model for the problem is thus defined. From the example, it is known that if one child bought n pieces of candy, the other bought $2n$ pieces of candy. Since 15 pieces were bought in all, a mathematical sentence expressing the conditions of the problem is:

$$n + 2n = 15.$$

Step (2) is completed by deducing from this mathematical sentence the value of n. The procedure used is an example of the deductive reasoning characteristic of pure mathematics. The sentence $n + 2n = 15$ is taken as a premise and a succession of mathematical sentences leading to the conclusion that $n = 5$ are:

$n + 2n = 15$	Premise.
$(1 \times n) + (2 \times n) = 15$	Renaming n and $2n$.
$(1 + 2) \times n = 15$	Distributive property for multiplication.
$3 \times n = 15$	Renaming $1 + 2$.
$n = 15 \div 3$	Definition of division.
$n = 5$	Performing division.

The procedure is given in detail to make it perfectly clear that the reasoning is strictly deductive. Experience in problem solving makes it possible to go directly from the premise to $3n = 15$ to $n = 5$, supplying mentally the reasons for each part omitted or using methods from past experience in simplifying mathematical sentences.

Step (3): The meaning of the conclusion, $n = 5$, which was obtained in the second step is interpreted. The meaning is: Anne bought 5 pieces of candy and Mary bought 2×5, or 10, pieces of candy.

Step (4), the final step: The answer is tested to determine whether it meets all the conditions of the problem. The test is made by observing that $5 + 10$ does equal 15, the total number of pieces of candy bought. The solution of the problem is therefore complete.

Characteristics of the use of a model.   There are several observations about the procedure just described which are of value. *First*, there are many problems which will lead to the same mathematical model. For example, the following problem also leads to the model just used.

> Tom and Dick together ride 15 miles a day on their bicycles, delivering newspapers. Tom rides twice as far as Dick. How many miles does each boy ride to deliver the papers?

Second, the solution of the mathematical sentence in step two of any problem may follow essentially the same pattern even though the numbers in the problem are different. For example, if Anne and Mary bought 16 pieces of candy and Mary bought three times as many pieces as Anne, the mathematical model for this new problem would be $n + 3n = 16$, but the steps by which you may deduce that $n = 4$ follow exactly the same pattern as in the original example.

These observations are important, as they suggest that problems may be classified into types for which the same procedure of solution is appropriate. Part of the skill acquired in solving problems consists of a knowledge of common problem types, and an ability to recognize easily the type into which a given problem falls.

Third, a mathematical model for a problem may be defined in several ways. The model for the problem used as an example was defined by the single mathematical sentence $n + 2n = 15$. The model could, however, be defined by more than one sentence. For example, if m denotes the number of pieces of candy which Mary bought, the two sentences below also state the essence of the problem in mathematical symbols.

$$m = 2n, \qquad m + n = 15.$$

With these sentences it is not necessary to find n first. The value of m may first be deduced, then n is one-half m. The procedure for the solution of sentences stated in this way will not be considered here. If you wish to study this method further, consult an elementary algebra book.

Although there may be several mathematical models for a problem, the simplest is to be preferred. It usually shortens the deductive reasoning required for the second step of the solution. With practice, you can learn to formulate your problems in the simplest mathematical sentence.

Fourth, and finally, observe that in the second step of the solution, the mathematical model was defined by a single mathematical sentence, and the reasoning that led from the model to the desired conclusion was stated in a succession of single mathematical sentences. All the problems considered in this chapter lead to mathematical models with these two characteristics.

4. MATHEMATICAL MODELS IN PROBLEMS OF APPLIED MATHEMATICS

Pattern of problem solving. Before discussing more fully the particular kind of problems and mathematical sentences which are the concern of this chapter, the pattern of problem solving used in the example of Section 3 will be summarized. The pattern is of value because the same four steps may be used generally in the solution of any mathematical problem. The steps are:

(1) To examine the problem and isolate the essence of the problem.

(2) To translate the essence of the problem into a mathematical model and deduce from the model a mathematical conclusion.

(3) To interpret the meaning of the mathematical conclusion in the problem.

(4) To test the conclusion to determine whether it meets the conditions of the problem as a whole.

Use of the pattern of problem solving. The pattern described here is employed for solving the problems encountered as you or anyone else studies mathematics. It is the central pattern followed by all scientists in applying mathematics to their specialties. It is constantly used in solving problems in pure mathematics itself. The chief difficulty often lies in the deductive part of Step (2) since it may be very hard to discover a proof leading from the premises given by the mathematical model to the desired conclusion. You will not encounter this difficulty in the problems studied in this chapter. The mathematical models that you employ will be definable by a single mathematical sentence, and the procedure leading to the answer will consist in an intelligent use of the fundamental operations of arithmetic.

The great advantage of using mathematical models in problem solving is that problem solving can be learned by anyone willing to study the use of models in the solution of problems of his special interest. Naturally, difficult problems require a wider and deeper knowledge of mathematics, and problems on the frontier of knowledge may be extremely difficult to formulate in mathematical terms. In fact, their proper formulation may require the invention of new mathematics.

5. MATHEMATICAL SENTENCES

The mathematical model for solving the problems discussed in this chapter is the mathematical sentence. A mathematical sentence is a statement expressed in the symbols of mathematics. In this chapter, the statements will be concerned with numbers and their relations. The sentences may contain number names such as 5 or $\frac{12}{7}$. They may contain number symbols such as a, n, or x^2, which may be either variables whose domain is a set of numbers, or constants (see Chapter 2, Section 5). The situation of the problem will determine the kind of numbers that are appropriate.

A mathematical sentence may be a *proposition*, that is, either always true or always false, or a *propositional form* which may be either true or false according to the values assigned to the variables that appear in the sentence (see Chapter 3, Sections 5 through 7). For example, the mathematical sentences

$$5 + 2 = 7, \quad 25 = 20 + (2 \times 3), \quad 2n + n = 3n, \quad \text{and} \quad 0 \times n = 0$$

are propositions; but the mathematical sentences

$$n + 2 = 5, \quad 4n \neq 29, \quad \text{and} \quad n > 21$$

are propositional forms. Propositional forms are sometimes called *open sentences*.

Propositional forms such as $n + 2 = 5$ and $4n = 29$, which are true for at most one value of the variable n, are particularly important in problem solving, since the solution of a problem will usually depend on this type of mathematical sentence. The variable n or x in such mathematical sentences will be called an unknown.

Verbs in mathematical sentences. Mathematical sentences of the form considered in this chapter have verbs which express the relationship of equality or inequality between two numbers. The verb of a sentence is either $=$, $\neq$, $>$, or $<$. The relationship with which this chapter is especially concerned is that of equality.

Examples of mathematical sentences. Considering only the relationship of equality between numbers, we find that mathematical sentences may have the following forms (among others):

$$a + b = c, \quad c - a = b, \quad ab = c, \quad b = \frac{c}{a};$$

$$a + b + c = d, \quad abc = d, \quad a(b + c) = d;$$

$$\frac{a + b}{c} = d, \quad a + \frac{b}{c} = d, \quad a - b - c = d, \quad \frac{a}{b} - \frac{c}{d} = e.$$

Note that these mathematical sentences usually indicate one or more operations on numbers. If the numbers to be operated on are the numbers of arithmetic, the sentence may be simplified at once, provided the order of operations is understood.

Order of operations. In mathematical sentences parentheses are used to ensure the correct meaning, just as commas are used in word sentences. For example, if $5 \times 4 - 2$ is interpreted as $(5 \times 4) - 2$, it has a different meaning than if it is interpreted as $5 \times (4 - 2)$. The parentheses in $5 \times (4 - 2) = 18$ are needed to give the sentence meaning just as a comma is needed in the sentence, "When she had finished eating Mary Jane fell asleep" to give it the meaning intended.

Parentheses are also needed in sentences like these:

$$(a + b) - (c + d) = 4; \quad a \div (2 + 3) = p;$$

$$a(b - c) = ab - ac; \quad (a + b) \div c = a \div c + b \div c;$$

$$(a + b) \div (b + c) = d.$$

Some mathematical sentences, for example,

$$5 \times 2 - 8 \div 2 + 5^2 = n,$$

indicate a series of operations without introducing parentheses. In such sentences, any possible danger of misinterpreting the order of operations is avoided by following the order which has been agreed on by mathematicians. This order can be described as follows. First, raise all numbers to powers and extract roots. For example, the sentence

$$5 \times 2 - 8 \div 2 + 5^2 = n$$

is first simplified by renaming 5^2 as 25. Second, perform all multiplications and divisions in the order in which they are indicated. For example, the sentence

$$5 \times 2 - 8 \div 2 + 25 = n$$

is now simplified as

$$10 - 4 + 25 = n.$$

Last, perform all additions and subtractions. For example, the sentence

$$10 - 4 + 25 = n \qquad \text{becomes} \qquad n = 31.$$

6. SPECIAL MATHEMATICAL SENTENCES—FORMULAS

Certain problem situations require mathematical sentences that have the same definite pattern. These mathematical sentences are identified, called formulas, and used as models for problems of similar types. For example, the model $a + b = s$ is used to find the sum of two known addends, and the model $c = \pi d$ is used to determine the circumference of a circle when the diameter is known.

Algebraic formulas, that is, formulas which are true for all values of the variables that appear in them, are also useful in problem solving. The sentence $a + b = b + a$ is a formula of this type. It expresses the pattern for the commutative property for addition and is true for any numbers a and b. Other useful algebraic formulas with which you are familiar are

$$ab = ba; \qquad a \cdot \frac{1}{a} = 1 \quad \text{if} \quad a \neq 0; \qquad \text{and} \qquad \frac{a + b}{c} = \frac{a}{c} + \frac{b}{c}.$$

The formulas discussed in the first paragraph of this section are not algebraic formulas. For example, the formula $c = \pi d$ is not true for all values of the variables c and d. The formula is false, for example, if $d = 1$ and $c = 3$, since $\pi \neq 3$. It is true, however, when d denotes the length of the diameter of a circle and c denotes the length of the circumference of the same circle. The formula $c = \pi d$ may be used, therefore, to determine the circumference of a circle if the diameter is known, or of the diameter if the circumference is known.

Both types of formulas are of value in problem solving. The power of a formula is that it is a general mathematical sentence which describes many situations and hence is so frequently used that some steps in the reasoning underlying its derivation become commonplace and may be abbreviated or omitted.

7. REWRITING A MATHEMATICAL SENTENCE— AN ACT OF DEDUCTION

Mathematical sentences are often rewritten in another form for purposes of reemphasis, simplification, or—and most important—for the purpose of deducing the value of the unknown in the sentence. Successive rewriting of a sentence is a part of the procedures of deduction described in Section 3.

You have rewritten many mathematical sentences in the exercises of previous chapters. The following will serve as a review.

Performing operations and renaming

$$3a + 2a = 9 - 2 \qquad \text{rewritten as} \qquad 5a = 7$$
$$3 \times 4 \times a = 48 \div 3 \qquad \text{rewritten as} \qquad 12a = 16$$

Commutative property for addition and multiplication

$$a + 5 = n \qquad \text{rewritten as} \qquad 5 + a = n$$
$$ab = n \qquad \text{rewritten as} \qquad ba = n$$
$$(a + b)c = pq \qquad \text{rewritten as} \qquad c(b + a) = qp$$

Associative property for addition and multiplication

$$(a + b) + c = n \qquad \text{rewritten as} \qquad a + (b + c) = n$$
$$(ab)c = p \qquad \text{rewritten as} \qquad a(bc) = p$$

Inverseness of operations

$$a + b = n \qquad \text{rewritten as} \qquad n - a = b \quad \text{or} \quad n - b = a$$
$$ab = 8 \qquad \text{rewritten as} \qquad \frac{8}{a} = b \quad \text{or} \quad \frac{8}{b} = a$$

Identity element for multiplication

$$\frac{a}{2} + \frac{b}{5} = c \qquad \text{rewritten as} \qquad \frac{5a}{10} + \frac{2b}{10} = c$$
$$2.5p = 2.75 \qquad \text{rewritten as} \qquad 250p = 275$$

Distributive property for multiplication and division

$$\frac{a + b}{3} = n \qquad \text{rewritten as} \qquad \frac{a}{3} + \frac{b}{3} = n$$
$$5(a + b) = p \qquad \text{rewritten as} \qquad 5a + 5b = p$$

Cancellation property for addition and multiplication

$$a + b + 5 = n + 5 \qquad \text{rewritten as} \qquad a + b = n$$
$$ab = an \qquad \text{rewritten as} \qquad b = n$$

8. THE SOLUTION OF A MATHEMATICAL SENTENCE

If sentences are of the form that involves only one unknown, say n, repeated simplification of the sentence results in a sentence of the form $n = 5$. In such a case, the unknown n is identified.

Three solutions of mathematical sentences follow. Each time the sentences are rewritten, the property which justifies the rewriting is stated to the right. The purpose of each step is to simplify the sentence so that the unknown may be identified.

ILLUSTRATION I: $3n - 4 = 8$.

$$3n = 8 + 4 \qquad \text{Inverseness of addition and subtraction.}$$
$$3n = 12 \qquad \text{Operation of addition.}$$
$$n = 4 \qquad \text{Inverseness of multiplication and division.}$$

ILLUSTRATION II. $3(x + 1) = \dfrac{6x + 12}{3}$.

$$3x + 3 = 2x + 4 \qquad \text{Distributive property for multiplication and for division.}$$
$$2x + x + 3 = 2x + 1 + 3 \qquad \text{Renaming } 3x \text{ and } 4.$$
$$x = 1 \qquad \text{Cancellation property for addition.}$$

ILLUSTRATION III: $\dfrac{3m}{2} - \dfrac{4m}{3} = 5$.

$$\frac{9m}{6} - \frac{8m}{6} = 5 \qquad \text{Identity element for multiplication.}$$
$$\frac{m}{6} = 5 \qquad \text{Operation of subtraction.}$$
$$m = 30 \qquad \text{Inverseness of multiplication and division.}$$

There are usually several series of sentences which may be used in the solution of a mathematical sentence. Some are simpler than others. Part of the skill in problem solving is choosing the simplest series of sentences. As you gain more experience in problem solving you will be able to choose economical methods.

The solution, $n = 4$, in Illustration I indicates that 4 is another name for n. By replacing n by 4 in the given sentence $3n - 4 = 8$, the solution may be tested for accuracy. If $n = 4$, then

$$3n - 4 = 8$$

becomes

$$3 \cdot 4 - 4 = 8 \qquad \text{or} \qquad 8 = 8.$$

The other solutions may be tested in a similar way. It is advantageous to check all solutions either in writing or mentally.

EXERCISE SET 10–1

1. Are the following sentences true or false or are they open sentences?
    (a) n is 5 greater than a.
    (b) The sum of a and b is the same as the sum of b and a.
    (c) The sum of the numbers represented by the digits of 25 is the same as the remainder obtained when 25 is divided by 7.
    (d) $\frac{73}{146}$ is a decimal number.
    (e) The square of 9 equals the square root of 81.
    (f) The prime number a is greater than 17.

2. Are the following sentences true or false or are they open sentences?
    (a) $5 + 2 = 7$
    (b) $5^2 - 5 < 4^2 + 4$
    (c) $a > 2 + 7$
    (d) $(5 - 2)(6 - 4) = (a + 8)$
    (e) $\dfrac{a + b}{2} = \dfrac{a}{2} + \dfrac{b}{2}$
    (f) $\dfrac{a}{b} = \dfrac{a}{b} \cdot \dfrac{c}{c}$
    (g) $3a - 7 = 5 \cdot 4$
    (h) $4 + 3a = 12$
    (i) $12 - 2 = 3 \cdot 4 - 1 - 1$
    (j) $3(m + n) = 3m + n$
    (k) $abc = (bc)a$
    (l) $a = \dfrac{c}{b}$

3. What is the verb in each of the sentences below? (In the word sentences choose the verb of the independent clause.)
    (a) A man who lost 31 lb now weighs 207 lb.
    (b) A number is 4 more than twice 23.
    (c) If $\frac{1}{4}$ of a number is decreased by 12, the result is 18.
    (d) The $10-book sells for $3 more than a person has to spend.

4. What is the verb in each of these sentences? (Write the answers in words.)
    (a) $A \supseteq B$
    (b) $C \approx D$
    (c) $E = F$
    (d) $A \cup B \subseteq BC$
    (e) $AB \parallel BC$
    (f) $5 + 9 > 0$
    (g) $a + b \neq c - d$
    (h) $m + n < mn$
    (i) $\dfrac{a}{b} = \dfrac{2a}{2b}$
    (j) $(a + b)7 = 7(a + b)$
    (k) $n(A) = 5$
    (l) $\dfrac{a}{b} \neq \dfrac{b}{a}$

5. Find n in each of the following. Observe the grouping indicated and the convention for order of operations.
    (a) $n = 5 - 2 + 6 + 3$
    (b) $n = (5 - 2) + (6 + 3)$
    (c) $n = (5 \cdot 2) + (6 \cdot 3)$
    (d) $n = 5(2 + 6)3$
    (e) $n = 6 \cdot 3 + 18 \div 6 \cdot 2 - 1$
    (f) $n = (4 + 3)(5 - 3) + 7$
    (g) $n = 4 + 3 \cdot 5 - 3 + 7$
    (h) $n = (3 + 2)^2 + (3 + 2^2)$

6. State the property which made it possible to rewrite the first sentence as the second sentence in each of the following.
    (a) $12 = 5a;\ \frac{12}{5} = a$
    (b) $n - 3 = 7;\ n = 7 + 3$
    (c) $2(3 + 4n) - 7 = 12 - 7;\ 2(3 + 4n) = 12$
    (d) $\dfrac{2}{5} + \dfrac{a}{3} = 7;\ \dfrac{6}{15} + \dfrac{5a}{15} = 7$

(e) $2(3 + 4n) = 12; 6 + 8n = 12$

(f) $15 = \dfrac{3 + 12x}{3}; 15 = 1 + 4x$

(g) $15 = 2a + (5a - 2); 15 = (2a + 5a) - 2$

(h) $m + 3m = 20; 4m = 20$

7. For each sentence in the column on the left choose, from the column on the right, a sentence (or sentences) which is a different form of the same sentence. State the property which makes it possible for both sentences to express the same relationship.

(a) $7 + a = 25$ $A = 18$
(b) $5a = 25$ $a = 25$
(c) $30 \div 3a = 37$
(d) $3(4 + a) = 27$
(e) $30 + 3a = 5a + 8a$
(f) $\dfrac{14a + 8}{2} = 24$

(1) $13a = 30 + 3a$
(2) $a = 5$
(3) $7a + 4 = 24$
(4) $12 + 3a = 27$
(5) $a = 25 - 7$
(6) $3a = 7$
(7) $14a + 8 = 48$
(8) $4 + a = 9$
(9) $25 = a + 7$

8. Use the property indicated to rewrite the mathematical sentence preceding it.

(a) $5a = 15$ — Inverseness of multiplication and division.

(b) $\dfrac{12a + 3}{3} = 7.$ — Distributive property for division.

(c) $4a + 1 = 7$ — Cancellation property for addition.

(d) $a - 5 = 4$ — Inverseness of addition and subtraction.

(e) $2a + 9 = 15$ — Inverseness of addition and subtraction.

(f) $25 = 3(2a + 7) - 4$ — Distributive property for multiplication.

(g) $3a + 4a = 9 + 19$ — Renaming by operation of addition.

(h) $\dfrac{2a}{3} - \dfrac{a}{2} = 2$ — Identity element for multiplication.

9. Rewrite the following sentences in two simpler ways. State the property which makes it possible to write each new sentence.

(a) $7 = a + 3 + 2$

(b) $5a - 2a = 27$

(c) $16 = 2(3a + 5)$

(d) $\dfrac{3}{4} = \dfrac{2a}{3}$

(e) $28 = 3a + a$

(f) $5a + 4a = 20 + 4a$

(g) $\dfrac{12a + 6}{2} = 8$

(h) $2a - 5 = 13$

10. The solutions of four mathematical sentences are given below. For each step state a property which made it possible to rewrite the previous sentence.

(a) $8 = 2a + 5$
　(1) $3 + 5 = 2a + 5$
　(2) $\quad 3 = 2a$
　(3) $\quad a = \frac{3}{2}$

(b) $2(b + 4) = 26$
　(1) $2b + 8 = 26$
　(2) $2b + 8 = 18 + 8$
　(3) $\quad 2b = 18$
　(4) $\quad b = 9$

(c) $\dfrac{15a + 12}{3} - 2 = 3a + 2$

(1) $5a + 4 - 2 = 3a + 2$
(2) $ 5a + 2 = 3a + 2$
(3) $2a + 3a + 2 = 3a + 2$
(4) $ 2a + 2 = 2$
(5) $ 2a = 0$
(6) $ a = 0$

(d) $\dfrac{3a}{2} + a = 10$

(1) $\dfrac{3a}{2} + \dfrac{2a}{2} = 10$

(2) $\dfrac{5a}{2} = 10$

(3) $5a = 20$

(4) $a = 4$

11. Solve each of the mathematical sentences below by applying the properties of mathematics which you know.

(a) $\dfrac{12a + 15}{3} = 21$

(b) $6b = 10$

(c) $6c = 10 + c$

(d) $12 + 3n = 72$

(e) $7(4 + 8a) - 3 = 6a + 75$

(f) $\dfrac{3m}{4} = 9$

(g) $7b - 4 = 24$

(h) $5a - 2a = 7a - 6a + 16$

(i) $15 = 2d + (d + 3)$

(j) $8(m + 3) = 88$

(k) $n - 9 = 15$

(l) $5a - 2a = \frac{3}{2}$

12. Check each of the mathematical sentences below against the solution given. State whether the solution is correct. If it is not, find the correct solution.

(a) $5b + 3 = 18$
    Answer: $b = 2$

(b) $5(b + 8) = b + 40$
    Answer: $b = 0$

(c) $36 = b + b + b$
    Answer: $b = 12$

(d) $18 = \dfrac{20b + 10}{5}$
    Answer: $b = 2$

(e) $b + \frac{2}{3} = \frac{2}{3}$
    Answer: $b = 1$

(f) $12b - 8b = 3b - 2b + 120$
    Answer: $b = 40$

(g) $\dfrac{b}{2} + \dfrac{3b}{4} = 20$
    Answer: $b = 16$

(h) $24 = 3b + 3$
    Answer: $b = 9$

(i) $\frac{2}{9}b = \frac{8}{3}$
    Answer: $b = 12$

(j) $m + 12 = 5m - 12$
    Answer: $m = 0$

9. THE ESSENCE OF A PROBLEM EXPRESSED IN A WORD SENTENCE

This section and the following sections will provide examples that illustrate the four steps in problem solving, identify difficulties, and suggest helpful techniques.

Statement of the problem. The first step in problem solving is the identification and statement of the essence of the problem in a clear concise word sentence. The word sentence may be verbalized, i.e., spoken or written, or it may exist in the form of mental awareness. If you are not skilled in problem solving, you will find that writing word sentences which express the relationship existing among the numbers in problems is helpful in the development of a problem-solving technique. However, the writing of the word sentence should soon cease.

The word sentence is formulated by isolating all pertinent data and eliminating all unnecessary data. This demands that the problem be thoroughly understood. The basic idea in a problem may emerge from answers to questions such as, What question is asked in the problem? What data are given? Are all the given data necessary? Are there sufficient data? How are the data related? Is a diagram needed to determine relationships? Can all the necessary data and the unknown be expressed in a clear concise word sentence?

Illustrations of problems and their word sentences. Note that some problems are themselves word sentences describing the essence of the problem, e.g., Problem A below; others are more complicated.

PROBLEM A: How long is an 8-furlong race in miles?

This problem is itself a clear concise statement of the relationship of the data given. (You will need additional information, however, to solve the problem.) Other problems require very little simplification. Consider this example.

PROBLEM B: If a rocket travels 400 miles in two minutes, what is its speed in miles per second?

The problem has no unnecessary facts. It involves three quantities, speed, distance, and time. The speed is unknown in the problem, the distance is 400 miles, and the time is 2 minutes, or 120 seconds. The essence of the problem may then be stated as, "What is the speed of a rocket which travels 400 miles in 2×60 seconds?"

Statements of other problems require more study. They may require one or all of the following procedures: the separation of the problem into parts; a restatement of part or all of the problem; a recall of the definition of terms and of mathematical ideas involved; a diagram to identify the relationship of the elements; or a reconsideration of the question. For example,

PROBLEM C: A rocket traveling at 18,000 miles per hour can take a photograph of an 1800-mile arc of the earth's horizon from an altitude of 450 miles. What is the minimum number of shots required to photograph the entire circumference at the equator?

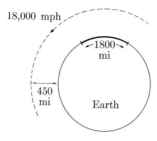

18,000 mph

1800 mi

450 mi

Earth

FIGURE 10–1

This problem is not itself a concise statement. It may be necessary to read the problem several times and to consider carefully the question asked. It may occur to you to draw a diagram similar to Fig. 10–1.

A study of the diagram reveals the data that are needed. It is not necessary to know that the rocket is moving at a speed of 18,000 miles per hour or that it has an altitude of 450 miles. Omitting these data, we restate the problem as "A rocket can take a photograph of an 1800-mile arc of the earth's horizon. What is the minimum number of shots required to photograph the entire circumference at the equator?"

If you have no simple statement ready at this point, further study of Fig. 10–1 may reveal that some additional information is needed. Once the circumference of the earth at the equator is identified as approximately 25,000 miles, you may restate the problem including this information. The essence of the problem is a word sentence similar to: How many 1800-mile arcs are there in the 25,000-mile circumference of the earth?

10. TRANSLATING WORD SENTENCES INTO MATHEMATICAL SENTENCES

The act of translating the essence of a problem into a word sentence was discussed and illustrated in Section 9. When the word sentence is stated, the words are then changed to mathematical symbols and a mathematical sentence is created. For example, Problem A is a simple word sentence itself. The translation may be made as follows.

PROBLEM A: How long is an 8-furlong race in miles?
$$\begin{array}{cccc} \downarrow & \downarrow & \downarrow & \downarrow \\ n & = & 8 & \times & \frac{1}{8} \end{array}$$

The word statements of Problems B and C may be translated similarly.

PROBLEM B: What is the speed . . . travels 400 miles in 2 · 60 seconds?

$$n \;=\; \qquad\qquad 400 \;\div\; 2 \cdot 60$$

PROBLEM C: What is . . . number of 1800-mile arcs in 25,000 . . . of earth?

$$n \;=\; \qquad 25,000 \;\div\; 1800$$

In Problems D, E, and F below it is left for you to identify the word sentences and the mathematical sentences which express the essence of the problems. (The complete solution of the problems will be discussed in later sections.)

PROBLEM D: The highest point on the earth is Mt. Everest at 29,028 feet and the lowest is the Dead Sea at 1286 feet below sea level. The highest point in the United States is Mt. McKinley, Alaska, at 20,320 feet and the lowest is Death Valley at 282 feet below sea level. What is the difference in altitude of the highest point on the earth and the highest point in the United States?

PROBLEM E: At the beginning of a trip the odometer reads 25,782 and at the end it reads 26,276. If the automobile has been traveling for 8 hours and 30 minutes, what was the average speed?

PROBLEM F: A retailer advertises a reduction of 50% on all coats, 25% on all shoes, and 10% on all other items. What was the original marked price of a dress whose sale tag reads $31.95?

11. THE USE OF FORMULAS IN PROBLEM SOLVING

A knowledge of formulas and their use facilitates the processes of translating the ideas of problems into mathematical sentences and of finding the solution to the problems. The more formulas you know, the greater is your problem-solving potential.

Formulas are mathematical sentences which may be used for many problems. For example, the formula $d = rt$ was a model for the formulation of the mathematical sentences in both Problems B and E. You will find that it is applicable to a wide range of problems. The value of this and other formulas will be apparent as you work through the problem sets of this chapter.

EXERCISE SET 10–2

1. Assume that each of the following concise word statements expresses the main mathematical idea of a problem. Write a word problem corresponding to each of these statements. (Study the example given.)

EXAMPLE

Word statement: Find the average of 64 numbers, given that their sum is 16,000.

Problem (one of many): Sixty-four newsboys sold 16,000 papers in one day. What was the average number sold by each?

(a) What number is 3 more than twice 18?

(b) 80% of an amount is $750. What is the amount?

(c) If two numbers are in the ratio of 3 to 5 and the larger number is 12, what is the other number?

(d) If 6 is subtracted from a number, the result is 10.

(e) What will it cost to varnish the floor of a 15 ft by 30 ft room if a pint of $1.20 varnish covers 50 sq ft?

2. Assume that each of the following concise word statements expresses the main mathematical idea of a problem. Write a word problem corresponding to each of these statements.

(a) How many $\frac{2}{3}$-gal containers can be filled from 50 gal of liquid?

(b) What is $4\frac{1}{2}$% of $5000?

(c) If $\frac{1}{4}$, then $\frac{5}{16}$, then $\frac{1}{8}$, and then $\frac{1}{8}$ of $7280 is used and the rest is saved, how much money is saved?

(d) If a train traveled a distance of 480 mi in $7\frac{1}{2}$ hr, what was its speed?

(e) How much is left from $4498 if 57 items are purchased at $52 each?

3. Write a mathematical sentence for each part of Exercise 1. Solve each.

4. Write a mathematical sentence for each part of Exercise 2. Solve each.

5. State the essence of each of the following in a clear concise sentence.

(a) A clothing store paid $214.71 for electric current. This was $33.33 more than was budgeted for it. How much did the budget earmark for electric current?

(b) A firm made a gross profit of $\frac{1}{4}$ of its receipt of sales. If the gross profit was $247,000, what was the receipt of sales?

(c) It is estimated that in a certain hatchery 80% of the eggs placed in an incubator hatch. How many eggs must be placed in an incubator to fill an order for 1000 chicks?

(d) The price of a share of stock decreased from 48 to 42. Express the decrease in percent.

(e) Two men are paid a salary of $500 per month. *A*'s salary was first raised 10% and later lowered 10%. *B*'s salary was first lowered 10% and then raised 10%. What is the difference in their present salaries?

6. State the essence of each of the following in a clear concise sentence.

(a) The circumference of an automobile tire is 85 in. How many revolutions will it make during a 500-mi trip?

(b) Each of the 45 girls in a club is given a badge made from a 4-in. piece of ribbon. The ribbon sells for 45 cents a yard. What is the total cost of the ribbon?

(c) It is recommended that a classroom of a particular department provide 15 sq ft of floor space for each student. How many students will a room 24 ft by 40 ft accommodate?

(d) At the price of 3 for 25 cents, what will two dozen bars of soap cost?

(e) At the beginning of a 750-mi trip, the odometer of an automobile reads 12,062. The automobile stopped because the gas tank was empty when the odometer read 12,406. If the 16-gal gas tank was full at the beginning of the trip, how many miles per gallon was the car averaging?

7. Write a mathematical sentence for each of the word sentences you wrote for Exercise 5. Solve each.

8. Write a mathematical sentence for each of the word sentences you wrote for Exercise 6. Solve each.

9. Write each of the following mathematical sentences as a word sentence. (Study the example.)

EXAMPLE

Mathematical sentence: $5x - 3 = 2 + x$.
Word sentence: Five times a number less 3 is the same as two more than the number.

(a) $\frac{1}{2}x + 5 = 7$ (b) $x - \frac{1}{5} \cdot 75 = 43$ (c) $\dfrac{15 + 27}{2} = x + 6$

(d) $\dfrac{5}{2} = \dfrac{x}{10}$ (e) $4x = \frac{1}{2} \cdot 18$ (f) $25 = 7x - 4$

10. Solve each of the mathematical sentences of Exercise 9.

11. Sketch a diagram to help you understand each of the following problems.

(a) The circumference of an automobile tire is 85 in. How many revolutions will it make during a 500-mi trip?

(b) It is recommended that a classroom of a particular department of a school provide 15 sq ft of floor space for each student. How many students will a room 24 ft by 40 ft accommodate?

12. Write a problem for which each of the following mathematical sentences may express the main idea.

(a) $5x = 125$ (b) $x = \frac{1}{4} \cdot 92$
(c) $\frac{2}{3}x = 12,988$ (d) $x + 250 = 1175$
(e) $n + 2n = 42$ (f) $x - (5 \cdot 3 + 4 \cdot 5) = 5$

13. From the formulas listed below, choose one which will serve as a model for a mathematical sentence for each of the following problems. Use the formula and write a mathematical sentence for each problem. Given formulas:

$$A = lw; \qquad P = 2l + 2w; \qquad C = \tfrac{5}{9}(F - 32)$$
$$i = prt; \qquad c = 2\pi r \quad (\pi = 3.14)$$

(a) The thermometer in the United States reads 77°. How should I change this reading so that my friend in France will understand it?

(b) What is the distance around a rectangular field which is 100 yd long and 75 yd wide?

(c) What is the area of the field in (b)?

(d) What is the circumference of a circle which has a diameter of 14 ft?

(e) What is the interest I must pay on a $3000 loan each month, given that the rate is 6%?

14. Write a word sentence which means the same as each of the five formulas of Exercise 13.

15. (a) Find and list three other formulas from the area of science or mathematics or from your own experience.

 (b) Write the meaning of each of these in a word sentence.

 (c) Write two problems which require the use of each of the formulas.

16. Find and list four formulas found in previous chapters of this book. Explain their meaning by translating them into a word sentence.

12. USE OF MATHEMATICAL SENTENCES IN PROBLEM SOLVING

Once the essence of the problem situation is understood and the word sentence and the mathematical sentence are written, the plan for a solution is implied. The mathematical sentence identifies this plan. The complete process of deducing the value of the unknown from the sentence was described in Section 3 and shortened in Section 7. The mathematical sentence is solved by a deductive procedure which consists of a successive rewriting of the sentence until it is of the form $n = a$.

In Problem D, Section 10, the sentence

$$f = 29{,}028 - 20{,}320$$

clearly indicates a plan for rewriting the sentence. The number f is found by performing the subtraction $29{,}028 - 20{,}320$.

PROBLEM D: $\qquad\qquad\qquad\qquad f = 29{,}028 - 20{,}320,$

$\qquad\qquad\qquad\qquad\qquad\quad f = 8708.$

The sentence,

$$31.95 = a - .10a$$

of Problem F does not indicate a plan as clearly as D does, but a plan is there to be followed. Whereas the plan for Problem D is one step, that for Problem F consists of two steps. First, the number $a - .10a$ may be renamed by performing the subtraction, $a - .10a = .90a$. The sentence

$\qquad 31.95 = a - .10a \qquad$ is rewritten as $\qquad 31.95 = .90a.$

This form of the sentence implies the second step, the use of the inverse of multiplication to find the missing factor a. Upon division, $a = 35.50$.

PROBLEM F: $\qquad\qquad\qquad\qquad 31.95 = a - .10a,$

$\qquad\qquad\qquad\qquad\qquad 31.95 = .90a,$

$\qquad\qquad\qquad\qquad\qquad 35.50 = a.$

These examples, and others which may be examined, show that the value of mathematical sentences lies not only in the simplicity with which they express the essence of a problem but in their ability to suggest a plan for the solution of the problem.

13. USING THE SOLUTION OF MATHEMATICAL SENTENCES

A problem asks a question about a number or about several numbers. This number, or the principal number among several, is symbolized in the mathematical sentence as n or some other letter of the alphabet. The object of solving a mathematical sentence is to identify the number called the unknown which n represents, say, $n = 8$. Once the unknown has been identified, the question asked in the problem may be answered.

Thus Problem D asked, "What is the difference in altitude of the highest point on the earth and the highest point in the United States?" When the mathematical sentence was formulated and solved, the result was the sentence $f = 8708$. The question in the problem may now be answered:

"The highest point on the earth is 8708 feet higher than the highest point in the United States."

In Problem F, it was found that $a = 35.50$. The question, "What was the marked price of a dress whose sale tag reads "$31.95?," may now be answered,

"The marked price of the dress was $35.50."

Note that a mathematical sentence removes numbers from a problem situation and presents them in a mathematical setting. However, to answer the question asked in the problem, the number which is the solution of a mathematical sentence is returned to the problem situation.

You should find the mathematical solution for Problems A, B, and C and use the solution to answer the question asked in the problems.

14. EXAMINING THE PROBLEM AS A WHOLE

When the question asked in a problem has been answered, the entire problem situation should be examined. The purpose of this step, Step (4) (Section 3), is to determine whether the complete data which now include the solution fit the pattern of the problem. Questions which help one make this check are, "Is the question in the problem answered?," "Is it a reasonable answer?," "Do the data fit in with the complete situation of the problem?"

For example, in Problem F the answer, "The marked price of the dress was $35.50," is examined to determine whether it is compatible with the problem. The price of $35.50 is a reasonable price. The data fit in with the complete problem situation.

15. WRITTEN FORM OF PROBLEM SOLUTIONS; EXAMPLES

The written form for problem solving includes fewer steps than the general plan for problem solving described in Section 3. The written form may or may not include the first step. It may be omitted by a skillful problem solver. The written form does not include Step (4), an examination of the problem and its data as a whole. Step (4) is a mental step.

Examples of the written form of two problems follow the statements of the problem below. Each written form is supplemented by some comments which help identify procedures that are not recorded.

PROBLEM G: A rectangular lot, 72 yards by 65 yards, is to be fertilized with a brand of fertilizer that recommends a 22-pound bag for each 5500 square-foot area. If the bags sell for $4.35 each, what will it cost to fertilize the lot?

Written form
(1) Word sentence: What is the cost of fertilizing a 72 by 65 yard lot if each 5500 square-foot area requires a bag of fertilizer and each bag costs $4.35?
(2) Mathematical sentence:

$$\frac{(72 \times 65) \times 9}{5500} \times 4.35 = c,$$

$$8 \times 4.35 = c,$$

$$c = 34.80.$$

(3) Answer to question in problem: The eight bags of fertilizer required for the lot will cost $34.80.

Comments: There are at least three points at which a person solving this problem might pause for thought. First, he might pause in the formulation of the word sentence describing the essence of the problem. The weight, 22 pounds, of the bag of fertilizer must be identified as excess data. Second, he might pause in the formulation of the mathematical sentence. The area of the lot must be changed from square yards to square feet in order to determine the number of 5500 square-foot regions in the lot. Third, he might pause before deciding that the number of bags of fertilizer must be rounded to a whole number since only whole bags may be purchased.

PROBLEM H: John picked twice as many strawberries as Mike, and Sam picked as many as John and Mike together. The boys picked 180 quarts. How many quarts did each boy pick?

Written form
   (1) Word sentence: Of the 180 quarts of berries, John picked twice as many as Mike, and Sam picked as many as John and Mike together. How many quarts did each boy pick?
   (2) Mathematical sentence:

$$180 = 2a + a + 3a,$$
$$180 = 6a,$$
$$a = 30.$$

   (3) Answer to question in problem: John picked 60 quarts, Mike picked 30 quarts, and Sam picked 90 quarts of strawberries.

Comments: Once the essence of the problem has been stated as a word sentence, a decision has to be made concerning the amount of strawberries picked by a particular boy which will serve as basis of comparison. There are several ways of writing the mathematical sentence depending on which boy's work is chosen as a basis of comparison. Since the amount of John's work is compared to Mike's, and Sam's is then compared to that of both of the other boys, it is simplest to think of Mike picking a quarts of berries. When this is decided upon, the word sentence tells you that 180 is the sum of "twice a," and "a," and "twice a and a." In mathematical sentence form this is $180 = 2a + a + 3a$.

16. DISCOVERING PROBLEM-SOLVING TECHNIQUES THROUGH THE STUDY OF PROBLEM SOLUTIONS

   Problem solving is a learned skill, learned as problems are solved. Further improvement can result, however, from the study of completed solutions as well as the study of mathematics. After a solution is understood, answers to questions similar to those listed below will help you identify problem-solving techniques.

   What were the essential steps in the solution? Are they steps that I should remember to use in other problems?

   What were the nonessential steps? How can I avoid nonessential steps?

   Is this problem similar to others I have solved? Is it one which falls into a pattern? Is there a model I should remember and use in other problems of this type?

Is this problem different from others I have solved? Did it require a different technique? If so, is it one I should remember?

Is there another way of solving the problem? If so, how do the solutions compare? Which method is better for me and why?

Can I solve a similar problem more easily after studying this solution? Why?

What guides do the answers to the preceding questions give me for solving problems?

Answers to questions similar to the above, especially the answer to the last question, result in an expanding set of techniques which in turn increase your ability to solve problems.

17. USING PROBLEM-SOLVING PATTERN

Flexibility within a problem-solving pattern. The four-step pattern of problem solving suggested in this chapter is not assumed to be *the* procedure but it is considered *a* recommended plan for solving most problems. As you develop skill, you will find that you can omit steps, e.g., the formulation of the word sentence, and that other steps merge into a workable procedure of your own design. It is recommended, however, that the pattern of problem solving suggested be used until some degree of skill is developed and that the pattern not be discarded but kept in reserve for problems which present difficulty.

There is really no detailed set of rules which can be provided to solve all problems. A general pattern as the one suggested may be followed, but within that plan, flexibility is demanded by the very nature of problems.

Problems differ in the relationships of the numbers involved. As the relationships differ, so do the details within a plan for solving the problems. However, you will find that with an adequate background in mathematics and experience in problem solving these relationships are easily identified. Knowledge and experience make problems fall into groups which present similar mathematical relationships and require similar plans of solution.

Problems also differ with respect to the situation which they describe. A problem may involve the speed of a rocket, an automobile, or a snail; it may involve the cost of several similar garments, the total number of cans in five cartons, or the length, in miles, of 12 furlongs. In each of these examples the mathematical model $a = bc$ is needed, but the data to be used must be separated from the sentences which compose the problem. There is no one detailed plan to follow as the data and their relationship are identified. Each problem must be considered individually within a general plan.

Attitude of a problem solver. Some people solve problems for enjoyment and satisfaction; all of us solve problems from necessity. Whatever the reason, it is an activity which requires our total attention and our concern or desire to find the answer to the question raised in the problem.

Most problems are not solved by one trial and no errors. Many plans may suggest themselves. If the first is successful, or even the second, you are lucky. Problem solving requires some determination, willingness to persevere, and acceptance of some failures along with successes.

Knowledge and experience. The more is known of the situation of the problem and of mathematical concepts involved, the easier the task of problem solving. You bring to the problem knowledge of the situation and of mathematics. This knowledge is helpful to each step of a general procedure.

The experience gained from solving many problems and analyzing their solutions increases your skill and hence your success. You will recognize similar patterns and use model sentences; you will identify analogous problems; and you will encounter familiar obstacles in the process. But since you have overcome these obstacles in problems you have solved, there will be no discouragement. Indeed, you may draw on your past experiences to master present difficulties. The value of past experience to problem solving cannot be overestimated.

EXERCISE SET 10–3

1. Each problem below has been partially solved, and the solution to its mathematical sentence is given. Use this solution to answer the question asked in the problem. (Answer in complete sentences.)
   (a) One number is twice another. Their sum is two more than twice their difference. What is the smaller number? $n = 2$.
   (b) A book containing 360 pages is $\frac{5}{8}$ in. thick. What is the thickness of each sheet? $n = \frac{1}{576}$.
   (c) A family with an income of \$6500 spends $\frac{1}{4}$ of it for food, $\frac{1}{5}$ for rent, $\frac{3}{20}$ for operating expenses, $\frac{1}{5}$ for clothing; the remainder is available for miscellaneous expenses and savings. What part of the income remains for the last category? $p = \frac{1}{5}$.
   (d) If tomatoes average 4 to the pound, approximately how many pounds can be sold from a bin containing 300 tomatoes? $a = 75$.
   (e) Several years ago the average rent in a certain apartment building was \$62. Since that time rents have increased 120%. What is the average rent for one of the apartments today? $p = 136.40$.

(f) What is the weekly production of an automobile plant which published data indicating that an automobile was completed every 4 min? Assume that the plant operates each hour of the day. $a = 2520$.

2. Answers are given to the questions in each of the following problems. Check each to find whether it is reasonable. If it is not, explain why.

(a) An object traveling at 138.45 ft/sec overtakes another object traveling 129.54 ft/sec. How far apart are they one minute after one passes the other? (The objects will be 534.6 ft apart one minute after they pass each other.)

(b) A room is $18\frac{2}{3}$ ft long and $12\frac{5}{12}$ ft wide. Find its perimeter. (The perimeter of the room is $31\frac{1}{12}$ ft.)

(c) A salesman sells an item for $3.50. He earns a 20% commission. How many items must he sell if he wishes to earn a commission of $56 per week? (The salesman must sell 80 items each week to earn a commission of $56.)

(d) If 12 pages of a book are read in 3 min, and this rate is maintained, how long will it take to read an 844-page book? (It will take 3 hr 31 min to read an 844-page book.)

(e) Two parcels of fencing, one 450 ft long and the other 50 ft long, were purchased to enclose a lot. When building the fence, the contractor found that 15 ft more fencing was needed. How many feet of material were actually needed for the fence? (485 ft of fencing were needed to build the fence.)

3. Solve the following problems.

(a) A college student needed to save $500 during vacation. He banked $56 in June, $225 in July, and $100 in the first half of August. How much does he still need to reach his goal?

(b) A book of 688 pages has 16 chapters. How many pages does each chapter contain on the average?

(c) An article whose price was reduced by $\frac{1}{3}$ sold for $62. What was the price before reduction?

(d) A salesman receives a salary of $300 a month and a commission of 4% on his sales. He sells $49,080 worth of goods in a year. What is his annual income?

4. Solve the following problems.

(a) A mixture of milk, water, and sugar is made up of 24 oz of milk, 11 oz of water, and 1 oz of sugar. What part of the mixture is milk?

(b) Light travels approximately 186,000 mi/sec. Find the distance traveled by a ray of light in one year.

(c) There were 2,800,000 passenger automobiles sold in the United States in 1930 and 4,200,000 in 1958. What was the percent increase in sales in 1958?

(d) A rocket on its way to the sun passed the moon. Assuming that the earth, sun, and moon are in a straight line, and that the sun is 93,000,000 mi from the earth and the moon is 240,000 mi from the earth, determine what part of the trip to the sun a rocket had completed when it passed the moon.

5. Solve the following problems.

   (a) If a man walks on the average $2\frac{1}{2}$ mi per day, how far will he have walked if he lives to be 70 years old, and had begun to walk at age 2?

   (b) Water expands about $\frac{1}{10}$ of its volume upon freezing. Given that one cubic foot of water weighs approximately 62.5 lb, find the approximate weight of one cubic foot of ice.

   (c) The distance from the earth to the moon is 240,000 mi. How many miles per hour would an object have to move to get to the moon and back again in 30 days?

   (d) A 200-lb man gained 10% in weight in one month and then lost 10% in weight in the succeeding month. What was his weight at the end of the second month?

6. Examine the solutions below and answer the questions (a) through (d).

    PROBLEM I. An automobile traveled 380 mi in 8 hr. What was its average speed?

Solution (i)	Solution (ii)
Word sentence: The distance of 380 mi traveled is 8 times the average speed of the automobile.	*Word sentence:* The average number of miles traveled in one hour is $\frac{1}{8}$ of 380 mi.
Mathematical sentence (i): $$380 = 8a.$$	*Mathematical sentence* (ii): $$a = \frac{1}{8} \cdot 380.$$
Solution to sentence (i): $$a = 47\frac{1}{2}.$$	*Solution to sentence* (ii): $$a = 47\frac{1}{2}.$$

    Answer to question in the problem. The average speed of the automobile was $47\frac{1}{2}$ mi/hr.

   (a) Which of the given plans might you have used to solve Problem I, (i) or (ii)? Why?

   (b) What do the two numbers, 380 and $8a$, of sentence (i) have in common (other than being equal) as they relate to the problem?

   (c) What do the two numbers, a and $\frac{1}{8} \cdot 380$, have in common (other than being equal) as they relate to the problem?

   (d) Using your answer to (b) and (c), explain why both solutions to the problem are correct.

7. Examine the solutions below and answer the questions which follow the solutions.

    PROBLEM II. A college student spends $24 of his weekly allowance of $36 for board and room. If he spends an average of one-half of the rest of his allowance for clothing, what part (fraction) is available for miscellaneous expenses?

Solution (i)	Solution (ii)
Word sentence (i): The student spends \$24 of his allowance of \$36 and then $\frac{1}{2}$ of what is left; the remaining allowance is a part of \$36 and is used for miscellaneous expenses.	*Word sentence* (ii): The part that \$24 is of \$36, and the part that \$36 less \$24 is of \$36, and the part used for miscellaneous expenses constitute one whole of the allowance.
Mathematical sentence (i): $36 - 24 - \frac{1}{2}(36 - 24) = n \cdot 36.$	*Mathematical sentence* (ii): $\dfrac{24}{36} + \dfrac{\frac{1}{2}(36 - 24)}{36} + n = 1.$
Solution to sentence (i): $12 - 6 = n \cdot 36,$ $6 = 36n,$ $n = \frac{6}{36},$ $n = \frac{1}{6}.$	*Solution to sentence* (ii): $\frac{2}{3} + \frac{6}{36} + n = 1,$ $n = 1 - \frac{2}{3} - \frac{1}{6},$ $n = \frac{1}{6}.$

Answer to question in problem. The student had $\frac{1}{6}$ of his allowance of \$36 left for miscellaneous expenses.

(a) Which of the plans might you have used to solve Problem II, (i) or (ii)? Why?

(b) What do the four numbers,

$$36, \qquad 24, \qquad \tfrac{1}{2}(36 - 24), \qquad \text{and} \qquad n \cdot 36,$$

of mathematical sentence (i) have in common as they relate to the problem?

(c) What do these four numbers,

$$\tfrac{24}{36}, \qquad \frac{\frac{1}{2}(36 - 24)}{36}, \qquad n, \qquad \text{and} \qquad 1,$$

of mathematical sentence (ii) have in common as they relate to the problem?

(d) Using your answers to (b) and (c), explain why both solutions to the problem are correct.

8. Why do you think that two people might choose different plans for solving these or any other problems?

9. Solve each of the following problems and then answer questions (a) through (c).

(i) An employee of a firm was given a 15% salary increase effective at once and was promised an increase of 10% in 3 months and another increase of 15% in 6 months. What will his salary be next week if he is earning \$125 now.

(ii) A firm sold $3\frac{1}{2}$ cartons each containing 1728 objects. The objects were sold at \$24 per gross. What was the bill for the sale?

(iii) An article was purchased at $524 in a state which collects a sales tax of $2\frac{1}{2}\%$. If a luxury tax of 10% was also collected, what was the total amount paid by the customer?

(a) Are there insufficient data in any of the problems? What are they?

(b) Are there excess data in any of the problems? What are they?

(c) Are there just sufficient data in any of the problems?

10. (a) Classify the problems involving mathematics which you encounter out of school as having excess data, insufficient data, or just enough data.

(b) What effect does the amount of data have on the ease with which problems are solved?

11. Solve the following problem. Use a diagram to help you in the solution.

The goal of a firm is to increase its sales by 20%. The sales for this year are $92,545. What is the goal for next year?

12. Solve the following problem. Show how an analogous problem may be of help in the solution.

A trip by sea is 460 nautical miles. Translate this distance into statute miles. (A nautical mile is 1.15 statute miles.)

13. Solve the problem below. Show how the substitution of a simpler situation may be of help in the solution.

The Department of Agriculture estimated that 97,481,200 acres of wheat were harvested in the United States during a recent year. Given that the average yield was 15 bushels to the acre and the average price paid the farmer was $1.71 per bushel, find the value of the crop.

14. Explain how diagrams, analogous problems, and simpler situations help you plan the solution of a problem.

15. What is the significance of the expression, "It is easy if you know," in problem solving?

EXERCISE SET 10-4 (SUPPLEMENTARY)

Use the most effective and efficient procedure of problem solving that you know, to solve the following.

1. A recipe received from a friend directs you to bake a roast at 150°C. At what temperature should you set an oven manufactured for use in the United States?

2. If a man can walk one mile in $\frac{1}{4}$ hr, how far can he walk in $2\frac{1}{2}$ hr?

3. If the average playing time for 518 long-playing records is 55 min, and you are able to listen two hours per day, how many days will it take to listen to each record once?

4. One box weighs $15\frac{1}{2}$ lb more than another. Together they weigh $73\frac{5}{8}$ lb. What is the weight of each box?

5. How many cups of coffee can be served from the 2,700,000,000 lb of coffee imported into the United States in a recent year, given that one pound makes 55 cups of coffee?

6. The annual profit in a business was $36,000. Mr. *A* has $37,500, Mr. *B* has $30,000, and Mr. *C* has $22,500 invested in the business. If the profits are distributed according to the amount each partner has invested, what is Mr. *A*'s share of the annual profit?

7. If a train averages 48 mi/hr between two cities that are 376 mi apart, how many hours will it take to make the trip?

8. Fifteen of 24 students were present one day. Eight were absent because of illness. What percent of the class was absent?

9. According to the label, a large can of orange juice contains 36 fluid ounces. How many pints does it contain?

10. A basketball team won 12 games and lost 8. What part of their games was won?

11. Three pieces of wire measuring 2.2, 7.8, and 9.2 in. were cut from a piece 40.5 in. long. How much wire was left?

12. In 1950 the population of a town was 2000, in 1955 it was 3500, and in 1960 it was 6500. What was the percent increase from 1950 to 1960?

13. A man traveled 256.4 mi in 2.5 hr. At this same rate, how far can he travel in 18 hr?

14. What is the weight of the water which fills a 72 cubic-foot tank?

15. A rectangular park, 725 yd by 650 yd, is to be fertilized with a brand of fertilizer that recommends a 22-lb bag for 5000 sq ft. If bags sell at $4.35 each, what will it cost to fertilize the park?

16. Three chickens which were marked $3\frac{1}{2}$ lb, $2\frac{3}{4}$ lb, and $3\frac{1}{4}$ lb were purchased for $3.61. Disregarding any tax, determine the price of the chicken per pound.

17. In a recent year 5,532,572 gal of gasoline were used in the state of California. If the federal government collected $.04/gal and the state collected $.06/gal, what was the total tax collected on the gasoline?

18. If a family buys on the average 3 gal of milk every two days and 3 pt of cream each week, what is the annual bill for these items if milk is selling at $.90 per gallon and cream at $.38 per half-pint?

19. How many cartons of 9 in. by 9 in. floor tile must be purchased to cover the floor of a 14 ft by 20 ft room, given that a carton contains 48 tiles?

20. The sum of three consecutive even numbers is 72. What are the numbers?

21. *A* is 6 years older than *B*. The sum of their ages will double in 22 years. How old are they today?

22. A 24-in. length of ribbon can be cut into three pieces so that one piece is three times as long as the shortest piece, and the longest piece is four times as long as the shortest piece. What is the length of each of the three pieces?

23. How many days will it take a truck which can haul 5 tons of corn per load and makes 8 trips per day, to haul away the 700,000,000 bushels of corn produced in Iowa in a recent year? One bushel of corn weighs 56 pounds.

24. A certain brand of motor oil is advertised at $.32/qt or $5.95 /5-gal can. How much can be saved on one gallon by purchasing 5 gal at a time?

25. The motor oil of Exercise 24 may also be purchased in a 55-gal drum for $48.95. How much can be saved on 55 gal if the oil is bought by the drum rather than by the quart?

26. A machine can produce 2430 items in 8 hr. Five percent of these must be discarded as waste. How many salable objects can be produced, given that the machine operates 24 hr a day for a year and no time is lost?

27. In the preparation of an invoice for a $1250 item a clerk computed a 40% discount rather than successive discounts of 10% and 30%. What difference did his error make in the amount for which the customer was billed?

28. A small can of vegetables which contains 14 oz sells for $.28 and a large can which contains 32 oz sells for $.56. How much is saved on 32 oz by buying the larger can?

29. A warehouse sold 130 boxes of apples. The bill itemized a price of $7.58 per box, a commission of 5% of the cost of the apples, and an additional $.16 per box for storage. What was the amount due for the 130 boxes of apples?

30. A man is five times as old as his son, and the son is three years younger than a sister. The sum of their ages is 66 years. How old is each?

REFERENCES

Banks, J. Houston, *Learning and Teaching Arithmetic*. Boston: Allyn and Bacon, Inc., 1959, pp. 364–380.

Brumfiel, Charles F., Robert E. Eicholz, and Merrill E. Shanks, *Fundamental Concepts of Elementary Mathematics*. Reading, Massachusetts: Addison-Wesley Publishing Company, Inc., 1962, pp. 226–236.

Johnson, Donovan A., and William H. Glenn, *Exploring Mathematics on Your Own*. Garden City, New York: Doubleday and Company, Inc., 1961, pp. 53–94, 235–274.

Pólya, G., *How to Solve It*. Garden City, New York: Doubleday and Company, Inc., 1957, 253 pp.

Williams, Sammie M., H. Garland Read, Jr., and Frank L. Williams, *Modern Mathematics in the Elementary and Junior High Schools*. Syracuse, New York: The L. W. Singer Company, Inc., 1961, pp. 103–108.

CHAPTER ELEVEN

THE INTEGERS

1. ORIGIN AND IMPORTANCE

The set of whole numbers and the set of fractional numbers have their origin in counting situations. So does the set of integers. It was invented to meet the need to count and measure in whole units with respect to a fixed reference point when the direction of counting or measuring relative to the reference point is important. Examples of such situations are the measurement of temperatures, in degrees, and altitude, in feet. A temperature might be 30 degrees above zero or 30 degrees below zero, and an altitude might be 300 feet above sea level or 300 feet below sea level. If integers are used, the temperatures are written as $^+30$ degrees or $^-30$ degrees and the altitudes as $^+300$ feet or $^-300$ feet. Situations such as these are common both in daily life and in science. They give the integers their practical importance.

The integers will be denoted by

$$\ldots\ ^-2,\ ^-1,\ 0,\ ^+1,\ ^+2,\ \ldots$$

and read: ... "negative two," "negative one," "zero," "positive one," "positive two," ... The superscripts $^-$ and $^+$ describe the relation of the integer to the reference number zero. Pairs of integers such as $^+1$ and $^-1$, or $^+2$ and $^-2$ are said to be *opposite integers*. Thus $^-2$ is the opposite of $^+2$, and $^+2$ is the opposite of $^-2$. Zero is written without a superscript. It is its own opposite.

2. GEOMETRIC REPRESENTATION

The integers may be represented geometrically as shown in Figs. 11–1 and 11–2.

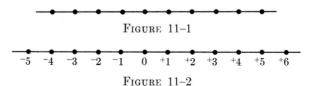

FIGURE 11–1

FIGURE 11–2

In Fig. 11–1, a portion of a straight line is shown, and a distinguished set of points on the line is indicated. These points are represented by equally spaced dots. The points of the distinguished set are such that the segments of the line joining any two adjacent points of the set are congruent to one another.

The points of the distinguished set are labeled as follows. A centrally located dot is chosen and labeled 0. The dots to the right of 0 are labeled successively $^+1$, $^+2$, $^+3$, . . . , and the dots to the left of 0 are labeled successively $^-1$, $^-2$, $^-3$, . . . This labeling is imagined to continue indefinitely; in Fig. 11–2 it is carried as far as is convenient.

Figure 11–2 may be regarded from two viewpoints: on the one hand, it is a *diagram representing integers* and relations among integers; on the other hand, it is a *geometric figure* representing a straight line and a distinguished set of points on this line to each of which a number name has been assigned.

From the first viewpoint, the essential feature of Fig. 11–2 is the fact that the dots are equally spaced. This serves to show that the integers are similar to one another. Any dot could have been labeled 0. Any integer can be obtained from any other integer by proceeding in uniform steps either to the right or to the left. The line is merely a guide which makes the relations among the integers apparent to the eye.

From the second viewpoint, it is the line and the segments of the line which join points of the distinguished set that are essential. The number symbols . . . $^-2$, $^-1$, 0, $^+1$, $^+2$, . . . name the points of the set in a convenient way, but it is the congruent line segments between adjacent points which show geometrically how the distinguished set is constituted.

The first viewpoint is adopted during the discussion of the general properties of the integers in this and the following sections. The second viewpoint is adopted in Section 4 to give another geometric representation of the integers, which is useful in considering the operations of addition and subtraction.

Ordering the integers. Figure 11–2 makes it apparent that the positive integers may be thought of as extending indefinitely to the right of zero, and the negative integers as extending indefinitely to the left of zero. Pairs of opposite integers such as $^-4$ and $^+4$ are represented by pairs of dots spaced symmetrically about zero.

The dots in Fig. 11–2 present themselves to the eye as naturally ordered from left to right. The integers are ordered in the same way: $^+5$ is greater than $^+2$, and $^+2$ is less than $^+5$; $^+2$ is greater than $^-13$ and $^-13$ is less than $^+2$; $^-2$ is greater than $^-5$ and $^-5$ is less than $^-2$. These inequalities may be stated in mathematical sentences:

$$^+5 > {}^+2, \quad ^+2 < {}^+5, \quad ^+2 > {}^-13, \quad ^-13 < {}^+2, \quad ^-2 > {}^-5, \quad ^-5 < {}^-2.$$

The integers are totally ordered, and naturally separate into three disjoint sets: the positive integers, zero, and the negative integers. Zero is less than every positive integer and greater than every negative integer, and any positive integer is greater than any negative integer.

3. COUNTING AND OPERATIONS WITH INTEGERS

Operations on whole numbers. As was shown in Chapter 6, Sections 7 through 12, each of the fundamental operations on whole numbers may be performed by either finding the number of an appropriately selected finite set or by a counting procedure. Consider, for example, the operations of addition and subtraction. The sum $5 + 3$ may be found by starting with 5 and counting forward 6, 7, 8; the difference $5 - 3$ may be found by starting with 5 and counting backward 4, 3, 2. Operations on integers may also be performed by counting. But the fact that counting backward as well as counting forward may be continued indefinitely makes the interpretation of the operations as counting processes more complicated for operations on integers than it was for operations on whole numbers.

Counting with integers. Starting with any integer, $^+3$ for example, one can count forward by ones,

$$^+3, {}^+4, {}^+5, {}^+6, \ldots,$$

or backward by ones,

$$^+3, {}^+2, {}^+1, 0, {}^-1, {}^-2, \ldots,$$

as far as is needed. The counting forward or backward may be done by numbers other than by ones, e.g., forward by fours,

$$^+3, {}^+7, {}^+11, \ldots,$$

or backward by sixes,

$$^+3, {}^-3, {}^-9, {}^-15, \ldots$$

Adding integers by counting. The addition of integers may be thought of as a counting process. For example, the sum $^+5 + {}^+4$ may be thought of as the result of counting forward four from $^+5$:

$$^+5 + {}^+4 = {}^+9.$$

The sum $^+5 + {}^-6$ may be thought of as the result of counting backward six from $^+5$:

$$^+5 + {}^-6 = {}^-1.$$

Although the reduction of both addition and subtraction of integers to counting is always possible, a geometric method of visualizing and performing the operations will be adopted as better fitted to show the properties of these operations. Once these properties are understood, direct methods for operating with integers will be introduced.

4. THE REPRESENTATION OF INTEGERS BY VECTORS

Vectors. A geometric representation of integers will be used in this section to develop the properties of the operations of addition and subtraction of integers. Integers will be represented by vectors, that is, by directed line segments. (See Chapter 8, Section 7.) To develop this representation, Fig. 11–2 will be regarded from the second viewpoint described in Section 2, that is, as a geometric figure.

The line in Fig. 11–2 will be called a *number line*, and the distinguished set of points on it will be called *integral points*. Each point of this set will be named by the number symbol associated with it. Thus reference will be made to the point $^+2$, the point 0, the point $^-7$, etc.

There is a set of vectors which is naturally associated with the integral points. All are the directed segments of the number line joining the integral points. This set of vectors will be referred to as the set V. Three vectors α, β, and γ of V are shown in Fig. 11–3. They are represented above the line for purposes of identification.

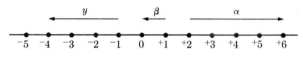

FIGURE 11–3

Any directed segment is specified by giving its end points in a definite order. For example, the vector α extends from the point $^+2$ to the point $^+6$. It may therefore be specified by the ordered pair of integers, $[^+2, {}^+6]$. Brackets, rather than parentheses, are used here to indicate that a directed segment is meant, and not the ordered pair $(^+2, {}^+6)$ corresponding to the end points of the segment. With this interpretation, any ordered pair of integers specifies a vector. The particular pair $[^+1, 0]$ specifies the vector β in Fig. 11–3, which extends from $^+1$ to 0. Similarly, each of the infinite set of ordered pair of integers specifies a vector. In general, then,

The set of vectors V and the set of all ordered pairs, $[m, n]$, of unequal integers m and n, are in a one-to-one correspondence.

Ordered pairs such as $[^+1, {}^+1]$ or $[^-2, {}^-2]$ are exceptional. Their geometric significance will be discussed later. They do not correspond to vectors of V as defined above.

Naming a vector. Because of the correspondence between ordered pairs of integers and vectors, $[^+2, {}^+6]$, $[^+1, 0]$, and $[^-1, {}^-4]$ may be thought of as names for the corresponding vectors α, β and γ. "The vector $[^+4, {}^-7]$" means the vector on the number line extending from $^+4$ to $^-7$.

Direction of a vector. The integer $^+2$ is less than $^+6$, and the vector α, $[^+2, {}^+6]$, points to the right; $^-1$ is greater than $^-4$, and the vector γ, $[^-1, {}^-4]$, points to the left. In general, the vector $[m, n]$ points to the right if $m < n$ and to the left if $m > n$.

Measure of a vector. If the segment joining the points 0 and $^+1$ is chosen as a unit segment and assigned the measure one, the measure of any other segment joining integral points is a whole number. All segments joining adjacent integral points are congruent to the unit segment joining 0 and $^+1$. These segments will also be referred to as unit segments.

Congruent vectors. Two vectors of V are said to be *congruent* if they have the same direction and if their line segments have the same measure. For example, $[^+2, {}^+6]$, and $[^-3, {}^+1]$ are congruent vectors. The set A of vectors congruent to α is given below. Each vector of the set extends from left to right, and each of their segments has measure 4. They differ only in their position on the number line.

$$A = \{\ldots, [^-1, {}^+3], [0, {}^+4], [^+1, {}^+5], [^+2, {}^+6], \ldots\}.$$

The set G of vectors congruent to γ is given below. Each vector of this set points to the left, and each of their segments has a measure of 3. They differ only in their position on the number line.

$$G = \{\ldots, [^-2, {}^-5], [^-1, {}^-4], [0, {}^-3], [^+1, {}^-2], \ldots\}.$$

Among the vectors of A and G, the two vectors $[0, {}^+4]$ and $[0, {}^-3]$ are noteworthy. Both start from the point zero. Both have their direction and measure given immediately by the integers $^+4$ and $^-3$ which denote their terminal points. Since all vectors congruent to $[0, {}^+4]$ belong to A, and all vectors congruent to $[0, {}^-3]$ belong to G, the measure $^+4$ is assigned to every vector of A, and the measure $^-3$ is assigned to every vector of G.

In general, every vector $[r, s]$, where r and s are integers, $r \neq s$, is congruent to exactly one vector $[0, m]$. The integer m is called the measure of the vector $[r, s]$. *The measure of a vector is an integer which specifies both the measure of the line segment and the direction of the vector.* Furthermore, two vectors are congruent if and only if they have the same measure. Thus a new geometric interpretation for an integer may be given.

Every nonzero integer is the measure of a set of congruent vectors.

The measures of the vectors α, β, and γ in Fig. 11–3 are $^+4$, $^-1$, and $^-3$.

Null vectors. The correspondence between ordered pairs of integers and vectors of V is at present incomplete, since ordered pairs such as $[0, 0]$, $[^+1, ^+1]$, and $[^-4, ^-4]$ do not correspond to vectors of V. The correspondence between integers as measures of vectors and vectors is also incomplete, since there is no vector of V of measure zero.

To make the correspondence complete and to allow the use of vectors to represent operations on integers, the convention is adopted of calling $[0, 0]$, $[^+1, ^+1]$, and $[^-4, ^-4]$ *null vectors* and assigning to each the measure zero. The justification for this convention is the same as that for considering the empty set as a set or zero as a whole number. The introduction of null vectors simplifies thinking about vectors and their relation to the integers.

The null vectors will now be considered as elements of set V. They form the subset

$$\{\ldots, [^-2, ^-2], [^-1, ^-1], [0, 0], [^+1, ^+1], [^+2, ^+2], \ldots\}.$$

On a number line, a null vector such as $[^-2, ^-2]$ has position, since it begins and ends at the point $^-2$, and it has no direction since the integer zero is its own opposite.

EXERCISE SET 11–1

1. What are the opposites of these integers?
   (a) $^+5$ (b) $^-2$ (c) 0 (d) $^-8$
   (e) ^-a (f) ^+b (g) $^-(ab)$ (h) $^+(a + b)$
2. Order each of the following sets of integers from smallest to greatest.
   (a) $0, ^-5, ^+5$ (b) $^-2, ^-8, ^-6$
   (c) $^+1, ^+7, ^+3$ (d) $0, ^-8, ^+3, ^-2, ^+4$
   (e) $^-5, ^-2, ^-8, 0, ^+8, ^+1$ (f) $^+5, ^+9, ^+6, ^-5, ^-2, ^-1$
3. Use the procedure of counting to find the sum of the following numbers.
   (a) $^+3, ^+7$ (b) $^-2, ^-9$ (c) $^-3, ^-2$ (d) $^+8, ^-2$
   (e) $^-5, ^+5$ (f) $^-3, ^-3$ (g) $^-2, ^-3, ^-5$ (h) $^+3, ^+6, ^-5$
4. Begin at each of the points below on a number line and add $^+5$ by counting.
   (a) $^+5$ (b) $^-5$ (c) 0 (d) $^+7$
   (e) $^-2$ (f) $^-8$ (g) $^-12$ (h) $^+4$
5. Repeat Exercise 4, adding $^-3$ to each number by counting.
6. Repeat Exercise 4, adding $^-1$ to each number by counting.
7. What ordered pair of integers name each of the vectors in Fig. 11–4?
8. What ordered pair of integers name each of the vectors in Fig. 11–5?
9. In what direction does each of the vectors of Exercises 7 and 8 point, right or left? If a vector points to the right, indicate direction with "$+$"; if it points to the left indicate direction with "$-$."
10. What is the measure of the line segments determined by each of the vectors of Exercises 7 and 8?
11. What is the measure of each of the vectors of Exercises 7 and 8?

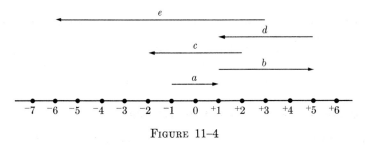

FIGURE 11–4

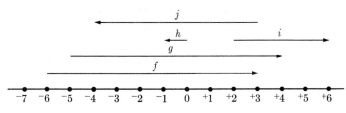

FIGURE 11–5

12. Sketch an integer line. Above it draw vectors to represent each of the following ordered pairs. Label them a, b, c, etc.
    (a) $[^+3, ^-1]$
    (b) $[^-6, 0]$
    (c) $[^+3, ^+2]$
    (d) $[^-3, ^+3]$
    (e) $[0, ^-6]$
    (f) $[^-2, ^-3]$
    (g) $[^-1, ^+5]$
    (h) $[^+7, ^+3]$
    (i) $[^-5, ^-5]$

13. In what direction, positive or negative, does each of the vectors of Exercise 12 point?

14. What is the measure of the line segments determined by each of the vectors of Exercise 12?

15. What integer does each of the vectors of Exercise 12 represent?

16. (a) Are any of the vectors of Exercises 7 and 8 congruent? If so, name them.
    (b) Are any of the vectors of Exercise 12 congruent? If so, name them.
    (c) Give three other examples of congruent vectors.

17. (a) Are any of the vectors of Exercises 7 and 8 null vectors? Why?
    (b) Are any of the vectors of Exercise 12 null vectors? Why?
    (c) Give three examples of null vectors.

18. Sketch each of the following vectors on a number line. Label each with the measure of the vector.
    (a) $[^+4, ^-4]$
    (b) $[^+3, ^+8]$
    (c) $[0, ^+6]$
    (d) $[^-2, ^+2]$
    (e) $[^+2, ^-2]$
    (f) $[^+5, ^-1]$
    (g) $[^+5, ^+1]$
    (h) $[^+1, ^+4]$
    (i) $[^-1, ^-4]$
    (j) $[^-5, ^-2]$
    (k) $[^+3, ^-8]$
    (l) $[^-3, ^-3]$

19. (a) Are any of the vectors of Exercise 18 congruent? If so, name them.
    (b) Are any of the vectors of Exercise 18 null vectors? If so, why?

20. Draw three other vectors congruent to each of the following vectors.
    (a) $[0, ^+3]$
    (b) $[0, ^-4]$
    (c) $[^-2, ^+3]$
    (d) $[^+6, ^+3]$
    (e) $[^+1, ^+2]$
    (f) $[^-5, ^-7]$

21. What ordered pair of integers names the vectors for each of your answers in Exercise 20?

22. Sketch three vectors which may be used to represent each of the following integers. Be sure that one vector representing each integer begins at zero.
(a) $^+4$ (b) $^-5$ (c) $^+2$ (d) $^-4$ (e) $^+7$ (f) $^-8$

5. ADDITION OF VECTORS AND INTEGERS

Abutting vectors. Two vectors in a prescribed order are said to abut or be abutting vectors if the terminal point of the first is the initial point of the second. For example, the vectors $[^+2, ^+6]$ and $[^+6, ^+4]$ abut, and so do the vectors $[^+2, ^+6]$ and $[^+6, ^-6]$. On the other hand, the vectors $[^+2, ^+6]$ and $[^+2, ^+4]$ do not abut and neither do the vectors $[^+6, ^+4]$ and $[^+2, ^+6]$.

Given vectors:

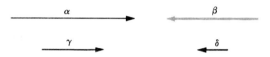

Abutting vectors:

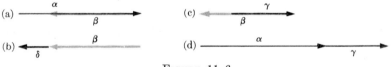

FIGURE 11–6

Figure 11–6 shows a few of the twelve ways in which the given vectors α, β, γ, and δ may abut. You may be interested in sketching others.

Arrow representation of vectors. To perceive more easily the relations between abutting vectors, it is often convenient to represent the positions of vectors on the number line by drawing arrows directly above the line. Each such arrow is then labeled with the measure of the vector which it represents. In Fig. 11–7, arrows are sketched for the three vectors $[^+3, ^-1]$, $[^-4, ^+3]$, and $[^+5, ^+3]$. The vectors of measures $^+7$ and $^-4$ are abutting vectors as are the vectors of measures $^-2$ and $^-4$. Those with measures of $^+7$ and $^-2$ do not abut.

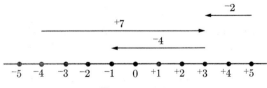

FIGURE 11–7

Vector addition. An important geometric operation, called *vector addition*, may be performed on abutting vectors. It is used here to show the meaning of the addition of integers, and will be employed again in Chapter 13 to show the meaning of the addition of rational numbers. Vector addition is continually used in the application of mathematics to science and engineering. It will also be used further by those who pursue the study of mathematics.

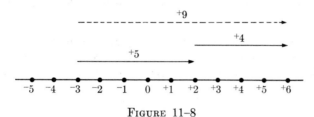

FIGURE 11–8

Vector addition is best explained by examples. Figure 11–8 shows two abutting vectors, [⁻3, ⁺2] and [⁺2, ⁺6]. The vector [⁻3, ⁺6], indicated by a dashed arrow, is defined to be their sum:

$$[^-3, {}^+2] + [^+2, {}^+6] = [^-3, {}^+6].$$

The initial point ⁻3 of the sum is the initial point of the first vector, [⁻3, ⁺2], and the terminal point ⁺6 of the sum is the terminal point of the second abutting vector, [⁺2, ⁺6].

When the abutting vectors have opposite directions, the sum,

$$[0, {}^+3] + [^+3, {}^-5] = [0, {}^-5]$$

is indicated as in Fig. 11–9. The sum is again denoted by a dashed arrow.

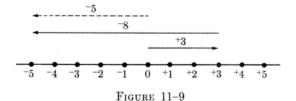

FIGURE 11–9

Note that the initial point 0 of the sum [0, ⁻5] is the initial point of the first abutting vector, and the terminal point ⁻5 is the terminal point of the second abutting vector.

There is an important special case of the sum of two abutting vectors which should be noted. The vectors [0, ⁺6] and [⁺6, 0] abut, and their sum is the null vector, [0, 0]; the vectors [$^+$6, $^-$3] and [$^-$3, $^+$6] abut, and their sum is the null vector, [$^+$6, $^+$6]. In general, if m and n are any integers, the vectors [m, n] and [n, m] abut, and their sum is the null vector [m, m].

Addition of integers. In both of the cases illustrated in Figs. 11–8 and 11–9,

The sum of the measures of the two abutting vectors is the measure of their sum.

This is true of any vector addition. For example, the vector [0, $^+$3] has measure $^+$3; the vector [$^+$3, $^-$5] has measure $^-$8, and their sum, [0, $^-$5], has measure $^-$5. Indeed, counting backward eight from $^+$3 gives $^-$5:

$$^+3 + {}^-8 = {}^-5.$$

Similarly, the vectors [$^-$3, $^+$2] and [$^+$2, $^+$6] have measures $^+$5 and $^+$4, and their sum, [$^-$3, $^+$6], has measure $^+$9; and counting forward four from $^+$5 gives $^+$9:

$$^+5 + {}^+4 = {}^+9.$$

Thus the geometric addition of abutting vectors corresponds to the numerical addition of their measures.

Performing the operation of addition. Due to the correspondence between geometric addition of vectors and numerical addition of integers, it is possible to find the sum of two or more integers geometrically. For example, to find the sum $^+$4 + $^-$9, two abutting vectors with measures $^+$4 and $^-$9 are chosen. The measure of their sum is then $^+$4 + $^-$9. The procedure is illustrated in Fig. 11–10, where the vectors are indicated by arrows.

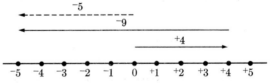

FIGURE 11–10

First an arrow is drawn, representing the vector [0, $^+$4]. Any other vector of measure $^+$4 could be taken, but [0, $^+$4] gives the simplest construction. Next, starting from $^+$4, an arrow is drawn of measure $^-$9. This arrow terminates at the point $^-$5. It represents the abutting vector [$^+$4, $^-$5]:

$$[0, {}^+4] + [{}^+4, {}^-5] = [0, {}^-5].$$

The dashed arrow extending from 0 to $^-5$ represents the sum $[0, {}^-5]$; its measure is $^-5$ and hence

$$^+4 + {}^-9 = {}^-5.$$

It is not necessary to continue using vector addition to perform the addition of integers. Rather, by examining the results of vector addition, a procedure for the addition of integers may be derived. For example, study the following:

(a) The addition of two positive integers:

$$^+2 + {}^+5 = {}^+7; \quad {}^+3 + {}^+7 = {}^+10; \quad {}^+4 + {}^+9 = {}^+13; \quad {}^+1 + {}^+6 = {}^+7.$$

(b) The addition of two negative integers:

$$^-2 + {}^-5 = {}^-7; \quad {}^-3 + {}^-7 = {}^-10; \quad {}^-4 + {}^-9 = {}^-13; \quad {}^-1 + {}^-6 = {}^-7.$$

(c) The addition of a positive integer and a negative integer:

$$^-2 + {}^+5 = {}^+3; \quad {}^+3 + {}^-7 = {}^-4; \quad {}^+4 + {}^-9 = {}^-5; \quad {}^-1 + {}^+6 = {}^+5.$$

A careful study of these and other examples leads to the following generalizations.

The sum of two positive integers or of two negative integers is an integer whose whole number is the same as the sum of the corresponding whole numbers of the addends and whose direction is the same as that of the addends.

The sum of two integers, one positive and one negative, is an integer whose whole number is the same as the difference in their corresponding whole numbers and whose direction is the same as that of the integer which has the greater corresponding whole number.

Properties of addition of integers. It may be shown that the operation of addition of integers has the *closure property,* and is both *associative* and *commutative.* Furthermore, *zero is the identity element for addition,* and *addition has the cancellation property.* In short, the addition of integers has all the operational properties of the addition of whole numbers. Not all these properties may be exhibited directly by comparison with the operation of addition of vectors. For, although the sum

$$[^+2, {}^+4] + [^+4, {}^+7] = [^+2, {}^+7],$$

corresponds to $^+2 + {}^+3 = {}^+5$, the sum $^+3 + {}^+2 = {}^+5$ corresponds to a different vector sum, because the vectors $[^+4, {}^+7]$ and $[^+2, {}^+4]$ do not abut.

The additive inverse. The operation of addition of integers has one very important property which the operation of addition of whole numbers lacks. The vector sum $[0, {}^+6] + [{}^+6, 0]$ is the null vector $[0, 0]$. The measures of $[0, {}^+6]$, $[{}^+6, 0]$, and $[0, 0]$ are ${}^+6$, ${}^-6$, and 0. Hence ${}^+6 + {}^-6 = 0$. This example illustrates the following general principle: the sum of any integer and its opposite is zero; or

For every integer u, there exists another integer u' such that $u + u' = u' + u = 0$.

The number v' is called the *additive inverse* of u. The additive inverse of ${}^-5$ is ${}^+5$, of ${}^+2$ is ${}^-2$.

6. SUBTRACTION OF VECTORS AND OF INTEGERS

Vector subtraction, the inverse of addition. Vector addition has the cancellation property; that is, if α, β, and γ are vectors such that $\alpha + \beta = \alpha + \gamma$, then $\beta = \gamma$. Vector subtraction may consequently be viewed as the operation inverse to vector addition. But not every two vectors may be subtracted. A geometric condition must be satisfied for subtraction to be possible.

To find this condition, observe that it follows from the definition of the sum of two vectors, that if a, b, and c denote any integers, then

$$[a, b] + [b, c] = [a, c].$$

Consequently, since subtraction is the inverse of addition,

$$[a, c] - [a, b] = [b, c]; \quad \text{and} \quad [a, c] - [b, c] = [a, b].$$

Note that the vector representing the unknown addend begins at the terminal point of the vector representing the known addend and ends at the terminal point of the vector representing the sum. Therefore,

Two vectors may be subtracted if and only if they have the same initial points or the same terminal points.

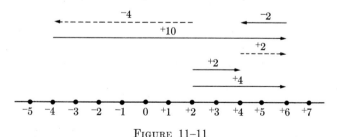

FIGURE 11–11

For example, from Fig. 11–11

$$[^+2, \,^+6] - [^+2, \,^+4] = [^+4, \,^+6] \quad \text{and} \quad [^+2, \,^+6] - [^-4, \,^+6] = [^+2, \,^-4];$$

but $[^+2, \,^+6]$ and $[^+6, \,^+4]$ cannot be subtracted.

Subtraction of integers. Since the operation of addition of integers has the cancellation property, subtraction of integers may be viewed as the inverse of the operation of addition. Subtraction may therefore be performed geometrically by subtracting suitably chosen vectors. It will suffice to illustrate this statement by one or two examples.

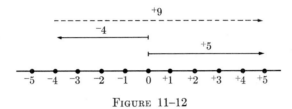

Figure 11–12

To subtract the integers $^+5 - {}^-4$, vectors must be chosen of measures $^+5$ and $^-4$ which have either the same initial point or the same terminal point. The choice of vectors with the same initial point is more natural, and will be the only one considered. Taking zero as the initial point, the two chosen vectors are $[0, \,^+5]$ and $[0, \,^-4]$ (see Fig. 11–12). The vector representing the missing addend in Fig. 11–12 is the vector which when added to $[0, \,^-4]$ equals $[0, \,^+5]$. It is drawn from the terminal point of the known addend to the terminal point of the sum. Therefore,

$$[0, \,^+5] - [0, \,^-4] = [^-4, \,^+5],$$

and

$$^+5 - {}^-4 = {}^+9.$$

The subtraction $^+3 - {}^+8$ is illustrated in Fig. 11–13. It shows that

$$[0, \,^+3] - [0, \,^+8] = [^+8, \,^+3].$$

Figure 11–13 further shows that

$$^+3 - {}^+8 = {}^-5.$$

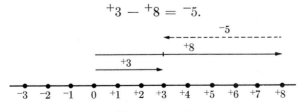

Figure 11–13

Since addition and subtraction are inverse operations, the performance of the subtractions $^+5 - {}^-4$ and $^+3 - {}^+8$ may be thought of as finding the missing addend m in the mathematical sentences

$$^-4 + m = {}^+5 \quad \text{and} \quad {}^+8 + m = {}^+3.$$

Note that in both Figs. 11–12 and 11–13 the dashed vector which corresponds to the missing addend extends from the terminal point of the vector representing the given addend to the terminal point of the vector representing the given sum. This is always true for the type of geometric construction used here, regardless of the integers being subtracted.

Performing the operation of subtraction. Study and comparison of the addition of integers illustrated in Figs. 11–8 and 11–9 and the subtraction of integers illustrated in Figs. 11–12 and 11–13 reveal another important property of subtraction:

To subtract an integer, its opposite may be added.

For example, from Fig. 11–12, $^+5 - {}^-4 = {}^+9$, and from Fig. 11–8, $^+5 + {}^+4 = {}^+9$. Therefore,

$$^+5 - {}^-4 = {}^+5 + {}^+4 = 9.$$

From Fig. 11–13, $^+3 - {}^+8 = {}^-5$, and from Fig. 11–9, $^+3 + {}^-8 = {}^-5$. Therefore,

$$^+3 - {}^+8 = {}^+3 + {}^-8 = {}^-5,$$

and

$$a - u = a + u'.$$

Properties of subtraction. The integers are *closed* under the operation of subtraction; and if any integer is subtracted from itself, the result is zero, $m - m = 0$.

You should note that the addition and subtraction of integers has all the properties of addition and subtraction of whole numbers and the additional property of closure under subtraction; subtraction is always possible within the set of integers.

EXERCISE SET 11–2

1. Which of the following name abutting vectors?
   (a) $[^-3, {}^+2], [^+2, {}^+3]$ (b) $[^-3, {}^-4], [^-2, {}^-4]$ (c) $[^-5, {}^-6], [^-5, {}^-8]$
   (d) $[^+2, {}^-3], [^-3, {}^+2]$ (e) $[^+7, {}^+9], [^+9, {}^-5]$ (f) $[^+4, {}^-6], [^+4, {}^-2]$
   (g) $[0, {}^-5], [^-5, 0]$ (h) $[0, {}^-5], [^-5, {}^-8]$ (i) $[0, {}^-5], [^-5, {}^+2]$

2. Sketch the pairs of vectors of Exercise 1 that are abutting vectors.
3. Make sketches to show the vector addition of each of the following.
   (a) $[^+2, {}^+3] + [^+3, {}^+7]$ (b) $[^-2, 0] + [0, {}^+6]$
   (c) $[0, {}^-3] + [^-3, {}^-4]$ (d) $[^-2, {}^-8] + [^-8, {}^-4]$
   (e) $[^-2, {}^+3] + [^+3, {}^-5]$ (f) $[^+5, {}^-2] + [^-2, {}^+5]$
   (g) $[^+7, {}^+2] + [^+2, {}^+9]$ (h) $[^+7, {}^+2] + [^+2, {}^+4]$
4. Write a mathematical sentence for each of the vector additions sketched in Exercise 3.
5. Using the integers which each of the vectors of Exercise 3 may represent, rewrite the mathematical sentences of Exercise 4, substituting integers for vector names.
6. Sketch three vectors which may be used to represent each of the following integers.
   (a) $^+3$ (b) $^-3$ (c) $^+7$ (d) $^-6$
   (e) $^+4$ (f) $^+6$ (g) $^-2$ (h) $^-1$
7. (a) Choose and mark with an asterisk the vectors of Exercise 6 which most conveniently represent each of the integers. (If you have not sketched the most convenient one, do so, and mark with an asterisk.)
   (b) Describe the vector which most conveniently represents an integer?
8. Draw the vector which most conveniently represents the following integers.
   (a) $^-7$ (b) $^+7$ (c) $^+3$ (d) $^+4$
   (e) $^-2$ (f) $^-6$ (g) $^-5$ (h) $^+8$
9. Sketch the abutting vectors that represent the addends given below. Sketch the vector which represents the sum.
   (a) $^+2 + {}^+3$ (b) $^-3 + {}^-2$ (c) $^+4 + {}^-2$
   (d) $^+4 + {}^-6$ (e) $^+4 + {}^-4$ (f) $^+7 + {}^-5$
   (g) $^-5 + {}^-2$ (h) $^-5 + {}^+7$ (i) $^-5 + {}^+3$
10. Write a mathematical sentence for each addition sketched in Exercise 9.
11. What are the opposites of these integers?
    (a) $^-5$ (b) $^+7$ (c) $^-8$
    (d) 0 (e) $^+2$ (f) $^-5$
12. Show by vector diagrams that the sum of each of the integers of Exercise 11 and its opposite is zero.
13. What is the additive inverse of $^-5$, $^+6$, $^-2$, 0, and $^+8$?
14. (a) Illustrate the sum of $^+2$ and $^+3$ by a vector diagram.
    (b) By extending the diagram for (a) show the addition of the result in (a) to $^-8$.
    (c) Does the diagram of (b) show the sum $(^+2 + {}^+3) + {}^-8 = n$? What is n?
15. (a) Illustrate the sum of $^+3$ and $^-8$ by a vector diagram.
    (b) By extending the diagram for (a) show the addition of $^+2$ to the result in (a).
    (c) Does the diagram of (b) show the sum $^+2 + (^+3 + {}^-8) = p$? What is p?
16. (a) Compare the results of Exercises 14(c) and 15(c).
    (b) What property does this comparison illustrate?
    (c) State the property.

17. (a) Use vector diagrams of the sentences $^+5 + {}^-2 = n$ and $^-2 + {}^+5 = n$ to illustrate that the commutative property holds for the addition of integers.

(b) Explain the diagram.

18. Which of the pairs of vectors listed below have either the same terminal point or the same initial point?

(a) $[^-3, {}^+2], [^+2, {}^+3]$ (b) $[^-6, {}^-2], [^-6, {}^+2]$ (c) $[^-6, {}^-2], [^+3, {}^-2]$
(d) $[0, {}^-8], [0, {}^+2]$ (e) $[^+2, {}^-2], [^-2, {}^+2]$ (f) $[^+2, {}^-5], [^+2, {}^-8]$
(g) $[^+6, {}^+9], [0, {}^+9]$ (h) $[^-2, 0], [5, {}^-2]$ (i) $[^+3, 0], [^+3, {}^-1]$

19. Sketch the pairs of vectors of Exercise 18 which have either the same terminal or the same initial point. Label each vector with the integer it represents.

20. Make sketches to show the vector subtraction of each of the following. Label each vector with the integer it represents.

(a) $[^+2, {}^+7] - [^+2, {}^+5]$ (b) $[^+1, {}^+4] - [^+1, {}^+8]$
(c) $[0, {}^-3] - [0, {}^+2]$ (d) $[0, {}^-2] - [0, {}^-5]$
(e) $[0, {}^-7] - [0, {}^-2]$ (f) $[^+2, {}^-5] - [^+6, {}^-5]$
(g) $[^+8, 0] - [^-2, 0]$ (h) $[^-3, 0] - [^+1, 0]$

21. Write a mathematical sentence for each of the vector subtractions sketched in Exercise 20.

22. Using integers which each of the vectors of Exercise 20 may represent, rewrite the mathematical sentences, substituting integers for vector names.

23. Sketch the vectors which represent the subtraction of the integers below. Sketch the vector which represents the missing addend.

(a) $^+7 - {}^+3$ (b) $^+2 - {}^+3$ (c) $^-3 - {}^-2$
(d) $^-2 - {}^-8$ (e) $^-2 - {}^+8$ (f) $^+3 - {}^-5$
(g) $^+3 - {}^-1$ (h) $^-7 - {}^+2$ (i) $0 - {}^-2$

24. Write a mathematical sentence for each of the subtractions sketched in Exercise 23.

25. (a) Illustrate $^+5 - {}^+2$ by a vector diagram.

(b) From the result obtained in (a) subtract $^+8$.

(c) Does the diagram in (b) show n in the sentence $(^+5 - {}^+2) - {}^+8 = n$? What is n?

26. (a) Show $^+2 - {}^+8$ by a vector diagram.

(b) Subtract the result in (a) from $^+5$.

(c) Does the diagram in (b) show n in the sentence $^+5 - (^+2 - {}^+8) = n$? What is n?

27. (a) Are the results of 25(c) and 26(c) the same?

(b) What does your answer to (a) indicate? State as a generalization.

28. Use the integers $^+5$ and $^-3$ to show by means of vector diagrams that the subtraction of integers is a noncommutative operation.

29. Solve the following by means of vector diagrams.

(a) $a = {}^+2 + {}^-8$ (b) $^-8 + {}^-5 = b$ (c) $c = {}^-8 - {}^-2$
(d) $d = {}^+7 + {}^-2$ (e) $^+2 - {}^-5 = e$ (f) $^-3 + {}^+3 = f$
(g) $g = {}^-2 - {}^-6$ (h) $^+7 - {}^-2 = h$ (i) $^+5 - {}^-5 = i$

30. (a) Solve the following by means of vector diagrams.

$^+5 + {}^+3 = n;$ $^+8 + {}^+1 = p;$ $^+2 + {}^+3 = q;$ $^+4 + {}^+7 = r.$

(b) Study the results in (a) and devise a method of finding the sum of two positive integers without the use of vector diagrams.

31. Use the generalization made in Exercise 30 to solve the following.

(a) $a = {}^+8 + {}^+7$ (b) ${}^+18 + {}^+92 = b$ (c) ${}^+124 + {}^+49 = c$

(d) $d = {}^+45 + {}^+85$ (e) ${}^+99 + {}^+101 = e$ (f) $f = {}^+8 + {}^+91$

32. (a) Solve the following by means of vector diagrams.

$${}^-6 + {}^-2 = n; \quad {}^-4 + {}^-8 = p; \quad q = {}^-2 + {}^-4; \quad r = {}^-2 + {}^-9.$$

(b) Study the results in (a) and devise a method of finding the sum of two negative integers without the use of vector diagrams.

33. Use the generalizations made in Exercises 30 and 32 to solve the following.

(a) $a = {}^-9 + {}^-7$ (b) ${}^-14 + {}^-17 = b$ (c) $c = {}^+15 + {}^+6$

(d) ${}^+14 + {}^+9 = d$ (e) $e = {}^-44 + {}^-78$ (f) ${}^+76 + {}^+4 = f$

34. (a) Solve the following by means of vector diagrams.

$$n = {}^+8 + {}^-2; \quad {}^-8 + {}^+2 = p; \quad q = {}^-8 + {}^+8; \quad r = {}^+12 + {}^-10.$$

(b) Study the results of (a) and devise a method of adding a positive integer and a negative integer without the use of vector diagrams.

35. Use the generalizations made in Exercises 30, 32, and 34 to solve the following.

(a) $a = {}^+7 + {}^-2$ (b) $b = {}^-6 + {}^-4$ (c) $c = {}^-8 + {}^-12$

(d) ${}^-12 + {}^+8 = d$ (e) ${}^-25 + {}^-45 = e$ (f) ${}^-33 + {}^+18 = f$

(g) ${}^+29 + {}^+78 = g$ (h) $h = {}^-19 + {}^+40$ (i) $i = {}^-100 + {}^+32$

(j) ${}^+49 + {}^+256 = j$ (k) ${}^-75 + {}^-44 = k$ (l) $l = {}^-92 + {}^+128$

36. (a) Solve: ${}^+5 - {}^+7 = n$ and ${}^+5 + {}^-7 = p$.

(b) Compare n and p of (a). What do you know about ${}^+5 - {}^+7$ and ${}^+5 + {}^-7$?

37. (a) Solve: ${}^-12 - {}^-2 = q$ and ${}^-12 + {}^+2 = r$.

(b) Compare q and r of (a). What do you know about ${}^-12 - {}^-2$ and ${}^-12 + {}^+2$?

38. (a) Study the pairs of sentences of Exercises 36(a) and those of 37(a) and describe how they differ.

(b) How are they alike?

(c) What important generalization do they illustrate?

(d) Give three other pairs of sentences which illustrate the same generalization.

7. MULTIPLICATION OF INTEGERS

Multiplication of whole numbers. Properties of the operation of multiplication on whole numbers, such as closure or distributivity, ultimately depend on the nature of multiplication as a counting process. Consider, for example, distributing 5 over the sum $2 + 2$,

$$5 \times 4 = (5 \times 2) + (5 \times 2).$$

The product $5 \times 4 = 20$ records in compact form the fact that if you count by fives four times, the number twenty results. But it is equally true that counting by pairs of fives twice also produces twenty.

It is also interesting that, conversely, the nature of multiplication as a counting process is determined by the properties of multiplication as an operation. Consider, for example, the process of multiplying by five. The products, $5 \times 1, 5 \times 2, 5 \times 3, \ldots$, are equal to

$$5 \times (1), \qquad 5 \times (1 + 1), \qquad 5 \times (1 + 1 + 1), \ldots$$

Since multiplication is distributive with respect to addition, these products are equal to

$$5 \times 1, \qquad (5 \times 1) + (5 \times 1), \qquad (5 \times 1) + (5 \times 1) + (5 \times 1), \ldots$$

Finally, since 1 is an identity element for multiplication, the last series of products written are equal to $5, 5 + 5, 5 + 5 + 5, \ldots$

This shows that the multiplication of 5 by $1, 2, 3, \ldots$ may be performed by counting by fives, once, twice, thrice, $\ldots$ It may be shown in the same manner that if m and n are whole numbers and $n \neq 0$, then

$$m \times n = m + m + m + \cdots + m \quad \text{or} \quad m \quad \text{counted} \quad n \quad \text{times.}$$

In developing a definition of the multiplication of integers, we shall require that it have the same properties as the multiplication of whole numbers so that the arithmetics of the two sets will be similar. This requirement determines how the multiplication on integers is to be performed and, therefore, the nature of the operation as a counting process.

Properties of multiplication of integers. For convenience of reference, the properties of multiplication discussed in Chapter 6 for whole numbers are restated here for the integers.

CLOSURE PROPERTY. If u and v are integers, then $u \cdot v$ is an integer uniquely determined by u and v.

COMMUTATIVE PROPERTY. If u and v are integers, then $u \cdot v = v \cdot u$.

ASSOCIATIVE PROPERTY. If u, v, and w are integers, then

$$u \cdot (v \cdot w) = (u \cdot v) \cdot w.$$

EXISTENCE OF IDENTITY. For every integer u, there exists an integer i such that $i \cdot u = u \cdot i = u$.

CANCELLATION PROPERTY. If u, w, and v are integers, and $w \neq 0$, then $w \cdot u = w \cdot v$ implies that $u = v$.

DISTRIBUTIVE PROPERTY.   If u, v, and w are integers, then

$$u \cdot (v + w) = (u \cdot v) + (u \cdot w),$$
$$(v + w) \cdot u = v \cdot u + w \cdot u.$$

Definition of multiplication of integers.   Since the operation must resemble the operation on whole numbers, the integer $^{+}1$ is chosen as an identity element for the operation.

(1)   For any integer u, $u \cdot {}^{+}1 = {}^{+}1 \cdot u = u$.

The following two properties of the operation may be proved from (1) and the properties already assumed:

(2)   For any integer u, $u \cdot 0 = 0 \cdot u = 0$.

(3)   For any integer u, the opposite of u is $(^{-}1) \cdot u$.

(If u is $^{+}5$, its opposite is $^{-}5$; if u is $^{-}5$, its opposite is $^{+}5$.)
    Since $^{+}1$ is the opposite of $^{-}1$, it follows from (3) that

(4) $^{+}1 = {}^{-}1 \cdot {}^{-}1$.

The product of two positive integers may be derived by applying some of the Principles (1) through (4) above, together with other ideas from mathematics.   The product of $^{+}5 \cdot {}^{+}3$ then is (reasons for each step are included):

$$
\begin{aligned}
{}^{+}5 \cdot {}^{+}3 &= {}^{+}5({}^{+}1 + {}^{+}1 + {}^{+}1) & &{}^{+}3 \text{ renamed.}\\
&= {}^{+}5 \cdot {}^{+}1 + {}^{+}5 \cdot {}^{+}1 + {}^{+}5 \cdot {}^{+}1 & &\text{Distributive property.}\\
&= {}^{+}5 + {}^{+}5 + {}^{+}5 & &\text{Principle (1)}\\
& & &\text{(identity elements).}\\
&= {}^{+}15 & &\text{Addition of integers.}
\end{aligned}
$$

(5) $\quad {}^{+}5 \cdot {}^{+}3 = {}^{+}(5 \cdot 3) \qquad\qquad\qquad {}^{+}15$ renamed.

The product of a positive and a negative integer may be derived similarly. The product of $^{+}5$ and $^{-}3$ is:

$$
\begin{aligned}
{}^{+}5 \cdot {}^{-}3 &= {}^{+}5 \cdot ({}^{-}1 \cdot {}^{+}3) & &\text{Renamed } {}^{-}3 \text{ as } {}^{-}1 \cdot {}^{+}3.\\
&= {}^{-}1({}^{+}5 \cdot {}^{+}3) & &\text{Commutative and associative properties.}\\
&= {}^{-}1 \cdot {}^{+}(5 \cdot 3) & &\text{Principle (5).}
\end{aligned}
$$

(6) $^{+}5 \cdot {}^{-}3 = {}^{-}(5 \cdot 3) \qquad\qquad$ Principle (3).
    or
$\quad {}^{-}5 \cdot {}^{+}3 = {}^{-}(5 \cdot 3) \qquad\qquad$ Derivation similar to that for $^{+}5 \cdot {}^{-}3$.

The product of two negative integers, ⁻5 and ⁻3, may be derived as follows.

$$\begin{aligned} {}^{-}5 \cdot {}^{-}3 &= ({}^{-}1 \cdot {}^{+}5) \cdot ({}^{-}1 \cdot {}^{+}3) && \text{Each factor renamed.} \\ &= ({}^{-}1 \cdot {}^{-}1) \cdot ({}^{+}5 \cdot {}^{+}3) && \text{Commutative and associative} \\ &&& \text{properties.} \\ &= {}^{+}1 \cdot {}^{+}(5 \cdot 3) && \text{Principles (4) and (5).} \end{aligned}$$

$$(7) \qquad {}^{-}5 \cdot {}^{-}3 = {}^{+}(5 \cdot 3) \qquad\qquad \text{Principle (1).}$$

The product of two integers. It has been shown that the multiplication of the integers associated with the whole numbers 5 and 3 is performed by multiplying 5 and 3 and then defining the product to be ⁺(5 · 3) if the integers are both positive or both negative, and ⁻(5 · 3) if one of the integers is positive and the other is negative.

It may be proved that the procedure just used applies to the multiplication of any two integers. The operation is accordingly defined over the set of integers as follows.

If u and v are any two integers, and m and n are the whole numbers associated with them, then:

$$u \cdot v = {}^{+}(m \cdot n) \qquad \text{if } u \text{ and } v \text{ are both positive}$$
$$\text{or both negative;}$$

$$u \cdot v = {}^{-}(m \cdot n) \qquad \text{if either } u \text{ or } v \text{ is positive}$$
$$\text{and the other is negative;}$$

$$u \cdot v = 0 \qquad\qquad\;\; \text{if } u \text{ or } v \text{ is zero.}$$

With this definition for the multiplication of integers, it is possible to prove that the operation has all the properties of the multiplication of whole numbers. The proofs are left for you to develop.

Division of integers. Since the operation of multiplication of integers has all the properties of the multiplication of whole numbers, an inverse operation of the division of integers may be defined. It is evident that since the division of whole numbers is not always possible, the division of integers is not always possible. For example, the quotient 5 ÷ 2 cannot be represented by a whole number, and neither can the quotient ⁻5 ÷ ⁺2 be represented by an integer. *The set of integers is not closed under the operation of division.*

The division ⁺12 ÷ ⁻4 requires that the missing factor u be found in the product $u \cdot {}^{-}4 = {}^{+}12$. Since the product, ⁺12, is positive and the known factor, ⁻4, is negative, it follows from the definition of the multiplication of integers, that the other factor, u, is negative. Since 3 · 4 = 12, the unknown factor is $^-3$. The integer u is obtained by dividing 12 by 4 and associating the whole number 3 with the integer $^-3$. Similarly,

$$^-12 \div\ ^-6 =\ ^+2 \quad \text{and} \quad ^-18 \div\ ^+3 =\ ^-6.$$

In general then, if $v \neq 0$, the quotient $u \div v$ is positive if u and v are both positive or both negative; otherwise the quotient is negative. Further, division of two integers can be performed if and only if division of the corresponding whole numbers can be performed.

8. THE INTEGERS AS AN EXTENSION OF THE WHOLE NUMBERS

The set of fractional numbers has a subset P_1, the fractions with denominators one, which can replace the set of whole numbers for all arithmetical purposes. (See Chapter 9, Section 8.) The fractional numbers are therefore said to be an *extension* of the whole numbers. The members of the new set may be used for all the purposes for which whole numbers can be used and for many other purposes as well. Throughout the history of mathematics this replacement of one set of numbers by another more extensive set has occurred many times as a need arose.

The set of integers is also an extension of the set of whole numbers. This is true because a subset of the integers exists which can replace the whole numbers for all arithmetical purposes. The subset is the set P of the positive integers and zero:

$$P = \{0,\ ^+1,\ ^+2,\ ^+3, \ldots\}.$$

Note that P and W, the set of whole numbers, may be placed in a one-to-one correspondence which preserves both order and the fundamental operations of arithmetic.

$$P = \{0,\ ^+1,\ ^+2,\ ^+3, \ldots\},$$
$$\updownarrow \quad \updownarrow \quad \updownarrow \quad \updownarrow$$
$$W = \{0,\quad 1,\quad 2,\quad 3, \ldots\}.$$

For example,

$$^+3 <\ ^+5 \text{ and } 3 < 5; \quad ^+9 +\ ^+3 =\ ^+12 \text{ and } 9 + 3 = 12;$$
$$^+9 -\ ^+3 =\ ^+6 \text{ and } 9 - 3 = 6; \quad ^+9 \times\ ^+3 =\ ^+27 \text{ and } 9 \times 3 = 27;$$
$$^+12 \div\ ^+3 =\ ^+4 \quad \text{and} \quad 12 \div 3 = 4.$$

Furthermore, the ordered set $(^+1,\ ^+2,\ ^+3, \ldots)$ can be used as a counting set just as the ordered set of fractions $(\frac{1}{1}, \frac{2}{1}, \frac{3}{1}, \ldots)$ can.

Note that the extension of the number concept to include the integers was dependent on the fact that addition and multiplication of whole numbers and integers have similar properties.

EXERCISE SET 11–3

1. Solve the following.
   (a) $a = (^+5)(^+3)$ (b) $b = (^-6)(^-2)$ (c) $c = (^+2)(^-3)$
   (d) $(^-3)(^+8) = d$ (e) $e = (0)(^-5)$ (f) $f = (^+2)(^+3)$
   (g) $(^-3)(^-3) = g$ (h) $(^+2)(0) = h$ (i) $i = (^+7)(^-5)$

2. Solve the following.
   (a) $a = (^+12) \div (^+2)$ (b) $b = (^+12) \div (^-2)$ (c) $c = (^-12) \div (^+2)$
   (d) $^-2d = ^-12$ (e) $e = (^+24) \div (^-3)$ (f) $^-4f = ^+4$
   (g) $(^-8) \div (^-2) = g$ (h) $(0) \div (^-5) = h$ (i) $^+3i = ^-15$

3. Solve the following.
   (a) $a = ^+5 + ^-2$ (b) $b = ^+6 - ^-5$
   (c) $c = (^+25)(^-3)$ (d) $d = (^-144) \div (^-12)$
   (e) $^+12 + e = ^+3$ (f) $^-7f = ^+91$
   (g) $^-5 + ^-8 = g$ (h) $h = (^-12)(^-9)$
   (i) $^-9 = ^-2 + i$ (j) $^-25 + ^+16 = j$
   (k) $^+72 = ^-6k$ (l) $(^+2)(^-7)(^-10) = l$
   (m) $^+125 \div ^+5 = m$ (n) $n = (^+18)(^-100)$
   (o) $^-8 - ^-3 = p$ (p) $q = ^-7 + ^-2 + ^+6 + ^-3$

4. State a general rule for adding two integers, based on operations with their corresponding whole numbers.

5. State a general rule for subtracting two integers.

6. State a general rule for multiplying two integers, based on operations with their corresponding whole numbers.

7. State a general rule for dividing two integers, based on operations with their corresponding whole numbers.

8. (a) Is the set of integers closed under all the four basic operations?
   (b) If your answer is "no," prove your statement by giving an example(s) which has no integer as the result of an operation on two integers.

9. (a) Use the sentence below to illustrate the distributive property for the multiplication of integers in three ways:

$$n = (^-4)(^-32).$$

   (b) Use the sentence below to illustrate the distributive property for the division of integers in three ways:

$$p = (^-693) \div (^+3).$$

10. The normal annual temperature range is given below for some locations in the United States. Find the number of degrees and the direction the temperature must change to rise or fall from the first reading given to the second.
    (a) Mobile, Alabama: 104°, 11°
    (b) Little Rock, Arkansas: −5°, 107°
    (c) Denver, Colorado: 104°, −30°
    (d) Miami, Florida: 32°, 98°
    (e) Bismark, North Dakota: −44°, 109°
    (f) Juneau, Alaska: 84°, −21°

(g) Honolulu, Hawaii: 55°, 93°   (h) New York City: —14°, 102°

(i) Chicago: 104°, —15°   (j) San Francisco: 20°, 104°

11. If deposits to an account are represented by positive integers and with-
drawals by negative integers, and if an account has a balance of $290,
what is the balance after each of the following consecutive transactions?
Write a mathematical sentence for each.

(a) Deposit $750   (b) Deposit $98   (c) Withdraw $45

(d) Deposit $1250   (e) Withdraw $985   (f) Withdraw $35

12. (a) If $125 are deposited in an account each month, how much money is
deposited in a year?

(b) If $32 are withdrawn from an account each month, how much money
is withdrawn in a year?

(c) What is the total effect of (a) and (b)?

13. The altitudes of the highest and lowest points for some states of the United
States are given below. By how many feet does the altitude change when
you move from the first location to the second? Write a mathematical
sentence for each move and solve.

(a) Louisiana: 535 ft, —5 ft   (b) Illinois: 279 ft, 1241 ft

(c) California: 14,495 ft, —282 ft   (d) Alaska: 0 ft, 20,320 ft

(e) Colorado: 3350 ft, 14,431 ft   (f) Florida: 345 ft, 0 ft

14. The average altitudes of the floor of some oceans and seas of the world are
given in the following exercises. Find the difference in altitude between
the first location and the second. Write a mathematical sentence for each
part and solve.

(a) Pacific Ocean, $^-$14,048 ft,   (b) Persian Gulf, $^-$82 ft,
    Arctic Ocean, $^-$3953 ft   Indian Ocean, $^-$13,002 ft

(c) North Sea, $^-$308 ft,   (d) Atlantic Ocean, $^-$12,880 ft,
    English Channel, $^-$190 ft   Pacific Ocean, $^-$14,048 ft

15. In each of the following find the difference in altitude between the first
point named and the second. Write a mathematical sentence for each
and solve.

(a) Mount Everest, 29,028 ft,   (b) Death Valley, $^-$282 ft,
    Dead Sea, $^-$1286 ft   Dead Sea, $^-$1286 ft

(c) Death Valley, $^-$282 ft,   (d) Mount McKinley, $^+$20,320 ft,
    Mount McKinley, $^+$20,320 ft   Mount Everest, $^+$29,028 ft

(e) Mount Blanc, $^+$15,771 ft,   (f) Dead Sea, $^-$1286 ft,
    Mount McKinley, $^+$20,320 ft   Caspian Sea, $^-$92 ft

16. If a grasshopper starts at the point given on a line and makes jumps measuring the number of feet indicated in each of the following, what is his
final location? Write a mathematical sentence for each part and solve.

(a) Starting point: 0. Jumps: $^-$3, $^-$5, $^-$3

(b) Starting point: $^+$7. Jumps: $^+$8, $^-$15, $^+$7

(c) Starting point: $^-$3. Jumps: $^+$8, $^+$5, $^-$7, $^-$2, $^-$3

(d) Starting point: $^+$4. Jumps: $^-$6, $^-$4, $^+$3, $^+$4, $^-$10

17. If two grasshoppers start at the point indicated on a line and make jumps measuring the number of feet indicated for each, which one will win the races in (a) through (c)? Write mathematical sentences for each grasshopper's series of jumps, solve, and answer the question.

    (a) Starting point: 0. Jumps of grasshopper M: $^+8$, $^+12$, $^+3$, $^-17$. Jumps of grasshopper R: $^-4$, $^-6$, $^+8$, $^+2$, $^+10$.

    (b) Starting point: $^+12$. Jumps of grasshopper N: $^+210$, $^-172$, $^+402$, $^-78$. Jumps of grasshopper S: $^+578$, $^-50$, $^-62$, $^-37$, $^-67$.

    (c) Starting point: $^-215$. Jumps of grasshopper P: $^-87$, $^-78$, $^+305$, $^+72$. Jumps of grasshopper T: $^+45$, $^+92$, $^+125$, $^-76$.

REFERENCES

Banks, J. Houston, *Elements of Mathematics.* Boston: Allyn and Bacon, Inc., 1961, pp. 148–153.

Brumfiel, Charles F., Robert E. Eicholz, and Merrill E. Shanks, *Fundamental Concepts of Elementary Mathematics.* Reading, Massachusetts: Addison-Wesley Publishing Company, Inc., 1962, pp. 198–213.

Peterson, John A., and Joseph Hashisaki, *Theory of Arithmetic.* New York: John Wiley and Sons, Inc., 1963, pp. 112–124.

Schaaf, William L., *Basic Concepts of Elementary Mathematics.* New York: John Wiley and Sons, Inc., 1960, pp. 121–129.

School Mathematics Study Group, "Number Systems," in *Studies in Mathematics.* Volume VI. New Haven, Connecticut: Yale University, 1961, pp. 167–215.

Swain, Robert L., *Understanding Arithmetic.* New York: Rinehart and Company, Inc., 1957, pp. 170–181.

CHAPTER TWELVE

THE RATIONAL NUMBERS

1. IMPORTANCE

The rational numbers are continually used in mathematics, science, and everyday life and are second in importance only to the whole numbers. The reasons for their importance can best be understood by examining what they are and by relating them to familiar number systems. Their properties will be discussed later in the chapter.

Counting situations and rational numbers. The need for rational numbers arises in certain counting situations for which integers or fractions alone are inadequate, that is, when it is necessary to count or measure both in units and subunits and in one or the other direction from a fixed reference point. For example, if distances above and below sea level are to be measured and the results are to be stated in integers only, then distances of, say, 19 feet 4 inches above sea level and 17 feet 6 inches below sea level must be measured in inch units, e.g., $^+232$ inches or $^-210$ inches. If it is desired, however, to state the distances in feet, a new number symbol is required. Proceeding by analogy with fractions, you might speak of distances of

$$\frac{^+232}{12} \text{ feet} \quad \text{and} \quad \frac{^-210}{12} \text{ feet.}$$

The numbers used here are examples of *rational numbers*. They have the character of both integers and fractions.

Rational numbers are represented by fractions whose numerators are integers, but whose denominators are whole numbers excluding zero. The meaning of these symbols expresses the counting situations which gave rise to them. For example, in the rational fraction $\frac{^-210}{12}$, the denominator 12 expresses the relation between the inch unit and the foot unit in which the distance "17 feet 6 inches below sea level" is expressed. The numerator $^-210$ expresses the fact that the inch units are to be counted in the negative sense corresponding to a distance below sea level. The mixed form, $^-17\frac{1}{2}$ feet, expresses the same fact, for $\frac{^-210}{12} = {}^-17\frac{1}{2}$ because the same number is being named in each case.

Many other examples could be given, such as temperatures above and below zero measured in degrees and tenths of a degree, times before or after a zero hour measured in minutes and seconds. You should identify other examples where the quantities involved require rational numbers.

The number systems of arithmetic. Any kind of number used in arithmetic, e.g., the whole numbers, has two aspects. First, the whole numbers are *mathematical ideas* applicable to certain counting activities. Secondly, the whole numbers are *mathematical objects* whose properties may be studied independently of their origin and use in counting. As mathematical objects, their properties ultimately depend upon certain precisely defined relations and operations that can be performed on them. The relations are the order relations and the operations are the four fundamental operations of arithmetic. When the whole numbers are thought of in this manner, they are said to form a *number system*.

Three number systems have already been considered: the whole numbers, the fractions, and the integers. The rational numbers form still another number system. All four systems resemble one another in certain important respects:

(a) *The numbers of each system are totally ordered.*

(b) *The basic arithmetic operations of addition and multiplication may be unrestrictedly performed in each system.*

(c) *Each system may be interpreted geometrically on a number line.*

There are also important differences among the four number systems. The most important difference concerns the inverse operations of subtraction and division. The whole numbers are neither closed under subtraction nor closed under division. The fractions excluding zero are closed under division, but not under subtraction. The integers are closed under subtraction, but not under division. The rational numbers, however, are closed under both subtraction and division. It is understood that division by zero is excluded.

Another important difference among the four systems concerns their inclusiveness. Both the fractions and the integers are extensions of the

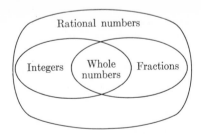

FIG. 12–1. The number systems of arithmetic.

whole numbers (Chapter 9, Section 8; Chapter 11, Section 8). Hence they may be thought of as including the whole number system which is identified, in the one case, with the nonnegative integers, and in the other case, with the fractions of denominator one. The rational number system is an extension of all the other three number systems and hence may be thought of as including all of them. Each of these number systems may be identified as a distinguished subsystem of the rational numbers. The relationship among the four subsystems is shown schematically in Fig. 12–1.

2. THE RATIONAL NUMBER LINE

A number line helps to clarify the meaning of the rational numbers and their order relations, as it did with other number systems.

FIG. 12–2. The rational number line.

Figure 12–2 makes it evident that both integers and fractions correspond to rational numbers. For example, the integers $^-2$, $^-1$, 0, $^+1$, $^+2$, correspond to the rational fractions

$$\frac{^-2}{1}, \quad \frac{^-1}{1}, \quad \frac{0}{1}, \quad \frac{^+1}{1}, \quad \frac{^+2}{1}$$

while fractions such as $\frac{1}{5}$, $.75$, $\frac{10}{3}$, correspond to the positive rationals

$$\frac{^+1}{5}, \quad \frac{^+75}{100}, \quad \frac{^+10}{3}.$$

Furthermore, these correspondences preserve order since corresponding numbers are represented by the same point on the number line.

It will be shown later that the above-mentioned correspondences between integers and rational numbers and between fractions and rational numbers preserve not only order, but the fundamental arithmetical operations as well. This fact is the justification for regarding the rational number system as an extension of both the integers and the fractions.

3. SIMPLIFIED NOTATION FOR INTEGERS AND RATIONALS

The operations of addition and multiplication of rational numbers are performed, as with fractions, on the numerators and denominators of the fractional symbols which represent the numbers. The denominators may be thought of as positive integers, but the numerators may be either positive or negative integers. Consequently, operating with rational numbers requires repeated arithmetical operations on integers. For these purposes, the use of the $+$ and $-$ signs as superscripts to distinguish the positive integers, $^{+}1$, $^{+}2$, $^{+}3$, ..., from the negative integers, $^{-}1$, $^{-}2$, $^{-}3$, ..., becomes very cumbersome. The simplification universally adopted is to drop the superscript $^{+}$ from the positive integers, denoting them by 1, 2, 3, ..., and to lower the superscript $^{-}$ on the negative integers, denoting them by -1, -2, -3, ...

The first simplification is justified by the one-to-one correspondence between the whole numbers and the positive integers, which was described in Chapter 11. The positive sign may be reintroduced, if necessary. For example, if it desired to emphasize that the integer "positive two" is meant rather than the whole number two, one writes $+2$.

The disadvantage of using $+$ and $-$ both as symbols for operations and as the criterion distinguishing between different kinds of integers is offset by the advantages of simplicity in writing integers and flexibility in operating on integers. The numbers -1, -2, -3, ..., etc., are read "negative one," "negative two," "negative three," ...

When used to designate integers, $+$ and $-$ are called the *signs* of the integers. Thus, the sign of 2 or $+2$ is $+$; the sign of -2 is $-$, and opposite integers like 4 and -4 are said to differ only in sign.

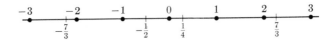

FIG. 12–3.   Rational number line.

On the rational number line in Fig. 12–3, a few of the representative points are depicted in the simplified notation.

Operations on integers expressed in simplified notation.   One of the main advantages of the simplified notation is the ease with which it allows arithmetical operations on integers to be performed. For example, since

$$^{+}5 + {}^{-}4 = {}^{+}5 - {}^{+}4,$$

$$^{+}5 + {}^{-}4 \qquad \text{is written} \qquad 5 - 4,$$

and since

$$^{+}5 - {}^{-}4 = {}^{+}5 + {}^{+}4,$$

$$^{+}5 - {}^{-}4 \qquad \text{is written} \qquad 5 + 4.$$

In general, if a minus sign and a plus sign are juxtaposed as in $5 + {}^{-}4$

or $5 - {}^+4$, the plus sign may be omitted; thus ${}^-13 - {}^+8$ may be written $-13 - 8$. If two minus signs are juxtaposed as in $5 - {}^-4$, they are replaced by a plus sign; thus ${}^+5 - {}^-4$ may be written $5 + 4$.

The following important property of an integer and its opposite was developed in Chapter 11: if u is a positive integer, then

$$-u = (-1) \cdot u \qquad \text{and} \qquad (-1) \cdot (-1) = +1.$$

In simplified notation these results may be restated as follows:

The integers u and u' are opposite   if and only if $u' = (-1) \cdot u$. (1)

For example, 8 and -8 are opposite integers. Consequently, $-8 = (-1) \cdot 8$ and $8 = (-1) \cdot (-8)$ since

$$(-1) \cdot (-8) = (-1) \cdot (-1) \cdot 8 = 1 \cdot 8 = 8.$$

When you add and multiply rationals the operations are performed on the numerators and denominators of the fractions representing them. The following formulas for addition and subtraction of integers are useful (u and v denote any integers).

$$v - u = v + u';$$ (2a)

$$-u - v = -(u + v);$$ (2b)

$$u + v = -(-u - v);$$ (2c)

$$u - v = -(v - u).$$ (2d)

For example, by (2a), $5 - (-2) = 5 + 2$. By (2b), $-8 - 13 = -(8 + 13) = -21$. By (2c), $-13 + 8 = -(13 - 8) = -5$. By (2d), $8 - 13 = -(13 - 8) = -5$.

The following formulas may be used in a similar manner to simplify the multiplication of rationals.

$$(-u) \cdot (-v) = u \cdot v.$$ (3)

$$(-u) \cdot v = u \cdot (-v) = -(u \cdot v).$$ (4)

For example,

$$(-4) \cdot (-3) = 4 \cdot 3 = 4 \times 3 = 12$$

and

$$(-4) \cdot 3 = 4 \cdot (-3) = -(4 \cdot 3) = -12.$$

The simplified notation for integers described in this section will now be used without further mention. Opportunities for practice will be found in the exercises.

4. GEOMETRIC ADDITION AND SUBTRACTION OF RATIONALS

It is possible to define and perform addition and subtraction of rational numbers geometrically, using vectors and arrow diagrams on the number line precisely as was done in Chapter 11 for the addition and subtraction of integers. Vectors representing the rational numbers $\frac{5}{4}$ and $-\frac{5}{4}$ are indicated by arrows in Fig. 12–4.

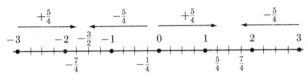

FIGURE 12–4

The geometric interpretation of the addition and subtraction of rationals is left for you in the exercises.

The development of addition and subtraction given in the next section follows the plan used for the addition and subtraction of fractions in Chapter 9, and is arithmetic, rather than geometric, in character.

EXERCISE SET 12–1

1. (a) Sketch a number line and locate the following points:

$$0, \quad \frac{^+1}{1}, \quad \frac{^+5}{1}, \quad \frac{3}{2}, \quad \frac{7}{3}, \quad \frac{^-5}{1}, \quad \frac{^-1}{1}, \quad \frac{1}{4}, \quad \frac{^-3}{1}.$$

   (b) Use a plus sign to label all numbers to the right of point 0 (positive integers).
   (c) Show the symmetry between any opposites which you located in (a), by connecting them with arrows.
   (d) Locate and label the opposite of any number for which you have not found an opposite. Connect the opposite with arrows.
2. Write the rational number which describes the following counting situations.
   (a) The accounts showed a deficit of $545.25.
   (b) The city is 30°30' north of the equator.
   (c) The city is 45°15' west of the Greenwich meridian.
   (d) The temperature recorded was $232\frac{1}{2}°$ below zero.
3. Illustrate each of the following, using the system of whole numbers.
   (a) The numbers of the system are totally ordered.
   (b) The basic arithmetic operations of addition and multiplication may be unrestrictedly performed.
   (c) The numbers may be interpreted geometrically on a number line.
4. Use the system of fractions to illustrate each of the statements of Exercise 3.
5. Using the system of integers, illustrate each of the statements of Exercise 3.

6. (a) Which of the three number systems, whole numbers, fractions, and integers, are not closed with respect to subtraction?

   (b) Prove your answer to (a) by giving one illustration to show that the sets are not closed.

7. (a) Which of the number systems, whole numbers, fractions, and integers, are not closed with respect to division?

   (b) Prove your answer to (a) by giving one illustration showing that the sets are not closed.

8. What number(s) must be excluded from the set mentioned in each of the following statements to make them true?

   (a) A whole number has neither an additive nor a multiplicative inverse.

   (b) A fractional number has no additive inverse.

   (c) An integer has no multiplicative inverse.

   (d) A rational number has both an additive and a multiplicative inverse.

9. If W is the set of whole numbers, F is the set of fractions, and I is the set of integers, indicate which of the following are true and which are false.

   (a) $F \supset W$ (b) $F \cup I \supset W$ (c) $W \subseteq I$

   (d) $I \cap F = W$ (e) $W \cap F = W \cap I$ (f) $W \cup F = I \cup W$

10. Express the following rational numbers in the simplified notation described in Section 3.

   (a) $^{+}5$ (b) $^{-}7$ (c) $^{+}7 + {}^{+}3$

   (d) $^{+}7 + {}^{-}3$ (e) $^{+}7 - {}^{+}3$ (f) $^{+}7 - {}^{-}3$

   (g) $^{-}4 + {}^{+}3$ (h) $^{-}4 + {}^{-}3$ (i) $^{-}4 - {}^{+}3$

   (j) $^{-}4 - {}^{-}3$ (k) $^{-}2 + {}^{-}3 + {}^{+}7$ (l) $^{-}5 - {}^{-}6 + {}^{-}4$

11. Show by vector addition or subtraction (Chapter 11, Sections 5 and 6) each of the following.

   (a) $\dfrac{^{+}5}{2} + \dfrac{^{-}3}{2}$ (b) $\dfrac{^{-}7}{4} + \dfrac{^{-}5}{4}$ (c) $\dfrac{^{-}5}{2} - \dfrac{^{-}3}{2}$ (d) $\dfrac{^{-}5}{2} - \dfrac{^{+}3}{2}$

12. Verify each of the following by vector diagrams.

   (a) $\dfrac{5}{3} + \dfrac{^{-}7}{3} = \dfrac{5}{3} - \dfrac{7}{3}$ (b) $\dfrac{5}{3} - \dfrac{^{-}7}{3} = \dfrac{5}{3} + \dfrac{7}{3}$

5. OPERATIONS AND RELATIONS OF THE RATIONAL NUMBER SYSTEM

The properties of the rational number system will now be considered in detail. To facilitate comparison with other systems, the properties of addition and multiplication which have been previously developed are summarized in Table 12–1. It is assumed that a number system is under consideration over which an addition, a multiplication, and an order relation are defined and that these have some or all of the properties listed. The letters u, v, and w are variables whose domain is the set of numbers being considered. For example, if the number system of the integers is under consideration, u, v, and w denote integers.

TABLE 12–1.   PROPERTIES OF ADDITION AND MULTIPLICATION

ADDITION	MULTIPLICATION
CLOSURE	
I. If u and v are elements in the system, then $u + v$ is in the system and is uniquely determined by u and v.	If u and v are elements in the system, then $u \cdot v$ is in the system and is uniquely determined by u and v.
ASSOCIATIVITY	
II. For any elements u, v, and w, $$(u + v) + w = u + (v + w).$$	For any elements u, v, and w, $$(u \cdot v) \cdot w = u \cdot (v \cdot w).$$
EXISTENCE OF IDENTITY	
III. An element 0 exists in the system so that for any u, $$0 + u = u + 0 = u.$$	An element 1 exists in the system so that for any u, $$1 \cdot u = u \cdot 1 = u.$$
CANCELLATION PROPERTY	
IV. For any elements v, w, and u, $$u + v = u + w$$ implies that $v = w$.	For any elements v, w, and $u (u \neq 0)$, $$u \cdot v = u \cdot w$$ implies that $v = w$.
COMMUTATIVITY	
V. For any elements u and v, $$u + v = v + u.$$	For any elements u and v, $$u \cdot v = v \cdot u.$$
EXISTENCE OF ADDITIVE AND MULTIPLICATIVE INVERSES	
VI. For any element u, there exists an element u' so that $$u + u' = u' + u = 0.$$	For any element $u (u \neq 0)$, there exists an element u^* so that $$u \cdot u^* = u^* \cdot u = 1.$$

DISTRIBUTIVE PROPERTY

VII. For any three elements u, v, and w,

$$u \cdot (v + w) = u \cdot v + u \cdot w,$$

and

$$(v + w) \cdot u = v \cdot u + w \cdot u.$$

Properties of operations in a number system

TABLE 12–2

PROPERTIES OF OPERATIONS IN NUMBER SYSTEMS

	Closure	Closure	Associativity	Associativity	Identity	Identity	Cancellation	Cancellation	Commutativity	Commutativity	Additive inverse	Multiplicative inverse	Distributivity
Property	I	I	II	II	III	III	IV	IV	V	V	VI	VI	VII
Operation	+	×	+	×	+	×	+	×	+	×	+	×	×
Whole numbers	✓	✓	✓	✓	✓	✓	✓	✓	✓	✓	No	No	✓
Fractions	✓	✓	✓	✓	✓	✓	✓	✓	✓	✓	No	✓	✓
Integers	✓	✓	✓	✓	✓	✓	✓	✓	✓	✓	✓	No	✓
Rationals	✓	✓	✓	✓	✓	✓	✓	✓	✓	✓	✓	✓	✓

With the properties of operations summarized, it is now possible to compare and contrast the four number systems that are familiar to you (Table 12–2).

It is clear from Table 12–2 that although a whole number, an integer, a fraction, and a rational number are conceptually different, their properties as members of a number system are very much alike. In fact, the only difference is the existence of additive and multiplicative inverses. Further, the rational number system is the only one of the systems whose operations have all the properties.

Properties of order relation in a number system. In addition to the properties of operations a number system may also have three properties of order relation.

VIII. *Total ordering.* If u and v denote any two elements, exactly one of the following three relations is true:

(a) $u > v$;   (b) $v > u$;   (c) $u = v$.

IX. If u, v, and w are any three elements, then $v > w$ implies that

$$u + v > u + w.$$

X. If v and w are any any two elements and $u > 0$, then $v > w$ implies that
$$u \cdot v > u \cdot w.$$

Each of the four familiar number systems has the three order properties. For example,

$$0 < 1 < 2 < 3 < \cdots ; \qquad \tfrac{1}{2} < \tfrac{2}{2} < \tfrac{4}{3} < \tfrac{3}{2} < \cdots ;$$

$$-2 < -1 < 0 < +1 < \cdots ; \qquad \text{and} \qquad \frac{^-1}{3} < 0 < \frac{3}{3} < \frac{5}{3} < \cdots$$

Also, since
$$\frac{^-5}{3} > \frac{^-7}{3} , \qquad \text{then} \qquad \frac{^-6}{3} > \frac{^-8}{3}$$
and since
$$\frac{^-5}{3} > \frac{^-7}{3} , \qquad \text{then} \qquad \frac{^-15}{6} > \frac{^-21}{6} .$$

6. THE FIELD CONCEPT

A system of numbers in which an addition and a multiplication are defined with all the properties just listed is called a number field or simply a *field*. If, in addition, the order properties are satisfied, the number system is called an *ordered field*. The simplest example of an ordered field is the rational number system. There are many fields which cannot be ordered.

Rational field. Of the many fields of mathematics the *rational field* is the most important one not only for elementary arithmetic, but for applications of mathematics. This is true because all physical measurements and computations are carried out in the rational number system.

Some recent treatments of elementary algebra begin with the field concept. The numbers of the system are then mathematical objects which have the properties I through VII. These properties are postulates for a field analogous to the postulates for the rudimentary geometry described in Chapter 8, Section 5. In the properties of a field, "number" is an undefined term analogous to "point" in the postulates of geometry.

Example of a field. The meaning of the field concept can be further understood from an examination of a simple field. In the following, the numbers of modulo-five arithmetic will be examined in terms of each of the field properties I through VII and shown to be a field. (See Section 15, Chapter 6 for a review of the numbers of modular arithmetic.) Tables 12–3 and 12–4 are the addition and multiplication charts for modulo-five arithmetic.

TABLE 12–3
ADDITION CHART

+	0	1	2	3	4
0	0	1	2	3	4
1	1	2	3	4	0
2	2	3	4	0	1
3	3	4	0	1	2
4	4	0	1	2	3

TABLE 12–4
MULTIPLICATION CHART

×	0	1	2	3	4
0	0	0	0	0	0
1	0	1	2	3	4
2	0	2	4	1	3
3	0	3	1	4	2
4	0	4	3	2	1

The modulo-five system of numbers is *closed* (Property I) with respect to each operation since each space in the two charts contains a number of the system. An examination of the charts also shows that the *identity* for *addition* is zero and the *identity* for *multiplication* is one. The numbers of modulo-five numbers have met the criteria of Property III.

The operations of addition and multiplication of modulo-five numbers are *commutative* (Property V) as the symmetry of the charts show. Both formulas,

$$u + v = v + u \quad \text{and} \quad u \cdot v = v \cdot u,$$

apply to modulo-five numbers.

Table 12–3 verifies that each number has an *additive inverse*. For example,

$$4 + 1 = 0, \quad 3 + 2 = 0, \quad 2 + 3 = 0,$$
$$1 + 4 = 0, \quad \text{and} \quad 0 + 0 = 0.$$

Table 12–4 verifies that each number other than zero has a *multiplicative inverse*. For example,

$$1 \times 1 = 1, \quad 2 \times 3 = 1, \quad 3 \times 2 = 1, \quad \text{and} \quad 4 \times 4 = 1.$$

The system satisfies field property VI.

The operations of addition and multiplication may be shown to be *associative* (Property II). For example, since

$$(2 + 3) + 4 = 0 + 4 = 4 \quad \text{and} \quad 2 + (3 + 4) = 2 + 2 = 4,$$

then $(2 + 3) + 4 = 2 + (3 + 4)$. Since

$$(1 \times 4) \times 3 = 4 \times 3 = 2 \quad \text{and} \quad 1 \times (4 \times 3) = 1 \times 2 = 2,$$

then

$$(1 \times 4) \times 3 = 1 \times (4 \times 3).$$

The operations of addition and multiplication also have the *cancellation property* (Property IV).   For example, if $4 + 1 + 2 = 0 + 2$, then $4 + 1 = 0$, and if $3 \times 4 \times 2 = 2 \times 2$, then $3 \times 4 = 2$.

The *distributive* property (Property VII) for the operations of multiplication may be verified from Table 12–4.   For example, since $2 \times 5 = 0$ and

$$2(2 + 3) = (2 \times 2) + (2 \times 3) = 4 + 1 = 0,$$

then

$$2 \times 5 = 2(2 + 3) = (2 \times 2) + (2 \times 3).$$

The numbers of modulo-five arithmetic form a field because they have all the properties of a field. You can verify that the system does not form an ordered field no matter how the order relation is defined.   For instance, if we assume

$$0 < 1 < 2 < 3 < 4,$$

Properties IX and X are not satisfied.

You should determine whether the numbers of other modular arithmetics form a field. See Exercises 21 and 22 of Exercise Set 12–2.

7.   OPERATIONS WITH RATIONALS

The addition and multiplication of rationals. To ensure that the rational number system shall be an extension of the fractional number system, the sum and product of two rational numbers are defined in terms of fractional numbers. The definitions are chosen so that the operations reduce to the corresponding operations on fractions whenever the rational numbers are nonnegative.

Suppose that $\frac{a}{c}$ and $\frac{b}{d}$ are two rational fractions, so that a and b are integers and c and d are positive integers.   Then the sum and the product of $\frac{a}{c}$ and $\frac{b}{d}$ are defined as follows:

$$\frac{a}{c} + \frac{b}{d} = \frac{a \cdot d + b \cdot c}{c \cdot d}, \tag{5}$$

and

$$\frac{a}{c} \times \frac{b}{d} = \frac{a \cdot b}{c \cdot d}. \tag{6}$$

Note that if the rational numbers are positive, a and b are positive integers and the definitions agree with the procedure for adding and multiplying fractions derived in Chapter 9. In any case, the multiplication and addition necessary to perform the operations are carried out in the system of integers.

It may be proved from these definitions that the addition and multiplication defined by formulas (5) and (6) have all the previously stated properties for addition and multiplication in a number field. It will suffice here to illustrate the distributive property by discussing a numerical example.

We first note the following criterion for equality which is used repeatedly in operating with rational fractions (see Chapter 9, Section 2).

$$\frac{a}{b} = \frac{c}{d} \quad \text{if and only if} \quad a \cdot d = b \cdot c \quad \text{and} \quad c \cdot d \neq 0. \qquad (7)$$

Thus, for example, we have

$$\frac{-25}{50} = \frac{-1}{2}$$

because $-25 \cdot 2 = -1 \cdot 50$. Then formula (3) justifies the dividing out of common factors from the numerator and denominator of a rational fraction. In this case, 25 is a common factor of -25 and 50. If the multiplication of rational numbers is distributive with respect to addition, then for

$$\frac{-6}{5}, \quad \frac{2}{3}, \quad \text{and} \quad \frac{-1}{4},$$

we must have

$$\frac{-6}{5} \times (\frac{2}{3} + \frac{-1}{4}) = (\frac{-6}{5} \times \frac{2}{3}) + (\frac{-6}{5} \times \frac{-1}{4}).$$

That the number expressions to the left (L) and to the right (R) of the equals sign are both equal to $\frac{-1}{2}$ may be verified by using formulas (5), (6), and (7) to simplify the number expressions. The computations are as follows.

$$L = \frac{-6}{5} \times (\frac{2}{3} - \frac{1}{4}) = \frac{-6}{5} \times (\frac{8}{12} - \frac{3}{12}) = \frac{-6}{5} \times \frac{5}{12} = \frac{-30}{60} = \frac{-1}{2}$$

and

$$R = (\frac{-6}{5} \times \frac{2}{3}) + (\frac{-6}{5} \times \frac{-1}{4}) = \frac{-12}{15} + \frac{3}{10} = \frac{-24}{30} + \frac{9}{30} = \frac{-15}{30} = \frac{-1}{2}.$$

Thus $L = R$, and the application to the rationals of the first of the two parts of the distributive property (VII, Table 12–1) was properly made.

The subtraction and division of rationals. If r and s denote any rationals, then the difference $r - s$ is defined by

$$r - s = r + s'. \qquad (8)$$

Here the element s' is the opposite of s and $r + s'$ is defined by formula (2). For example, if

$$r = \frac{10}{7} \quad \text{and} \quad s = \frac{-53}{7}, \quad \text{then} \quad s' = \frac{53}{7}.$$

Consequently,

$$\frac{10}{7} - \frac{-53}{7} = \frac{10}{7} + \frac{53}{7} = \frac{63}{7} = 9.$$

It may be proved that formula (8) is correct in every case because of the inverseness of addition and subtraction.

$$\text{If } \quad t + s = r, \qquad \text{then} \quad t = r - s. \tag{9}$$

But by the properties of addition,

$$(r + s') + s = r + (s' + s) = r + 0 = r.$$

Consequently, if r and s are given rationals, formula (9) is satisfied if $t = r + s'$. Therefore formula (8) must be true for any rationals r and s.

You should note that formula (8) is analogous to the principle proved in Chapter 11 for integers:

> *To subtract an integer, add its opposite.*

In the rational field it may also be stated,

> *To subtract a rational, add its opposite.*

Thus subtraction is not a separate operation in the rational field.

Division may be defined in terms of multiplication by following the same pattern, but replacing the operation of addition by the operation of multiplication. Observe first, that if s is a positive rational, the element s^*, the multiplicative inverse, is the reciprocal of s. For example, if $s = \frac{5}{3}$, then $s^* = \frac{3}{5}$ because $s \cdot s^* = \frac{5}{3} \times \frac{3}{5} = 1$. If s is negative, e.g., $\frac{-5}{3}$, then $s^* = \frac{-3}{5}$. Again,

$$s \cdot s^* = \frac{-5}{3} \times \frac{-3}{5} = \frac{(-5) \times (-3)}{3 \times 5} = \frac{15}{15} = 1.$$

This shows then that every nonzero rational number has a multiplicative inverse; that is, for any rational s excluding zero, its inverse s^* exists where s is positive or negative. Accordingly, if $s \neq 0$, $r \div s$ may be defined by

$$r \div s = r \times s^*. \tag{10}$$

Ordering of rational numbers. Rational numbers may be compared with respect to order by plotting their representative points on the rational number line. But a purely numerical definition of the relation "greater than" can be given from which Properties VIII, IX, and X follow. If $\frac{a}{b}$ and $\frac{c}{d}$ are any two rationals in fractional form, the relation $>$

is defined by

$$\frac{a}{b} > \frac{c}{d} \quad \text{if and only if} \quad a \cdot d > b \cdot c.$$

For example, $\dfrac{-7}{8} > \dfrac{-8}{9}$ because $-7 \cdot 9 > 8 \cdot (-8)$ or $-63 > -64$.

8. OTHER NUMBERS AND NUMBER SYSTEMS

The rational number system is sufficient for the purposes of elementary arithmetic. However, there is a need for another kind of number in algebra, geometry, and in the applications of algebra and geometry. This need can be met by a *further extension of the number system*. An important extension, the *real number system*, will be described in Chapter 13 in connection with the geometry of the Euclidean line. The simplest examples of useful numbers which are not rational are square roots such as $\sqrt{2}$, $\sqrt{3}$, $\sqrt{10}$, and $\sqrt{37}$. The following proposition, which will be used in Chapter 13, is theoretically important because it shows that the rational number system, although very extensive, does not contain all numbers which you need. For example,

There exists no rational number whose square is equal to 2.

The proof of this proposition was known to Euclid. It consists in showing that the assumption "A rational number r exists so that $r^2 = 2$" leads to a contradiction. The proof follows.

The rational number r may be represented as a fraction in its lowest terms. Let

$$r = \frac{n}{m}. \quad (n, m) = 1$$

relatively prime

Here n and m are positive integers which cannot both be even, since r is in its lowest terms. If it is assumed that $r^2 = 2$, then by implication

$$2 = \frac{n^2}{m^2}$$

and

$$n^2 = 2m^2.$$

The number $2m^2$ is even. Therefore n must be even. Let $n = 2p$, where p is a positive integer. Then substituting $2p$ for n in $n^2 = 2m^2$ gives $4p^2 = 2m^2$. Therefore $2p^2 = m^2$ by the cancellation property of multiplication. Since m^2 is even, m must also be even. But n and m cannot both be even. Therefore the assumption that $r^2 = 2$ is false, and the theorem must be true.

The rational number system was invented to satisfy the need for a system which had both an additive inverse and a multiplicative inverse, a system in which subtraction and division, excluding division by zero, are always possible. The proof that no rational number exists whose square is equal to 2 indicates, however, *a need for further extension of the number system.*

EXERCISE SET 12–2

1. Illustrate each of the following statements using the system of rational numbers.
   (a) The numbers of the system are totally ordered.
   (b) The basic arithmetical operations of addition and multiplication may be unrestrictedly performed.
   (c) The numbers may be interpreted geometrically on a number line.
2. (a) Is the operation of addition of rational numbers commutative? If so, state the property and illustrate.
   (b) Is the operation of multiplication of rational numbers commutative? If so, state the property and illustrate.
3. (a) Is the operation of addition of rational numbers associative? If so, state the property and illustrate.
   (b) Is the operation of multiplication of rational numbers associative? If so, state the property and illustrate.
4. (a) Does the operation of addition of rational numbers have an identity element? If so, what is the number? Illustrate.
   (b) Does the operation of multiplication of rational numbers have an identity element? If so, what is the number? Illustrate.
5. State the property of closure for the rational numbers with respect to the basic operations.
6. Illustrate the property of closure for the rational numbers

$$-\tfrac{5}{2}, \quad \tfrac{3}{4}, \quad \text{and} \quad \tfrac{1}{2}.$$

7. Give the additive inverse of each of the following:
   (a) $\tfrac{7}{8}$ (b) $-\tfrac{3}{2}$ (c) $+4$ (d) -6 (e) $-\tfrac{3}{7}$
8. (a) Does every rational number have an additive inverse? If so, state your observation as a property.
   (b) Illustrate the property with the rational number $\tfrac{5}{2}$.
9. Give the multiplicative inverse for each of the following:
   (a) $\tfrac{7}{8}$ (b) $-\tfrac{3}{2}$ (c) $+4$ (d) -6 (e) $-\tfrac{3}{7}$
10. (a) Does every rational number have a multiplicative inverse? If so, state this observation as a property.
    (b) Illustrate with the rational number $\tfrac{5}{2}$.
11. Illustrate the distributive property of multiplication of the rational numbers with respect to addition with the numbers $-\tfrac{1}{2}, \tfrac{2}{3}, -\tfrac{8}{3}$.

12. In (a) through (f) below, state the order relation of the first number to the second.

(a) $-\frac{2}{3}$, $-\frac{5}{2}$ (b) $\frac{7}{3}$, $\frac{21}{9}$ (c) $\frac{2}{3}$, $-\frac{5}{2}$

(d) $\frac{3}{1}$, $-\frac{3}{1}$ (e) $\frac{1}{2}$, $\frac{5}{2}$ (f) $-\frac{1}{2}$, $-\frac{5}{2}$

13. Order each of the following sets of numbers with respect to the "greater than" relationship.

(a) $\frac{1}{4}$, $\frac{5}{4}$, $-\frac{8}{4}$, -3, 0

(b) $\frac{3}{2}$, $-\frac{7}{8}$, $+\frac{3}{4}$, $-\frac{8}{4}$, $\frac{0}{4}$

(c) -6, $\frac{2}{3}$, $\frac{5}{6}$, $-\frac{8}{3}$, 2

(d) $-\frac{5}{8}$, $-\frac{3}{8}$, $\frac{8}{8}$, $\frac{1}{8}$, $\frac{0}{8}$

14. (a) Give one reason why the set of whole numbers does not constitute a number field.

(b) Give one reason why the set of integers does not constitute a number field.

(c) Give one reason why the set of fractions does not constitute a number field.

15. Solve the following:

(a) $\frac{2}{3} - \frac{5}{2} = a$

(b) $-\frac{5}{4} - \frac{7}{8} = b$

(c) $c = -\frac{5}{8} + \frac{1}{2} - \frac{5}{4}$

(d) $-\frac{2}{3} + \frac{7}{8} = d$

(e) $e = -\frac{3}{2} + 8 - \frac{7}{3}$

(f) $f = +\frac{5}{12} - \frac{2}{3} - \frac{11}{9}$

16. Solve the following:

(a) $(\frac{2}{3})(-\frac{1}{4}) = a$

(b) $b = (-\frac{7}{3})(-\frac{5}{2})$

(c) $c = (-\frac{2}{3})(\frac{6}{5})(\frac{3}{4})$

(d) $d = (-\frac{2}{5}) \div (\frac{1}{4})$

(e) $e = (-12) \div (\frac{2}{3})$

(f) $f = (\frac{7}{3}) \div (-\frac{1}{6})$

17. Solve the following for n:

(a) $n = -\frac{1}{2}(\frac{2}{3} - \frac{3}{4})$

(b) $n = -\frac{2}{3}(-\frac{6}{3} - \frac{9}{5})$

(c) $n = \frac{a}{b}(\frac{c}{d} + \frac{e}{f})$

(d) $(\frac{8}{5} - \frac{14}{3}) \div (-2) = n$

(e) $n = (-\frac{5}{2} - \frac{7}{2}) \div (\frac{1}{2})$

(f) $n = (\frac{c}{d} + \frac{e}{f}) \div \frac{a}{b}$

18. Illustrate each of the following on a number line with r and s as rational numbers. (Assume specific values for r and s.)

(a) If $r > s$, then $-s > -r$.

(b) If $r > s$, then $s > -r$.

(c) If $r > s$, then $r > -s$.

*19. Prove: There exists no rational number whose square is equal to 3.

20. If W is the set of whole numbers, F is the set of fractions, I is the set of integers, and R is the set of rationals, indicate which of the following are true and which are false.

(a) $R \supseteq F \cup W \cup I$

(b) $W = R \cap I \cap F$

(c) $F \supseteq W \cap R$

(d) $W \subset I \cup F$

(e) $R \approx F \cup W \cup I$

(f) $W \cap F \approx W \cap I$

21. Examine the addition and multiplication charts for modulo-six numbers in Section 15, Chapter 6, and answer the questions below.

(a) Are the numbers closed with respect to the two operations? Explain (Property I of a field).

(b) Are the operations of addition and multiplication associative? Illustrate (Property II).

(c) Does an identity exist for addition and for multiplication? Illustrate (Property III).

(d) Do the operations of addition and multiplication have the cancellation property? Illustrate (Property IV).

(e) Are the operations of addition and multiplication commutative? Illustrate (Property V).

(f) Do the numbers have an additive inverse? Illustrate (Property V—Addition).

(g) Do the numbers have a multiplicative inverse? Illustrate (Property V—Multiplication).

(h) Is the operation of multiplication distributive? Illustrate (Property VI).

(i) Do the numbers of modulo-six arithmetic form a field? Why?

22. Prepare addition and multiplication charts for modulo-three arithmetic and answer the questions of Exercise 21 regarding the numbers of the system.

23. Do the whole numbers form a field? Why?

24. Do the integers form a field? Why?

25. (a) By numerical examples and induction, discover and define what is meant by a negative decimal.

(b) State satisfactory rules for adding and multiplying positive and negative decimals.

26. (a) Prepare a generalization for dividing by a rational, analogous to the generalization, "To subtract a rational, add its opposite."

(b) Prove the generalization stated in (a).

27. Prove that there is no rational number r such that $r^3 = 2$.

REFERENCES

PETERSON, JOHN A., and JOSEPH HASHISAKI, *The Theory of Arithmetic*. New York: John Wiley and Sons, 1963, pp. 166–192.

School Mathematics Study Group, "Number Systems", *in Studies in Mathematics*, Volume VI. New Haven, Connecticut: Yale University, 1961, pp. 95–161.

CHAPTER THIRTEEN

GEOMETRY AND NUMBER

1. IMPORTANCE

A connection between geometry and number was shown earlier when number lines were introduced to illustrate properties of important kinds of numbers, e.g., fractions and integers. The number lines were used then primarily as diagrams of number relations. They were not thought of as geometric objects to be studied for their own sake.

The point of view adopted in the first part of this chapter is quite different. The nature of Euclidean line geometry is studied in order to discover what kinds of numbers will make possible a complete correspondence between points and numbers. In this manner a more extensive system of numbers, the *real numbers*, is introduced. These numbers are needed to express mathematically the meaning of concepts, such as length, area, and volume.

The real number system is an extension of the rational number system. It includes all the rational numbers. It also includes numbers such as $\sqrt{2}$, $\sqrt{3}$, and π that are not rational.

The objective of the first part of this chapter is to show how a one-to-one correspondence is established between the points of a Euclidean number line and the numbers of the real number system. This correspondence provides the theoretical foundation for describing, in mathematical language, all physical processes of measuring size, shape, position, and the many other quantities observed in the world around us. In the last part of this chapter, the ideas developed in the first part are extended to plane and solid geometry.

It should be noted that the geometric constructions used are to be thought of as mathematical operations in the space of Euclidean line geometry, leading to exact mathematical results. They are not to be thought of as physical constructions in experimental geometry with their unavoidable inaccuracies. Nevertheless, the discussions and definitions in the chapter are usually demonstrative. You should draw many figures and diagrams of your own to visualize the meaning of the ideas, and to familiarize yourself with the terminology.

2. LINE GEOMETRY

The purpose of this section is to describe those properties of Euclidean line geometry which are important for the understanding of the real numbers and their geometric representation. The space of line geometry will be denoted by the Greek letter Λ (lambda).

Directions on a line. The space Λ of line geometry is visualized as a line extending indefinitely in both directions. One direction is chosen and called the positive direction. The opposite direction is called the negative direction. Which direction is chosen to be positive is unimportant, but once the choice is made, it is left unchanged. In Fig. 13–1, the positive direction is from left to right, as indicated by the arrow.

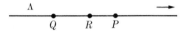

FIG. 13–1. Direction and order on a line.

Ordering of points on a line. Given two points P and Q of Λ: if the direction from Q to P is positive, then $P > Q$, read, "P is greater than Q"; if the direction from Q to P is negative, then $Q > P$; and finally, if P and Q coincide, $P = Q$.

It may be verified that the points of Λ are totally ordered by the "greater than" relationship. If $P > R$ and $R > Q$, then $P > R > Q$, read, "P is greater than R is greater than Q." If, as in Fig. 13–1, $Q > P$ is false, one writes $P \geq Q$, read, "P is greater than or equal to Q."

Intervals. Let P and Q be two points of Λ with $P < Q$, as shown in Fig. 13–2. Then the positively directed segment from P to Q can be distinguished from the negatively directed segment from Q to P.

Such directed segments, called vectors in Chapter 8, have already been used in Chapters 11 and 12 to illustrate the operations of addition and subtraction of integers and rational numbers. A *positively directed vector is called an interval.* It is a point set of Λ. The interval shown in Fig. 13–2 with end points P and Q is denoted by $[P, Q]$, read, "interval P, Q."

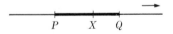

FIG. 13–2. An interval of Λ.

Intervals of Λ will be denoted by the Greek capital Γ (gamma). Subscripts or superscripts will be used, when convenient, as follows:

$$\Gamma, \quad \Gamma', \quad \Gamma_1, \quad \Gamma_2, \quad \ldots, \quad \Gamma_n, \quad \ldots$$

If Γ and Γ' are intervals and $\Gamma \supset \Gamma'$, Γ' is a proper subinterval of Γ.

Set intersections of intervals. There are various geometrical possibilities for the set intersection of two intervals, depending on the relative position of the intervals on the line. Some of these possibilities are illustrated in Fig. 13–3.

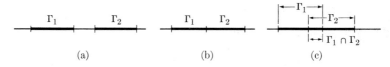

Fig. 13–3. (a) Disjoint intervals. (b) Abutting intervals. (c) Intersecting intervals.

If the two intervals are called Γ_1 and Γ_2, then Γ_1 and Γ_2 are said to be disjoint if $\Gamma_1 \cap \Gamma_2$ is the empty set, and they are said to abut if $\Gamma_1 \cap \Gamma_2$ is a single point. In all other cases, the intervals intersect in more than one point, and $\Gamma_1 \cap \Gamma_2$ is then an interval.

3. THE PRINCIPLE OF NESTED INTERVALS

The principle of nested intervals will be developed and then used to define

(1) irrational numbers, thereby completing the real number system,
(2) length and area, and
(3) coordinate systems.

Size of intervals. A method of comparing segments with respect to size, by using the congruence relation was shown in Chapter 8. The same method of comparison may be used for intervals.

Let Γ_1 and Γ_2 be two intervals. If Γ_1 may be superposed on Γ_2 so that the intervals completely coincide, then Γ_1 and Γ_2 are said to be congruent, $\Gamma_1 \cong \Gamma_2$, read "Γ_1 is congruent to Γ_2." If Γ_1 is congruent to a proper subinterval of Γ_2, then Γ_2 is said be larger than Γ_1.

Nested intervals. Consider any infinite sequence of intervals:

$$\Gamma_1, \quad \Gamma_2, \quad \Gamma_3, \quad \ldots, \quad \Gamma_n, \quad \Gamma_{n+1}, \quad \ldots \tag{1}$$

This sequence is said to be a sequence of nested intervals if the following two conditions are satisfied.

(a) $\Gamma_n \supset \Gamma_{n+1}$ for every positive integer n.
(b) The intervals become arbitrarily small as n becomes larger and larger. This implies that a definite plan is followed in defining the intervals of a sequence.

Two examples of sequences of nested intervals are given below.

EXAMPLE 1.   Choose for Γ_1 any interval $[P_1, Q_1]$ of Λ, as shown in Fig. 13–4. Let

Q_2 be the mid-point of $\overline{P_1Q_1}$, and $\Gamma_2 = [P_1, Q_2]$;

Q_3 be the mid-point of $\overline{P_1Q_2}$, and $\Gamma_3 = [P_1, Q_3]$;

Q_4 be the mid-point of $\overline{P_1Q_3}$, and $\Gamma_4 = [P_1, Q_4]$; etc.

FIG. 13–4. First example of a nested sequence.

The intervals Γ_1, Γ_2, Γ_3, ... , Γ_n, ... are well defined by this procedure. Furthermore, both condition (a) and condition (b) are satisfied because of the manner in which the end points Q_2, Q_3, Q_4, ... were chosen.

EXAMPLE 2.   Choose as Γ_1 the interval $[P_1, Q_1]$ in Fig. 13–5. Choose points P_2 and Q_2 such that $\overline{P_1Q_1}$ is divided into three congruent abutting intervals. Let $\Gamma_2 = [P_2, Q_2]$. Choose points P_3 and Q_3 such that $\overline{P_2Q_2}$ is divided into three congruent abutting intervals. Let $\Gamma_3 = [P_3, Q_3]$. Choose points P_4 and Q_4 such that $\overline{P_3Q_3}$ is divided into three congruent abutting intervals. Let $\Gamma_4 = [P_4, Q_4]$, ...

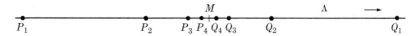

FIG. 13–5. Second example of a nested sequence.

The intervals Γ_1, Γ_2, Γ_3, ... are well defined by this procedure. Furthermore, both condition (a) and condition (b) are satisfied because of the manner in which the end points $P_2, Q_2; P_3, Q_3; P_4, Q_4; ...$ were chosen.

The principle of nested intervals. The two examples of nested sequences have an important common feature. There is exactly one point of the space Λ contained in every interval of each nested sequence. For the first example, this point is P_1, the left end point of all the intervals. For the second sequence, this point is M, the mid-point of each of the segments determined by the intervals of the sequence.

The principle of nested intervals asserts that for any sequence of intervals of Λ which satisfies both condition (a) and condition (b),

There exists exactly one point P of the space contained in every interval of the nested sequence; or

any sequence of nested intervals of the space Λ closes down on a point of Λ.

The geometric meaning of the principle is suggested in Fig. 13–6.

FIG. 13–6. A sequence nesting on the point P.

Since the principle asserts that there exists a point on the Euclidean line which is determined by any sequence of nested intervals, the principle is concerned with the mathematical nature of Euclidean space, not with the nature of physical space. In a deductive development of Euclidean geometry, the principle is either assumed as one of the postulates of the geometry, or else some other logically equivalent form is assumed and the principle proved as a theorem.

4. ASSIGNING COORDINATES TO POINTS OF A LINE

The geometric properties of the Euclidean line which are necessary to an understanding of the correspondence between numbers and points have now been discussed. It remains to show how the correspondence is established, and to describe the numbers which are needed to make the correspondence complete. Up to a certain point, the procedure by which this correspondence is brought about will be familiar to you, since it is the same as that by which a particular number system, such as the integers or fractions, is represented on a number line. The difference is that we do not start with a known number system, but with a line, namely the space Λ, and endeavor to represent all the points of Λ by numbers. The nature of these numbers, called "the real numbers," will emerge as the correspondence is developed.

Coordinate systems in the space Λ. Let O and I be two points of the space Λ with $I > O$, as shown in Fig. 13–7. Assign the number 0 to the point O and the number 1 to the point I. The numbers 0 and 1 are called the coordinates of the points O and I, and the points O and I are said to establish a coordinate system in the space Λ; O is called the origin of the coordinate system. Once a coordinate system is chosen in Λ, numbers can be systematically assigned to an extensive set of points on the line. The number assigned to a point is called the coordinate of that point.

Since it is possible to make an infinite number of choices of the points O and I, it follows that the number of coordinate systems in Euclidean line geometry is infinite. All the developments presented below are carried out for a fixed coordinate system which is chosen once and for all. The

FIG. 13–7. A coordinate system in Λ.

geometric figures introduced to illustrate features of the coordinate system are not always drawn to the same scale. Assigning coordinates to points is a mental process. The diagrams are to help you understand the process by the visual, intuitive methods of experimental geometry. The figures are therefore drawn to whatever scale may best help you to understand the coordinate system.

Points with integral coordinates. Choose a coordinate system on Λ by selecting two points O and I and then points P, Q, R, S, ... successively to the right of I, and points U, V, W, Y successively to the left of I, so that the intervals $[I, P]$, $[P, Q]$, $[Q, R]$, $[R, S]$, ... and $[U, O]$, $[V, U]$, $[W, V]$, $[Y, W]$, ... are all congruent to $[O, I]$, as illustrated in Fig. 13–8.

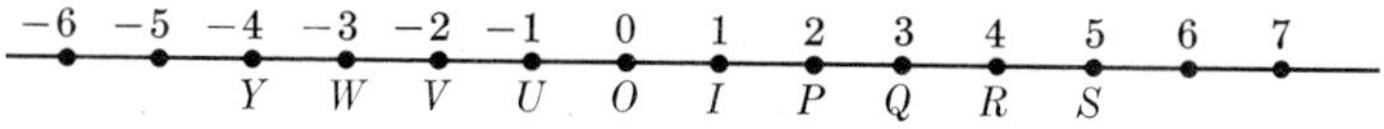

FIG. 13–8. The integral points of Λ.

Points O and I have been assigned coordinates 0 and 1, respectively. Point P is now assigned the coordinate 2, Q the coordinate 3, R the coordinate 4, etc. Similarly, assign U the coordinate -1, V the coordinate -2, W the coordinate -3, Y the coordinate -4, etc. In Fig. 13–8, the coordinates are shown above their corresponding points.

The set of all the points of a line which are obtained in this manner is called the set of *integral points* of the space Λ. This set has several important characteristics. First, integral points to the right of O have positive coordinates and the integral points to the left of O have negative coordinates, in agreement with the choice of positive and negative directions on the line. Second, a one-to-one correspondence has been established between the point set and the set of integers:

$$\{\ldots, \quad Y, \quad W, \quad V, \quad U, \quad O, \quad I, \quad P, \quad Q, \quad R, \quad \ldots\},$$
$$\{\ldots, \quad -4, \quad -3, \quad -2, \quad -1, \quad 0, \quad 1, \quad 2, \quad 3, \quad 4, \quad \ldots\}.$$

The sets are conceptually quite different, for the first set consists of points of Λ, while the second set consists of numbers. The correspondence preserves order in both sets. For example, $R > Q$ and $4 > 3$; $-2 > -3$ and $V > W$. Third, each integral point may be named and identified by its corresponding coordinate. This fact is illustrated in Fig. 13–8, where the integral points in the neighborhood of O have been indicated by their corresponding integral coordinates. Finally, the set of integral points determined in the space Λ depends on the initial choice of coordinate system. In general, for a different coordinate system, a different set of integral points will be obtained.

Number lines. Diagrams such as Fig. 13–8 are used in the development of elementary ideas of mathematics. The positive ray through O with the equally spaced points is a picture of the set of whole numbers and their order relations. It also enables you to visualize simple operations on whole numbers and to perform them graphically, that is, geometrically. When used in this way, the ray is referred to as a number line. Thus, for example, the line in Fig. 13–8 was used in Chapter 11 as a number line for the integers. The points of Λ to which coordinates have not been assigned play no role in the use of Fig. 13–8 as a number line for representing whole numbers or integers; all that is essential is the row of equally spaced dots.

Rational points. The procedure just described of pairing integers with points of Λ may be extended to pairing rational numbers with points of Λ. The following examples illustrate this extension.

Consider first the location of the rational number $\frac{5}{6}$. Divide the interval $[0, 1]$ into six congruent abutting segments. This process may be imagined to be carried out as illustrated in Chapter 8, Section 7. The end points of the segments now divide the interval exactly into six congruent parts. The fifth point, counting from the origin, is assigned the coordinate $\frac{5}{6}$. The other points in sequence have the coordinates $\frac{1}{6}$, $\frac{2}{6} = \frac{1}{3}$, $\frac{3}{6} = \frac{1}{2}$, $\frac{4}{6} = \frac{2}{3}$, as indicated in Fig. 13–9.

Fig. 13–9. Some rational points of Λ.

Consider the location of $\frac{13}{6}$ on Λ. Since $\frac{13}{6} = 2 + \frac{1}{6}$, the same procedure of dividing the interval $[2, 3]$ into sixths helps locate the point with coordinate $\frac{13}{6}$.

Finally, consider the location of $\frac{-41}{6}$ on the line. This number may be thought of as $-6 + \frac{-5}{6}$; and division of the interval $[-7, -6]$ into sixths shows that the point with coordinate $\frac{-41}{6}$ is the first point to the right of the point -7.

One of these procedures applies to the location of every rational number. Therefore to every rational number r may be assigned a point R. The number r is called the coordinate of R. The set of all points so obtained is called the set of rational points of Λ, or the rational number line.

If A, B, ... P, ... are the rational points, their corresponding coordinates are denoted by a, b, ..., p, ... The two sets are in a one-to-one correspondence, and this correspondence preserves order in both sets, that is, if $a > b$, $A > B$, and if $P > Q$, then $p > q$.

Note that the rational points of Λ include the integral points, and that if the coordinate system is changed, the rational points may change.

The existence of nonrational points. If the set of rational points included all the points on the line, the correspondence between points and numbers would be complete, and the space Λ could be described by the properties of the set of rational numbers. Fortunately or unfortunately, this is not the case. There exist points on the line which are not rational points. This fact would not be of too serious consequence, if such points were rare. They are not rare. *In any interval of the line Λ, there exists an infinite number of nonrational points.*

In fact, if K is any nonrational point, one can construct by the method described in Chapter 8 a point L either to the left or right of K such that the measure of $\overline{KL}$ is any rational number. In this manner the point L may be made to lie within any given interval. In Fig. 13–10 this fact is illustrated by the interval $[O, Q]$. Note that there are many choices possible for L in the interval.

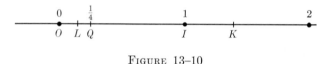

FIGURE 13–10

The point L cannot be rational. For if it were, the measure of $\overline{OL}$ would be a rational number. By construction the measure of $\overline{LK}$ is a rational number r. Consequently, the measure of $\overline{OK}$ would be the rational number $k = 1 + r$. Therefore K would have the rational coordinate k, contrary to the hypothesis that K is nonrational. Therefore L cannot have a rational coordinate.

A nonrational point may be located on the line as follows. The triangle ABC in Fig. 13–11 has a right angle at B, and the sides $\overline{AB}$ and $\overline{BC}$ are both congruent to $\overline{OI}$ on the line Λ. The segment $\overline{OK}$ of Λ is constructed so that $\overline{OK} \cong \overline{AC}$ and $K > 0$.

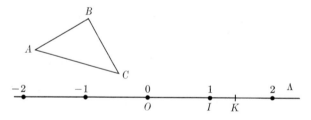

FIG. 13–11. Existence of irrational points on a line.

The point K thus located is either a rational point of the line, or a nonrational point. It will be shown that the assumption, "K is a rational point," leads to a contradiction.

Proof. Assume that K is a rational point. Then K has a rational co-ordinate k which is the measure of $\overline{OK}$. The number k is also the measure of $\overline{AC}$ since $\overline{AC} \cong \overline{OK}$ by construction. The measures of $\overline{AB}$ and $\overline{BC}$ are both 1 since $\overline{AB} \cong \overline{BC} \cong \overline{OI}$ by construction. By the Pythagorean theorem applied to the right $\triangle ABC$, $k^2 = 1^2 + 1^2 = 2$. But it was shown in Chapter 12, Section 8, that there exists no rational number whose square is equal to 2. Therefore the assumption that K is a rational point is false. Hence K is not a rational point; that is, K is a nonrational point.

The proper coordinate to assign to the point K is $\sqrt{2}$. However, $\sqrt{2}$ is not a member of the set of whole numbers or of the set of rational numbers. It is a member of a more inclusive set, the set of real numbers which includes the set of rational numbers. A real number which is not rational is said to be *irrational*. The terms "rational" and "irrational" are applied to points as well as numbers. For example, the point K is irrational. As might be expected, irrational points have irrational coordinates.

5. THE REAL NUMBERS AND THEIR DECIMAL REPRESENTATION

The real number system is used extensively in the calculus and its applications. You also used it in high-school trigonometry and algebra. It is an extension of the rational number system. It includes rational numbers, such as $\frac{1}{2}$, -1.413, $71\frac{3}{8}$, and also irrational numbers, such as $\sqrt{2}$, $\sqrt{17}$, π. There are many other irrational numbers. The square root of a positive integer is irrational unless the integer is a perfect square like 4 or 9. The logarithm of a decimal fraction is irrational unless the fraction is a power of 10. The values recorded for square roots and logarithms in tables are decimal fractions. But, in general, they give only approximations to the actual numbers which are irrational.

Every real number may be represented by a decimal. The form of this decimal representation depends on the nature of the number represented. If a real number is rational, there are two possibilities. Rationals such as $\frac{1}{2}$, $\frac{-5}{16}$, $17\frac{1}{8}$ may be represented as terminating decimals:

$$\tfrac{1}{2} = .5, \qquad \tfrac{-5}{16} = -.3125, \qquad 17\tfrac{1}{8} = 17.125.$$

Other rational numbers such as $\frac{1}{3}$, $\frac{-15}{7}$, and $17\frac{1}{6}$ cannot be represented as terminating decimals, but can be represented as nonterminating decimals:

$$\tfrac{1}{3} = .33333\ldots, \qquad \tfrac{-15}{7} = -2.142857142857\ldots,$$
$$17\tfrac{1}{6} = 17.16666\ldots$$

A method for obtaining such representations was given in Chapter 9, Section 9.

The three dots which are written to the right of each decimal above signify that there exists a well-defined process for finding as many digits in the decimal as may be desired. As in the case of terminating decimals, a decimal in this book is the name of a number, and not itself a number. These same remarks apply to the decimal representations of $\sqrt{2}$, $-\sqrt{10}$, and π which follow.

Note that in each of the examples, the digits of the decimal repeat after a certain point. For example, in the decimals for $\frac{1}{3}$ and $17\frac{1}{6}$, the digits 3 and 6 repeat indefinitely. In the decimal for $\frac{-15}{7}$, the series of digits 142857 repeat indefinitely. A similar repetition occurs in the decimal representation of any rational number.

Any terminating decimal may be thought of as a nonterminating decimal in which the digit 0 repeats indefinitely after a certain point. For example,

$$\tfrac{1}{2} = .50000\ldots\,; \qquad \tfrac{-5}{16} = -.3125000\ldots$$

Representations of terminating decimals by nonterminating decimals will not be used in this book. On occasion, as in Chapter 9, a decimal fraction such as $\frac{1}{2}$ may be written as .50 or .500. In this case, the decimal terminates with the last written zero.

If a real number is irrational, it is representable as a nonterminating, nonrepeating decimal. For example, the irrational numbers $\sqrt{2}$, $-\sqrt{10}$, and π have decimal representations which begin as follows:

$$\sqrt{2} = 1.414214\ldots, \qquad -\sqrt{10} = -3.162278\ldots,$$
$$\pi = 3.14159265358\ldots$$

In each case, as many decimal places may be found as desired, but the digits of the decimals neither terminate nor repeat.

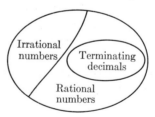

Fig. 13–12. The real number system.

The structure of the real number system is indicated in the Euler diagram of Fig. 13–12. The rational and irrational numbers are complementary sets in the set of real numbers.

6. THE SET **D** OF NUMBERS REPRESENTABLE AS TERMINATING DECIMALS

The set of all real numbers which may be represented as terminating decimals is an important distinguished subset of both the real numbers and the rational numbers. It will be denoted by a bold-face capital **D**, since ordinary capital letters denote points. For the same reason, the set of real numbers will be denoted by **R**.

The numbers of **D** are extensively used in computations, in recording the results of physical measurements, and in approximating other real numbers. These uses of **D** will be discussed in Chapter 14. The importance of **D** in this development, and in mathematics in general, is that by use of the numbers of **D** the correspondence between points of the line Λ and numbers of the set **R** is completed.

The set **D** contains both positive rationals and negative rationals. A rational number is an element of **D** if and only if the denominator of the fraction expressed in its simplest form is a product of powers of 2 and 5. For example, $\frac{323}{85}$ and $-\frac{1}{640}$ are both elements of **D**:

$$\frac{323}{85} = \frac{19}{5} = 3.8 \quad \text{and} \quad -\frac{1}{640} = -\frac{1}{2^7 \times 5} = -.0015625.$$

But $\frac{323}{86}$ and $-\frac{1}{639}$ are not elements of **D**, for both fractions are in simplest form, and their denominators contain prime factors other than 2 and 5.

Zero and the positive elements of **D** may be identified with the numbers of the set B_{10} discussed in Chapter 9, Sections 8 and 9. The negative elements of **D** are the opposites of these numbers. Thus the elements of **D** may be grouped in pairs of opposites such as .1 and $-.1$, .0734 and $-.0734$. Since $1 = 2^0 = 5^0$ is both a power of 2 and a power of 5, the set **D** contains all the integers.

The points of the line corresponding to terminating decimals.   Each terminating decimal d has a corresponding point D on the line. This point will have the number d as its coordinate. The set of all such points will be denoted by Δ (delta). An interval Γ whose end points D and D' are in Δ will be said to belong to Δ. Real numbers and points on the line are placed in a one-to-one correspondence by using sequences of nested intervals belonging to Δ.

Assigning points of the line to real numbers.   Consider the real number

$$\pi = 3.14159265358 \ldots$$

A sequence of intervals belonging to Δ may be defined by the decimal

FIG. 13–13. Intervals of Δ determined by π.

representation of π as follows. Consider the sequence of number intervals:

$$[3.1, 3.2], \qquad [3.14, 3.15], \qquad [3.141, 3.142], \qquad \dots$$

The corresponding sequence of point intervals is

$$\Gamma_1 = [D_1, D_1'], \qquad \Gamma_2 = [D_2, D_2'], \qquad \Gamma_3 = [D_3, D_3'], \qquad \dots$$

All belong to Δ. Thus 3.1 and 3.2 are the coordinates of D_1 and D_1', 3.14 and 3.15 are the coordinates of D_2 and D_2', 3.141 and 3.142 are the coordinates of D_3 and D_3', ... The intervals are shown on an enlarged scale in Fig. 13–13. In general, if d_n is the terminating decimal agreeing with the decimal representation of π to the first n decimal places, then $\Gamma_n = [D_n, D_n']$. Here D_n has the coordinate d_n, and D_n' has the coordinate

$$d_n' = d_n + \frac{1}{10^n}.$$

Therefore the measure of Γ_n is $\dfrac{1}{10^n}$.

For example, $d_5 = 3.14159$, $d_5' = 3.14160$ are the coordinates of D_5 and D_5', so that $\Gamma_5 = [D_5, D_5']$ has measure $1/10^5$. Note that for every n, $d_n < \pi < d_n'$. Thus there is associated with the real number π a sequence of intervals belonging to Δ:

$$\Gamma_1, \quad \Gamma_2, \quad \Gamma_3, \quad \dots, \quad \Gamma_n, \quad \Gamma_{n+1}, \quad \dots \tag{2}$$

From the manner in which these intervals are defined,

$$\Gamma_1 \supset \Gamma_2 \supset \Gamma_3 \supset \cdots \supset \Gamma_n \supset \Gamma_{n+1} \supset \dots$$

Furthermore, the successive intervals have measures

$$\frac{1}{10}, \quad \frac{1}{10^2}, \quad \frac{1}{10^3}, \quad \cdots \quad \frac{1}{10^n}, \quad \frac{1}{10^{n+1}}, \quad \cdots$$

Consequently, sequence (2) is a sequence of nested intervals. By the principle of nested intervals, sequence (1) closes down on a unique point P of Λ. The point P is assigned to π as its geometric image, and π is called the coordinate of P.

The reasonableness of making P and π correspond may be seen from the fact that for every positive integer n,

$$D_n < P < D'_n \qquad \text{and} \qquad d_n < \pi < d'_n.$$

Furthermore, from the manner in which the terminating decimals d_n and d'_n are defined, π is the only number of $\mathbf{R}$ contained in all the number intervals $[d_n, d'_n]$.

Now let α be any real number. If α is rational, it is the coordinate of a rational point A of Λ. If α is irrational, it may be represented by a non-terminating decimal. By the procedure illustrated for π, a sequence of nested intervals belonging to D is determined by the decimal representation of α. This sequence converges on a unique point A of Λ to which α is assigned as its coordinate. It therefore follows that

Every real number is the coordinate of a point of Λ.

Assigning coordinates to points of the line. It remains to be proved that *every point of Λ corresponds to a real number which is its coordinate.* It suffices to show that this statement is true for irrational points. The proof depends upon the construction of a suitable sequence of nested intervals belonging to Δ. The construction is entirely geometric, and determines the real number by its decimal representation.

The process of proof will be illustrated by the point K discussed in Section 4. This point was located on the line Λ by a geometric construction. In the discussion which follows, it is unnecessary to know the coordinate of K.

Imagine the line divided as far as convenient into congruent abutting intervals starting at 0 and each of measure $\frac{1}{10}$ (see Fig. 13–14). Since the point K is irrational, it is within one of these intervals of measure $\frac{1}{10}$. Call this interval Γ_1. If Γ_1 is divided into congruent abutting intervals of measure $\frac{1}{100}$, point K is within one of these. Call this interval Γ_2. If Γ_2 is divided into congruent abutting intervals of measure $\frac{1}{1000}$, point K is within one of these. Call this interval Γ_3. This process may be continued as far as desired.

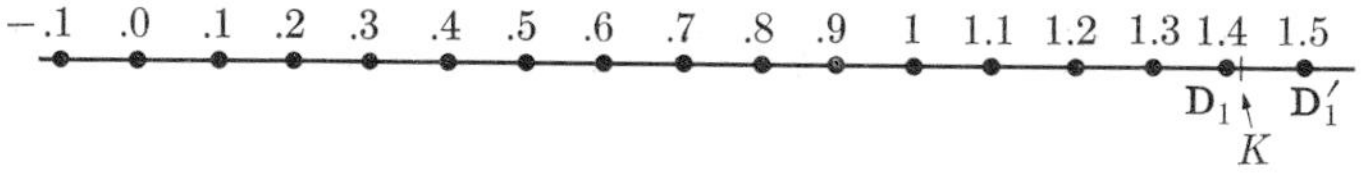

FIG. 13–14. Finding the coordinate of K.

Since there is a one-to-one correspondence between the points of Δ and the set of terminating decimals, D, there is also a one-to-one correspondence between the end points of Γ_1, Γ_2, Γ_3, ... and the coordinates of these points. For example, if the point interval Γ_n equals $[D_n, D'_n]$, then

TABLE 13–1

THE COORDINATE OF K

Point interval	Number interval	
Γ_n	d_n	d'_n
Γ_1	1.4	1.5
Γ_2	1.41	1.42
Γ_3	1.414	1.415
Γ_4	1.4142	1.4143
Γ_5	1.41421	1.41422
$\vdots$	$\vdots$	$\vdots$

the number interval determined by it is $[d_n, d'_n]$. Here d_n is the coordinate of D_n and d'_n is the coordinate of D'_n.

The decimals d_n and d'_n can be read from the line if it has a coordinate scale. For example, d_1, d'_1 and d_2, d'_2 are determined from Figs. 13–14 and 13–15 to be 1.4, 1.5 and 1.41, 1.42, respectively. By repeating the constructions of Figs. 13–14 and 13–15 on an increasingly larger scale, the data of Table 13–1 are obtained. It should be emphasized again that the decimal entries in the table are found by geometric constructions and not by an arithmetical procedure.

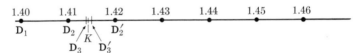

FIG. 13–15. Finding the coordinate of K.

In this manner, a real number κ is determined represented by the non-terminating decimal

$$1.41421 \ldots$$

As many decimal places as desired may be found. In the present case, κ may be renamed $\sqrt{2}$. It is possible, however, that if point K had been chosen arbitrarily on the line Λ and if the real-number coordinate κ had been determined by a geometric process, there might be no simpler way of naming κ than with a nonterminating decimal.

The real number line. It has been shown that to every point A of the line there corresponds a number α of the set **R**, and that the correspondence $A \leftrightarrow \alpha$ between the points on the line and their real number coordinates is one-to-one. The correspondence also preserves order; that is, if B is another point of Λ with the coordinate β, then

$$A > B \quad \text{if and only if} \quad \alpha > \beta.$$

Because of this correspondence, the space Λ is often referred to as the real number line. It has the same relation to the real number system as the rational number line has to the rational number system.

The use of the real number line allows relations and operations on real numbers to be visualized and interpreted geometrically. This is illustrated in the next section. The remainder of the chapter is devoted to applications and extensions of the coordinate concept which unites geometry and number.

The correspondence between numbers and points developed here is one of the most important mathematical inventions of all times. It was developed in France during the seventeenth century by the mathematician and philosopher René Descartes (1596–1650).

EXERCISE SET 13–1

1. Sketch a line and locate any point R on the line. Locate the following points according to the order indicated, assuming that the direction from left to right is positive.
   (a) $M > R$ (b) $N > M$ (c) $R < P < M$
   (d) $Q < R$ (e) $R > S > Q$ (f) $T > N$
2. Order all the points on the line of Exercise 1 by the "greater than" relationship.
3. Assuming that on line AF the direction from left to right is positive, state which of the following are intervals.
   (a) $\overline{AB}$ (b) $\overline{BA}$ (c) $[B, A]$
   (d) $[A, B]$ (e) $\overline{CE}$ (f) $\overline{DB}$
   (g) $[B, E]$ (h) $[F, A]$ (i) $[D, E]$
4. The points below are from Fig. 13–16. Order the points by placing $>$ or $<$ between pairs of points.
   (a) A, B (b) E, C (c) C, F (d) F, C
   (e) A, C, F (f) F, C, A (g) E, D, B (h) D, B, A

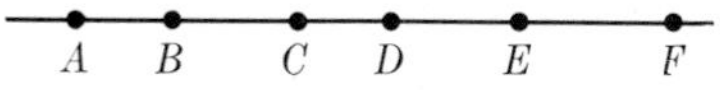

FIGURE 13–16

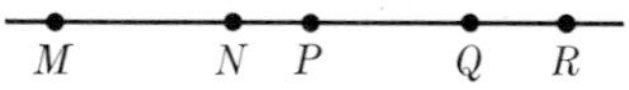

FIGURE 13–17

5. After consulting Fig. 13–17, place the symbol $\supseteq$ or $\subseteq$ between the pairs of intervals listed below.
   (a) $[P, R]; [Q, R]$ (b) $[Q, R]; [P, R]$
   (c) $[N, Q]; [N, P]$ (d) $[N, P]; [M, P]$
   (e) $[M, P]; [N, P]$ (f) $[P, R]; [M, R]$

6. Consult Fig. 13–17 and then state the results of the union or intersection of the following point sets.

(a) $[M, N] \cup [N, Q]$ (b) $[M, Q] \cap [P, R]$

(c) $[M, P] \cup [P, Q] \cup [Q, R]$ (d) $[N, R] \cap [Q, R]$

(e) $[M, N] \cap [N, P]$ (f) $[Q, R] \cup [N, Q]$

7. Identify the following pairs of intervals (from Fig. 13–18) as disjoint or intersecting. Also indicate those which abut.

(a) $[D, F]; [F, H]$ (b) $[D, E]; [F, H]$

(c) $[D, E]; [D, G]$ (d) $[F, H]; [F, G]$

(e) $[G, H]; [E, F]$ (f) $[D, E]; [E, H]$

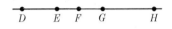

$$D \qquad E \quad F \quad G \qquad\qquad H$$

FIGURE 13–18

8. (a) Under what condition does $\Gamma_1 \cap \Gamma_2 = \Gamma_1$?

(b) Under what condition does $\Gamma_1 \cap \Gamma_2 = \{\}$?

(c) Under what condition does $\Gamma_1 \cup \Gamma_2 = \Gamma_1$?

9. Illustrate each of the following relations of point sets on a number line.

(a) When $\Gamma_1 \supseteq \Gamma_2$ (b) When $\Gamma_2 \supseteq \Gamma_1$

(c) When $\Gamma_2 \cap \Gamma_1 = \Gamma_3$ (d) When $\Gamma_1 \cup \Gamma_2 = \Gamma_3$

(e) When $(\Gamma_1 \cup \Gamma_2) \cap \Gamma_3 = \Gamma_3$ (f) When $\Gamma_1 \cup \Gamma_2 = \Gamma_2$

10. Show with a line that the "larger than" relation over the family of intervals of Λ is transitive. (If $\Gamma_1 > \Gamma_2$ and $\Gamma_2 > \Gamma_3$, then $\Gamma_1 > \Gamma_3$.)

11. Can a finite sequence of intervals, $\Gamma_1, \Gamma_2, \Gamma_3, \ldots, \Gamma_\kappa$, meet the conditions for a sequence of nested intervals? Why?

12. (a) Locate, on a line, the end points of the first five intervals of the sequence:

$$-1, 1; \quad \frac{-1}{2}, \frac{1}{2}; \quad \frac{-1}{3}, \frac{1}{3}; \quad \cdots; \quad \frac{-1}{n}, \frac{1}{n}; \quad \cdots$$

(b) Is this a sequence of nested intervals? If so, on what point does the sequence close down?

13. (a) On a line, locate the end points of the first five intervals of the sequence:

$$-1, 2; \quad \frac{-1}{2}, \frac{3}{2}; \quad \frac{-1}{3}, \frac{4}{3}; \quad \frac{-1}{4}, \frac{5}{4}; \quad \cdots; \quad \frac{-1}{n}, \frac{n+1}{n}$$

(b) Is the above sequence of nested intervals? If so, on what point does the sequence close down?

14. In Fig. 13–19, P_2 is located on the line below halfway between P_1 and A, P_3 is located halfway between P_2 and A, etc. Similarly, Q_2 is located halfway between Q_1 and B, Q_3 is located halfway between Q_2 and B, etc. Does

$$P_1 \qquad\qquad P_2 \quad P_3 P_4 \qquad A \qquad B \qquad Q_3 \quad Q_2 \qquad Q_1$$

FIGURE 13–19

the following sequence of intervals satisfy the conditions for a sequence of nested intervals? Why?

$$[P_1, Q_1]; \quad [P_2, Q_2]; \quad [P_3, Q_3]; \quad \ldots; \quad [P_n, Q_n]; \quad \ldots$$

15. Show by construction a sequence of circles closing down on a point.
    (a) The circles converge on the center of each circle of the sequence.
    (b) The circles converge on a point of the boundary of the first circle of the sequence.
16. Describe the location of points on which a sequence of spheres may converge.
17. Draw a line to represent Λ. Locate the points which have the following coordinates.

(a) 0	(b) $+3$	(c) -2	(d) 5
(e) -4	(f) 6	(g) -5	(h) -6

18. Draw a line to represent Λ. Locate the points which have the following coordinates.

(a) 0	(b) $\frac{1}{2}$	(c) $\frac{-3}{2}$	(d) $\frac{7}{2}$
(e) $\frac{-7}{4}$	(f) $\frac{-17}{8}$	(g) $\frac{19}{4}$	(h) $\frac{-24}{8}$

19. Which of the following are nonterminating decimals?

(a) $2\frac{3}{4}$	(b) $1\frac{1}{3}$	(c) $\frac{2}{7}$	(d) $\sqrt{9}$
(e) 3	(f) $5\frac{5}{6}$	(g) 12	(h) $\sqrt{1}$

20. Express each of the nonterminating decimals in Exercise 19 to eight decimal places.
21. (a) Consult a history of mathematics and determine to how many digits Archimedes computed π.
    (b) Consult a recent report and determine to how many digits π has been computed to date.
22. Express the following as nonterminating decimals and in each underline the sequence of digits which repeat indefinitely.

(a) $\frac{1}{9}$ (b) $\frac{1}{11}$ (c) $\frac{1}{13}$ (d) $\frac{1}{15}$ (e) $\frac{1}{19}$ (f) $\frac{1}{23}$

23. Show by example that set **D**, the set of numbers representable as terminating decimals, is closed under addition, subtraction, and multiplication, but not under division.
24. Show by example that **D** is closed under the averaging operation Δ discussed in Chapter 6, Section 2.
25. Show that as many elements of **D** as desired may be found within any given interval of **D**. Illustrate by repeatedly using the averaging operation of Exercise 24 with the interval $[.051, .052]$. Find at least five elements of **D** within the interval.
26. Sketch a figure to illustrate Exercise 25 for the interval $[.051, .052]$ by dividing the interval into 10 congruent intervals, then into 100 congruent intervals, then into 1000 congruent intervals, $\ldots$.
27. Is the statement of Exercise 25 true for a rational interval such as $[\frac{1}{3}, \frac{3}{4}]$?
28. By considering the nested sequence (2) of Section 6, show that the principle of nested intervals does not hold on the rational number line.
29. Give the decimal coordinates of three of the intervals which close down on the point whose coordinate is $\frac{9}{11}$.

30. A sequence of nested intervals begins as follows:

$$[3, 4], \quad [3.3, 3.4], \quad [3.33, 3.34], \quad [3.333, 3.334], \quad \ldots$$

(a) Give the next two intervals in the sequence.
(b) On what point are the intervals of (a) closing down?
31. Find the length of the segments below from the coordinates of their intervals.
(a) [5, 2]   (b) [−2, −9]   (c) [+8, −2]   (d) [β, 5]   (e) [β, σ]

7. PROPERTIES OF THE REAL NUMBER SYSTEM

The Greek letters α, β, σ, and τ will be used in this section to denote real numbers, whether they are rational or irrational. If a real number is known to be rational and a distinction is needed, a rational number will be denoted as previously by an italicized letter. Note that the Greek letter π always denotes the particular real number

$$\pi = 3.14159265358 \ldots$$

The number π has an important geometric meaning which will be discussed later in this chapter.

Order relations. The order relations between two or more real numbers may be determined from their decimal representations. For example,

$$\tfrac{22}{7} = 3.142 \ldots \qquad \text{and} \qquad \tfrac{355}{113} = 3.14159292 \ldots$$

Therefore $\tfrac{22}{7} > \tfrac{355}{113} > \pi$. Both of the fractions $\tfrac{22}{7}$ and $\tfrac{355}{113}$ are used as approximations to π.

Arithmetical operations. The real number system **R**, like the rational number system, is an ordered field under the operations of addition and of multiplication. Multiplication will often be denoted by juxtaposition, $\alpha\beta = \alpha \cdot \beta$. Subtraction may be defined either as finding a missing addend or as adding an additive inverse:

$$\sigma = \beta - \alpha \qquad \text{means} \qquad \alpha + \sigma = \beta \quad \text{or} \quad \sigma = \beta + (-\alpha).$$

Similarly, division may be defined in terms of multiplication. Some examples of arithmetical operations on real numbers are:

$$(\sqrt{2} + \sqrt{18})^2 = 2 + 2\sqrt{36} + 18 = 32,$$

$$\frac{1 + \sqrt{2}}{2} \cdot \frac{1 - \sqrt{2}}{2} = \frac{1 - 2}{4} = -\frac{1}{4},$$

$$\pi(17\tfrac{3}{4} - \sqrt{13}) = \pi 17\tfrac{3}{4} - \pi\sqrt{13}.$$

Geometrical representations. Because of the one-to-one correspondence between real numbers and points of the Euclidean line, real numbers may be represented as points on a number line. Real numbers may also be represented as vectors on a Euclidean line.

If $\overline{AB}$ is a segment of the line Λ, and α and β are the coordinates of A and B, then the measure of $\overline{AB}$ is whichever of the numbers $\alpha - \beta$ and $\beta - \alpha$ is positive. It follows that the directed segment or vector $\overrightarrow{AB}$ represents the real number $\beta - \alpha$, which is positive if $B > A$ and negative if $B < A$. For example, if

$$\alpha = \frac{1 - \sqrt{2}}{2} \qquad \text{and} \qquad \beta = \frac{1 + \sqrt{2}}{2},$$

then $\overrightarrow{AB}$ represents $\sqrt{2}$; $\sqrt{2}$ may also be represented as $\overrightarrow{OK}$ where K is the point with coordinate $\sqrt{2}$.

In general, every real number has an infinite number of vector representations all of which are congruent to one another. Addition and subtraction of real numbers may be visualized by adding and subtracting suitably chosen representative vectors, as was done in Chapters 11 and 12 for integers and rational numbers.

The principle of nested intervals for real numbers. The one-to-one correspondence between real numbers and points enables one to show that the principle of nested intervals holds for real numbers. The principle is used extensively in the remainder of this chapter. It may be formulated as follows.

Let $I = [\alpha, \beta]$ denote the interval made up of all real numbers τ such that $\alpha \leq \tau \leq \beta$. (It is assumed that $\beta > \alpha$.) Consider an infinite sequence of such number intervals:

$$I_1, \quad I_2, \quad I_3, \quad \ldots, \quad I_n, \quad I_{n+1}, \quad \ldots \tag{3}$$

Then if the following two conditions are satisfied, the sequence closes down on a unique number of **R**:

(a) $I_n \supset I_{n+1}$ for every positive integer n.

(b) The measure of each interval I_n becomes arbitrarily small as n becomes larger and larger.

Examples of sequences of nested intervals belonging to **D** have been given in Section 5. Another example is obtained by taking

$$I_n = \left[\frac{1 - \sqrt{2}}{n}, \quad \frac{1 + \sqrt{2}}{n} \right].$$

Then (a) is satisfied, and since the measure of $I_n = 2\sqrt{2}/n$, (b) is also satisfied. For example,

$$\frac{2\sqrt{2}}{n} < \left(\frac{1}{10}\right)^{10} \quad \text{if} \quad n > 2\sqrt{2} \cdot 10^{10}.$$

This particular nested sequence closes down on the number 0. The end points of all its intervals are irrational.

8. THE APPLICATION OF REAL NUMBERS TO THE MEASURE OF LENGTHS AND AREAS

Real numbers may be assigned as measures to certain curves and plane surfaces in the Euclidean plane. A few of the simplest cases will be considered here. The underlying procedure rests on the principle of nested intervals, and is basically the same in all instances.

To achieve agreement with common language usage, the measures assigned will be called the "length" of curves, the "area" of surfaces, etc. Once a unit of measurement has been chosen, the assigning of a measure to a geometric object (whenever possible) is an exact mathematical process leading to an exact numerical result. It should not be confused with the physical process of measurement with its unavoidable errors. The mathematical description of physical measurement always involves approximations and is discussed in Chapter 14.

Length of line segments. The simplest case is the assigning of lengths to line segments in the plane or in space. The procedure is as follows. Choose any segment $\overline{OI}$ as a unit of length, and let Λ be the line determined by the points O and I (Fig. 13–20). Assume that the direction from O to I is the positive direction of Λ and assign the coordinates 0 and 1 to the points O and I. Then a coordinate system is defined on Λ in which every segment has a definite length, namely its "measure" in the previous terminology of this chapter. In particular $\overline{OI}$ has length 1.

Let P and Q be any two distinct points of space. Then by a construction described in Chapter 8, a point T can be located on Λ such that $T > O$ and $\overline{OT} \cong \overline{PQ}$. The length of $\overline{OT}$ is τ, the coordinate of T on the line. By definition, τ is the length of $\overline{PQ}$.

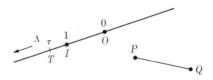

FIG. 13–20. Length of line segments.

Length has the following properties, by definition:

Every line segment of space has a unique length which is a positive real number; and congruent line segments have the same length.

The length of any simple polygonal path is the sum of the lengths of its sides. (See Chapter 8, Section 9.) The lengths of curved paths will be discussed later in this chapter.

Area of rectangles. The simplest case of measure of surface area of any plane figure is dependent on the measure of the area of rectangles. First a unit of area must be chosen. The simplest choice is a square whose sides are of length one. By definition, the area of this square is one. Consider a rectangle $\Re$. If the lengths of the sides of this rectangle are rational numbers a and b, then it follows from Chapter 9, Section 2, that the measure of $\Re$ is ab; therefore its area is also ab. In this case, $\Re$ is called a rational rectangle.

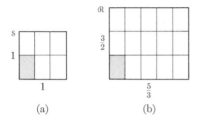

Fig. 13–21. Area of a rectangle with rational sides. (a) Unit square, S. (b) Rational rectangle, $\Re$.

For example, observe the unit square S and the rational rectangle $\Re$ whose sides are of length $\frac{3}{2}$ and $\frac{5}{3}$ (Fig. 13–21). The unit square is divided as shown into $2 \cdot 3$, or 6, small congruent rectangles. One of these, shown by shading, has an area of $\frac{1}{6}$. The rational rectangle $\Re$ can be exactly filled by $5 \cdot 3$, or 15, of these small rectangles. Consequently, the area of $\Re$ is

$$15 \times \tfrac{1}{6} \qquad \text{or} \qquad \tfrac{3}{2} \times \tfrac{5}{3}.$$

Note that the small shaded rectangle of area $\frac{1}{6}$ serves as a common subunit of area for both the unit square S and the rational rectangle $\Re$. The same considerations apply to any rational rectangle.

If a rectangle is not rational, there exists no common subunit of area for the rectangle and the unit square. Nevertheless, if the lengths of the sides of the rectangle are α and β, the area of the rectangle may be properly defined as the product $\alpha\beta$. To understand why this is so, suppose that

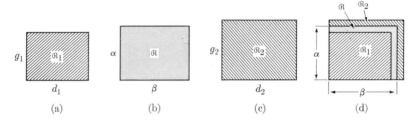

FIGURE 13–22

g_1, g_2, d_1, and d_2 are positive rational numbers such that

$$g_1 < \alpha < g_2 \qquad \text{and} \qquad d_1 < \beta < d_2. \tag{4}$$

Then

$$g_1 d_1 < \alpha\beta < g_2 d_2. \tag{5}$$

Inequalities (4) and (5) have a geometric interpretation. In Fig. 13–22, $\mathcal{R}_1$ and $\mathcal{R}_2$ are rational rectangles with sides of lengths g_1, d_1 and g_2, d_2. Inequality (4) shows that if these rectangles are superposed on the rectangle $\mathcal{R}$ with sides α and β (Fig. 13–22d) so that all three rectangles have a common vertex, then

$$\mathcal{R}_2 \supset \mathcal{R} \supset \mathcal{R}_1. \tag{6}$$

Thus $\mathcal{R}_2$ is larger than the rectangle $\mathcal{R}$, and $\mathcal{R}$ is larger than the rectangle $\mathcal{R}_1$.

Inequality (5), on the other hand, shows that the area of $\mathcal{R}_1$ is less than the real number $\alpha\beta$, and the number $\alpha\beta$ is less than the area of $\mathcal{R}_2$. Evidently, if a real number is to be assigned to the rectangle $\mathcal{R}$ to be called its area, it must be greater than the area of every rational rectangle smaller than $\mathcal{R}$, and less than the area of every rational rectangle larger than $\mathcal{R}$. It may be shown by the principle of nested intervals, that $\alpha\beta$ is the *only* real number which meets this requirement. Consequently, the area of rectangle $\mathcal{R}$ is defined to be the product $\alpha\beta$ of the lengths of two adjacent sides.

With this definition of the area of a rectangle, it is possible to visualize properties of addition and multiplication of real numbers geometrically, as was done for rational numbers in Chapter 12.

Note that a distinction in notation between rational and real numbers is no longer needed. Therefore italicized letters, a, b, c, . . . , will now be used to denote real numbers. The symbolism of geometry will also be simplified by denoting common geometric figures by script letters, for example, $\mathcal{C}$ for circle and $\mathcal{R}$ for rectangle.

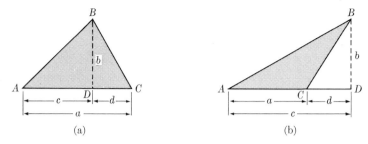

Fig. 13–23. Bases and corresponding altitudes of triangles.

The areas of triangles. There are various formulas for finding the area of a triangle which depend on what is known about the angles and lengths of the sides associated with the triangle. One of the simplest of these may be obtained from the formula for the area of a rectangle. It assumes that the length of one side and the length of the perpendicular from the opposite vertex to that side (or the side extended) are both known.

The given side is called a *base* of the triangle, and the perpendicular to this side from the opposite vertex is called an *altitude*, or the corresponding altitude. Figure 13–23 shows two cases. In both cases $\overline{AC}$ is the base and $\overline{BD}$ the corresponding altitude. In Fig. 13–23(a), the angles of $\triangle ABC$ at A, B, and C are acute; in Fig. 13–23(b), the angle at C is obtuse. In the acute-angled triangle, the altitude $\overline{BD}$ intersects the base $\overline{AC}$ at D and is inside the triangle. In the obtuse-angled case, the altitude intersects the extended base $\overline{AC}$ at D and is outside the triangle.

An intermediate case is shown in Fig. 13–24(a). The angle at C is a right angle and the altitude $\overline{BD}$ coincides with the side $\overline{BC}$.

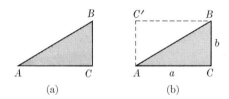

Fig. 13–24. The area of a right triangle.

In Fig. 13–24(b), note that $\triangle ABC$ may be thought of as one half of rectangle $ACBC'$ with the hypotenuse $\overline{AB}$ as a diagonal. If $\overline{AC}$ is of length a and $\overline{BC}$ is of length b, the area of $\triangle ABC$ is therefore $\frac{1}{2}ab$. In general then,

The area of any right triangle is one-half the product of the lengths of its legs.

A formula for the area of any triangle may be obtained from this formula for the area of a right triangle. Referring back to Fig. 13–23, let the line segments $\overline{BD}$, $\overline{AC}$, $\overline{AD}$, and $\overline{DC}$ have the lengths b, a, c, and d, respectively. In Fig. 13–23(a), $a = c + d$ and in Fig. 13–23(b), $a = c - d$. In both figures, triangles ABD and CDB are right triangles. Consequently, their areas are $\frac{1}{2}cb$ and $\frac{1}{2}db$. In Fig. 13–23(a), the area of $\triangle ABC$ is the sum of the areas of triangles ABD and CDB. Consequently, this area equals

$$\tfrac{1}{2}cb + \tfrac{1}{2}db = \tfrac{1}{2}(c + d)b = \tfrac{1}{2}ab.$$

In like manner, the area of $\triangle ABC$ is the difference of the areas of triangles ABD and CDB, which again is $\frac{1}{2}ab$. One may conclude then:

The area of any triangle is one-half the product of the length of a base of the triangle and the length of the corresponding altitude.

Length and area in general. The area of a rectangle has been defined as a certain real number, and this definition was shown to be valid by application of the principle of nested intervals. The same procedure is applicable to the problem of determining the area of more complicated geometric figures. The principle of nested intervals has enabled mathematicians to define precisely what is meant by the "area" of a plane region or the "length" of a plane curve. The definition has enabled them to prove in particular that every bounded convex region will have an area, and that every curve bounding such a region will have a length.

The difficulty in the case of more complicated geometric figures is that the real numbers assigned as lengths and areas are unknown, and must be determined from suitably chosen sequences of nested intervals. This procedure requires the use of the calculus in all except the simplest instances. However, in the following, the procedure will be illustrated by a discussion of the circle and a few simple convex figures naturally associated with it.

Area of a circle. Figure 13–25(a), (b), and (c), shows a circle $\mathcal{C}$ of unit radius. In Fig. 13–25(a), two three-sided regular polygons, that is, equilateral triangles, are respectively inscribed in, and circumscribed about, $\mathcal{C}$. In Fig. 13–25(b), two six-sided regular polygons are respectively inscribed in, and circumscribed about, $\mathcal{C}$. In Fig. 13–25(c), two twelve-sided regular polygons are inscribed in, and circumscribed about, $\mathcal{C}$. Note that the number of sides of the inscribed figures of this sequence doubled from step to step and equals $3 \times 2^{n-1}$ when n is the number of steps. For example, in step 1, $n = 1$ and $3 \times 2^{n-1} = 3$; a triangle is inscribed.

This process of inscribing and circumscribing regular polygons with an increasing number of sides in and about the circle $\mathcal{C}$ may be continued

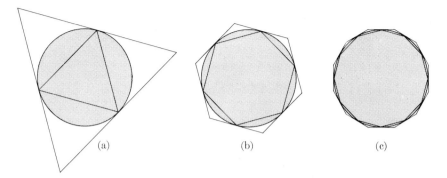

(a)   (b)   (c)

FIG. 13–25. Regular polygons inscribed in, and circumscribed about, a circle $\mathcal{C}$ of unit radius.

indefinitely. At the nth step, two regular polygons $\mathcal{P}_n$ and $\mathcal{P}'_n$ of $3 \times 2^{n-1}$ sides are inscribed in, and circumscribed about, $\mathcal{C}$; these enclose the boundary of the circle more and more closely as n increases. Also for every choice of n,

$$\mathcal{P}'_n \supset \mathcal{C} \supset \mathcal{P}_n. \tag{7}$$

Let a'_n be the area of the polygon $\mathcal{P}'_n$ and a_n the area of the polygon $\mathcal{P}_n$. The numbers

$$a_1, a'_1; \quad a_2, a'_2; \quad a_3, a'_3; \quad \ldots$$

may be computed step by step as far as desired. If a real number is assigned to the circle $\mathcal{C}$ to serve as its area, inequality (7) shows that this number must be contained in the number interval $[a_n, a'_n]$ for every value of n.

Finally, the sequence of intervals,

$$[a_1, a'_1], \quad [a_2, a'_2], \quad [a_3, a'_3], \quad \ldots, \quad [a_n, a'_n], \quad \ldots,$$

may be shown to be a nested sequence. Consequently, by the principle of nested intervals for real numbers, the sequence closes down on a unique real number. This number is called the area of the circle $\mathcal{C}$ of unit radius. You are already familiar with the number; it is π, and its decimal representation has been discussed earlier in this chapter.

Length of a circle. On examining Fig. 13–25, it appears that the length of the circle $\mathcal{C}$ is less than the perimeter of the circumscribed polygon $\mathcal{P}'_n$ and greater than the perimeter of the inscribed polygon $\mathcal{P}_n$ for every value of n. This property of the circle may be proved from the fact that it is a convex curve, and every bounded convex curve has a length. Therefore, the perimeters of the polygons $\mathcal{P}_n$, $\mathcal{P}'_n$ may be used to form a nested sequence which closes down on the number 2π. Thus π has the following geometric interpretation:

> *The real number π is the area of a circle of unit radius, and 2π is the length of the circumference of a circle of unit radius.*

If the radius of the circle $\mathcal{C}$ is of length r, it may be shown from this result that

> *The area of a circle of radius r is πr^2, and its circumference is of length $2\pi r$.*

The idea of inscribing and circumscribing regular polygons closing down on $\mathcal{C}$ with $3, 6, 12, \ldots$ sides is due to Archimedes (287–212 B.C.), one of the greatest mathematicians of antiquity. He computed the perimeters for the polygons $\mathcal{P}_6$ and $\mathcal{P}_6'$ of $3 \cdot 2^{6-1} = 96$ sides and obtained thereby the approximation 3.14 for π.

Sectors and arcs of circles. The same ideas may be applied to define the area of a sector of a circle and the length of an arc of a circle (Fig. 13–26). A sequence of convex polygons may be inscribed and circumscribed in a sector to determine a nested sequence of polygonal areas and lengths, defining the area of a sector and the length of its bounding arc.

If the circle $\mathcal{C}$ is of radius one and the arc of the circle from O to A is of length s, the area of the sector is $\frac{1}{2}s$. For example, since the circumference of $\mathcal{C}$ is of length 2π, the arc of the sector of a fourth of a circle is

$$\tfrac{1}{4}(2\pi) = \frac{\pi}{2}$$

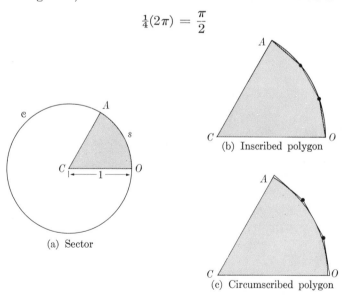

(a) Sector

(b) Inscribed polygon

(c) Circumscribed polygon

FIG. 13–26. Nested sequence for area of sector and length of arc.

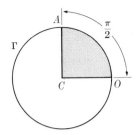

FIG. 13–27. A quadrant of the circle $\mathcal{C}$.

(see Fig. 13–27). Since the triangle has a right angle at C, the area of the sector is

$$\frac{1}{2}\left(\frac{\pi}{2}\right) = \frac{\pi}{4},$$

which is one fourth of the area of $\mathcal{C}$.

Measure of an angle. In this section a widely used method for measuring angles will be described. The measurement is based on the arc lengths of circles. The measure obtained is an important example of the correspondence between number and geometry.

A Euclidean angle with vertex P is shown in Fig. 13–28(a); $\overset{\frown}{AB}$ and $\overset{\frown}{A'B'}$ are circular arcs with center P and radii r and r'. Thus $\overline{PA}$ and $\overline{PB}$ are of length r, and $\overline{PA'}$ and $\overline{PB'}$ are of length r'. The lengths of $\overset{\frown}{AB}$ and $\overset{\frown}{A'B'}$ are s and s', as indicated in the figure.

It may be proved by the method of nested intervals that

$$\frac{s}{r} = \frac{s'}{r'}.$$

Consequently, the ratio $\frac{s}{r}$ is independent of the particular circle centered at P which was used to obtain $\frac{s}{r}$. If a circle of unit radius is used, and the length of arc obtained is denoted by θ, then $\frac{s}{r} = \theta$. A portion of a circle with unit radius centered at P is indicated by the dashed line in Fig. 13–28(a).

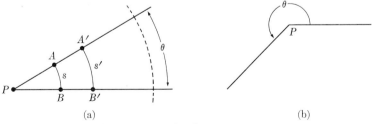

(a)   (b)

FIG. 13–28. Angle measurement.

The number θ is called the radian measure of the angle P. It is a positive real number. The radian measure of a right angle is $\frac{1}{2}\pi$, and that of a straight angle is π. Concisely, if $0 < \theta \leq \pi$, an angle with vertex P may be constructed with radian measure θ.

Since the length of the circumference of a circle of unit radius is 2π, the radian measure of a Euclidean angle suggests that the definition of a Euclidean angle be extended to angles greater than a straight angle (Fig. 13–28b). This extension is very useful in trigonometry and applied mathematics.

9. APPLICATIONS OF COORDINATE SYSTEMS TO PLANE GEOMETRY

Geometry and number are connected in the Euclidean plane by the introduction of coordinate systems. Only the simplest system of this kind will be described here. Called a *Cartesian coordinate system* in honor of the mathematician Descartes, it is the most widely used coordinate system in the geometry and trigonometry of the secondary school. It is also used in the calculus and the applications of the calculus to geometry, physics, and engineering.

To define a Cartesian coordinate system in the Euclidean plane, a point O is selected as an origin for the coordinate system. Then two perpendicular lines Λ_1 and Λ_2 are chosen passing through O (Fig. 13–29). These lines are called the *axes* of the coordinate system. Next a coordinate system is determined on each of the lines Λ_1 and Λ_2 by first assigning a positive direction, indicated by an arrow in the figure, and then choosing unit points I_1 and I_2 so that $\overline{OI_1} \cong \overline{OI_2}$. For brevity this coordinate system will be denoted by **C**.

Let T in Fig. 13–30 be any point of the plane. Coordinates are assigned to T in the coordinate system **C** as follows. Lines are drawn through T

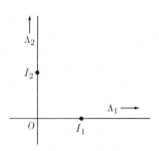

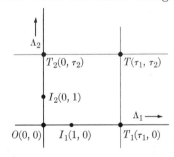

Fig. 13–29. A Cartesian coordinate system.

Fig. 13–30. Assigning coordinates to a point in the Cartesian coordinate system **C**.

parallel to the two coordinate axes and intersecting the axes in the points T_1 and T_2. Let τ_1 be the coordinate of T_1 on the line Λ_1, and τ_2 the coordinate of T_2 on the line Λ_2. Then the ordered pair of real numbers (τ_1, τ_2) is called the coordinate of T.

Certain special cases should be noted. If point T lies on the line Λ_1, the line which is parallel to Λ_2 through T meets Λ_1 in the point T, and the line which is parallel to Λ_1 through T coincides with Λ_1. It therefore meets the Λ_2-axis at the point O. The coordinate of T in this case is the ordered pair $(\tau, 0)$, where τ denotes the coordinate of the point T on the line Λ_1. Similarly, a point on the Λ_2-axis has as its coordinate an ordered pair of the form $(0, \tau)$. For example, the coordinates of the points O, I_1, and I_2 are $(0, 0)$, $(1, 0)$ and $(0, 1)$, respectively, whereas the coordinates of the points T_1 and T_2 are $(\tau_1, 0)$ and $(0, \tau_2)$, respectively.

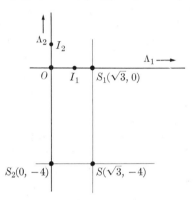

FIG. 13–31. Assigning points to coordinates in **C**.

Conversely, to any ordered pair of real numbers, there corresponds exactly one point of the plane which has this pair as its coordinates. For example, consider the ordered pair $(\sqrt{3}, -4)$. Let S_1 be the point on Λ_1 with coordinate $\sqrt{3}$, and let S_2 be the point on Λ_2 with coordinate -4 (Fig. 13–31). Let the line through S_1 parallel to Λ_2 meet the line through S_2 parallel to Λ_1 in the point S. The point S is uniquely determined by this construction, and its coordinate is $(\sqrt{3}, -4)$. The process of locating a point in the plane when its coordinates are given is called plotting the point.

The Cartesian coordinate system **C** which has been described establishes a one-to-one correspondence between the set of all points of the Euclidean plane and the set of all ordered pairs of real numbers. There are many other coordinate systems beside the Cartesian system, and no one coordinate system is best for all purposes. Plotting points is simplest, however, in Cartesian systems.

Other applications of coordinates. Cartesian coordinate systems may be extended to space, leading to a one-to-one correspondence between the set of all points in space and the set of all ordered triples of real numbers. An important extension of a different kind is to associate numbers with geometric figures. For example, let **F** be a family of concentric circles (Fig. 13–32). Then any circle $\mathcal{C}$ of the family **F** is known if the radius of $\mathcal{C}$ is known. Therefore if a unit of length is chosen, $\mathcal{C}$ corresponds to a positive real number γ, the length of the radius of $\mathcal{C}$. Consequently the pairing $\mathcal{C} \leftrightarrow \gamma$ establishes a one-to-one correspondence between the family **F** and the set of positive real numbers. The positive real numbers then serve as coordinates for the circles of the family.

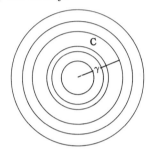

FIG. 13–32. The family **F** of concentric circles.

As a second example, consider the family **G** of all rays having a common end point R as in Fig. 13–33(a).

In Fig. 13–33(b), a fixed ray Δ_0 has been chosen. Any other ray Δ of **G** together with Δ_0, determines an angle with vertex at R. If the radian measure of this angle is ϕ, the ray Δ and the real number ϕ are in a one-to-one correspondence. To each ray of **G** there corresponds a real number ϕ in the interval $0 \leq \phi < 2\pi$, and to each number ϕ in the interval there

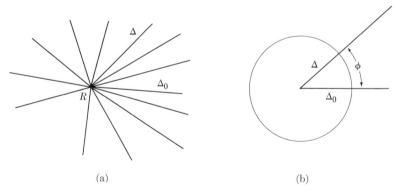

(a)   (b)

FIG. 13–33. (a) The family **G** of rays. (b) The coordinate of the ray Δ of **G**.

corresponds a ray of **G**. Thus the numbers ϕ are coordinates for the rays of **G**.

Coordinates may also be applied to surfaces in space, as well as to the points of space. One example may suffice. Figure 13–34 represents a cylinder whose base circle has a radius of length one. It is geometrically evident that to each point P on the surface of the cylinder may be assigned the coordinate pair (α, β), where α, β have the geometric meaning indicated in the figure. Thus α is the height of P above the base of the cylinder, that is, the length of the segment $\overline{PQ}$ in the figure; and β is the length of the arc OQ of the base circle.

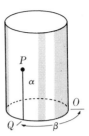

FIGURE 13–34

EXERCISE SET 13–2

1. Order the following numbers by the "greater than" relation:

$$\tfrac{3}{2}, \quad \tfrac{17}{12}, \quad \tfrac{577}{408}, \quad 1.414, \quad 2$$

2. (a) Square each of the numbers in Exercise 1 and express each as a terminating decimal or as a nonterminating decimal to five digits.
   (b) How closely does each of the squares approximate 2?
3. (a) Show that $\sqrt{2} + \sqrt{18} = 4\sqrt{2}$.
   (b) Show that

$$\frac{1 + \sqrt{5}}{2} \cdot \frac{1 - \sqrt{5}}{2} = -1.$$

4. (a) Is $\sqrt{2} + 7$ a rational or an irrational number? Why?
   (b) Is $\sqrt{2} - 7.5$ a rational or an irrational number? Why?
5. Prove that if a is an irrational number, then $a + 7$ is an irrational number.
6. Prove that if a is an irrational number, then $a - 7.5$ is an irrational number.
7. For what rational number r is $2 + \sqrt{r}$ rational? Give some examples.
8. Prove that $\sqrt{2} - \sqrt{3}$ is irrational. [*Hint:* Show that $(\sqrt{2} - \sqrt{3})^2$ cannot be rational.]
9. Formulate a generalization concerning the sum and difference of a rational and an irrational number as suggested by Exercises 4 through 8.
10. Order the following set of real numbers, using the "greater than" relationship.
    (a) $\{\pi, 3\tfrac{1}{3}, \tfrac{779}{256}\}$ (b) $\{\sqrt{2}, \tfrac{17}{12}, \tfrac{577}{408}\}$
11. On what point are the following intervals closing down?

$$[4, 5], \quad [4.1, 4.2], \quad [4.11, 4.12], \quad [4.111, 4.112], \quad \ldots$$

12. Give five intervals expressed in real-number coordinates which close down on the real number $\tfrac{1}{7}$.

13. (a) Show that
$$(\sqrt{2} \cdot \sqrt{3})^2 = (\sqrt{6})^2, \qquad (\sqrt{2} \cdot \sqrt{4})^2 = (\sqrt{8})^2,$$
and
$$(\sqrt{2} \cdot \sqrt{5})^2 = (\sqrt{10})^2.$$

(b) Does
$$\sqrt{2 \cdot 3} = \sqrt{2} \cdot \sqrt{3}, \qquad \sqrt{2 \cdot 4} = \sqrt{2} \cdot \sqrt{4},$$
and
$$\sqrt{2 \cdot 5} = \sqrt{2} \cdot \sqrt{5}?$$

(c) Study (a) and (b) and by induction write a generalization regarding $\sqrt{m \cdot n}$ when m and n are positive rationals.

14. From your observation in Exercise 13 show that
(a) $\sqrt{18} \cdot \sqrt{2}$ is rational and $\sqrt{18} \cdot \sqrt{3}$ is irrational.
(b) $(\sqrt{18} + \sqrt{2})^2 = 32$ and $(\sqrt{18} - \sqrt{2})^2 = 8$.

15. Show that:
(a) $\sqrt{20} = 2\sqrt{5}$ (b) $\sqrt{18} + \sqrt{2}$ is irrational.

16. Prove that if $\alpha + \pi = \frac{355}{113}$, then $\alpha < .000001$.

17. (a) Choose a convenient unit of length and construct a line of length $\sqrt{2}$. See Section 4.

(b) Draw a line and on the line locate points with the following coordinates:
$$\sqrt{2}; \ \ 1 + \sqrt{2}; \ \ 2\sqrt{2}; \ \ \sqrt{2} - 1$$

18. (a) Show by three dissimilar triangles that the sum of the lengths of two sides of a triangle is always greater than the length of the third side. This property of triangles is called the triangle inequality.

(b) If $\triangle ABC$ collapses so that C is a point on $\overline{BA}$, describe the relation of the three sides of the triangle.

19. In $\triangle ABC$, angle A is a right angle. The length of $\overline{BC}$ is a, that of $\overline{AC}$ is b, and that of $\overline{AB}$ is c.
(a) Show that $a > b$.
(b) Show that the triangle inequality is true for each side of $\triangle ABC$.

20. Sketch a pair of rational rectangles which are a part of the nested intervals which close down on the rectangle whose sides have lengths $\sqrt{3}$ and $\sqrt{5}$.

21. Derive the formula for the area of a parallelogram from the formula for the area of a triangle.

22. Derive the formula for the area of a regular hexagon from the formula for the area of a triangle.

23. Find the area of the figures sketched in Fig. 13–35.

(a)   (b)   (c)   (d)

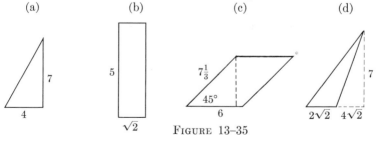

FIGURE 13–35

24. What is the perimeter of each of the geometric figures of Exercise 23?
25. Make a careful sketch of each of the following figures and show how each may be dissected into triangles for the purpose of determining area. What is the minimum number of triangles required for each figure below?

(a)   (b)   (c)

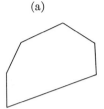 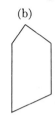 

FIGURE 13–36

26. Compute the altitude and area of equilateral triangles with sides of the following lengths.
    (a) 1   (b) 10   (c) 100   (d) $\sqrt{10}$
27. Compute the altitude and area of an equilateral triangle which has sides of length a.
28. (a) Compute the area of an isosceles triangle with sides of lengths 5, 5, and 8.
    (b) Compute the area of an isosceles triangle with sides of length 8, 8, and 5.
    (c) Does the triangle of (a) or (b) have the greater area? Approximately how much greater? Sketch a figure.
29. (a) If an isosceles triangle has sides of 4, 4, and a base of 3, find the altitude.
    (b) If an isosceles triangle has sides of 5, 5, and a base of 6, find the altitude.
    (c) If an isosceles triangle has sides of a, a, and a base of b, find the altitude.
30. (a) What is the area of a circle of radius 5?
    (b) What is the length of the boundary of a circle of radius 5?
    (c) What is the area of a semicircle of radius π?
31. What are the coordinates of points A through F in the Cartesian system of Fig. 13–37.

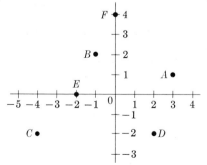

FIGURE 13–37

32. Sketch a Cartesian coordinate system and locate the points given below.
    (a) $(5, 7)$ (b) $(0, 0)$ (c) $(-2, -5)$ (d) $(3, -6)$
    (e) $(-3, 4)$ (f) $(0, -4)$ (g) $(-2, 3)$ (h) $(-4, 0)$

33. Sketch a Cartesian coordinate system and locate the following points.
    (a) $(\frac{1}{3}, \frac{2}{3})$ (b) $(0, -\frac{5}{3})$ (c) $(-\frac{2}{3}, -\frac{7}{3})$ (d) $(\frac{4}{3}, -\frac{5}{3})$
    (e) $(\frac{2}{3}, 0)$ (f) $(2, 1)$ (g) $(\frac{7}{3}, -3)$ (h) $(0, -2)$

34. Plot all the points in the plane with coordinates (a, a), where a is any real number. Use a Cartesian coordinate system.

35. If P is a point in a Cartesian coordinate system, find the distance of P from the origin, given that P has the following coordinates:
    (a) $(1, 1)$ (b) $(3, 4)$ (c) $(\sqrt{3}, \sqrt{13})$ (d) $(0, -\sqrt{\pi})$

36. If the distance of P from the origin is $\sqrt{2}$, where in the plane is P located?

37. Copy the coordinate system of Fig. 13–38 and on it locate the following points.
    (a) $(3, 4)$ (b) $(2, 7)$ (c) $(3, 2)$ (d) $(5, 6)$

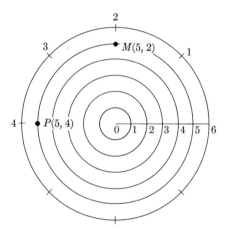

FIGURE 13–38

38. Answer the following by use of a carefully sketched figure. If the center point of all the circles of the family $\mathbf{F}$ is assigned the coordinate 0, to what sets of points in the plane do the intervals $[0, 1]$ and $[2, 3]$ correspond?

39. To what points in the plane of the family of rays, $\mathbf{G}$, do the intervals

$$\left[0, \frac{\pi}{2}\right] \quad \text{and} \quad \left[\frac{\pi}{6}, \frac{\pi}{4}\right]$$

correspond?

40. Show that two rays with the following coordinates are perpendicular to each other.

$$\frac{\pi}{4} \quad \text{and} \quad \frac{3\pi}{4}$$

REFERENCES

BANKS, J. HOUSTON, *Elements of Mathematics*. Boston: Allyn and Bacon, Inc., 1961, pp. 255–277.

BRUMFIEL, CHARLES F., ROBERT E. EICHOLZ, and MERRILL E. SHANKS, *Fundamental Concepts of Elementary Mathematics*. Reading, Massachusetts: Addison-Wesley Publishing Company, Inc., 1962, pp. 277–312.

LAY, L. CLARK, *Arithmetic: An Introduction to Mathematics*. New York: The Macmillan Company, 1961, pp. 164–195.

PETERSON, JOHN A., and JOSEPH HASHISAKI, *Theory of Arithmetic*. New York: John Wiley and Sons, Inc., 1963, pp. 193–225.

SCHAAF, WILLIAM L., *Basic Concepts of Elementary Mathematics*. New York: John Wiley and Sons, Inc., 1960, pp. 121–129.

School Mathematics Study Group, "Concepts of Informal Geometry," in *Studies in Mathematics*, Volume V. New Haven, Connecticut: Yale University, 1960, 270 pp.

School Mathematics Study Group, "Intuitive Geometry" in *Studies in Mathematics*, Volume VII. New Haven, Connecticut: Yale University, 1961, 227 pp.

SWAIN, ROBERT L., *Understanding Arithmetic*. New York: Rinehart and Company, Inc., 1957, pp. 170–191.

CHAPTER FOURTEEN

MEASUREMENT

1. THE APPROXIMATE NATURE OF MEASUREMENT

In the preceding chapter, real numbers were assigned as measures of various geometric figures in the Euclidean line or plane. A similar procedure can be applied to solids in Euclidean space. However, the underlying coordinate system is more complex for solids than for the plane or the line. For a given geometric figure, the appropriate number is uniquely determined by the choice of the coordinate system. The numbers used as measures in every case are expressible as either terminating or nonterminating decimals.

In everyday life, whole numbers and rational numbers are used to express lengths, areas, and volumes. One speaks of a room with a length of 18 feet, a farm with an area of 80 acres, or a space capsule with a volume of $2\frac{1}{2}$ cubic feet. Similar quantitative statements are commonly made about the measurement of time, weight, cost, temperature, and speed. The discussion here will be confined principally to lengths, areas, and volumes, but the ideas are also applicable to other measurable quantities.

The meaning of statements, such as "This room is 18 feet long" and "The space capsule Mark CXIV has a volume of $2\frac{1}{2}$ cubic feet," differ in two important respects from mathematical statements, such as "The length of the hypotenuse of a right triangle with sides of length 1 has length $\sqrt{2}$," and "A circle of unit radius has area π."

In the first place, *statements made about length, area, or volume in everyday life are not usually interpreted literally.* Whether the length of a room is 18 feet, 17 feet $11\frac{13}{16}$ inches, or 18 feet $\frac{3}{16}$ inch is often unimportant. The purpose for which the measurement is used determines how the number is interpreted. Because a metal space capsule is exposed to great extremes of temperature, and since temperature changes produce changes in the volume, the statement that the volume is $2\frac{1}{2}$ cubic feet must either be qualified by a further statement about the temperature, or interpreted in the broader context of the use to which the statement will be put. To a newspaper reader anxious to get some idea of the size of the capsule, the statement, "$2\frac{1}{2}$ cubic feet," means one thing; to the designer who must fit a number of delicate instruments into the interior of the capsule, "$2\frac{1}{2}$ cubic feet" means something quite different.

In the second place, the numbers expressing lengths, areas, and volumes are not usually obtained by deductive reasoning, but by various physical procedures summed up in the term *measurement*.

It is impossible to be sure that a room is exactly eighteen feet long. For example, suppose that the length is measured by pacing, or by laying a foot ruler on the floor at one end of the room, picking it up, and laying it down again until the length of the room is covered. Neither process is accurate enough to allow the statement, "This room is 18 feet long," to be interpreted literally. Indeed, in either case, there may be inaccuracy due to the human factor. All that can be said is that the number 18 probably represents the length of the room, in feet, better than either of the numbers 17 or 19.

If the measurement is done by two people using a steel surveyors' tape, the measurement may indeed be accurate to within an inch. But since the tape expands and contracts with temperature, and no ordinary floor is perfectly flat, the statement cannot be interpreted literally. All that can be said is that with present methods of measuring, the number 18 probably represents the length of the room, in feet, better than either of the numbers 17.9 or 18.1.

Another difficulty arises. Should the length of a room be measured at floor level as has been assumed, or at ceiling level, or five feet above the floor? The place of measuring will affect the measurement. No room has sides which are actually planes nor are the opposite sides of a room parallel to each other. For these reasons and others, it may be concluded that *all physical measurement is necessarily approximate.* Even if a standard of length is agreed upon so that the meaning of "one foot" is clear, it is not possible to assign one number to the length of a room as it is possible in Euclidean geometry to assign one number to the length of the hypotenuse of a right triangle whose sides are both of length one.

2. THE MATHEMATICAL MODEL FOR MEASUREMENT

Since all physical measurement is approximate, the exact length of a room, the exact distance between two cities, and indeed the exact measure of any measurable quantity are physically meaningless concepts. All that can be really determined about the length of a room is an interval within which the numbers expressing the result of the measurement lie. The size of this interval depends on factors such as the method of measuring selected, the purpose for which the measurement is made, and the care and skill with which the measurement is performed.

The mathematical model appropriate to a measuring situation is not a number, but a set of numbers; that is, *an interval of the rational number line*. Within this interval are found the numbers which express the results of the measurement in the units selected. Consequently, a mathematical model for a physical length is a *variable* whose domain is a specified interval on the rational number line.

In any given case, the interval associated with the measuring situation depends both on the measuring process and the units in which the measuring process is expressed. For example, if the measuring situation is the determination of the length of a room, and if this length has been found to be between $17\frac{1}{2}$ and $18\frac{1}{2}$ feet, the appropriate rational interval to use is $[17\frac{1}{2}, 18\frac{1}{2}]$. If the length were expressed in yards, the appropriate rational interval to use is $[5\frac{5}{6}, 6\frac{1}{6}]$. Therefore, before physical lengths can be understood, the units in which they are expressed must be known, and lengths can only be compared numerically when they are expressed in the same units. Before describing the mathematical model for measurement further, we shall present a short account of the history of measurement followed by a brief review of our present-day basic metric standards of measurement. These were originated by the French less than two centuries ago and are gradually being adopted by the majority of nations.

3. HISTORY OF UNITS

An essential feature of the mathematical method of Chapter 13 for assigning measures in Euclidean space was the choice of a line segment $\overline{OI}$ to serve as the standard unit. The choice of $\overline{OI}$ was completely arbitrary, but once chosen, all other lengths were fixed.

A similar choice of a standard unit must be made for the measurement of physical length. Indeed, in order to measure any magnitude, a suitable unit must first be selected as a standard with which the total magnitude can be compared. From earliest times, men have chosen such standards, and the choice has indeed been completely arbitrary.

Once a convenient standard of length had been agreed on, it would seem that it would gradually spread to other peoples and would persist unchanged for some time. Study reveals that the exact opposite has generally occurred. Not only was the selection of standards a matter of chance, but the standards changed from place to place and time to time in a most capricious way. The ensuing confusion has persisted to the present day. For example, an Indian unit of length, the "guz," is a yard in Bengal, $\frac{11}{12}$ of a yard in Madras, and $\frac{3}{4}$ of a yard in Bombay. The Spanish "pulgada" is .914 inch in Spain and in Chile. But in Mexico, the pulgada is .916 inch, while the Argentine pulgada is .947 inch. Canada uses both a 12-inch foot and a "French foot," which is 12.19 inches long. To this day, each country of Europe has its own interpretation of "foot." No two of them agree.

The situation was even more chaotic in times past. Thus, for example, in Italy, at the close of the eighteenth century, the term "foot" was applied to no less than two hundred different lengths, varying from about 9.5 inches to almost 14 inches.

The change of standards of length with time has been no less arbitrary. Eleven different yards were used in England from 1490 to 1760, varying in length from 35.924 inches to 36.00002 inches. The length of the yard in the United States was legally changed as recently as 1956.

The only standard of length which has remained unchanged for a considerable time is the royal Egyptian cubit. This standard was originally defined around 2650 B.C. as the distance from the elbow to the tip of the middle finger of the reigning Pharaoh and remained unchanged for over two thousand years. Cubits of different lengths were used in Mesopotamia, the Aegean Islands, and Palestine. The Bible gives the height of Goliath as "six cubits and a span" (a span is 9 inches). In Egyptian cubits, this would have made Goliath nearly eleven feet tall, but the Biblical cubit was considerably shorter (17 inches). The cubit still survives in an Arabian standard of 19 inches called the covido.

The custom of using the human body as a basis for choosing standards of length was common for a long period of time. The word "yard" is derived from an old Anglo-Saxon word meaning "girth." The English yard was later defined as the distance from the point of King Henry I's nose to the end of the thumb of his outstretched arm. The "hand" (4 inches), the "span" (9 inches), the "finger" and the "nail" ($2\frac{1}{4}$ inches) were similarly derived. This latter measure was actually the length of the outstretched thumb from the tip of the nail to the base joint.

Sometimes the standards chosen had their origins in the occupations of the people. The "furlong" was the length of a furrow along which an ox could pull the plow without stopping to rest. It is now 220 yards, but varied in the past with the stamina of the local oxen. The English "barley corn," the length of a grain of barley, used for many years and later standardized by an act of parliament, is still used as the unit of length for shoe sizes.

The custom of basing standards on occupations still persists. For example, sailors use "cable length," 120 fathoms; weavers use the "skein," 120 yards; surveyors use "link," 7.92 inches; and printers use "point," .013837 inch. The "fathom," a unit of six feet, although now used exclusively to measure water depth, originally meant "an embrace." It was defined in Tudor England as the distance from finger tip to finger tip of the outstretched arms.

It is evident from the history of measurement that lengths or any other measurable quantities cannot be compared effectively unless standards are established about which there is no disagreement. This is especially true now since the general technological progress has increased the demand for both refinement in measurement and universally interchangeable parts.

4. STANDARDIZATION

The English system. The standard units of measure used in the United States are the result of a modification of those developed in England. The Saxons and Romans first formulated the units, and since then there have been many attempts to clarify and adjust them.

The Magna Carta of 1215 guaranteed that the Saxon standards then several centuries old would continue. Subsequent laws were intended to define certain units more clearly. It was not until 1824 that the recommendations of a royal commission appointed to study standards of measure resulted in the enactment of a law which attempted to define the units of measure in use. This commission first described the meaning of yard, gallon, bushel, and pound in terms of their current use and then gave these units some scientific foundation by defining the yard in terms of the length of a pendulum, the gallon in terms of space occupied by a defined amount of water, etc. The act refined and systematized the standards, but it did not provide the invariance sought.

France. The same problems of multiple standards existed in early France. There was no attempt at standardization until an entirely new system, the metric system, was devised and adopted in the late eighteenth century. This system will be discussed in the next section.

United States. Although from its very inception the Congress of the United States was given the power to determine standards for measurement it did not exercise that right. The units used in the United States during its early history were principally those used in England and were nonuniform in nature.

President Washington in his first messsage to Congress urged uniformity, and Congress requested and received a plan from Secretary of State Jefferson on which it did not act. This lack of congressional action was repeated several times. Secretary of State John Quincy Adams presented a brilliant report in 1817 which was put aside because Congress hoped that several countries would cooperatively adopt standards. In the meantime standards were needed, and as a result individual states set their own. This procedure was not conducive to the establishment of smooth interstate commerce.

The United States Coast Survey, at the direction of the Treasury Department, standardized measures used at custom houses in 1830. A 36-inch yard, 7000-grain pound, 231-cubic-inch gallon, and a 2150-cubic-inch bushel were recommended. Congress which had nothing to do with this development adopted it informally by sending a copy of the standards to individual states for use. The Coast Survey at this time established the Office of Weights and Measures, which was replaced by the National Bureau of Standards in 1901. Congress made the metric system a part of the standards and established equivalents for the two systems in 1866.

The yard and pound which became standards in the United States were those adopted in England; the gallon and bushel were not. The United States gallon is about $\frac{1}{5}$ smaller than the English gallon, and the bushel is about $\frac{1}{30}$ smaller than the English bushel.

The International Bureau of Weights and Measures has now designated an international meter and kilogram, which since 1893 has been the basis for length and weight for metric and other units.

5. THE METRIC SYSTEM

History. We are in debt to the French for a simple and convenient system of measures, called the metric system. The essential simplification of the system, a simplification which we use in measuring money, is that of using decimal multiples and submultiples of a standard. The simplification was first suggested in 1595 by the Dutchman Simon Stevin (1548–1620), but the system presently used is a product of the French Revolution (1789–1799). The French reformers hoped that in time the metric system would universally be adopted by all mankind. They planned so well that their hope seems destined to be fulfilled, for the metric system is used now throughout the world. Its use is optional in all industrialized countries and obligatory in all western Europe save Great Britain.

In 1789 the French appointed a committee of five, including three of their greatest mathematicians, to decide upon the standards for the new system. It seemed desirable that the standards should be invariable and that their prototypes should occur in nature. The committee decided that the standard of length, the meter, should be one ten-millionth of the distance from the equator of the earth to the North Pole, measured along a meridian. It took French engineers, surveyors, and scientists, seven years to determine this distance. The task was difficult, and the final result of their computations, a length of 32,808,992 feet, has turned out to be in error by a significant amount. Nevertheless the carefully made metal bar about 3.2809 feet long which the French instrument makers completed in 1799 served as the standard meter for the world until the later part of the nineteenth century.

During the course of the nineteenth century, astronomers and geodesists discovered that the French had made an error in their calculation and hence that the actual standard meter was not one ten-millionth of the length from the equator to the North Pole. Worse yet, it was found that the lengths of different meridians were slightly different and that they fluctuated with the time of year. The standard of length chosen by the creators of the metric systems was therefore not invariable. To add to this difficulty, unforeseen discrepancies had appeared between the standards of the metric system for capacity and mass.

As a result, the French government in 1875 invited an International Committee of Scientists to reconsider the standards of the metric system. A deeper knowledge of metallurgy made it feasible to construct a standard more accurate and convenient than the old meter. However, during the 75 years of its existence, the metric system had been so widely adopted that it was deemed undesirable to change the actual length of the meter. The decision was therefore made that the new standard meter should have the same length as the old one.

The standard meter. In accordance with the decision of the International Committee, the international standard of length since 1889 has been a metal bar of a costly platinum-iridium alloy, called the standard meter. Near each end of the bar are two gold plugs. The distance between two lines engraved on these plugs when the bar is at a temperature of 0° centigrade is defined as *one meter*. One-hundredth of this distance, a *centimeter*, is the standard of length used in science. All other lengths throughout the world are defined ultimately by comparison with the standard meter. For example, the yard is now defined legally in the United States as

$$1 \text{ yard} = .9144 \text{ meter exactly.}$$

Table 14–1 shows how some other lengths are defined in terms of the standard meter and centimeter.

A convenient metric standard for small lengths is a newly minted nickel, which has a diameter of approximately two centimeters.

The metric system of weights and measures is employed in all scientific work and, to an increasing degree, in engineering and industry. It is easy to remember and use since it has a decimal base. It is slowly supplanting the cumbersome British system both in this country and in the British Commonwealth. Its use will expand further with the demands of the world market for interchangeable parts.

The standard meter is kept at the International Bureau of Weights and Measures at Sèvres, France. Because of its inaccessibility, copies of this primary standard have been made. One such copy, known as Meter No. 27,

TABLE 14–1

UNITS OF LENGTH

Unit	Length in meters	Length in centimeters
Inch	.0254	2.54
Foot	.3048	30.48
Yard	.9144	91.44
Mile	1609.344	160,934.4
Kilometer	1000	100,000
Centimeter	.01	1.
Micron	.000001	.0001
Angstrom	.000000001	.0000001

[*Note:* The micron which is one-millionth of a meter is used for measurements in microscopy, and the angstrom which is one-billionth of a meter is used to measure wavelengths and light.]

has been on deposit in the National Bureau of Standards in Washington since 1890. The accuracy of all measuring devices, such as meter sticks, yard sticks, rulers, and tapes, made in the United States is fixed by manufacturing specifications derived from this secondary standard.

Atomic standards of length. With the increasing need for precise measurements in physics and engineering, standards of length have been based on discoveries in atomic physics. An atomic standard of length, which may soon become the new world standard, is the wavelength of the orange light emitted by the atoms of a certain isotope of the rare gas, krypton. Since all krypton atoms are alike, this length furnishes an unchanging and readily available standard which is reproducible in any physics laboratory. The standard meter was found to be 1,650,763.73 times this wavelength. Using optical and spectroscopic methods, scientists can now measure lengths in angstroms; that is, length may be measured to an accuracy of one-billionth of a meter. All precise measurements of length are now made with light waves. The pioneer in the development of these methods was the American physicist, A. A. Michelson (1852–1931).

Other metric units. In the metric system, the unit of area is a *square meter*, the area of a square each of whose sides is exactly one meter in length. Similarly, the unit of volume is the *cubic meter*, the volume of a cube each of whose edges is one meter in length.

In scientific work, the unit of area is the square centimeter, and the unit of volume is the cubic centimeter. For example, syringes used for injecting drugs and antibiotics are graduated in cubic centimeters.

EXERCISE SET 14–1

1. (a) Is the statement, "There are exactly 18 ft in 6 yd," meaningful?
   (b) Why?
2. (a) Is it correct to say "18 ft equals 6 yd"?
   (b) Why?
3. What are three measurements that could be expressed by each of the following?
   (a) 7 ft   (b) 25 sq ft   (c) $-12°$
   (d) 780 lb   (e) 48 hr   (f) 25 gal
4. List at least three precautions you should observe in order to physically measure the length of a table, in inches, with accuracy.
5. What interval on the rational number line is used to describe the following measurements?
   (a) 5 ft   (b) $3\frac{3}{4}$ ft   (c) $3\frac{11}{16}$ ft
   (d) $3\frac{1}{2}$ ft   (e) $6\frac{3}{4}$ lb   (f) $6\frac{12}{16}$ lb
   (g) 6 lb 12 oz   (h) $\frac{1}{2}$ mi   (i) 2640 ft
6. Define each of these nonstandard units in terms of standard units:
   (a) jiffy   (b) pinch of salt
   (c) wink of an eye   (d) day's journey
   (e) whoop and holler   (f) one hour's drive
   (g) hop, skip, and jump   (h) week's salary
7. (a) What are two other nonstandard units of measure used by your family and friends?
   (b) Describe each in terms of standard units.
8. Why was there no agreement in eighteenth-century Italy on the length of the unit called "foot"?
9. What difficulties would arise for (a) through (d) if our legislative bodies adopted as the official unit of weight, the "pres," defined as the weight of the president of the United States at the time of his inauguration?
   (a) National Bureau of Standards   (b) Instruments of measure
   (c) Books, magazines, and other printed material
   (d) Teachers, students, and the curriculi of schools
10. (a) Determine the height of Goliath, using the Egyptian cubit.
    (b) Determine the height of Goliath, using the cubit defined in the Bible.
    (c) If you had been king instead of Pharaoh in 2650 B.C., how would the cubit have been defined in inches?
    (d) Using the cubit defined in (c), determine the height of Goliath.
11. (a) The length of a dollar bill is often used to make measurements of length. What is its approximate length?
    (b) Explain why it is a convenient instrument of measure?
12. What part of your body can you use to make the following measurements? Explain whether adjustments are necessary.
    (a) Inch   (b) Foot   (c) Yard   (d) Centimeter.
13. What lengths can you measure with the parts of your body listed in (a) through (d)?
    (a) Span from end of thumb to end of index finger
    (b) Length of foot

    (c) Width of hand at widest part

    (d) Span of outstretched arms from tip of finger on one hand to tip of finger on the other hand

14. Express a square foot in square meters.

15. Express a square inch in square centimeters.

16. (a) If the number you obtained in Exercise 14 is divided by the number you obtained in Exercise 15, what must the quotient be?

    (b) Test your answer either by division or multiplication.

17. Complete the following table.

Unit	Square meters	Square centimeters
Square foot	.09290204	(a)
Square yard (9 square feet)	(b)	(c)
Acre (4840 square yards)	(d)	(e)

18. Express an acre in square kilometers.

19. Using a table of square roots, determine the length of the side of an acre of land in the shape of a square:

    (a) to the nearest yard,   (b) to the nearest foot,

    (c) to the nearest tenth of a foot,

    (d) in meters to the nearest centimeter.

20. A frequently voiced criticism of the metric system is that the meter is too long a standard and that the foot is a much more convenient length.

    (a) With your knowledge of the history of measurement, imagine that you are on a committee organized for the purpose of combining the British and metric systems. What length would you advocate for the new "metric foot"?

    (b) A metric foot would have ten metric inches. How long would the new inch be in terms of the old inch?

    (c) What would be the length of three metric inches?

    (d) Could the length of a mile be adjusted to make it fit the metric system better?

6. EXPRESSING MEASUREMENTS BY NUMBERS

The use of real numbers in computations gives rise to problems quite similar to those that appear when measured quantities must be used in computations. Since a real number such as $\sqrt{2}$ is not rational, it must be replaced in computations by a rational approximation sufficiently accurate for the purposes at hand. From the study of such approximations, you may discover a method of describing the rational interval associated with a measurement by a number, a number which specifies both the interval and an approximation of the numerical measurement.

Rounding numbers. The decimals 3.14 and 3.1416 are often used as approximations to the number

$$\pi = 3.14159265358 \ldots$$

It is usually said that "3.14 approximates π to two decimal places." The meaning of this statement is that of all the fractions with denominators 100, the fraction $\frac{314}{100}$ or 3.14 differs the least from π. For example, we have

$$\pi - 3.13 = .01159 \ldots$$

and

$$3.15 - \pi = .008407 \ldots,$$

while $\pi - 3.14 = .00159 \ldots$ This last number is about one-seventh as large as $\pi - 3.13$, and less than one-fifth as large as $3.15 - \pi$.

The closeness of the approximation of 3.14 to π may be stated as an inequality:

$$3.135 < \pi < 3.145.$$

This inequality is depicted on the real number line in Fig. 14–1. Note that 3.14 is the *only* decimal with denominator 100 in the interval [3.135, 3.145].

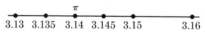

FIGURE 14–1

The approximation 3.14 determines a rational interval [3.135, 3.145] of length .01 to which π belongs. Since 3.14 is the middle point of this interval, the *decimal* 3.14 *differs from* π *by less than* .005, for .005 is half of .01. Indeed $\pi - 3.14 = .00159 \ldots$ is considerably smaller than .005.

Note that it is equally correct to say that "3.14 approximates *every* number in the interval [3.135, 3.145] to two decimal places." This is true because the decimal 3.14 differs from every number of the interval by no more than .005.

In a similar way, it may be shown that the decimal 3.1416 is closer to π than any other decimal with denominator 10,000. In particular, since $3.14 = 3.1400$, $3.1416 - \pi$ is less than $\pi - 3.14$.

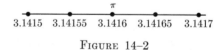

FIGURE 14–2

The approximation 3.1416 determines a rational interval [3.14155, 3.14165] of length .0001 to which π belongs. Furthermore 3.1416 is the middle point of this interval (Fig. 14–2) and is the only decimal with denominator 10,000 within this interval. Again note that 3.1416 approximates *every* number in the interval [3.14155, 3.14165] to four decimal places.

TABLE 14–2

CLOSEST DECIMAL APPROXIMATION TO π

Number of approximation	Approximation	Interval	Closeness of approximation
0	3.	$2.5 < \pi < 3.5$	$<.5$
1	3.1	$3.05 < \pi < 3.15$	$<.05$
2	3.14	$3.135 < \pi < 3.145$	$<.005$
3	3.142	$3.1415 < \pi < 3.1425$	$<.0005$
4	3.1416	$3.14155 < \pi < 3.14165$	$<.00005$
5	3.14159	$3.141585 < \pi < 3.141595$	$<.000005$
⋮	⋮	⋮ ⋮	⋮

By proceeding systematically in this manner you arrive at a table such as Table 14–2. The successive approximations are said to be obtained by "rounding" π to zero places, one place, two places, three places, etc. A given approximation such as 3.1416 is said to be "accurate to four decimal places." The process may be continued as far as desired and results in the construction of a sequence of nested intervals closing down on the real number π. In every case, the kth approximation is the middle point of the kth interval.

In rounding π, you must carefully note the differences in meaning between 3 and 3.0, 3.1 and 3.10, etc. Thus, 3.0 is *not* a closest decimal approximation to π, for if it were, π would have to lie in the interval [2.95, 3.05]. In other words, $\frac{30}{10}$ is not the decimal with denominator 10 which is closest to π. The distinction is that 3 has no significant digits to the right of the units place. The 0 in 3.0 is a significant digit, but not the correct digit to give the closest approximation to π.

Finite decimals may be rounded similarly. For example, the approximations to 3.0075898 are: 3., 3.0, 3.01, 3.008, 3.0076, 3.00759, 3.007590, and 3.0075898. All the zeros which appear in these approximations are significant digits.

Stating the results of measurements. There is a close analogy between measuring a physical quantity more and more precisely and approximating to a real number more and more closely. In each case, smaller and smaller intervals are obtained as the measurement becomes more precise and the decimal approximation becomes closer. The process, of course, terminates for physical measurement as soon as the ultimate level of precision of measurement is reached. The process of approximation for a nonrational real number does not terminate because it is a mental process which we can imagine to continue indefinitely.

Rounded decimals may be used to describe the results of measurements. Consider once more the statement, "This room is 18 feet long." The ambiguity in this statement may be removed by thinking of 18 as a rounded decimal with no significant digits to the right of the units' place. The meaning of the statement is that the length of the room is between 17.5 and 18.5 feet, so that the mathematical model associated with the measurement is the interval [17.5, 18.5]. Since 18 is the mid-point of this interval, the length of the room as found by measurement differs from 18 feet by less than 6 inches.

The statement, "This room is 18.0 feet long," would mean that the room is 18 feet long, with a maximum error of .05 foot or .6 inch. Note that the last statement is perfectly compatible with more refined measuring procedures, giving a length of 17.96 feet, with an error of less than .06 inch. Thus a single number, 18, or 18.0, or 17.96, specifies both the interval associated with the measurement *and* the precision of the measurement. Note how simply measurements can be stated in the metric system, where all subunits are obtainable from the standard unit by either multiplying or dividing by a power of ten.

7. THE SCIENTIFIC NOTATION FOR APPROXIMATING MEASUREMENTS

It is often necessary to approximate measures expressed in whole units. For example, a measured distance of 378 meters accurate to one-half of a meter can be approximated by 380 meters, accurate to five meters, or by 400 meters, accurate to fifty meters. The approximations, 380 or 400, may be thought of as obtained by "rounding" the number 378 just as the approximations .38 or .4 are obtained by rounding the number .378.

The rounding procedure leads to difficulties when zero must be used to indicate both a place value and a significant figure. For example, compare rounding 3.7896 with rounding 37,896. The approximations obtained are:

$$3.7896, \quad 3.790, \quad 3.79, \quad 3.8, \quad 4;$$
$$37,896, \quad 37,900, \quad 37,900, \quad 38,000, \quad 40,000.$$

The first and second approximations to 37,896 must be written exactly the same, although their meaning is quite different.

To remove this ambiguity, scientists write the number 37,896 as the product of a decimal between 1 and 10 and power of ten. For example,

$$37,896 = 3.7896 \times 10^4.$$

The rounding now proceeds without ambiguity:

$$3.790 \times 10^4, \quad 3.79 \times 10^4, \quad 3.8 \times 10^4, \quad 4 \times 10^4.$$

Note that the accuracy of each approximation is easily determined from its representation. Since 3.790 approximates 3.7896 to within 5×10^{-4} units, 3.790×10^4 approximates 37,896 to within 5 units. Similarly 3.79×10^4 approximates 37,896 to within 50 units.

The terminology for describing approximations. Scientists have devised a convenient terminology to describe such approximations, which is being widely adopted whenever measurements must be compared and discussed. In the representation of 37,896 as 3.7896×10^4, the power of 10 is called the *order of magnitude* of the number. It immediately shows that 37,896 lies between ten thousand and one hundred thousand. The digits 3, 7, 8, 9, and 6 of the decimal 3.7896 are called its *significant digits*. The number of significant digits describes the *accuracy* of the approximation. Thus one says that "3.79×10^4 is an approximation to 37,896, which is accurate to three significant digits," and "4×10^4 is an approximation to 37,896, which is accurate to one significant digit." The accuracy of the approximations to 37,896 decreases as the number of significant digits decreases, but each approximation is of the same order of magnitude as 37,896.

Products of measurements expressed in scientific notation. Scientific notation is well adapted to the task of estimating the products of measurements. It is based on the assumption that in a product of several factors no measurement is more precise than the least precise one. Suppose, for example, that it is necessary to estimate the product

$$37,896 \times .0000047 \times 1787.462,$$

where the factors express the results of measurements. The first step is to write the product as

$$3.7896 \times 10^4 \times 4.7 \times 10^{-6} \times 1.787462 \times 10^3.$$

Since the second factor is accurate only to two significant digits, the first and third factors must also be rounded to two significant digits. The product then becomes

$$3.8 \times 10^4 \times 4.7 \times 10^{-6} \times 1.8 \times 10^3 = (3.8 \times 4.7 \times 1.8) \times 10^1.$$

The product of the first three factors is $32.148 = 3.2148 \times 10^1$. Since only two digits of this product are significant, the final approximation is 3.2×10^2, and this number is the best estimate possible of the product of the given measurements. Note that further rounding affects the accuracy of the product. For example, if $(3.8 \times 4.7 \times 1.8) \times 10^1$ is rounded to $(4 \times 5 \times 2) \times 10^1$, the product is 4×10^2; this approximation is of the correct order of magnitude, but not accurate even to one significant digit.

8. OPERATING ON ROUNDED NUMBERS

Addition and multiplication of rounded numbers. In using 3.14 or 3.1416 as approximations to π or in using the number 9.3 in a statement such as "The distance from the earth to the sun is 9.3×10^7 miles," you are not using a new kind of approximate number; you are merely using familiar numbers for a new purpose. The decimals 3.14, 3.1416, 9.3 *as numbers*, that is, mathematical objects, are unaffected by the purpose for which they are employed. Consequently, these numbers may be added, subtracted, multiplied, and divided just like any other rational numbers. Unfortunately, such arithmetical operations often result in numbers which cannot be used for the original purposes of approximation or descriptions of measurement.

Suppose that the statement, "This room is 18 feet long," is true for three adjoining classrooms in a school. It is certainly true that $18 + 18 + 18 = 54$; however, the statement, "The total length of the three classrooms is 54 feet," does not follow. It means that the total length of the three rooms is between 53.5 feet and 54.5 feet. Imagine that careful measurements establish that the rooms are 17.52 feet, 17.60 feet, and 17.54 feet long. Then the three measurements are compatible with the first statement, but not with the second. The measurements imply that the total length of the three rooms is less than $17.525 + 17.605 + 17.545 = 52.675$ feet. The sum of the lengths of the three rooms is therefore actually less than 53 feet, so that the approximation, 54 feet, in the second statement is accurate only to one significant digit.

The same kind of difficulties is encountered when real numbers are rounded to terminating decimals. For example, since

$$\pi = 3.14159265358 \ldots \qquad \text{and} \qquad 8\pi = 25.13274122864 \ldots ,$$

3.142 approximates π accurately to four significant figures and 2.513×10^1 approximates 8π accurately to four significant figures. However $8 \times 3.142 = 25.136$ rounds to 2.514×10^1 and therefore approximates 8π accurately to only three significant figures.

These illustrations emphasize the fact that rounded numbers may be added only if the accumulated errors from the individual addends will not affect the final purpose for which the sum is to be used.

Repeated measurements and averaging. There is, however, an important and frequently occurring situation in which a set of measurements may be used to obtain an approximation that is more accurate than any member of the set. Let

$$M = \{m_1, m_2, m_3, \ldots, m_n\}$$

TABLE 14–3

MEASUREMENTS OF A ROOM

Measurement number	Measurement in feet	Deviation from 18.0 in tenths of a foot		
1	17.2	18.0		−.4
2	17.9	18.0		−.1
3	18.0	18.0		.0
4	18.0	18.0		.0
5	17.6	18.0		−.4
6	18.2	18.0		+.2
7	18.1	18.0		+.1
8	17.6	18.0		−.4
9	18.4	18.0		+.4
10	18.2	18.0		+.2
Sum	179.6	18.0		−.4
Mean	17.96	18.0		−.04
The mean rounds to 18.0 feet.				

be a set of n numbers representing the result of repeated measurements made under the same conditions. The mean of these measurements generally will be a more accurate approximation than any one of the individual measurements. The mean $\overline{m}$ of the numbers in set M is defined by the formula

$$\overline{m} = \frac{1}{n} (m_1 + m_2 + m_3 + \cdots + m_n).$$

Due to human errors in measurements, i.e., misplacements of measuring instruments, small inaccuracies in the reading of scales, and over- or underestimating, any one measurement may be less accurate than the mean of many measurements made by different people. The mean of the measurements tends to cancel human errors.

This observation may be checked by a simple experiment. If the length of a room is given as 18.0 feet and you wish to determine whether the mean of a series of measurements of the room yields 18.0 feet, follow these steps. Have a series of measurements made by 10 or more different people who use a foot ruler graduated in tenths of a foot. Record these measurements and find their mean. Your results may look like those listed in Table 14–3. Note that the measurements fluctuate from 17.6 feet to 18.4 feet and that the mean of the measurements is 18.0 feet.

The numerical data of Table 14–3 were not obtained by experimentation, but from a table of random numbers. However, if the experiment consists of a sufficient number of measurements, the mean will round to 18.0 feet. This result illustrates that the most accurate procedure leading to the most accurate measurement is to determine the mean of a number of measurements made by as many different persons.

EXERCISE SET 14–2

1. (a) When 66.666 ... is rounded to 67, what is meant by the statement

   $$66.5 < 67 < 67.5?$$

   (b) When 66.666 ... is rounded to 66.7, what is meant by the statement

   $$66.65 < 66.7 < 67.75?$$

2. (a) Illustrate Exercise 1(a) with a number line.
   (b) Illustrate Exercise 1(b) with a number line.
3. What rational interval is defined when 12.2745 ... is rounded to each of the following?
   (a) 12   (b) 12.3   (c) 12.27
4. (a) Approximate $\frac{16}{7}$ to twelve places to the right of the units' place.
   (b) Make a table for the closest decimal approximation to $\frac{16}{7}$ similar to that made for π in Section 6. Include approximations from no decimal places to five decimal places.
5. How many significant digits are there in each of the following decimal approximations of $\frac{1}{13} = .076923076923 \ldots$?
   (a) .08   (b) .077   (c) .0769231
   (d) .076923   (e) .0769230770   (f) .07692308
6. Round each of the following to four significant digits.
   (a) 2.3400   (b) 52.7689   (c) 3.333 ...
   (d) $66\frac{2}{3}$ (e) 3.141592 ...   (f) 9.29999
7. What is the maximum error in each of the following measurements?
   (a) 5 in.   (b) 12.3 m
   (c) 4.25 cm   (d) 17.253 gm
8. Express the following in scientific notation with two significant digits.
   (a) 6080.2 ft   (b) 5280 ft   (c) 92,900,000 mi
   (d) 253,000 ft   (e) 1089 ft   (f) 186,272 mi
9. Repeat Exercise 8, expressing each part in scientific notation with three significant digits.
10. What is the order of magnitude of each of the following?
    (a) 7926 mi   (b) 2159.9 mi   (c) 3.16×10^7
    (d) .454 kg   (e) 32.17 ft   (f) 33,136 cm
11. Express the following in scientific notation and perform the operation indicated. Assume that the numbers are the result of measurement and that no measurement in an exercise is more precise than the least precise one.
    (a) 5270×3000 (b) $5179.6 \times .00032$
    (c) 436×3.1416 (d) $26000 \times .006 \times 39426$

12. Have ten of your friends measure the length of your mathematics book, using a ruler graduated in tenths of an inch.

   (a) Record the measurements in a table similar to Table 14–3.

   (b) Find the mean of the measurements.

   (c) What is the maximum measurement recorded?

   (d) What is the minimum measurement recorded?

   (e) Does the mean seem to be a more accurate measurement than any of the others? Why?

REFERENCES

BANKS, J. HOUSTON, *Elements of Mathematics*. Boston: Allyn and Bacon, Inc., 1961, pp. 245–254, 294–297.

BRUMFIEL, CHARLES F., ROBERT E. EICHOLZ, and MERRILL E. SHANKS, *Fundamental Concepts of Elementary Mathematics*. Reading, Massachusetts: Addison-Wesley Publishing Company, Inc., 1962, pp. 253–260, 277–287, 214–225.

PAYNE, JOSEPH N., and ROBERT C. SEBER, "Measurement and Approximation," in *The Growth of Mathematical Ideas*, Twenty-fourth Yearbook of the National Council of Teachers of Mathematics. Washington, D. C.: The Council, 1959, pp. 182–229.

SWAIN, ROBERT L., *Understanding Arithmetic*. New York: Rinehart and Company, Inc., 1957, pp. 192–216.

CHAPTER FIFTEEN

MATHEMATICS AS A STUDY OF PATTERNS

---

1. PURPOSES OF THIS CHAPTER

This chapter has a threefold purpose. The first purpose is to reconsider the question of Chapter 1, "What is mathematics?", in the light of the additional knowledge you now possess, and to reemphasize the central theme of this book—the importance of patterns and the importance of the discovery of patterns to the learning and teaching of mathematics.

The second purpose of this chapter is to review and compare many of the patterns studied in previous chapters to show how they fit into the comprehensive pattern of mathematical thought. The third purpose is to give glimpses of the mathematical horizons which lie beyond elementary mathematics. This will be accomplished by presenting illustrative examples of familiar patterns applied to new situations. In this manner, you will better understand how new mathematical ideas grow out of known ideas.

2. MATHEMATICAL IDEAS AND PATTERNS

Mathematical ideas. Mathematics is both a way of thinking and a body of related ideas based on past thinking. When the essence of a problem is stated in a mathematical sentence, mathematics is used as a way of thinking. In solving the problem, it may be necessary to use a mathematical operation such as addition. When this addition is performed, a mathematical procedure is followed which makes use of known ideas. Once this procedure is understood, it is used without reflection on the reasons for every step. Skill in addition may be increased by practice. Knowledge of addition depends upon understanding the process as an application of mathematical ideas.

Some very important mathematical ideas are now familiar to you, for they were used in every chapter of this book. These are: the idea of a set, and a family of distinguished subsets, the idea of a relation, and the idea of an operation. In arithmetic the sets are number systems, and the distinguished subsets are numbers with some useful property, such as even numbers or decimal numbers. The relation of importance is the order relation, and the operations of importance are the four fundamental operations of arithmetic. In geometry, the sets are point sets either on a line, in a plane, or in space, and the distinguished subsets are the various geometric objects, such as lines, vectors, convex figures, and solid bodies, which are the subject matter of geometry. The important relations are congruence and similarity, and one of the most important operations is the assigning of coordinates to points, thus establishing a link between geometry and number.

Mathematical ideas can be studied either by the methods of deductive logic or by the methods of induction, but they are best first learned and understood by an inductive approach. In any application of mathematics which is not purely routine, both its inductive aspect and its deductive aspect must be utilized. The applications are made by the construction and use of appropriate mathematical models. Some models studied for this purpose in this book are mathematical sentences.

Mathematical objects, relations, and operations. Many useful, more specialized, mathematical ideas have been learned. Some are geometric objects, such as rays, segments, triangles, convex figures, planes, cones, cylinders, and neighborhoods. Others are arithmetical objects, such as prime numbers, square numbers, and decimals. Other mathematical ideas are special relations, such as set inclusion, parallelism, and the inverseness of two operations. Still other mathematical ideas are special operations, such as forming a Cartesian product, averaging two numbers, or finding the reciprocal of a fraction. Of particular importance are the ideas interpreting length, area, and volume as numbers associated with geometric objects. These latter concepts form the basis for quantitative comparisons not only of geometric objects, but physical objects in the world around us.

Organizing mathematical ideas. Mathematical ideas may be organized in various ways. Logicians organize them in hierarchies of sets and families of sets. Some nineteenth-century educators have organized mathematical ideas according to their practical usefulness, discarding all ideas for which no practical application could be seen. Historians organize mathematical ideas chronologically in order of their discovery. None of these ways are particularly helpful in a time of rapid change when new methods, new ideas, and unforeseen applications are constantly arising.

Mathematical patterns. A group of naturally connected ideas is called a pattern. The connections between the ideas are not arbitrary but arise from the very nature of the ideas themselves. A pattern makes it easier to understand the ideas concerned. Experience shows that patterns provide an effective way of thinking about mathematics. Because of your increased knowledge of mathematical ideas and how they are formed into patterns, you are now in a better position to understand mathematics and use it than when you began the study of this book.

The importance of the deliberate search for patterns has only been recently recognized. This awareness is one reason for the phenomenal growth of modern mathematics.

Important mathematical patterns arise in many situations. Equivalence relations are used in logic, in arithmetic, in geometry as well as in many other branches of mathematics. But every equivalence relation has the same pattern. The operation of addition has a pattern which is described by such properties as closure and associativity. This pattern persists whether whole numbers, fractions, integers, rational numbers, or real numbers are added. The processes by which these different kinds of numbers are added are different; however, the operation of addition has the same properties in each case. Consequently, understanding the pattern for the addition operation on one kind of number makes it easier to understand the addition operation on other kinds of numbers.

The fact that patterns reoccur and that the same pattern applies to many situations is a comparatively recent discovery. Different parts of mathematics, such as geometry, algebra, trigonometry, and calculus, have been presented in the past as unrelated subjects. Similarity of patterns was not emphasized. Recognition of patterns and of relations among patterns has led to a better understanding of the structure of mathematics. As a result the subject has become more unified. There is no strict break between elementary mathematics and other mathematics. Arithmetic does not suddenly stop and algebra begin. The same patterns and ideas reoccur in both subjects. New mathematical ideas grow out of the elementary mathematics you are studying, as well as out of more advanced mathematics.

The purposes of this chapter will be accomplished by illustrating (1) various ways in which patterns, some familiar some unfamiliar, are used and (2) how familiar patterns are related to one another.

3. ALGORITHMS AS PATTERNS

Patterns play an important role in the study and use of algorithms, or more generally, in any clearly defined mathematical procedure leading to a definite result. An algorithm such as that for addition of whole numbers has a pattern which anyone familiar with the algorithm employs. Several addends are written in columns, the numbers in the columns are added, and the sums recorded in a definite order. This *physical pattern* is important, since it minimizes the chances of error and shortens the work. But there is a still more important pattern, a hidden pattern, which the algorithm follows. It is this pattern which enables one to understand why the algorithm yields the sum. This hidden pattern is a *pattern of deductive reasoning*. Its premises are the meaning of our place-value system of numeration and the pattern of the operation of addition—properties such as associativity and commutativity that characterize the operation. This pattern need not be consciously followed every time one adds; in fact, the algorithm is planned so as to make this unnecessary. But the pattern must be thought about and understood if the algorithm is to be used intelligently. An example of this deductive pattern, which is described in Chapter 7, is given here to refresh your memory.

Consider the addition $27 + 94$. The successive steps in a performance of this addition may be written horizontally as follows:

$$27 + 94 = (20 + 7) + (90 + 4) = (20 + 90) + (7 + 4)$$
$$= 100 + 10 + 10 + 1 = 121.$$

Each step may be justified either by the meaning of our system of numeration or by one or more of the properties of addition. The calculation as presented is in reality a pattern of deductive reasoning carried out exclusively in mathematical symbols, and with the reasons justifying the successive steps omitted. The algorithm

$$\begin{array}{r} 27 \\ 94 \\ \hline 121 \end{array}$$

simply records the essential steps of this deductive pattern in a compact and convenient form. The physical pattern of the algorithm can be learned and followed by rote. To understand the algorithm and the reasons for its success requires thinking of the deductive pattern which determines the algorithm.

4. FORMULAS AS PATTERNS

An algebraic formula was defined in Chapter 3 as a proposition containing variables and stating an equality which is true for all values of the variables. The variables have as their domain some universal set. You have used many such formulas. For example, in Chapter 12 the conditions defining the field of rational numbers were stated as formulas. One of these is the formula $u + v = v + u$ for the commutative property for the addition of any two rational numbers u and v. Another slightly more complicated formula which illustrates more clearly how an algebraic formula may be regarded as a *pattern* is the formula

$$u^2 - v^2 = (u + v)(u - v).$$

This formula may be interpreted in terms of deductive logic. Its meaning is then conceived to be purely formal. Interpreted in this way, the formula $u^2 - v^2 = (u + v)(u - v)$ is a proposition which states that whatever rational numbers u and v denote, the expressions

$$u^2 - v^2 \quad \text{and} \quad (u + v)(u - v)$$

both name the same number, or $u^2 - v^2$ may be renamed $(u + v)(u - v)$. For example, if $u = 10$ and $v = 8$,

$$u^2 - v^2 = 100 - 64 = 36 \quad \text{and} \quad (u + v)(u - v) = 18 \times 2 = 36.$$

Therefore $10^2 - 8^2$ may be renamed 18×2. Evidently any algebraic formula may be thought of as a renaming. Although this interpretation is valuable, it does not convey meaning to *a* particular formula.

Approaches to the meaning of a formula. The approaches which are most effective in conveying the meaning of *a* particular formula are to view it as a pattern to be discovered, to be applied, or to be verified and then to be used for prediction. In each case the approach is demonstrative, involves induction and allows you to discover some aspect of the formula for yourself.

The first approach is to presuppose that you do not know the formula and to use the inductive procedures described in Chapter 5 as a guide to develop it. Thus, for example, observations that

$$2^2 - 1^2 = 3 \times 1, \quad 3^2 - 1^2 = 4 \times 2, \quad 4^2 - 1^2 = 5 \times 3, \ldots$$

suggest the generalization

$$u^2 - 1^2 = (u + 1)(u - 1),$$

which might be tested by computing

$$30^2 - 1^2 \quad \text{and} \quad 29 \times 31,$$
$$100^2 - 1^2 \quad \text{and} \quad 101 \times 99.$$

Similarly, the pattern

$$3^2 - 2^2 = 5 \times 1, \quad 4^2 - 2^2 = 6 \times 2, \quad 5^2 - 2^2 = 7 \times 3, \ldots$$

suggests that

$$u^2 - 2^2 = (u + 2)(u - 2);$$

also the pattern

$$4^2 - 3^2 = 7 \times 1, \quad 5^2 - 3^2 = 8 \times 2, \quad 6^2 - 3^2 = 9 \times 3, \ldots$$

suggests that

$$u^2 - 3^2 = (u + 3)(u - 3).$$

Finally, the pattern

$$u^2 - 1^2 = (u + 1)(u - 1), \qquad u^2 - 2^2 = (u + 2)(u - 2),$$
$$(u^2 - 3^2) = (u + 3)(u - 3)$$

suggests the generalization

$$u^2 - v^2 = (u + v)(u - v).$$

The generalization should then be tested by specializing u and v.

For those who have learned the formula in high-school algebra, the inductive procedure just described is time consuming. Furthermore, it does not prove the formula. Nevertheless, the examination of particular cases reveals the *meaning of the formula* as a numerical pattern, and successful testing reveals its meaning as a pattern of prediction. The required computations also show the arithmetical utility of the formula. $30^2 - 1^2$ not only renames the product 29×31, but it gives it an arithmetically simpler name. *An algebraic formula may often be used to replace a complicated numerical pattern by a simpler one.* This fact is so important that another example will be given.

Consider the formula for finding the sum of consecutive natural numbers when n denotes any positive integer:

$$1 + 2 + 3 + \cdots + (n - 2) + (n - 1) + n = \tfrac{1}{2}n(n + 1).$$

The indicated addition requires adding the first n positive integers. This procedure is laborious for large values of n, such as 100. The multiplication pattern is so simple, however, that for $n = 100$, it may be followed mentally. It may be concluded that the sum of the first hundred positive integers is 5050. Whatever positive integer n may be, the expressions $1 + 2 + 3 + \cdots + n$ and $\tfrac{1}{2}n(n + 1)$ both name the same number. What makes the formula useful is that one renaming is much simpler than the other.

The second approach makes an application of a formula the basis for understanding. A geometric application of a formula will first be presented because such an application is useful for algebraic formulas. The purpose of the approach is to give a formula, for example,

$$u^2 - v^2 = (u + v)(u - v),$$

a geometric interpretation which will make its truth evident. What follows may be regarded either from the standpoint of experimental geometry

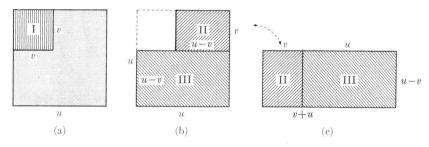

FIG. 15–1.   Geometric proof of the formula $u^2 - v^2 = (u + v)(u - v)$.

described in Chapter 8, or from the standpoint of the relation between number and geometry described in Chapter 13. From the latter standpoint, the geometric interpretation is simultaneously a proof of the formula.

Figure 15–1(a) shows a large square with side of length u and in the upper left-hand corner of this square, there is a smaller square I of side length v. In Fig. 15–1(b), the square I has been removed, and a horizontal line separates the large square into the rectangles II and III. The total area of these two rectangles is $u^2 - v^2$, and the lengths of their sides are as indicated in the figure.

In Fig. 15–1(c), II and III are fitted together to form a rectangle whose sides are of lengths $u + v$ and $u - v$. Since the area of this rectangle is the same as the area of figure (b),

$$u^2 - v^2 = (u + v)(u - v).$$

Thus the truth of the formula has been made geometrically evident. To understand the arithmetical meaning of the formula and its use as a pattern for prediction, it must be tested by giving u and v numerical values as was done in the first approach.

It is interesting to note that Fermat made the formula $u^2 - v^2 = (u + v)(u - v)$ the basis for a method of factoring large numbers. Two hundred years ago, the formula was utilized in conjunction with a table of squares so that multiplication of whole numbers could be performed by subtracting appropriately chosen squares. Thus, for example, the product 251×249 equals 62,499, for if $u = 250$ and $v = 1$,

$$(u + v)(u - v) = 251 \times 249 \quad \text{and} \quad u^2 - v^2 = 250^2 - 1^2 = 62,500 - 1.$$

Many other applications could be presented; in general an approach using applications provides a basis for understanding a formula.

The third approach to the meaning of a formula is its verification by use of the properties of the fundamental operations of arithmetic. In numerical cases, verification is done by indicating computations rather than by carrying them out as in the first approach. Verifying the formula

$$u^2 - v^2 = (u + v)(u - v)$$

by this approach requires a knowledge of the distributive property of multiplication with respect to addition and subtraction. Thus, since

$$a(b - c) = ab - ac,$$

it follows that if $a = 10 + 4$, $b = 10$, and $c = 4$, then

$$(10 + 4)(10 - 4) = (10 + 4)10 - (10 + 4)4,$$
$$(10 + 4)(10 - 4) = 10 \times 10 + 4 \times 10 - 10 \times 4 - 4 \times 4,$$
$$(10 + 4)(10 - 4) = 10 \times 10 - 4 \times 4,$$
$$(10 + 4)(10 - 4) = 10^2 - 4^2.$$

You should supply the reasons for the steps in this demonstration. Note that it has been possible to show that the formula $u^2 - v^2 = (u + v)(u - v)$ is true for $u = 10$ and $v = 4$ without performing the computations $(10 + 4)(10 - 4) = 84$, $10^2 - 4^2 = 84$. In like manner,

$$(15 + 7)(15 - 7) = (15 + 7)15 - (15 + 7)7,$$
$$(15 + 7)(15 - 7) = 15 \times 15 + 7 \times 15 - 15 \times 7 - 7 \times 7,$$
$$(15 + 7)(15 - 7) = 15 \times 15 - 7 \times 7,$$
$$(15 + 7)(15 - 7) = 15^2 - 7^2.$$

Therefore the formula is true for $u = 15$ and $v = 7$.

By further illustrations it is possible to accumulate inductive evidence for the truth of the formula. The illustrations do not follow the computational pattern of the formula itself, but the operational patterns of multiplication. In this manner, no matter what numbers u and v are chosen, it is possible to show that the expression $u^2 - v^2$ is equal to the expression $(u + v)(u - v)$, without performing the indicated computation.

Proof of a formula. The numerical examples of the third approach illustrates the pattern for a *deductive proof* of the formula illustrated. If you recall mathematical ideas from this book or if you remember high-school algebra, you will be able to follow the steps of the proof just as you were able to follow the steps of the numerical examples. The proof is as follows:

$$(u + v)(u - v) = (u + v)u - (u + v)v,$$
$$(u + v)(u - v) = u \cdot u + v \cdot u - u \cdot v - v \cdot v,$$
$$(u + v)(u - v) = u \cdot u - v \cdot v,$$
$$(u + v)(u - v) = u^2 - v^2.$$

Observe that the pattern of reasoning is exactly the same as in the numerical examples. The proof is algebraic because the reasoning is being carried out with variables instead of with particular numbers. This proof is another example indicating how the mathematical patterns used in arithmetic are also used in more advanced mathematics.

5. USING PATTERNS TO UNDERSTAND MATHEMATICAL IDEAS

Comparing patterns. Patterns may be compared with one another to find similarities. Recognizing these similarities brings out the analogies among patterns and facilitates understanding. An important example developed in Chapter 6 was the similarity in pattern between the operations of addition and the operation of multiplication of whole numbers. Both operations have the same properties of closure, associativity, commutativity, cancellation, and existence of identity elements.

The similarity of pattern indicates a relationship between the inverse operations of subtraction and division. To subtract 17 from 85 is to name the missing addend n in the mathematical sentence $17 + n = 85$. To divide 85 by 17 is to name the missing factor m in the mathematical sentence $17 \times m = 85$. The algorithms for performing subtraction and division are different. Yet as operations, subtraction and division are quite similar.

Contrasting patterns. Patterns may be contrasted. Recognizing the differences in patterns often gives a better understanding of the mathematical concepts linked in the patterns. For example, in contrasting the cancellation property of addition and multiplication the following difference is observed:

The cancellation property for addition, if $a + b = a + c$, then $b = c$, is true when $a = 0$.
However, the cancellation property for multiplication, if $a \times b = a \times c$, then $b = c$, is not true when $a = 0$.

This difference points up the fact that zero as an addend and zero as a factor have different properties.

A result of this difference is that division by zero is impossible. By contrast, it is always possible to add zero, subtract zero, and multiply zero.

Extending patterns. Patterns may be extended to new situations to give them meaning. New ideas often result when an extension is attempted even when the extension is not successful. An example of extension is the application of each property found for the addition of whole numbers to the addition of fractional numbers, integers, and rational numbers.

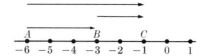

FIG. 15–2.   Addition of vectors on a line.

The addition of integers was developed by representing the integers as vectors between integral points on a number line and then adding the vectors geometrically. The geometric addition was found to represent the arithmetic addition of integers. In Fig. 15–2, the addition of two such vectors is illustrated. The vector $\overrightarrow{AB}$ extending from -6 to -3 represents the integer $^+3$, the vector $\overrightarrow{BC}$ extending from -3 to -1 represents the integer $^+2$. The sum of the two vectors is the vector $\overrightarrow{AC}$ extending from -6 to -1. It represents the integer $^+5$. The geometrical addition corresponds to the arithmetical addition $^+3 + {^+2} = {^+5}$.

FIG. 15–3.   Addition of vectors in a plane.

The ideas just described may be thought of as a single pattern linking geometrical objects and a geometrical operation with arithmetical objects and an arithmetical operation. The geometric aspect of this pattern may be extended to the plane. In Fig. 15–3, two plane vectors $\overrightarrow{AB}$ and $\overrightarrow{BC}$ are shown. The vector $\overrightarrow{AC}$ is defined to be their sum.

This new pattern is incomplete, for no numbers are linked with the geometrical objects. This defect is remedied in high-school mathematics when complex numbers are introduced. It is then shown by the coordinate methods described in Chapter 13 how complex numbers may be represented by vectors in the plane just as integers are represented by vectors on a line. Furthermore, it turns out that the geometric addition of vectors corresponds to the arithmetic addition of the complex numbers which they represent. Consequently the whole pattern may be extended with no structural change to a new situation.

The extension just described is of great historic importance. It was by devising a geometric representation of complex numbers and operations on complex numbers that the great mathematician Gauss won acceptance for complex numbers among other mathematicians. Complex numbers and their vector representations are widely used now in science and engineering. The first chapter of almost any electrical engineering text begins with a discussion of complex numbers and their vector representation. Without these mathematical ideas it is impossible to describe the nature of alternating currents.

The extension of vector addition from the line to the plane was chosen as an example to provide a glimpse of some of the mathematics which lies beyond what has been considered here, and to show you how it is connected with the elementary mathematics you are studying by examining the similarity of patterns.

6. REVEALING PATTERNS BY GEOMETRIC FIGURES

A geometric figure or diagram is often helpful in understanding a mathematical pattern. Such figures have been repeatedly used in this book. Number lines were employed to show the order pattern of numbers. Line segments and rectangular regions were used to represent the addition of integers and the multiplication of fractional numbers. Figures were used as a problem-solving technique to help reveal the essence of the problem.

The use of geometric figures and diagrams to illustrate and explain more abstract mathematical ideas is extremely common in everyday life. Statistical data are often presented graphically, so that their pattern can be understood at a glance. Trends, that is causal and functional relations of all kinds, are illustrated by graphs and diagrams. Engineers and scientists continually employ graphical methods and geometric diagrams in their work.

As you study mathematics you should be alert to the significance of using appropriate figures and diagrams. A few illustrative examples follow. They have not been previously presented in this book.

Representing formulas by geometric figures. Geometric figures often help the student to understand a formula. Such figures may be used (a) to illustrate the meaning of the formula by experimental geometry or (b) to give a geometric proof of the formula by utilizing the connection between number and geometry as was done in the discussion of the formula

$$1 + 2 + 3 + \cdots + (n - 1) + n = \tfrac{1}{2}n(n + 1).$$

The principle that the area of a rectangle is the product of its base and altitude is frequently useful. Figure 15–4 illustrates the geometric meaning of the distributive and associative properties of multiplication.

The rectangle shown in Fig. 15–4(a) has an altitude of length p and a base of length $(q + r)$. Its area consequently is $p(q + r)$. The rectangle has been divided by a vertical segment into two smaller rectangles. The first rectangle has an altitude of length p and a base of length q, and the

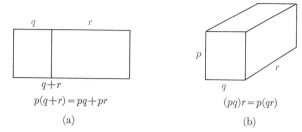

FIG. 15–4.   The distributive and associative properties of multiplication.

second rectangle has an altitude of length p and a base of length r. Since the areas of these rectangles are pq and pr, the distributive property is evident. You may work out the geometrical meaning of the associative property of multiplication by computing the volume of the rectangular solid of Fig. 15–4(b) in two different ways. The sides of the solid are of lengths p, q, and r.

Geometric illustration of propositions of logic. In Chapter 2, Section 10, sets were represented by regions in the plane, and this representation made it possible to visualize set relations and set operations geometrically. The same geometric representation helps you understand the meaning of propositions and patterns of reasoning used in ordinary logic. When geometric figures are employed to illustrate set concepts, they are called "Venn diagrams" rather than Euler diagrams because the English logician Venn first used them effectively for this purpose.

The possibility of making a connection with geometry is based on the fact that the meaning of statements such as, "A horse is an animal" or "Gold is a precious metal," may be expressed in the language of sets as

The set of horses is contained in the set of animals

or

Gold is an element of the set of precious metals.

Aristotle studied methods of arranging statements in simple deductive patterns consisting of three statements, two premises and a conclusion. Such a pattern is called a "syllogism." If one accepts the premises of a syllogism, one must accept the conclusion. An example of a syllogism is the following:

(a)   All horses have four legs.

(b)   All horses are mammals.

Therefore,

(c)   Some mammals have four legs.

Since the premises (a) and (b) are true, the conclusion (c) must also be true. Venn diagrams may be used to represent the meaning of syllogisms geometrically.

The following conventions are employed when Venn diagrams are used. The universal set U is represented by a square region. If a subset of U is nonempty, a star (*) is placed within the corresponding region in the diagram. If a subset of U is empty, the corresponding region is shaded. If it is not known whether a set is empty or nonempty, the corresponding region is unshaded.

In elementary logic, the complement of A is usually called "not A." Furthermore, the universal set U is assumed to be nonempty. Consequently, if x is an element of U and A is a subset of U, either x is an element of A or x is an element of "not A."

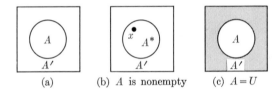

(a)   (b) A is nonempty   (c) $A = U$

FIG. 15–5.   Relations between a set and its complements.

Figure 15–5 illustrates various possible relations between a set A and its complement "not A," denoted by A'.

Figure 15–6 illustrates various possible relations between two subsets A and B of U. In Fig. 15–6(a), nothing is known about the relations between A and B; hence the diagram is unshaded. In Fig. 15–6(b), the star in the region $A \cap B$ indicates that A and B have elements in common.

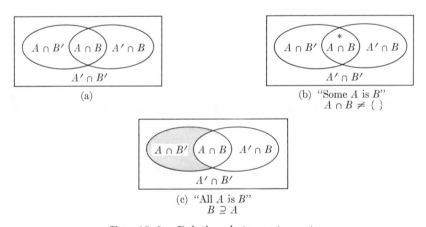

(a)

(b) "Some A is B"
$A \cap B \neq \{\,\}$

(c) "All A is B"
$B \supseteq A$

FIG. 15–6.   Relations between two sets.

Various ways of stating this fact are: "Some A is B," or "Some B is A," or "$A \cap B \neq \{ \}$." In Fig. 15–6(c), the shading indicates that $A \cap B'$ is an empty set. Consequently, if x is in A, x is in B. Therefore the diagram represents the statements "All A is B," or "B includes A," or "$B \supseteq A$." Note, that since no star appears in the region $A \cap B$, the statement $B \supseteq A$ does not exclude the possibility that A is an empty set.

There is a difference in logical meaning between statements such as "Jones is a man" and "Men are human beings." The first statement is a relation between an element of a set and a set. Its meaning is shown in Fig. 15–5(b), where the element x is indicated as belonging to the set A; the element x is visualized as a point, but A itself is a point set. The second statement is a relation between two sets. It is illustrated in Fig. 15–6(c). Until comparatively recently, logicians confused these two different types of statements. The Venn diagram makes the distinction quite evident.

Observe from the Venn diagram in Fig. 15–6(c) that the statements, "All A is B" and "All 'not B' is 'not A'" have the same meaning. This equivalence and many others studied in elementary logic were discovered by Aristotle.

7. DISCOVERING PATTERNS

Simple mathematical patterns are usually discovered by the inductive procedures of observation, generalization, and testing described in Chapter 5. More abstract patterns are often the outcome of a deliberate search instigated in the course of investigating the structure of mathematical systems. Mathematicians sometimes create a new pattern by modifying an existing pattern. Such a modification is an act of discovery, and may reveal an unsuspected simplicity. The introduction of the empty set, the whole number zero, and the null vectors are examples of this procedure. In each case, the operational pattern of set intersection, numerical addition, and vectorial addition was simplified.

Since you know many patterns and are conscious of pattern, the discussion which follows will be confined to procedures which have been proved useful when a deliberate search for pattern is made. Two of the most important of these procedures are generalization and specialization.

Generalization and specialization. Both the procedures of generalization and specialization were used more times than you probably realized as you studied this book. Every time an illustrative example was given to show the meaning of a general mathematical idea, a specialization of the idea was made. A general idea was often presented by first showing particular examples and then formulating the generalization from them. For example, $2 + 5 = 5 + 2$ is a specialization of the commutative property of addition.   The formula $u + v = v + u$, which states this property in mathematical language, is a generalization from numerical examples such as

$$2 + 5 = 5 + 2, \quad 7 + 3 = 3 + 7, \quad \text{and} \quad 139 + 447 = 447 + 139.$$

The following definitions of generalization and specialization which are due to George Pólya* should help you to understand their relationship to the idea of a set.

Generalization is passing from the consideration of a given set of objects to that of a larger set containing the given one.

Specialization is passing from the consideration of a given set of objects to that of a smaller set contained in the given one.

In the illustration above of the commutative property of addition, the given set consists of the following three pairs of sums:

$$\{2 + 5 \quad \text{and} \quad 5 + 2; 7 + 3 \quad \text{and} \quad 3 + 7; 139 + 447 \quad \text{and} \quad 447 + 139\}.$$

The larger set consists of all pairs of sums:

$$\{u + v \quad \text{and} \quad v + u \mid u, v \quad \text{any whole numbers}\}.$$

The generalization consists in the assertion that since in the smaller set each pair of sums is equal, the same will be true in the larger set.

Generalization is one of the three procedures of induction, and was fully discussed from this standpoint in Chapter 5. A pattern which does not have a certain generality will not have wide applicability and therefore is not likely to be useful. A most important kind of generalization is one which links several patterns into a single overall pattern of which the individual patterns may be viewed as special cases.

The American, E. H. Moore (1862–1932), was one of the first mathematicians to be aware of the importance of this kind of generalization and to use it systematically in his researches. An example of this type of pattern is given below to illustrate once more how mathematics is developed.

The identical nature of the patterns for the operations of addition of integers and multiplication of fractions has already been pointed out in Chapter 12. Many other examples of the same pattern were discovered in the nineteenth century. These examples suggested to mathematicians the idea of studying the properties of an abstract binary operation $x \circ y$ defined over a set and having all the properties of addition of integers or multipli-

---

* Pólya, George: *Induction and Analogy in Mathematics*, Volume I. Princeton, N. J.: Princeton University Press, 1954, pp. 12–13.

cation of fractions, with the possible exception of commutativity. The mathematical system consisting of a set and such an operation is called a *group*.

In this manner, an entire new branch of mathematics, group theory, was created to which American mathematicians have made important contributions. Group theory began as a branch of pure mathematics without any thought of applications. It has turned out to have very important practical applications, and is almost indispensable to theoretical physics. Moreover, it is one of the great unifying patterns in modern mathematics. More information about groups may be found in an article by Dean.*

Problems leading to new patterns. The problems of mathematics have patterns. The study of the method of solution of one problem may be applied to a whole set of problems with the same pattern. This fact is also true for the more complicated problems that occur in science and industry to which mathematics may be applied. Experience has shown, however, that the problem which does not fit into any existing pattern is often the one that leads to new, useful patterns. Solving such a problem may require new methods, and these methods lead to new patterns for solving other problems. Encountering problems which cannot be solved by the methods already known is often an incentive to a further study of mathematics.

In pure mathematics, the progress which has been made could well be measured by the number of difficult problems that previous generations of mathematicians could not solve, but which have been solved by mathematicians of the twentieth century. Indeed, in 1900, the great German mathematician, Hilbert, presented a list of twenty-three important problems which had been left unsolved by nineteenth-century mathematicians. Many of these problems have been solved, some by Americans, and in the course of solving them entirely new methods and new patterns of mathematical ideas have been created.

Problems are as important in learning mathematics as they are in developing new mathematics. George Pólya's† book, *How to Solve It*, approaches the whole subject of inductive methods in mathematics through well-chosen problems suggested by high-school geometry. Quite aside from their practical importance, problems can be very stimulating. They are particularly valuable if they are thought of as an opportunity to discover and recognize patterns.

---

* Dean, Richard A. "Group Theory for School Mathematics," in *Mathematics Teacher*, February 1962, pp. 98–105.

† Pólya, George, *How to Solve It*. Garden City, New York: Doubleday and Company, Inc., 1957. Also valuable is: Pólya, George, *Mathematical Discovery*, Volume I. New York: John Wiley and Sons, Inc., 1962.

8. CONCLUSION

If the purpose of this book has been attained, you know some important mathematical ideas and you know that these ideas may be united into larger groups called patterns.   There is, however, more to learn.   Your knowledge of mathematics and skill in using it will increase with study and practice. With the knowledge you now possess, you can pursue mathematics further, and help others in its study.   Experience with discovery should have convinced you of the importance of discovery as a method of learning to think with the ideas of mathematics. To teach you this method of thinking is the purpose of this book.

EXERCISE SET   15–1

1. (a) Write the first ten multiples of nine that are natural numbers.
   (b) Examine the symbols for the multiples and identify two patterns which exist among them.
2. Given: $2, 5 \rightarrow 14$; $3, 4 \rightarrow 14$; $9, 0 \rightarrow 18$; $6, 5 \rightarrow 22$.
   (a) Using the pattern illustrated above, complete the following by finding p, q, r, and s:

$$5, 7 \rightarrow p; \quad 12, 12 \rightarrow q; \quad 4, \tfrac{7}{2} \rightarrow r; \quad a, b \rightarrow s.$$

   (b) Describe the pattern used.
   (c) Use the same pattern and find t, u, v, and w in the following:

$$6, t \rightarrow 36; \quad 5, u \rightarrow 12; \quad v, a \rightarrow b; \quad c, w \rightarrow 7.$$

3. Draw several right triangles ABC with the same hypotenuse, $\overline{AC}$. What geometric pattern is suggested by the vertices of the triangles?
4. Draw several right triangles ABC with the same base, $\overline{AC}$.
   (a) Describe the triangle which appears to have the largest area.
   (b) Describe the apparent change in the area of the triangles as the length of $\overline{AB}$ changes from very small to larger and larger.
5. Explain how patterns are used to construct a Sieve of Eratosthenes.
6. Organize all the number systems considered in this book into an Euler diagram.
7. (a) List four fractions which are terminating decimals, e.g. $\frac{1}{2}$ and $\frac{1}{10}$, in the fum system.
   (b) Examine the denominators of these fractions for a pattern. Define a method of predicting from an examination of a denominator whether a fraction is a terminating decimal.
8. (a) Find the sum S_1 of the squares of the digits of 58; find the sum S_2 of the squares of the digits of S_1; find the sum S_3 of the squares of the digits of S_2. Continue this process until S_{20} is determined.
   (b) List the sums in the sequence (a) from S_1 to S_{20}. Describe the pattern emerging from this sequence of numbers.

9. (a) Repeat the process of forming successive sums of the squares of a number as was done in Exercise 8, beginning with each of the first ten natural numbers. If possible carry each to S_{20}. For example,

(i) 1

(ii) 2, 4, 16, 37, 58, 89, 145, 42, 20, 4, 16, 37, 58, 89, 145, 42, 20, 4, 16, 37, 58, . . .

(b) Do any of the sequences terminate? What is the final sum in each of these?

(c) Examine the nonterminating sequences for a common pattern. What is it?

(d) In the same manner, prepare sequences with the number symbols given below and determine whether the patterns of (b) and (c) apply.

$$32; \qquad 44; \qquad 645; \qquad 24{,}763; \qquad \text{and} \qquad 5{,}267{,}841$$

10. Can a floor be made entirely of whole tile of each of the following shapes? Illustrate your answer with a sketch.
    (a) Congruent squares
    (b) Congruent equilateral triangles
    (c) Congruent isosceles triangles
    (d) Congruent regular pentagons
    (e) Congruent regular hexagons
    (f) Congruent rectangles

11. (a) Make a list of the numbers whose squares have a number symbol with units' digit "6."

(b) Is there any pattern to the units' digit of the numbers listed in (a)?

12. (a) How many subsets does an empty set have? a set of one member? a set of two members? a set of three members? etc.

(b) Continue (a) until a pattern is recognized. What is the pattern? Express it as a formula.

13. (a) In the formula

$$1 + 2 + 3 + \cdots + (n - 1) + n = \tfrac{1}{2}n(n + 1)$$

for finding the sum of consecutive natural numbers, estimate how large n must be for the sum to exceed ten thousand.

(b) Calculate the sum for the estimate of n made in (a).

14. Inductive evidence for the formula of Exercise 13 may be obtained by determining one-half of a series of sums as follows:

$$\frac{(1 + 2 + 3) + (3 + 2 + 1)}{2} = \frac{(1 + 3) + (2 + 2) + (3 + 1)}{2} = \frac{3 \cdot 4}{2} = 6$$

or

$$\frac{(1 + 2 + 3 + 4) + (4 + 3 + 2 + 1)}{2}$$

$$= \frac{(1 + 4) + (2 + 3) + (3 + 2) + (4 + 1)}{2} = \frac{4 \cdot 5}{2} = 20.$$

    (a) Find the sum in a similar manner when $n = 5$ and $n = 10$.

    (b) Explain why the sum of 1, 2, 3, ... , 100 equals $\frac{1}{2}(100 + 101)$ by the evidence collected in (a).

15. (a) The property $n - n = 0$ holds for subtraction. What is its analogue for division?

    (b) Is there any exception for division?

16. (a) If the processes are known, is it generally easier to subtract or to divide whole numbers?

    (b) If the processes are known, is it generally easier to subtract or to divide fractional numbers?

    (c) What are the patterns called which you use to make it convenient to perform operations with numbers?

17. (a) What are the first five natural numbers which it is possible to rename as the sum of 1's? $(1 + 1 + 1 + \cdots)$

    (b) Give the first five natural numbers which it is possible to rename as sums of 2's. $(2 + 2 + \cdots)$

    (c) Give the first five natural numbers which it is possible to rename as sums of 3's.

    (d) Every whole number may be expressed as the sum of a series of 1's. May every whole number be expressed as the sum of a series of any other natural number? If so, list them.

18. List three formulas which are special cases of the mathematical model $ab = c$.

19. Use Fig. 15–4(b) of Section 6 to explain the associative property for multiplication.

20. Can the geometric meaning of the distributive property, as developed in Section 7, be extended to real numbers?

21. (a) What is the similarity between the operations $A \cup B$ on two sets and $a + b$ on two numbers?

    (b) What is the difference between these two operations?

22. The formula $A \cup B = C$ is analogous to $a + b = c$. Does $A \cup A = A$ have an analogous formula?

23. Express the following statements in the language of sets.

    (a) Some girls have blue eyes and red hair.

    (b) No girls have red eyes and blue hair.

    (c) Pie is a superb breakfast food.

    (d) A square is both a rectangle and a rhombus.

    (e) A number which is a multiple of 12 is also a multiple of 2, 3, 4, and 6.

    (f) The symbol of a number which is a square does not have a units' digit of three.

24. Illustrate each of the following propositions with a Venn diagram.

    (a) Not all is gold that glistens.

    (b) The integers are real numbers.

    (c) A square is both a rectangle and a rhombus.

    (d) A multiple of both 4 and 9 is a multiple of 6.

    (e) Some A is not B.

    (f) Some "not A" is "not B."

25. Sketch Venn diagrams for each pair of the following and decide whether the first statement implies the second.
   (a) All fire-breathing dragons are green;
       some fire-breathing dragons are green.
   (b) All human beings nineteen feet tall live in Chicago;
       some human beings nineteen feet tall live in Chicago.
   (c) All A is B; some A is B.
26. (a) Illustrate "Some A is B" and "Some B is not A" with two pairs of statements similar to those of Exercise 25.
   (b) Does the first statement of each of your pair of statements imply the second?
   (c) Does "Some A is B" imply "Some B is not A"?
   (d) Find an example of the type of reasoning suggested in (c) from a magazine advertisement.
27. Show by a Venn diagram the error in the following reasoning. All fine automobiles have good brakes; my automobile has good brakes; therefore I have a fine automobile.
28. (a) Does "Some A is B" have the same meaning as "Some B is A"?
   (b) Does "All A is B" have the same meaning as "All B is A"?
29. The figure below represents two squares, one inscribed in the other. Show geometrically that the area of the inscribed square is half the area of the other square.

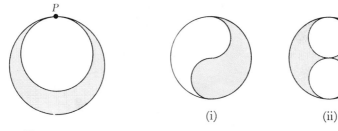

FIGURE 15-7

30. The shaded crescent-shaped figure below is bounded by two circles intersecting at P. If the area of the crescent is the same as the area of the inner circle and the radius of the outer circle is 2, what is the radius of the inner circle?

FIGURE 15-8   FIGURE 15-9

(i)   (ii)

31. (a) The pattern in Fig. 15-9(i) is common in Chinese art. What is its geometric relation to the pattern in Fig. 15-9(ii)?
   (b) Show that the shaded areas of the two figures are equal.

REFERENCES

BAKST, AARON, *Mathematics, Its Magic and Mastery*. New York: Van Nostrand Company, Inc., 1941, 790 pp.

DEAN, RICHARD A., "Group Theory for School Mathematics," in *Mathematics Teacher*, February, 1962, pp. 98–105.

JOHNSON, DONOVAN A., and WILLIAM H. GLENN, *Exploring Mathematics on Your Own*. Garden City, New York: Doubleday and Company, Inc., 1961, 303 pp.

KASNER, EDWARD, and JAMES NEWMAN, *Mathematics and the Imagination*. New York: Simon and Schuster, 1940, 380 pp.

PÓLYA, G., *How to Solve It*. Garden City, New York: Doubleday and Company, Inc., 1957, 253 pp.

PÓLYA, G., *Mathematical Discovery*, Volume I. New York: John Wiley and Sons, Inc., 1962, 216 pp.

APPENDIXES

POWERS AND ROOTS

N	N^2	$\sqrt{N}$	N	N^2	$\sqrt{N}$
1	1	1	51	2,601	7.141
2	4	1.414	52	2,704	7.211
3	9	1.732	53	2,809	7.280
4	16	2	54	2,916	7.348
5	25	2.236	55	3,025	7.416
6	36	2.449	56	3,136	7.483
7	49	2.646	57	3,249	7.550
8	64	2.828	58	3,364	7.616
9	81	3	59	3,481	7.681
10	100	3.162	60	3,600	7.746
11	121	3.317	61	3,721	7.810
12	144	3.464	62	3,844	7.874
13	169	3.606	63	3,969	7.937
14	196	3.742	64	4,096	8
15	225	3.873	65	4,225	8.062
16	256	4	66	4,356	8.124
17	289	4.123	67	4,489	8.185
18	324	4.243	68	4,624	8.246
19	361	4.359	69	4,761	8.307
20	400	4.472	70	4,900	8.367
21	441	4.583	71	5,041	8.426
22	484	4.690	72	5,184	8.485
23	529	4.796	73	5,329	8.544
24	576	4.899	74	5,476	8.602
25	625	5	75	5,625	8.660
26	676	5.099	76	5,776	8.718
27	729	5.196	77	5,929	8.775
28	784	5.292	78	6,084	8.832
29	841	5.385	79	6,241	8.888
30	900	5.477	80	6,400	8.944
31	961	5.568	81	6,561	9
32	1,024	5.657	82	6,724	9.055
33	1,089	5.745	83	6,889	9.110
34	1,156	5.831	84	7,056	9.165
35	1,225	5.916	85	7,225	9.220
36	1,296	6	86	7,396	9.274
37	1,369	6.083	87	7,569	9.327
38	1,444	6.164	88	7,744	9.381
39	1,521	6.245	89	7,921	9.434
40	1,600	6.325	90	8,100	9.487
41	1,681	6.403	91	8,281	9.539
42	1,764	6.481	92	8,464	9.592
43	1,849	6.557	93	8,649	9.644
44	1,936	6.633	94	8,836	9.695
45	2,025	6.708	95	9,025	9.747
46	2,116	6.782	96	9,216	9.798
47	2,209	6.856	97	9,409	9.849
48	2,304	6.928	98	9,604	9.899
49	2,401	7	99	9,801	9.950
50	2,500	7.071	100	10,000	10

SKILLS TESTS

The three tests which follow may be used as a series of self-evaluating instruments by students. They are not intended to test a student's understanding of the material of this book but rather to test the skills in arithmetic assumed as a background for the use of this book.

TEST I

(1) Divide: 6597.76 ÷ 9.76.   (2) What is $\frac{1}{2}$ of 5 cu yd 3 cu ft?

(3) Find 250% of 425.

(4) What is the approximate square root of 74? (Express to nearest tenth.)

(5) 6% of $49.50 is ____.   (6) $12\frac{1}{2}\%$ of $____ is $324.18.

(7) Arrange from smallest to largest: $\frac{3}{5}$, 62%, $\frac{5}{8}$, .7, and $\frac{2}{3}$.

(8) Multiply 6987 × 90.   (9) 35.8 × 100 is ____.

(10) 17.8 ÷ 10 is ____.

(11) Write MDCXLVI as a decimal number symbol.

(12) Write 1492 as a Roman numeral.

(13) The price of coffee which sold for 30 cents per pound in 1930 had increased by 200% in 1950. In the 10-year period from 1950 to 1960 the price decreased by 20%. What was the 1960 price?

(14) $\frac{7}{6}$ of $2\frac{1}{4}$ is ____.   (15) Subtract $19\frac{3}{5}$ from 400.

(16) $42\frac{1}{2} ÷ 3\frac{3}{4}$ is ____.   (17) What is 5% less than 90 ft?

(18) Round .125 to tenths.   (19) Round 47,343 to hundreds.

(20) $6\frac{1}{4}\%$ = ____ (common fraction).   (21) $\frac{5}{6}$ = ____%.

(22) Multiply 74.9 × 7.08.   (23) Add $48\frac{1}{10} + 53\frac{1}{5}$.

(24) Multiply $45\frac{3}{4} × 16\frac{2}{5}$.

(25) Divide the product of 22, 54, and 75 by the product of 45 and 90.

(26) .011 = ____ (common fraction).   (27) 225% = ____ (decimal fraction).

(28) Subtract 3700 ft from 4 mi 2200 ft.

(29) 12 is what percent of 21?   (30) Subtract 500.03 − 194.16.

(31) If 49 of the exercises on this test are correct, what percent is correct?

(32) Arrange from largest to smallest: .78; .087; .9; 87%; and $\frac{7}{8}$.

(33) Divide   60.375 ÷ .75.

(34) What is the sum of $.45, $6.92, $5, and $68.43?

(35) Subtract $19\frac{2}{3}$ from $48\frac{1}{15}$.   (36) $13 ÷ \frac{4}{5}$ = ____.

(37) $.3\frac{1}{2}$ = ____%.   (38) $\frac{7}{8}$ = ____ (decimal fraction).

(39) $\frac{1}{3}\%$ of $60 is ____.   (40) $12 is 30% of ____.

(41) Multiply 7 weeks 4 days 16 hours by 3.

(42) $.5^4 =$ ____.

(43) $372 \times 36\frac{2}{3} =$ ____.

(44) $\frac{7}{8}$ of $\frac{3}{4}$ is ____.

(45) 6 is what percent of 5?

(46) Divide $\frac{7}{16} \div \frac{3}{4} =$ ____.

(47) $883 - 384.94 =$ ____.

(48) Which number does 8% equal: .08, .125, .12$\frac{1}{2}$, or $\frac{1}{12}$?

(49) Find the mean of the following: $64\frac{1}{2}$ in., $49\frac{3}{4}$ in., $61\frac{3}{4}$ in., and 63 in.

(50) A house was bought for \$18,000 and sold for \$20,000. By how many percent did the price increase?

TEST II

(1) Divide 1728 by the product of 12, 24, and 6.

(2) If a 300-lb man gains 20% in one month and then loses 20% the next month, what is his weight at the end of the second month?

(3) $\frac{5}{6}$ of $4\frac{1}{2}$ is ____.

(4) Subtract $3\frac{3}{8}$ from 200.

(5) $12\frac{1}{2} \div 4\frac{3}{8}$ is ____.

(6) What is 3% less than \$30?

(7) 3.42×1000 is ____.

(8) $7.9 \div 100$ is ____.

(9) $3\frac{1}{2}\% =$ ____ (common fraction).

(10) Multiply $.867 \times 7.9$.

(11) Change .3 to a common fraction.

(12) $.3 =$ ____$\%$.

(13) Add $38\frac{3}{8}$ and $54\frac{1}{4}$.

(14) Multiply $35\frac{1}{8} \times 8\frac{4}{5}$.

(15) $72\% =$ ____ (common fraction).

(16) Which of the following is the largest: .8750, $87\frac{1}{2}\%$, .875, or $\frac{7}{8}$?

(17) 3 is what percent of 28?

(18) From 500.07 subtract 469.77.

(19) Divide $.03392 \div .32$.

(20) Subtract $15\frac{2}{7}$ from $42\frac{1}{14}$.

(21) Divide $31 \div \frac{2}{3}$.

(22) Subtract 6 lb 7 oz from 11 lb.

(23) $175\% =$ ____ (decimal fraction).

(24) Find 325% of 85.

(25) Arrange from smallest to largest: $\frac{1}{3}$, .3, $34\frac{1}{2}\%$, and $\frac{7}{20}$.

(26) $\frac{1}{8} =$ ____$\%$.

(27) Find the mean of the following: $35\frac{1}{2}$ hr, $72\frac{3}{4}$ hr, $85\frac{24}{60}$ hr.

(28) An automobile was marked up from \$1000 to \$1200. What was the percent of markup?

(29) $745 \times 24\frac{3}{5} =$ ____.

(30) \$14 is 35% of \$____.

(31) Multiply 5 yd 2 ft 8 in. by 6.

(32) $\frac{3}{4} =$ ____ (decimal fraction).

(33) $5^3 =$ ____.

(34) How many of the exercises on this test should you get correct to have 70% correct?

(35) $6.3 + 48.9 + 4.8 + 43.05 =$ ____.

(36) Multiply $53.28 \times .806$.

(37) Add $14\frac{2}{3}$, $14\frac{3}{8}$, and $7\frac{5}{6}$.

(38) $\frac{3}{4}$ of $\frac{5}{6}$ is ____.

(39) Which of the numbers does $12\frac{1}{2}\%$ equal? .12$\frac{1}{2}$, .08, .8, or .125.

(40) What percent is 4 of 4?

(41) $675 - 86.37 =$ ____.

(42) Round .739 to hundredths.

(43) Round 7942 to tens.

(44) Divide $15.54 \div 1.85$.

(45) Find $\frac{1}{3}$ of 7 gal 3 qt 1 pt.

(46) Find $\frac{1}{2}\%$ of \$90.

(47) What is the approximate square root of 8? (Express to the nearest tenth.)

(48) $62\frac{1}{2}\%$ of \$20.80 is ____.

(49) $66\frac{2}{3}\%$ of \$____ is \$19.44.

(50) Multiply 678×800.

TEST III

(1) $775 - 575.49 =$ _____.   (2) $\frac{4}{5}$ of $\frac{7}{9}$ is _____.

(3) What percent of 4 is 3?   (4) $\frac{5}{12} \div \frac{3}{4} =$ _____.

(5) Which of the following equals 4%: .4, $\frac{1}{25}$, .004, or .25?

(6) $5\frac{1}{2}\% =$ _____ (common fraction).

(7) $\frac{4}{3} =$ _____$\%$.   (8) Divide $9812.50 \div 12.50$.

(9) Find $\frac{1}{4}$ of 25 hr 42 min.   (10) 150% of $_____ is $972.

(11) What is the approximate square root of 13? (Express to nearest tenth.)

(12) Arrange from largest to smallest: $\frac{9}{10}$, $\frac{7}{8}$, 81%, and .8.

(13) $12\frac{1}{2}\%$ of $17.28 is _____.   (14) What is 2% less than $50?

(15) $\frac{5}{16}$ of $2\frac{2}{3}$ is _____.   (16) $76.2 \div 1000$ is _____.

(17) 5.7×10 is _____.

(18) Change MCMLIX to a decimal number symbol.

(19) Change 1066 to Roman numerals.

(20) Multiply 6987×600.   (21) Subtract $743\frac{5}{9}$ from 7000.

(22) $37\frac{1}{2} \div 2\frac{2}{3}$ is _____.   (23) $3 is 75% of $_____.

(24) $\frac{1}{4}\%$ of $64 is _____.   (25) $3^4 =$ _____.

(26) A farmer sold a quantity of cattle to a wholesaler for $7000. The wholesaler then sold the cattle at a 10% loss to a retailer. The retailer in turn sold the cattle at a loss of 50%. At what price did the retailer sell the cattle? (The cost of business operation is ignored.)

(27) What is 5% of $726?   (28) Round .378 to tenths.

(29) Multiply $43\frac{2}{3} \times 747$.

(30) Divide the product of 75 and 98 by 20.

(31) Multiply $.687 \times 9.3$.   (32) Add $18\frac{1}{6}$ and $36\frac{1}{3}$.

(33) Subtract 2 sq ft 100 sq in. from 5 sq ft.

(34) Add 7 qt 1 pt and 4 qt 1 pt.   (35) Subtract $16\frac{3}{4}$ from $25\frac{1}{12}$.

(36) $11 \div \frac{2}{3} =$ _____.   (37) Find 225% of 84.

(38) A coat was marked down from $75 to $50. What was the percent of reduction?

(39) Round 256,540 to thousands.

(40) Which of the following is the largest: .74, .407, .470, or .0704?

(41) 27 is what percent of 18?   (42) Multiply 5 tons 800 lb by 4.

(43) $38\% =$ _____ (common fraction).   (44) $\frac{4}{5} =$ _____ (decimal fraction).

(45) Multiply $48\frac{1}{4} \times 66\frac{2}{3}$.

(46) How many of the exercises on this test are correct, given that 80% are correct?

(47) Change .13 to percent notation.

(48) $125\% =$ _____ (decimal fraction).

(49) Divide $59.045 \div 9.8$.

(50) Find the mean of the following: $3\frac{3}{4}$ lb, $12\frac{5}{16}$ lb, $19\frac{3}{8}$ lb.

SELECTED ANSWERS

CHAPTER ONE

Exercise Set 1–1, pp. 11–16

1. (a) Rename 191 as 180 and 11. Subtract: $11 - 9$ and $180 - 80$. Change 191 to $190 + 11$, an increase of 10. Subtract $11 - 9$ and $190 - 90$. Note that 80 was also increased by 10.

8. (a) Vertices of the squares are in similar position; the large square regions are the same size, and the small square regions are the same size; both patterns are formed by perpendicular and parallel lines; the number of small squares is the same in each.

9. (b) If the divisor remains unchanged and the number divided is decreased, the result is also decreased.

10. (a) 10, 12, 14, 16, 18
    (c) $\frac{1}{64}$, $\frac{1}{128}$, $\frac{1}{256}$, $\frac{1}{512}$, $\frac{1}{1024}$

13. (b) Each of two players is assigned a cross ($\times$) or a circle ($\bigcirc$) and they take turns placing the marks in the regions of a 3 by 3 grid. The first player draws the grid

and places his mark in any one of the nine regions. Player two then places his mark in any one of the remaining regions. The players continue to play until one player has three of his marks in a vertical, horizontal, or diagonal row. He is the winner. If neither player forms a row of his marks, the game is a draw and is replayed.

18. $(a + b) \div c = a \div c + b \div c$

22. (a) Idea   (b) Symbol
    (c) Idea   (d) Symbol
    (e) Idea

23. (c) Angle 1 and angle 2 equal ninety degrees;* the sum of angles 1 and 2 is 90°; the sum of angles 1 and 2 equals 90°.

25. (b) Omit "Mary is pretty."

34. (c) The letters which spell "tip": t, i, p.

35. (d) It will be even because $(16 - 1)$ is a multiple of three.

36. (a) Answers will vary.
    Triangles are formed by rows 1 and 2, by rows 1, 2 and 3, etc.
    Remove the 1's, and the remaining numbers form a triangle.
    Two diagonal rows of 1, 2, 3, 4, and 5 intersect at 2.

CHAPTER TWO

Exercise Set 2–1, pp. 19–20

1. (b) B is the set whose members are 2, 4, 6, and 8.
9. The members of set A are numbers, whereas the members of set B are sets.
10. (b) Set B has as members multiples of three greater than zero and less than 12. Set B has as members numbers which are less than 36 and can be represented by the digits of "936."

Exercise Set 2–2, pp. 26–28

3. A set is well defined if it makes clear whether an object does or does not belong to the set.
6. $\{6, 7, 8\} = \{8, 6, 7\}$
9. (a) 1, 6   (b) 1, 7, 8   (c) 1, 2, 8   (d) 1, 3
    (e) 1, 5   (f) 1, 2, 4, 7, 8   (g) 1, 2, 4, 8   (h) 1
13. (a) The empty set and sets with one element
    (b) Sets with two or more members
18. (a) No.
    (b) Tested by division to determine whether 566,127 is a multiple of 853.
    (c) Test the given number by division to decide whether it is a multiple; test to determine whether the given number has the property defined.

Exercise Set 2–3, pp. 33–36

2. (f) $\{0, 10, 20, 30, \ldots\}$
5. (a) Unequal, disjoint, $A \supseteq B$
9. (a) $\{0, 2, 4, 6, 8\}$ (b) $\{4, 5, 6, \ldots\}$
16. (a) If

comp $(\{1, 3, 4, 7\} \cup \{1, 2, 3, 8\})$
$$= \text{comp } \{1, 3, 4, 7\} \cap \text{comp } \{1, 2, 3, 8\},$$
then

comp $\{1, 2, 3, 4, 7, 8\} = \{2, 5, 6, 8, 9, 10\} \cap \{4, 5, 6, 7, 9, 10\}$

and
$$\{5, 6, 9, 10\} = \{5, 6, 9, 10\}.$$

18. (d) $\{1, 2, 3\} \cup \{0, 4\} = M$
23. Each member is classified and classified once and only once.
28.

30. (d) The set union of any three sets is the smallest set containing each of the three sets. The set intersection of any three sets is the largest set contained in each of the sets.

Exercise Set 2–4, pp. 41–43

2. $(15, 5)$, $(1, \frac{1}{3})$, $(\frac{9}{5}, \frac{3}{5})$, $(1, \frac{1}{3})$, $\left(b, \dfrac{b}{3} \right)$, $(6b, 2b)$, $(3a, a)$, $\left(2a, \dfrac{2a}{3} \right)$, $(15b, 5b)$.

5. (a) $A \otimes B \neq B \otimes C$ (b) $A \approx B$ (c) $C \approx D$
    (d) $n(A) = n(B)$ (e) $n(C) < n\{5, 7, 9, 8\}$

9. "Love" is not reflexive. A may not love A. "Love" is not symmetric. If A loves B, B may or may not love A. "Love" is not transitive. If A loves B and B loves C, it does not follow that A loves C.

11. The equality relation of sets is reflexive, symmetric, and transitive: $A = A$. If $A = B$, then $B = A$. If $A = B$ and $B = C$, then $A = C$.

16. $T = \{1, 2, 4, 8, 16, 32, \ldots\}$
    $$\updownarrow \; \updownarrow \; \updownarrow \; \updownarrow \; \updownarrow \; \updownarrow$$
    $N = (1, 2, 3, 4, \; 5, \; 6, \; \ldots\}$
    $$T \approx N$$

20. If $D \approx N$, the set of natural numbers, then D is infinite. Let set E be set D with one element removed. Then E is an infinite set, $D \supset E$, and $D \approx E$.

23. Yes. The transitive property applies to the equality, inclusion, and included-in relationships, but not to inequality.

CHAPTER THREE

Exercise Set 3–1, pp. 51–53

5. (a) Both statements are of the form "x is an element of the set X."

8. (a) Proposition   (b) Propositional form

12. (a) $\{174\}$ (b) $\{2548\}$ (g) $\{0\}$ (h) $\{(1, 2), (2, 4)\}$
    (i) $\{(1, y), (2, y)|y > 0\}$
    (j) Set of forty-four ordered pairs:

    $$\{(0, 6), \ldots, (0, 9); (1, 5), \ldots, (1, 8); \ldots ; (8, 0), (8, 1); (9, 0)\}$$

Exercise Set 3–2, pp. 59–60

1. (a) There exists a whole number x such that $2x$ equals x.
    (b) Seven is an even number.

7. The statement of each of steps (2), (3), (4), (5) is true by the law of deduction.

10. (a) $\mathbf{a} \Rightarrow \mathbf{b}$ (b) $\mathbf{a} \Rightarrow \mathbf{b}$

12. There are four possibilities: $\mathbf{a}$ and $\mathbf{b}$ are both true; $\mathbf{a}$ and $\mathbf{b}$ are both false; $\mathbf{a}$ is true, $\mathbf{b}$ is false; $\mathbf{a}$ is false, $\mathbf{b}$ is true. Since if $\mathbf{a} \Leftrightarrow \mathbf{b}$, $\mathbf{a} \Rightarrow \mathbf{b}$. Therefore $\mathbf{a}$ true, $\mathbf{b}$ false is impossible. Similarly, $\mathbf{b} \Rightarrow \mathbf{a}$. Therefore $\mathbf{b}$ true, $\mathbf{a}$ false is impossible.

16. Assume $\mathbf{a}$ true. Then if $\mathbf{b}$ is true, $\mathbf{a}$ and $-\mathbf{b}$ are incompatible. Therefore $\mathbf{a} \Rightarrow \mathbf{b}$ is true. But $\mathbf{a} \Rightarrow \mathbf{b}$ is false. Therefore $\mathbf{b}$ cannot be true; that is, $\mathbf{b}$ is false.

17. Only $\mathbf{c} \Rightarrow \mathbf{a}$ is true.

CHAPTER FOUR

Exercise Set 4–1, pp. 71–72

2. Fe, fi, fo, fum, fum and fi, fum and fe, fum and fi, fum and fo, fi fum, fi fum and fe,
fi fum and fi, fi fum and fo, fo fum, fo fum and fe, fo fum and fi, fo
fum and fo, gum, gum and fe, gum and fi, gum and fo, gum and fum, gum
and fum and fe, gum and fum and fi, gum and fum and fo, gum and fi fum,
gum and fi fum and fe, gum and fi fum and fi.

5. (a) 20,122

7. (b) 240

9. (a) Hindu-Arabic   (b) All   (c) Roman
   (d) Roman, Japanese-Chinese   (e) Roman, Egyptian.

Exercise Set 4–2, pp. 78–79

1. (d) 12^3, 12^2, 12^1, 12^0

2. (a) 167

6. (a) $1001_{(two)}$

9. (a) $100_{(three)}$

11. 1, 2, 3, 4, 5, 6, 7, 8, 9, 10, 11, 12, 1, 2, 3, 4, 5, 6, 7, 8, 9, 10, 11, 12, 1, 2, 3, 4, 5

Exercise Set 4–3, pp. 83–84

1. (f) $\{0, 1, 2, 3, 4, 5, 6, 7, 8, 9, \ldots\}$

4. (c) Each member of the ordered set M_9 is 9 more than the preceding
member of the set. Adding 9 is the same as adding 10 and subtracting 1.
A number like 36 when increased by 9 becomes $36 + 10 - 1$, or 45.
The tens' digit is increased by 1 and the units' digit is decreased by 1.

6. (a) Comp M_2 is the set of all whole numbers not divisible by 2.

9. (a) The intersection of the set of multiples of 2 and 3 is the set of multiples of 6.

11. (a) M_1, M_2, M_3, M_4, M_6, M_8, M_{12}, M_{24}

13. (b) $M_2 \cap M_6 = M_6$

15. (a) The numbers 524, 1388, and 10,508 are not multiples of 8 even though
the number formed by the last two digits of each of the numbers
listed is a multiple of 8.

17. (a) $\{3n | n$ any whole number$\}$

Exercise Set 4–4, pp. 92–93

3. 961; 625; 529; 400; 81

4. (b) 27   (f) 24

8. (c) comp $D_0 = \{0\}$

10. (c) C is a multiple of d and $M_c \subseteq M_d$.

11. (c) 1, 100; 2, 50; 4, 25; 5, 20; 10, 10

13. (e) Composite: 5, 847

15. (b) $299 = 13 \times 23$

18. (a) $12 \times 30 = 360$; $6 \times 60 = 360$

22. (a) $24 = 2 \times 2 \times 2 \times 3$; $56 = 2 \times 2 \times 2 \times 7$; GCD $= 2 \times 2 \times 2 = 8$
    (c) $4 = 2 \times 2$; $14 = 2 \times 7$; $696 = 2 \times 348 = \cdots$; GCD $= 2$

23. $\{3^0, 3^1, 3^2, 3^3, 3^4, \ldots\}$

CHAPTER FIVE

Exercise Set 5–1, pp. 101–103

5. (b) A square always has an odd number of divisors.
6. (b) There exist ordered sets of three consecutive composite numbers of N. The first such set is (279, 289, 299). However, (279, 289, 299, 309, 329, 339) is an ordered subset of six composite numbers.
9. (a) The set T consists of the squares of the elements of P.
    (b) Answers will vary. (The product of two distinct elements of P is always an element of F.)
12. (a) The numbers are even but not divisible by four.
    (b) Yes. None of them are squares; each is twice an odd number.

Exercise Set 5–2, pp. 108–110

3. (a) 3, 6, 7, 11, 12, 14, 15, 19, 21, 22, 23, 24, 27, 28, 30, 31, 33, 35, 38, 39, 42, 43, 44, 46, 47, 48
    (b) No odd number of the form $4n + 3$ is a sum of two squares.
7. (b) $na = a + a + \cdots + a$ with n addends is analogous to

$$a^n = a \times a \times \cdots \times a$$

with n factors.

Exercise Set 5–2

8. (d) $S \supseteq T$
11. (a) If $a|b$ and $b|c$, then $a|c$. If $a|b$ and $b|a$, then $a = b$. $a|a$ is always true. There exists a number 1 such that $1|a$ for every a.
    (b) The universal set U corresponds to the number 1, and the empty set $\{\ \}$ to the number 0. $U \supseteq A$ for every set A. $A \supseteq \{\ \}$ for every set A.

CHAPTER SIX

Exercise Set 6–1, pp. 120–122

3. (a) No   (b) 2   (c) No   (d) Process cannot be performed.
5. (a) $a \ominus b = a + b + 6$
9. The set of whole numbers is closed under the following operations: $\ominus$, ℊ, $\wedge$.
11. (c) The operation is associative and commutative, and has no identity element.
13. No. It is not performable.
16. (a) When $a + b$ is divisible by 3.
    (b) The sum of a and b must be a multiple of 3.
17. (a) 12   (b) 8

Exercise Set 6–2, pp. 132–134

4. (b) Yes. $\boxtimes$ is commutative; 5 is the identity element.
7. (a) The process of intersection is performable and always has a unique result.
    (b) Yes   (c) Yes   (d) Yes   (e) Yes (the set W)   (f) No
    (g) All sets

9. (a) The operation $\triangledown$ is doubling the second number and subtracting the first number.

(b) $c \triangledown a = 2c - a$

14. (e)

17. $40 + 50 = (4 \times 10) + (5 \times 10) = (4 + 5) \times 10 = 9 \times 10 = 90$

19. (a) Correct

(b) Incorrect. $4 \div 2 = 2$ and $4 \div 2 = 5$. Therefore $4 \div 2 \neq 2 \div 4$.

CHAPTER SEVEN

Exercise Set 7–1, pp. 143–144

2. (a) 547 and 126 renamed

(b) Commutative and associative properties for addition

(c) Subtraction performed

(d) Addition performed

5. (c) $n = 200 + 50 + 1$ (Subtraction performed)

$n - 251$ (Addition performed)

$n = (700 + 20 + 8) + (400 + 30 + 6)$ (Addends renamed)

$n = (700 + 400) + (20 + 30) + (8 + 6)$ (Commutative and associative properties for addition)

$n = 1100 + 50 + 14$ (Addition performed)

$n = 1100 + (50 + 10) + 4$ (14 renamed)

$n = 1100 + 60 + 4$ (Addition performed)

$n = 1164$ (Addition performed)

8. (a) 821
   343
   ─────
   478

(b)
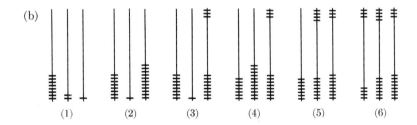

    (1)   (2)   (3)   (4)   (5)   (6)

11. (b) $400 + 110 + 18$

Exercise Set 7–2, pp. 153–155

1. (d) $n = (6 + 40) \times (3 + 50 + 200)$ (Factors renamed and commutative property for multiplication)

$n = 6(3 + 50 + 200)$ [6 and 40 each distributed over
$\quad + 40(3 + 50 + 200)$ $(3 + 50 + 200)$]

$$n = (6 \times 3) + (6 \times 50)$$
$$+ (6 \times 200) + (40 \times 3)$$
$$+ (40 \times 50) + (40 \times 200)$$

(6 distributed over 3, 50 and 200;
200 distributed over 3, 50 and
200)

$$n = (18 + 300 + 1200)$$
$$+ (120 + 2000 + 8000)$$

(Multiplication performed)

$$n = 1518 + 10,120$$

(Addition performed)

$$n = 11,638$$

(Addition performed)

4.   Answers will vary.   Example illustrated: 25×17.

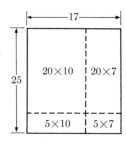

$$25 \times 17 = (5 + 20) \times (7 + 10)$$
$$= (5 \times 7) + (5 \times 10)$$
$$+ (20 \times 70) + (20 \times 10)$$

8.   Answers will vary.
  (b) $\frac{1728}{24} = \frac{1200}{24} + \frac{480}{24} + \frac{24}{24} + \frac{24}{24} = 50 + 20 + 1 + 1 = 72$

11.   Answers will vary.
  (a) $120 + 24;$* $60 + 60 + 24;$ $30 + 30 + 60 + 24;$ $60 + 60 + 12 + 12;$
      $120 + 18 + 6;$* $60 + 60 + 6 + 6 + 6$

15.   (b) The 1200 is immediately recognized as 1200 and not as 12, and the
      480 is recognized 480 and not as 48.

Exercise Set 7–3, pp. 162–165

1.   (d)   2̶
        1̶0̶0̶
        3̶4̶5̶6̶   148
        2444
        22

4.   (a) 1776

7.

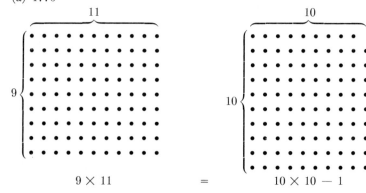

$$9 \times 11 \qquad = \qquad 10 \times 10 - 1$$

10. (b) To multiply a number by 25, first multiply the number by 100 and then multiply the result by $\frac{1}{4}$. ($n \times 25 = n \times 100 \times \frac{1}{4}$.)

15. (1) Seven

19. (b) Nine

22.

+	0	1	2	3	4	5
0	0	1	2	3	4	5
1	1	2	3	4	5	10
2	2	3	4	5	10	11
3	3	4	5	10	11	12
4	4	5	10	11	12	13
5	5	10	11	12	13	14

×	0	1	2	3	4	5
0	0	0	0	0	0	0
1	0	1	2	3	4	5
2	0	2	4	10	12	14
3	0	3	10	13	20	23
4	0	4	12	20	24	32
5	0	5	14	23	32	41

23. (c)
$$\begin{array}{r} 235\frac{2}{4} \\ 4\overline{)1434} \\ 1200 \\ \hline 234 \\ 200 \\ \hline 34 \\ 32 \\ \hline 2 \end{array}$$

24. (a) 194t

CHAPTER EIGHT

Exercise Set 8–1, pp. 174–176

1. (a) 1, 4, 9, 16, 25, 36, 49, 64, 81, 100

3.

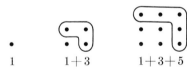

1   1+3   1+3+5

10. (b) Answers may vary. Assumptions 8 and 9 below must be stated. Assumptions 10, 11, 12 below may be stated among others.

ASSUMPTION 8. There exists a family of distinguished subsets of S, called "planes."

ASSUMPTION 9. There exist at least three planes in S.

ASSUMPTION 10. If α and β are distinct planes, there exists at most one line contained in both α and β.

ASSUMPTION 11. If A, B, and C are three distinct points of S which are not contained in a line, there exists one and only one plane containing A, B, and C.

ASSUMPTION 12. If a line l of S and a plane Π of S have more than one point in common, Π contains l.

Exercise Set 8–2, pp. 188–190

1. (a) True   (b) True   (c) False   (d) False   (e) True
5. A Euclidean triangle is the boundary of a triangle as defined in this book. A triangle is the set union of a Euclidean triangle and the region interior to the Euclidean triangle.
8. (c) The sector of the circle common to the square
10. (a) Yes   (b) Yes   (c) Yes   (d) Yes   (e) No   (f) No
22. Only (a) is an equivalence relation because: (1) A line is parallel to itself. (2) If $AB \parallel CD$ then $DF \parallel AB$. (3) If $AB \parallel CD$ and $CD \parallel EF$, then $AB \parallel EF$. (b) Perpendicularity is not a symmetric relation. (c) Intersection is not a transitive relation.

Exercise Set 8–3, pp. 201–204

4. A perpendicular from the vertex of the largest angle of a triangle to the opposite side separates the triangle into two right triangles.
12. A triangular region is a polygon because it consists of a simple closed path and its interior. An Euclidean triangle is not a polygon.
15. (a) 170   (b) $\dfrac{n(n-3)}{2}$
20. (d) Yes. Lines perpendicular to the same line are parallel to one another.
24. (a) A set is bounded in space if it may be included in a sphere.
26. (a) A solid Γ is convex if for every two points P and Q of Γ, the line segment $\overline{PG}$ is contained in Γ.
29. (b) Two planes may intersect so that all points of one plane are points of the other, they may intersect in a line, or they may not intersect.
31. (b) A cube is the set union of a Euclidean cube and its interior.

Exercise Set 9–1, pp. 213–215

3. (a) Symbol   (b) Idea   (c) Symbol   (d) Idea   (e) Idea
8. (f) 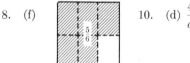   10. (d) $\dfrac{4}{a}$

16. (c) $\frac{7}{9} > \frac{6}{9}$ 17. (c) $7 \cdot 3 > 9 \cdot 2;\ \frac{7}{9} > \frac{2}{3}$
18. There are two procedures: (1) Rename the fractions so they have the same denominator. Examine the numerators. If the numerators are equal, the fractions are equal. (2) Find the product of the numerator of the first fraction and the denominator of the second fraction. Find the product of the denominator of the first fractions and the numerator of the second fractions. Compare the products. If the products are equal, the fractions are equal.
21. (a) $\{\frac{3}{4}, \frac{1}{2}, \frac{5}{16}, \frac{0}{2}\}$
24. (a) False   (b) True   (c) False   (d) False

CHAPTER NINE

Exercise Set 9–2, pp. 218

4. (h) $\frac{21}{24} - \frac{16}{24} = \frac{5}{24}$

8. Since there is no fractional number p that can be used in the sentence $\frac{2}{3} - \frac{5}{3} = p$, and $n = 1$ in the sentence $\frac{5}{3} - \frac{2}{3} = n$, the two statements $\frac{2}{3} - \frac{5}{3}$ and $\frac{5}{3} - \frac{2}{3}$ are not equal. Subtraction of fractional numbers is not commutative.

9. (b) $\{12, 24, 36, \ldots\}$

10. (i) $M_{36} = \{0, 36, 72, \ldots, 180, \ldots\}$
    $M_{30} = \{0, 30, 60, \ldots, 180, \ldots\}$
    $M_{12} = \{0, 12, 24, \ldots, 180, \ldots\}$
    The LCM, which can be used as a denominator, is 180.

    (ii) $36 = 2 \cdot 2 \cdot 3 \cdot 3$
    $30 = 2 \cdot \quad 3 \cdot \quad 5$
    $12 = 2 \cdot 2 \cdot 3$
    The LCM, which can be used as a denominator, is $2 \cdot 2 \cdot 3 \cdot 3 \cdot 5 = 180$.

    (iii) 2|36;   30;   12

    2|18;   15;   6

    3| 9;   15;   3

       3;   5;   1
    The LCM, which can be used as a denominator, is $2 \cdot 2 \cdot 3 \cdot 3 \cdot 5 = 180$.

Exercise Set 9–3, pp. 227–230

5. (b) $\frac{3}{5}$

7. (c) $\dfrac{33\frac{1}{3}}{33\frac{1}{3}}$

10. (a) Distributive property

13. (a) Yes. Zero cannot be used as a denominator.
    (b) Yes. In (e) $b \neq 0$, and in (f) $a \neq 0$.

17. To divide a fraction a/b by the fraction c/d, multiply a/b by the reciprocal of c/d.
$$\frac{a}{b} \div \frac{c}{d} = \frac{a}{b} \times \frac{d}{c}$$

21. (a) The resulting fraction is the reciprocal of the known factor.
    (b) Yes. When 1 is divided by a fraction, the result is the reciprocal of the fraction.

24. (b) $41\frac{2}{3}$

28. (m) $20\frac{1}{4}$

Exercise Set 9–4, pp. 239–241

4. $B_1 = \{\frac{1}{1}, \frac{2}{1}, \frac{3}{1}, \frac{4}{1}, \frac{5}{1}, \ldots\}$
   $\quad\quad\; \updownarrow \;\; \updownarrow \;\; \updownarrow \;\; \updownarrow \;\; \updownarrow$
   $W = \{0, 1, 2, 3, 4, \ldots\}$

10. (a) $\frac{1}{100}$

11. (e) $\frac{4}{100}$

12. (e) 2.35

16. (a) No decimal fraction form

18. (d) 4.0; .6

20. (e) $\frac{9}{8}$; 1.125

21. The set of decimal numbers is not closed under the operation of division.

CHAPTER TEN

Exercise Set 10–1, pp. 251–253

2. (a) T   (b) F   (c) Open   (d) Open   (e) T   (f) T
   (g) Open   (h) Open   (i) T   (j) Open   (k) T   (l) Open
4. (l) Dos not equal
5. (c) 28
6. (c) Inverseness of addition and subtraction or cancellation property for addition
8. (h) $\dfrac{4a}{6} - \dfrac{3a}{6} = 2$
9. Answers will vary.
   (f) $5a = 20$ (Cancellation property for addition or inverseness of addition and subtraction)
10. (a) (1) Renaming 8
    (2) Cancellation property for addition or inverseness of addition and subtraction
    (3) Inverseness of multiplication and division
12. (j) F, $m = 6$

Exercise Set 10–2, pp. 256–259

2. Answers will vary.
   (c) From a family income of $7280, $\frac{1}{4}$ is spent for rent, $\frac{5}{16}$ for food, $\frac{1}{8}$ for clothing, $\frac{1}{8}$ for miscellaneous items, and the rest is saved. How much of the income is saved?
3. (c) $7280 - (\frac{1}{4} + \frac{5}{16} + \frac{1}{8} + \frac{1}{8})7280 = s$; $7280 - \frac{13}{16} \cdot 7280 = s$; $7280 - 5915 = s$; $s = 1365$
6. (d) What is the cost of two dozen items which sell at a price of three for 25¢?
7. Mathematical sentences may be expressed in various forms:
   (e) $d = [500 + \frac{1}{10} \cdot 500 - \frac{1}{10}(500 + \frac{1}{10} \cdot 500)]$
   $\quad\quad - [500 - \frac{1}{10} \cdot 500 + \frac{1}{10}(500 - \frac{1}{10} \cdot 500)]$,
   $\quad d = [500 + 50 - \frac{1}{10}(500 + 50)] - [500 - 50 + \frac{1}{10}(500 - 50)]$,
   $\quad d = (550 - 55) - (450 + 45)$
   $\quad d = 495 - 495$
   $\quad d = 0$
12. Answers will vary:
    (e) I bought a red sweater, and my sister bought a blue sweater and a green sweater of the same type which I bought. The total cost was $42. What was the price of each?
13. (e) $i = 3000 \cdot \frac{6}{100} \cdot \frac{1}{12}$
14. (d) The circumference of a circle is the product of 2, π, and the radius of the circle.

Exercise Set 10–3, pp. 264–268

2. (b) No. $31\frac{1}{12}$ ft is one-half of the perimeter.

3. Sentences will vary.

    (a) *Word sentence:* How much money does the student need to add to $56, $225, and $100 to have $500?

    Mathematical sentence:

$$n + 56 + 225 + 100 = 500,$$
$$n + 381 = 500,$$
$$n = 119.$$

    Answer to question in the problem: The college student still needs to save $119.

5. (c) *Word sentence:* How many miles per hour must an object move to make two trips of 240,000 mi in 30 days?

    Mathematical sentence:

$$2 \cdot 240{,}000 = r \cdot 30 \cdot 24,$$
$$480{,}000 = 720r,$$
$$r = 666\tfrac{2}{3}.$$

    Answer to question in problem: An object would have to move at the rate of $666\tfrac{2}{3}$ mi/hr in order to get to the moon and back in 30 days.

9. (ii) $3\tfrac{1}{2}$ cartons each containing 1728 objects sell at a price of $24 per gross of the objects.

$$\frac{3\tfrac{1}{2} \times 1728}{144} \times 24 = c,$$
$$42 \times 24 = c,$$
$$c = 1008$$

    Answer to question in the problem: The $3\tfrac{1}{2}$ cartons sold for $1008.

    (b) Excess data were given in (i). I did not need to know that there was to be a 10% increase in 3 months or a 15% increase in 6 months.

13. Answers will vary.

    Simpler problem situation: Thirty acres of wheat give an average yield of 3 bushels per acre. If wheat sells for $2 per bushel, what is the value of the harvest? ($d = 30 \cdot 3 \cdot 2$; $d = 180$.) The solution of this simpler problem is a guide in solving the following problem.

    Word sentence: What is the value of 97,481,200 acres of wheat with a yield of 15 bushels per acre, given that the wheat sells for $1.71 per bushel?

    Mathematical sentence:

$$d = 97{,}481{,}200 \cdot 15 \cdot 1.71,$$
$$d = 2{,}500{,}392{,}780.$$

    Answer to question in the problem: The value of the annual wheat crop for a recent year was $2,500,392,780.

Exercise Set 10–4 (Supplementary), pp. 268–270

Note: Mathematical sentences will vary. The information given below for each problem consists of a mathematical sentence, the solution of the sentence, and the answer to the question asked in the problem.

4. $b + (b + 15\frac{1}{2}) = 73\frac{5}{8}$; $b = 29\frac{1}{16}$. The weight of the boxes is $29\frac{1}{16}$ lb and $44\frac{9}{16}$ lb, respectively.

15. $c = \dfrac{9(725 \cdot 650)}{5000} \cdot 4.35$; $c = 3693.15$. It will cost \$3693.15 to fertilize the park. (The number of bags of fertilizer was rounded to 849 since one cannot purchase a part of a bag.)

20. $n + (n + 2) + (n + 4) = 72$; $n = 22$. The three consecutive even numbers whose sum is 72 are 22, 24, and 26.

26. $n = \dfrac{(2430 - .05 \cdot 2430)}{8} \cdot 24 \cdot 365$; $n = 2{,}527{,}807.5$. The machine can produce 2,527,807 articles by operating 24 hr/day for one year.

CHAPTER ELEVEN

Exercise Set 11–1, pp. 276–278

1. (g) $^+(ab)$ 2. (f) $^-5$, $^-2$, $^-1$, $^+5$, $^+6$, $^+9$
3. (g) $^-10$ 7. e: $[^+3, ^-6]$
10. a: 2, b: 4, c: 4, d: 4, e: 9, f: 9, g: 9, h: 1, i: 4, j: 7
15. a: $^-4$, b: $^+6$, c: $^-1$, d: $^+6$, e: $^-6$, f: $^-1$, g: $^+6$, h: $^-4$, i: 0
16. (b) a and h; b, d, and g; c and f
17. (b) $[-5, -5]$ is a null vector. It has measure zero.

Exercise Set 11–2, pp. 284–287

1. (a), (d), (e), (g), (h), (i)
3. (b)

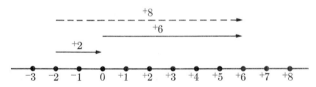

4. (f) $[^+5, ^-2] + [^-2, ^+5] = [^+5, ^+5]$
5. (g) $^-5 + {}^+7 = {}^+2$
7. (b) The vector which most conveniently represents an integer is one whose initial point is zero.
9. (d)

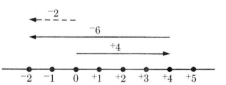

10. (d) $^+4 + {}^-6 = {}^-2$
18. Pairs of vectors with the same terminal points are (c) and (g). Pairs of vectors with the same initial points are (b), (d), (f), and (i).

23. (e)

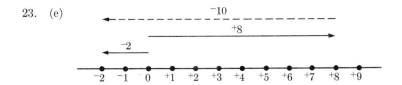

24. (e) $^-2 - {}^+8 = {}^-10$

29. (b)

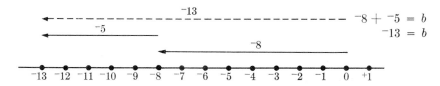

$^-8 + {}^-5 = b$

$^-13 = b$

37. (a) $q = {}^-10$; $r = {}^-10$ (b) $r = q$; $^-12 - {}^-2 = {}^-12 + {}^+2$

Exercise Set. 11–3, pp. 292–294

1. (e) $e = 0$ 3. (p) $p = {}^-6$

6. The product of two given integers of the same direction is a positive integer whose whole number is the product of the whole number of the given integers. The product of two given integers of different direction is a negative integer whose whole number is the product of the whole numbers of the given integers.

8. (a) No   (b) Answers will vary. $n = {}^+5 \div {}^-2$

11. (c) $^+1138 + {}^-45 = {}^+1093$

13. (e) $e = {}^+14{,}431 - {}^+3350$; $e = {}^+11{,}081$

15. (b) $b = {}^-282 - {}^-1286$; $b = {}^+1004$

17. (b) $N = {}^+12 + {}^+210 + {}^-172 + {}^+402 + {}^-78$; $N = {}^+374$
    $S = {}^+12 + {}^+578 + {}^-50 + {}^-62 + {}^-37 + {}^-67$; $S = {}^+374$
    Neither grasshopper will win.

CHAPTER TWELVE

Exercise Set 12–1, pp. 300–301

2. (a) -545.25 7. (a) Whole numbers; the integers

8. (c) $^+1$ and $^-1$ 10. (e) $7 - 3$

11. (b)

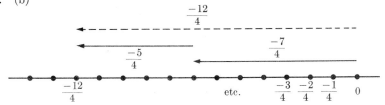

Exercise Set 12–2, pp. 310–312

2. (b) Yes. If a and b are rational numbers, then $ab = ba$. Illustrations will vary.

3. (a) Yes. If a, b, and c are rational numbers, then $(a+b)+c = a+(b+c)$. Illustrations will vary.

4. (b) Yes. One is the identity element for multiplication. For any rational number a, $a \cdot 1 = 1 \cdot a = a$.

8. Yes. If a is any rational number, there exists a rational a' such that $a + a' = a' + a = 0$.

   (b) $\dfrac{5}{2} + \dfrac{-5}{2} = \dfrac{5-5}{2} = 0$

11. $-\dfrac{1}{2}\left(\dfrac{2}{3} + \dfrac{-8}{3}\right) = \left(-\dfrac{1}{2}\right)\left(\dfrac{2}{3}\right) + \left(-\dfrac{1}{2}\right)\left(\dfrac{-8}{3}\right) = -\dfrac{1}{3} + \dfrac{4}{3} = \dfrac{3}{3} = 1$

12. (a) $-\frac{2}{3} > -\frac{5}{2}$

14. Other answers may be possible.

    (b) The set of integers has no multiplicative inverse.

17. (c) $c = -\dfrac{acf + ade}{bdf}$

19. (The proof follows the pattern in Section 8, where it was shown that there exists no rational number r such that $r^2 = 2$.) If it is assumed that there exists a rational number r such that $r^2 = 3$, the result is the following contradiction: If such a rational r exists, it may be assumed that $r = a/b$, where a/b is a fraction in simplest form. Therefore, $a^2/b^2 = 3$ and $a^2 = 3b^2$. It follows from this last equation that both a and b are divisible by 3, which contradicts the assumption that a/b is a fraction in simplest form. Therefore no rational number r exists such that $r^2 = 3$.

21. (b) Yes. $(3+4)+2 = 3+(4+2)$ because $(3+4)+2 = 1+2 = 3$ and $3 + (4 + 2) = 3 + 0 = 3$. $(3 \cdot 4) \cdot 2 = 3(4 \cdot 2)$ because $(3 \cdot 4) \cdot 2 = 0 \cdot 2 = 0$ and $3(4 \cdot 2) = 3 \cdot 2 = 0$.

25. (a) $-\frac{1}{2}$; $-.5$; $-\frac{7}{125}$ and $-.056$ are examples. A negative decimal is a rational number which when represented by a fraction in lowest terms has a negative numerator and a denominator which is a product of powers of 2 and 5.

CHAPTER THIRTEEN

Exercise Set 13–1, pp. 327–330

4. (f) $F > C > A$

5. (e) $[M, P] \supseteq [M, P]$

6. (f) $[N, R]$

7. (e) Disjoint   (f) Abut

13. (a)

(b) No. The second condition for a sequence of nested intervals is not satisfied.

18.

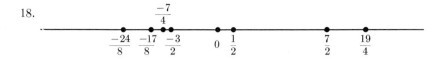

22. (d) $\frac{1}{15} = .0\underline{6}66\ldots$

26. The first subdivision gives

$$.0510, .0511, .0512, \ldots, .0519, .0520, \ldots,$$

The second subdivision gives

$$.0510, .05101, .05102, \ldots, .05109, .05110, \ldots,$$

etc.

29. Since $\frac{9}{11} = .8181\ldots$, the intervals $[.8, .9], [.81, .82], \ldots, [.818, .819]$ close down on $\frac{9}{11}$.

Exercise Set 13–2, pp. 343–346

2. (b) $.25, .0069, .00012, .00060, 2.000\ldots$

8. Suppose $r = \sqrt{2} - \sqrt{3}$ is rational, then r^2 is rational. But

$$r^2 = (\sqrt{2})^2 - 2\sqrt{2} \cdot \sqrt{3} + (\sqrt{3})^2 = 2 - 2\sqrt{6} + 3 = 5 - 2\sqrt{6}.$$

Since $5 - 2\sqrt{6}$ is not rational, then r^2 is not rational. Therefore r is not rational.

12. $[1, 2], [1.1, 1.2], [1.14, 1.15], [1.142, 1.143], [1.1428, 1.1429], \ldots$

14. (a) $\sqrt{18} \cdot \sqrt{2} = \sqrt{36} = 6.$ Rational

$\sqrt{18} \cdot \sqrt{3} = \sqrt{54} = \sqrt{9 \cdot 6} = 3\sqrt{6}.$ Irrational

16. $\pi = 3.14159265\ldots$; $\frac{355}{113} = 3.14159283$; $\frac{355}{113} - \pi = .00000013.$ Hence $\alpha < .000001.$

21. Parallelogram $ABCD$ of the figure is separated into triangular regions by altitudes $\overline{BE}$ and $\overline{DF}$ and by line $\overleftrightarrow{EF}$. The area of the parallelogram is then the sum of the areas of the four triangles.

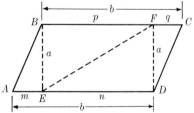

$A = \frac{1}{2}am + \frac{1}{2}an + \frac{1}{2}ap + \frac{1}{2}aq,$
$A = \frac{1}{2}a(m + n + p + q),$
$A = \frac{1}{2}a(2b),$
$A = ab.$

30. (a) 25π (b) 10π (c) $\pi^3/2$

31. $A(3, 1), B(-1, 2), C(-4, -2), D(2, -2), E(-2, 0), F(0, 4)$

35. (d) $\sqrt{\pi}$

39. The first interval corresponds to an angle of π/a radians, and the second corresponds to an angle of $\pi/12$ radians.

CHAPTER FOURTEEN

Exercise Set 14–1, pp. 356–357

2. (a) Yes and no.
   (b) Yes, if you are not seeking precision. The statement will mean, "The measure of approximately 18 ft equals the approximate measure of 6 yd." However, if you are seeking precision, a measurement of 18 ft is more precise than a measurement of 6 yd because the unit *foot* is smaller than the unit *yard*. The smaller the unit of measure used the more precise the measure.

5. (g) $[6\frac{23}{32}, 6\frac{25}{32}]$ 15. 6.45 sq. cm
19. (a) 70 yd   (c) 208.7 ft

Exercise Set 14–2, pp. 364–365

1. (b) 66.7 is the only number between 66.5 and 67.5 with denominator 10 and is the best approximation in the denomination for 66.666 . . .
5. (e) 10   6. (e) 3.1416
7. (a) .5 in.   8. (d) 2.5×10^5 ft
10. (d) -1
11. (b) $5.2 \times 10^3 \times 3.2 \times 10^{-4} = 16.64 \times 10^{-1} = 1.7$

CHAPTER FIFTEEN

Exercise Set 15–1, pp. 382–385

2. (c) $t = 12$; $u = 1$; $v = b/2 - a$; $w = \frac{7}{2} - c$
4. (b) If the length of $\overline{AC}$ is b for the isosceles right triangle in (a), the length of $\overline{AB}$ is $a/\sqrt{2}$ and the area is $a^2/4$. Therefore as the length of $\overline{AB}$ changes from 0 to $a/\sqrt{2}$, the areas of the right triangles change from 0 to $a^2/4$.
7. (a) $\frac{1}{2}, \frac{1}{10}, \frac{3}{10}, \frac{1}{20}, \frac{3}{20}, \frac{1}{100} \cdots$
8. (b) The numbers keep repeating after the first eight sums have been determined. For example,

$$S_1 = S_9 = S_{17} = 89; \quad S_2 = S_{10} = S_{18} = 145; \quad \ldots$$

9. (c) Each of the numbers 2 and 4 yields the same periodic sequence of eight numbers, which is the same as the one for 89 in Exercise 8. Each of the numbers 3, 5, 6, 8, and 9 yields the same periodic sequence which, however, is preceded by some nonrepeating numbers.
13. (a) By the conditions given, $n(n+1) > 2 \cdot 10^4$. A good estimate for n is obtained by noting that $(n + \frac{1}{2})^2 = n(n+1) + \frac{1}{4}$. Therefore, $(n + \frac{1}{2})^2 > 2 \cdot 10^4$, and hence $n + \frac{1}{2} > \sqrt{2} \cdot 10^2$ or $n + \frac{1}{2} > 141.4$. Consequently, $n = 141$ should suffice.
15. (a) $n \div n = 1$
    (b) Yes. The number n cannot be zero.
17. (b) 2, 4, 6, 8, 10. For example, $4 = (2 + 2)$
21. (b) The operation of addition of numbers has the cancellation property, and the operation of union of sets does not.

23. (d) The intersection of the set of rectangles and the set of rhombuses is the set of squares.

24. (c)

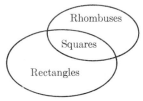

26. (a) Answers will vary. (Example: Some students are men. Some men are not students.)

30. If r is the radius of the inner circle, its area is πr^2. By the given conditions, the area of the outer circle is $2^2\pi$ or 4π, and $2(\pi r^2) = 4\pi$. Therefore, $r^2 = 2$ and $r = \sqrt{2}$.

APPENDIX I

Test I (Many of these answers may be written in another form.)

2. 2 cu. yd 15 cu. ft

7. $\frac{3}{5}$; 62%; $\frac{5}{8}$; $\frac{2}{3}$; .7

13. $.72

18. .1

24. $750\frac{3}{10}$

29. $57\frac{1}{7}\%$

36. $16\frac{1}{4}$

41. 23 weeks

48. None

50. $11\frac{1}{9}\%$

Test II

2. 288 lb

5. $2\frac{6}{7}$

12. 30%

13. $92\frac{5}{8}$

20. $26\frac{11}{14}$

24. $276\frac{1}{4}$

28. 20%

31. 35 yd 1 ft

36. 42.94368

37. $36\frac{7}{8}$

42. .74

47. 2.8

49. $29.16

Test III

2. $\frac{28}{45}$

4. $\frac{5}{9}$

10. $648

11. 3.6

17. 57

19. MLXVI

26. $3150

30. $367\frac{1}{2}$

34. 12 qt

40. .74

50. $11\frac{13}{16}$ lb

INDEX

GLOSSARY OF TERMS

Symbol	Meaning	Page
$A = \{1, 2\}$	A is the set whose elements are 1 and 2	19
$=$	Equality; names the same mathematical object	21 and 77
$\neq$	Inequality	21
$\supseteq$	Set inclusion	21
$\supset$	Proper set inclusion	21
$\{\ \}$	The empty set	24
$\{n/n \text{ with property } P\}$	Set definition	24–26
$\cup$	Set union	29
$\cap$	Set intersection	29
U	Universal set	30
comp A	Complement of set A	30
$>$	Greater than	25
$<$	Less than	25
$\geq$	Greater than or equal to	50
(a, b, c)	Ordered set	37
(a, b)	Ordered pair	37
N	Set of natural numbers	40–41
N_n	Counting set with number n	40
$\otimes$	Cartesian product	37
$\approx$	Set equivalence	38
$n(A)$ or $n\{a, b, c\}$	Number of a set	39
$\mathbf{a}, \mathbf{b}, \ldots, \mathbf{p}$	Propositions	53
$-\mathbf{a}, -\mathbf{b}, \ldots, -\mathbf{p}$	Negatives of propositions	53
$\Rightarrow$	Implication	54
$\Leftrightarrow$	Logical equivalence	55
W	Set of whole numbers	79
F	Set of fractional numbers	206
I	Set of integers	273
R	Set of rationals	295
$\mathcal{R}$	Set of real numbers	321
M_n	Multiples of n	80
D_n	Divisors of n	86
P	Prime numbers	86
GCD	Greatest common divisor	89

ABCDE69876543

Mike Tipolo